Silent Voices, Sacred Lives

WOMEN'S READINGS FOR THE LITURGICAL YEAR

Compiled and edited by

Barbara Bowe, R.S.C.J.
Kathleen Hughes, R.S.C.J.
Sharon Karam, R.S.C.J.
Carolyn Osiek, R.S.C.J.

Paulist Press ■ *New York/Mahwah*

Library of Congress Cataloging-in-Publication Data

Silent voices, sacred lives: women's readings for the liturgical year/compiled and edited by Barbara Bowe . . . [et al.].
    p. cm.
    Includes bibliographical references.
    ISBN 0-8091-3336-9 (pbk.)
    1. Women—Prayer-books and devotions—English. 2. Catholic Church—Prayer-books and devotions—English. 3. Church year—Prayer-books and devotions—English. I. Bowe, Barbara Ellen.
BX2170.W7S55 1992
264'.029—dc20   92-26234
                                                 CIP

Published by Paulist Press
997 Macarthur Blvd.
Mahwah, N.J. 07430

Printed and bound in the United States of America

CONTENTS

DEDICATION

To all who long
for a more just society
a more inclusive church
and a more inviting worship,
and to all who will find here
their history and their hopes

THANKS AND ACKNOWLEDGMENTS

We are grateful to the students in "Feminist Hermeneutics and Worship" (Winter, 1990) for encouraging us to launch this project and for all the women and men of Catholic Theological Union, students, faculty and staff alike, who labor for a more inclusive church and who have provided us an environment conducive to this pursuit.

We thank Barbara Quinn, R.S.C.J., for suggesting some passages from the life of Hadewijch, the mystic.

We are particularly indebted to Frances Krumpelman, S.C.N., for her tireless research and secretarial support.

We wish to acknowledge the use of the following materials:

For the pronunciation guides:

Martyrology Pronouncing Dictionary, Anthony I. Russo-Alesi. New York: Edward O'Toole Company, Inc., 1939.

NBC Handbook of Pronunciation, originally compiled by James F. Bender, revised and enlarged by Thomas L. Crowell, Jr. New York: Thomas Y. Crowell, 1943/1964.

"A Dictionary of Noted Names in Fiction, Mythology, Legend," and "A Dictionary of Scripture Proper Names and Foreign Words," in Webster's *New Twentieth Century Dictionary*, 2nd ed. Collins World, 1976.

For entries in the sanctoral calendar:

The Sacramentary and *The Roman Martyrology*.

The Publisher gratefully acknowledges use of the following materials: *Egeria's Travels to the Holy Land*, rev. ed., translated by J. Wilkinson, copyright © 1981, Ariel Publishing House, Jerusalem, Israel; *The Anglo-Saxon Missionaries in Germany*, edited and translated by Charles H. Talbot, copyright © 1954, Sheed & Ward, Division of National Catholic Reporter, Kansas City, Missouri; *The Writings of Medieval Women*, translated and introduced by Marcelle Thiébaux, Vol. 14 of Garland Series of Medieval Literature, Series B. copyright © 1987, Garland Publishing Inc., New York, New York; Reprints from *Maenads, Martyrs, Matrons, Monastics*, edited by Ross S. Kraemer, copyright © 1988, Fortress Press. Used by permission of Augsburg Fortress, Minneapolis, Minnesota; Selections from *Ante-Nicene Fathers*, Vol. 3 and 4 on Tertullian, edited by Alexander Roberts and James Donaldson; Selections from *Nicene and Postnicene Fathers*, series 2, Vol. 2, 1952, edited by Philip Schaff; Selections from *Church History*, vol. 2 on Socrates Scholasticus, edited by Philip Schaff; and *Jerome, Letters*, vol. 6, edited by Philip Schaff, published by William B. Eerdmans Publishing Company, Grand Rapids, Michigan; *Jerome, Chrysostom and Friends*, translated by Elizabeth Clark, copyright © 1979, The Edwin Mellen Press, Lewiston, New York; Excerpts from *The Nag Hammadi Library*, edited by James M. Robinsin, copyright © 1978 by E.J. Brill. Reprinted by permission of HarperCollins Publishers; Selections from *Holy Women of the Syrian Orient*, introduction and translation by Sebastian P. Brock and Susan Ashbrook Harvey, copyright © 1987, The Regents of the University of California; *Medieval Women Writers*, edited by Katharina M. Wilson, copyright © 1984, The University of Georgia Press, Athens, Georgia; *Ascetical Works*, translated by Virginia Woods Callahan, copyright © 1967, The Catholic University of America Press, Washington, D.C.; *The Acts of the Christian Martyrs*, translated by H. Musurillo, copyright © 1971, Oxford University Press, United Kingdom; Reprints from *New Testament Apocrypha* (Volume I: Gospels and Related Writings), by Edgar Hennecke, edited by Wilhelm Schneemelcher; English translation edited by R. McL. Wilson. Copyright © 1964, J.C.B. Mohr (Paul Siebeck), Tübingen; English translation © 1965, Lutterworth Press. Reprinted and used by permission of Westminster/John Knox Press. Reprints from *The Old Testament Pseudepigrapha* by James H. Charlesworth, copyright © 1983, 1985, by James H. Charlesworth. Used by permission of Doubleday, a division of Bantam Doubleday Dell Publishing Group, Inc., New York, New York. Reprints from *The Fire and the Cloud: An Anthology of Catholic Spirituality*, edited by David A. Fleming, S.M., copyright © 1978, Paulist Press, Mahwah, New Jersey. Reprints from *Hadewijch: The Complete Works*, translated and introduced by Mother Columba Hart, O.S.B., copyright © 1980, Paulist Press, Mahwah, New Jersey. Reprints from *Catherine of Siena: Dialogue*, translated and introduced by Suzanne Noffke, O.P., copyright © 1980, Paulist Press, Mahwah, New Jersey. Reprints from *Julian of Norwich: Showings*, translated by Edmund Colledge, O.S.A. and James Walsh, S.J., copyright © 1978, Paulist Press, Mahwah, New Jersey. Reprints from *Augustine of Hippo: Confessions*, translated by Mary T. Clark, copyright © 1984, Paulist Press, Mahwah, New Jersey. Reprints from *The Desert Christian*, translated by Benedicta Ward. Reprinted with permission from Cassell PLC, London, England.

INTRODUCTION

Story-tellers all, our most natural instinct is to preserve those tales which have shaped us. We remember the joys and the sufferings, the crisis moments and their resolutions, the characters who have peopled our daily lives and those special folk who have brought hope to our world. We tell stories over the dinner table; we reminisce in moments by the fire; we eulogize at wakes and toast with stories at our weddings. And sometimes the stories which have shaped our lives are written down for those who will come after us. Such is the origin of the book we call the lectionary.

The book is rigid down the aisle,
a book embraced, held high, held dear:
the common carrier of the tales
on fiber come from cotton fields
and pulp from forest cut in Maine.
What earth has given hands have made
flat, thin and bound between two boards,
the pages covered now with marks
that image sound that image all:
the picture of pictures only
are letters gathered into words
and words lined up and bundled, tied—
yet here's the kernel of ourselves:
the poems, genealogies,
laws, letters, sayings, prophecies,
psalms, stories, visions handed on
from mouth to mouth and tongue to tongue
and page to page: a year or three
to tell it round again, this book

1

that dances now in incense sweet
and sweet its alphabet to kiss.

G. Huck "Book," *Assembly* 8 (1981) 139

What a lovely, poetic description of a lectionary, treasured container of a faith-filled community's history and its dreams.

This introduction will explore the evolution of lectionaries, their style, content, and use in Christian tradition. It will situate the readings in this present collection, *Silent Voices, Sacred Lives*, as supplementary to the official lectionaries available in the Christian churches, and will explain why the editors judged it urgent to provide "a richer fare at the table of God's word." A description of the content of this collection and suggestions for its use will follow.

What Is a Lectionary?

A lectionary, most simply stated, is a collection of readings arranged in an orderly sequence by a particular faith community for use in its public worship. As a collection of readings, a lectionary is like an anthology of writings by different authors from different times and places—but with this difference: no particular genre binds the collection together. A lectionary is not solely poetry, nor solely history, nor law, nor prophecy, but it is all of these as well as travelogue, biography, romance, testament, apocalyptic, genealogy, parable, and hagiography. It is every form of story in a community's repertoire, a repertoire which has developed over time and is the product of many different authors in quite particular human circumstances.

Lectionaries emerge out of the human framework of particular cultures and concrete human circumstances, for the stories they contain are told in a context, often in response to a question, a problem, or a need, and always conditioned by the writer and by the distinctive culture within which that story-teller's words have been shaped. Jesus' parables, for example, were generally stories told in order to illuminate a particular question: "Who can be saved?" "What must I do to gain eternal life?" "Who is my neighbor?" "How often must I forgive?" The parables Jesus told in response to such questions were about ordinary people and commonplace events familiar to the listeners of his day because they mirrored the listeners' world. Similarly, whether we are speaking of letters, sayings, visions, or poems, the writings incorporated in a lectionary are "mundane" in the best sense of that word.

Each genre of story could be examined in turn, and each would suggest a quite specific human framework as its origin. Laws, for example, capture ways a community has resolved to structure its life; biography preserves the memory of those men and women whose personal struggle may in some way clarify our own; prophecy often erupts when a community loses touch with "the kernel of itself" and needs to be called back to the heart of its story. While lectionaries are designed precisely to preserve for other times and places what appears to be of enduring and universal interest, it cannot be ignored that their stories are cultural products. Rightly, therefore, lectionaries are revised periodically in order to ensure pastoral sensitivity to communities now some generations removed from the culture which spawned the collection.

Just as a family or a clan has favorite stories which are told over and over again, so too with faith communities. A lectionary might even be called a "canon within a canon" since it represents a judicious selection of texts from the canonical books of the Hebrew and Christian scriptures. "Canonicity" is another way of speaking about what the community decides to "censor in" and "censor out," what has been determined as vital for the community's memory and its hopes, binding one community to another and one generation to the next.

In other words, a lectionary contains all of—and only—what a community has determined is worthy of proclamation at public worship on a regularly recurring basis. A community's beliefs, its ethical concerns, its emerging ritual patterns, and even historical events have influenced the lections which are included: some lections become associated with a particular season such as Isaiah's traditional place in Advent; sometimes sacramental practices such as preparation for baptism at the Easter vigil have determined the focus of the readings in those days surrounding the sacramental event; nature's seasons have prompted the appropriate placement (at least for those living in the same hemisphere) of lections about sowing and reaping and about laborers in the vineyard; even the gradual evolution of the sanctoral cycle has suggested particular scripture passages which help to illustrate a saint's unique living of the holy life.

The readings of the lectionary are called "pericopes"—literally "cuttings." That means that a passage has been "cut" from a larger book. Typically, the cuttings are arranged on a continuous, semi-continuous, or discrete basis. If readings are continuous or semi-continuous, whole books or long portions thereof are read in sequence with no (continuous) or little (semi-continuous) omission. If the cutting is "discrete," that means that the excerpt is an isolated selection.

Lectionaries are structured in a variety of ways. The three-year pattern of the *Roman Lectionary* for Sunday readings during ordinary time, for example, has been built around a semi-continuous reading of the synoptic gospels, combined with Hebrew scriptures which harmonize in some way with the gospel, and a second reading, generally from the epistles, which is semi-continuous and not related to the other two. During the major seasons of the church year, however, all three readings have a greater affinity with each other because the ethos of the season has strongly colored their selection. Readings appointed for sacramental rites, on the other hand, are arranged more like a smorgasbord, allowing a community a free hand in selecting pertinent readings from a wide array of texts. Interestingly, whatever the principle of arrangement, the juxtaposition of readings or their assignment to a particular feast often yields a further meaning to the individual selections.

Why a Supplementary Collection of Readings?

The last several decades have witnessed the preparation and revision of lectionaries in nearly every major, mainline Christian denomination, a labor largely inspired by the liturgical reform of the Second Vatican Council. Why then, with ink barely dry on their pages, do we propose a supplementary collection of readings?

Critique of various lectionary efforts has included: criticism of the way pericopes have been "cut," sometimes eliminating verses deemed important; objection to the occasionally tenuous relationship of the Hebrew and Christian scriptures appointed for a given Sunday; negative judgment about some of the typological uses of the Hebrew scriptures; and concern that particular passages were not included, especially some of the great narratives of the Hebrew scriptures. Some have challenged the structuring of a lectionary around the gospel stories; others have debated the inclusion of the so-called apocryphal or deutero-canonical books.

Now add to these concerns the feminist critique.

More and more women are asking of the lectionary: Where are our voices? Where are our memories and our hopes? Does this collection of texts really represent "the kernel of ourselves"? If the word of God is a two-edged sword, where is the other edge?

Why are prominent women from the Hebrew and Christian scriptures missing from the lectionary or included in such an attenuated fashion? Where is Hannah's prayer, for example, or the great story of Esther or Judith? Where are the daughters of Philip who prophesy, or Phoebe and Lois and those other women who ministered alongside Paul?

Why are some pericopes "cut" in such a way as to eliminate references to women? Why, for example, would a lectionary include the story of David dancing before the ark while the few verses about Michal "who despised David as he danced" are censored out? Analogously, why do we occasionally discover that "short forms" of the readings eliminate references to women: Palm Sunday's shortened reading of the passion according to Mark stops before we hear of the faithful women at the foot of the cross; the story of the woman afflicted with a hemorrhage for twelve years drops out of the shortened gospel on the Thirteenth Sunday of the Year. In addition, some key readings are assigned to less significant days in the calendar; some readings give a negative interpretation of women, perpetuating the patriarchal "household codes" of behavior, for example, or outrageous analogies such as "conduct like the defilement of a menstruous woman" (Ez 36:17)—the latter proclaimed during that most holy of nights, the vigil of Easter? Why have those who shaped the lectionary allowed readings so antithetical to contemporary cultural sensitivities to remain in our "canon within a canon" as, for example, those on the feast of the Holy Family when wives are enjoined to be submissive to their husbands—a proclamation which regularly prompts nudges, broad grins, even snickers as it is proclaimed, a proclamation which has also justified domestic violence!

Such anomalies and inconsistencies are not insignificant! Women may well ask: Where are our histories and our hopes? What helps to link us to the great women of our tradition? Where do we look for exemplars of strength and tenderness in living out the Christian life?

There is a reciprocal relationship between identity and history as the oppressed of every age—and feminists of our day—have discovered. The more sensitive we become to history, the more conscious we are of our present identity and our future possibilities. The stronger our identity, the more we cultivate a deeper knowledge of our past. A supplementary collection of readings which has something significant to say to women about women's salvation history is needed precisely to harvest the power of our history and to present the *total* mystery of salvation in Christ, salvation yet to be completed in us.

What's in *Silent Voices, Sacred Lives?*

Gathering this collection of supplementary reading, *Silent Voices, Sacred Lives,* was inspired by a class held at the Catholic Theological Union in the Winter Quarter of 1990. Kathleen Hughes and Carolyn Osiek teamed up to offer a course in "Feminist Hermeneutics and Worship"; Sharon Karam was on sabbatical at CTU and participated in the class; Barbara Bowe became involved in the subject through conversations over the dinner table.

It was Sharon who initially suggested the need for such a collection of texts after trying, unsuccessfully, to identify good resources for the brief prayer which began each class. Where was the other edge? Where were women's voices and women's lives preserved in the tradition? Why were texts by and about women, texts contemporaneous with the establishment of the canon of scripture, not included in its formation? Why was the lectionary, that canon within a canon, so often unsatisfying? What could we learn from some of the early intertestamental literature, non-canonical early church sources, church orders, mystical literature, poetry, gnostic writings, diaries, visions, and epitaphs which might have a bearing on our lives—which might express that kernel of ourselves so elusive in official lectionaries?

In the literature we reviewed we encountered alternative images of God, women, church, ministry and spirituality. During the class and in subsequent conversations, we became convinced of the contemporary relevance of many early literary sources for our lives. Why, we wondered, were these sources not generally known and how could we make them more readily available? To this end, an appendix gives sufficient background for each of the texts cited in this collection in order for readers to locate our sources and continue the research begun in these pages.

We discovered writings which disturbed as well as consoled; we uncovered literature which offered answers to some of the great human dilemmas and sometimes posed their own set of questions for which we had no answers. In particular, we found and delighted in writings about God and our relationship with God as well as with God's definitive self-revelation, Jesus Christ. The paradox at the heart of the paschal mystery of Christ, namely the reversals of strength in weakness, salvation through infamy, liberty in discipleship, life through death—all of this is mirrored in the faithful women whose voices we have retrieved in these pages.

We found sayings, epitaphs, accounts of martyrdoms, even some few descriptions of women at worship, which expressed women's religious experience, often to heroic lengths. And we did not shy away from the less than sterling foremothers of the tradition. It is salutary to reflect on the avarice of Sapphira, the treachery of Jezebel, and the power struggle between Athaliah and Jehosheba. Surely we are not exempt from the same temptations!

In the course of our research we also examined some traditional lectionary texts and proposed to one another alternative interpretations of these scripture texts—and these alternative interpretations have found their way into this book as well. Each reading presented here is prefaced by a sentence or two of introduction. These introductions sometimes give the provenance of the writing but more often suggest a fresh interpretation. Did Lot's wife, for example, look back with reluctance, or was she motivated by compassion? Why is it that women were among the first to be witnesses of the Risen One and yet among the last to be believed?

The design of the book is simple. One reading has been appointed for each day of the church year beginning with the First Sunday of Advent. Many of the readings in this collection are "discrete" readings, isolated selections of the work from which they have been taken. But we have also decided to incorporate some wonderful narratives, and these are spread over several days at a time. *The Acts of Perpetua and Felicitas*, *The Life of Marcella*, and the stories of *The Holy Women of the Syrian Orient*, for example, are too good to shorten any further. These latter texts are arranged in continuous and semi-continuous fashion, and to a certain extent their impact will be dependent on use of the full story over several days. In all cases, the particular genre determined the appropriate length of the selection: epitaphs proved to be the shortest selections, narratives the longest.

Scripture passages which also appear in the Roman Lectionary for Sundays and weekdays were first assembled and most often were assigned to the same day as in the Lectionary. When a reading has synoptic parallels, we generally selected only one rendering of the story and gave the others as cross-referenced citations. A notable exception to this rule is our treatment of events surrounding the passion as well as the post-Easter apparitions. Most of these parallel passages at the heart of the gospel story have been retained.

Next we assigned readings as they seemed to us appropriate for particular feasts or seasons, either as an echo of the traditional themes of these days or as a counterpoint to traditional interpretation. An example of the latter is our placement of John 12:1-8, the woman's anointing of Jesus' body, on the eve of Corpus Christi lest we too quickly spiritualize the feast of the Body of Christ. The reader will find in the section entitled The Church Year a quick reference to discrete and continuous readings as appointed in the calendar.

There is a calendar of women's feasts in the appendix. We decided not to include a set of readings appointed for this "sanctoral cycle." By leaving the sanctoral calendar open we wish to encourage local communities to fill out this feast-day calendar with people and events important to the life of their community and to find readings here or elsewhere which will illuminate these days. Only thus will communities preserve God's ongoing revelation which is as particular and local as the daily lives of their members.

Use of This Book

We imagine this book to be useful to communities both large and small which gather for public prayer on a regular or occasional basis. Feminist groups may choose to begin or end their meetings with prayer; small intentional communities may find these readings conducive to reflective conversation over the dinner table; religious communities who gather regularly for informal prayer may find here a helpful addition to their resources for faith-sharing. Any community pattern of prayer in which daily readings are used may be enriched through the use of this material. In fact, communities may find here a living word, a liberating word, a saving word—a richer fare for our day at the table of the word.

While lectionaries are designed primarily for use in public worship, they are also frequently used for solitary prayer, for spiritual reading, for study and reflection, for days of private retreat. So, too, this supplementary collection of texts may prove a fruitful source of nourishment for individual study, reflection and prayer.

Whether used in common prayer or solitary meditation, these readings may also contribute to what has come to be called "bibliotherapy," that is, the use of reading to correct wounded memories, to fill in gaps in one's identity, to help us all identify vicariously with the human-religious experiences of the women whose lives are captured in these pages as mirrors of our own. These women tried to be faithful to the holy life to which God had called them, and struggled and doubted and were tempted just as we—and most prevailed thanks to the fidelity of God and the love of their sisters. For that alone, their memory should be treasured.

A Few Final Notes

The short introductions to each reading help to situate the text in a context, to highlight feminist interpretation, and sometimes to demythologize traditional interpretation. These introductions may prove to be useful in suggesting a tone or style of proclamation or in giving an insight for homiletic reflection. In general, they are not meant to be read aloud.

Some editorial judgments were made along the way. Most gender exclusive masculine references have been edited out of the text or have been altered. "The Son of Man," for example, is rendered "The Child of Humanity." References to God as "Father" have been altered; the title "Lord"—after long discussion and in light of some womanist concerns—has been retained. Reference to the human community is invariably inclusive.

The opening and closing phrases of many readings have been altered to assure comprehension of the setting or appropriate transitions. We have also sometimes shortened sentences, removed some archaic language, and placed citations to biblical allusions in the text.

Some texts in this collection do contain a good number of unfamiliar proper names. A pronunciation guide has been provided in order to indicate which syllable should be accented in proper names; some proper names already familiar to the scripturally literate have not been marked. The reader should attempt to be consistent and, however unfamiliar the text, to speak with authority.

Conclusion

This book is filled with the stories of sacred lives, many of them long forgotten. As you tell stories over the dinner table, reminisce in moments by the fire, eulogize at wakes, and toast with stories at your weddings, as you gather for prayer and praise or meditate in solitude, let these tales enrich your repertoire of the ways God has moved among us and the ways women have struggled to respond with integrity—for here is the kernel of ourselves.

Kathleen Hughes, R.S.C.J.

THE CHURCH YEAR

ADVENT SEASON
First Week of Advent
    Sunday   Revelation 12:1–6
    Monday   1 Enoch 42:1–3
    Tuesday   Sirach 1:1–10
    Wednesday   Sirach 4:11–18
    Thursday   Sirach 6:18–31
    Friday   Sirach 24:1–12
    Saturday   Sirach 24:13–14, 19–21

Second Week of Advent
    Sunday   Genesis 16:1–12, 15–16
    Monday   *Martyrdom of Saint Crispina*
    Tuesday   *Martyrdom of Saint Crispina*
    Wednesday   *Martyrdom of Saint Crispina*
    Thursday   *Sibylline Oracle* 3:1–23
    Friday   2 Kings 22:8, 11–20
    Saturday   John 16:20–22

Third Week of Advent
    Sunday   Luke 1:26–38
    Monday   Hadewijch, "To Learn Mary's Humility"
    Tuesday   *Testament of the Three Patriarchs* 5:9–6:8
    Wednesday   Genesis 38:13–18, 24–27
    Thursday   Acts 21:8–14
    Friday   Hippolytus, *Refutation of All Heresies* 8.19

Fourth Week of Advent
    Sunday   Luke 1:39–56

Weekdays of Advent

December 17	Sirach 51:12b–20
December 18	1 Samuel 4:4–22
December 19	Romans 8:35–39
December 20	Isaiah 54:7–8
December 21	Zephaniah 3:14–18
December 22	Galatians 4:4–7
December 23	Matthew 1:18–23

CHRISTMAS SEASON

Vigil	Hildegaard of Bingen
Mass at Midnight	*Sibylline Oracles* 8: 456–479
Mass during Day	Luke 2:1–14
Sunday in Octave of Christmas	
Holy Family	Julian of Norwich, *Showings* 59
December 26	Julian of Norwich, *Showings* 49
December 27	Exodus 1:15–22
December 28	Luke 2:15–19
December 29	Luke 2:22–35
December 30	Luke 2:36–40
December 31	Luke 2:41–52
January 1	
Solemnity of Mary, Mother of God	Epiphanius, *Medicine Box* 78.23
Second Sunday after Christmas	Clement of Alexandria, *Who Is the Rich One Who Can Be Saved?* 37
January 2	Hosea 11:1–9
January 3	*Protoevangelium of James* 4.1–9
January 4	*Protoevangelium of James* 5.1–6.1

January 5	*Protoevangelium of James* 6.2
January 6 Epiphany	*Sibylline Oracles* 2: 1–5, 32–55
Sunday after January 6 Baptism of the Lord	Wisdom of Solomon 7:21–28
January 7 or Monday after Epiphany	*Acts of Peter* 7:20
January 8 or Tuesday after Epiphany	*Acts of Peter* 7:21
January 9 or Wednesday after Epiphany	Galatians 3:23–28
January 10 or Thursday after Epiphany	2 Samuel 6:12–23
January 11 or Friday after Epiphany	2 Samuel 11:1–17, 26–27
January 12 or Saturday after Epiphany	2 Kings 11:1–4, 9–16, 20

LENTEN SEASON

Ash Wednesday	*Joseph and Aseneth* 21:11–21
Thursday after Ash Wednesday	Wisdom of Solomon 6:12–19
Friday after Ash Wednesday	Wisdom of Solomon 7:7–14b
Saturday after Ash Wednesday	James 3:13–18

First Week of Lent

Sunday	Mechtild of Magdeburg, "True Sorrow"
Monday	Catherine of Siena, *Dialogue*
Tuesday	Hadewijch, *Letters* 151, 163
Wednesday	Philippians 4:1–9
Thursday	Esther (Greek) C 14:18b, 3–5, 12–15a
Friday	*Joseph and Aseneth* 11:3–14
Saturday	*Joseph and Aseneth* 11:19–12:4

Second Week of Lent

Sunday	Mechtild of Magdeburg, "Praise of God"
Monday	Isaiah 46:3–4
Tuesday	*Acts of Peter*
Wednesday	Matthew 20:17–28
Thursday	Socrates, *Church History* 1.17

Friday　　　　　Socrates, *Church History* 1.17
Saturday　　　　Galatians 4:24–5:1

Third Week of Lent
　Sunday　　　　John 4:5–30, 39–42
　Monday　　　　*Testament of Job* 21:1–22:3
　Tuesday　　　　*Testament of Job* 23:1–24:10
　Wednesday　　　*Testament of Job* 39:1–40:14
　Thursday　　　*Testament of Job* 46:1–51:4
　Friday　　　　*Holy Women of the Syrian Orient*: Ruhm
　Saturday　　　*Holy Women of the Syrian Orient*: Ruhm

Fourth Week of Lent
　Sunday　　　　*Martyrs of Lyon and Vienne* 16–19
　Monday　　　　*Sayings of the Desert Mother Syncletica*
　Tuesday　　　　*Sayings of the Desert Mother Syncletica*
　Wednesday　　　*Sayings of the Desert Mother Syncletica*
　Thursday　　　*Sayings of the Desert Mother Syncletica*
　Friday　　　　*Sayings of the Desert Mother Syncletica*
　Saturday　　　*Sayings of the Desert Mother Syncletica*

Fifth Week of Lent
　Sunday　　　　John 8:2–11
　Monday　　　　Daniel 13:1–9, 15–17, 19–27
　Tuesday　　　　Daniel 13:28–30, 33–43
　Wednesday　　　Daniel 13:44–60, 62–63
　Thursday　　　2 Kings 4:1–7
　Friday　　　　2 Kings 4:8–17
　Saturday　　　2 Kings 4:18–37

Holy Week
　Passion Sunday (Palm Sunday)　　Mark 14:3–9
　Monday　　　　　　　　　　　　Matthew 27:15–26
　Tuesday　　　　　　　　　　　Luke 23:26–31
　Wednesday　　　　　　　　　　Mark 14:66–72

EASTER TRIDUUM AND EASTER SEASON
　Mass of the Lord's Supper　　John 19:25–27
　Good Friday　　　　　　　　*Martyrs of Lyon and Vienne*
　　　　　　　　　　　　　　40–42

Holy Saturday Meditation   *Martyrs of Lyon and Vienne*
                                  53–56
Easter Vigil   Luke 24:1–12
Easter Sunday   John 20:1–2, 11–18

Octave of Easter
    Monday   *Gospel of Mary* [Magdalene] 9.6–10.16
    Tuesday   Song of Solomon 3:1–4
    Wednesday   Gertrude, *Spiritual Exercises*
    Thursday   Matthew 27:55–61
    Friday   *Apocalypse of Elijah* 4:1–6
    Saturday   Mark 16:9–13

Second Week of Easter
    Sunday   *Odes of Solomon* 19:1–7
    Monday   Julian of Norwich, *Showings* 59
    Tuesday   Acts 16:11–15
    Wednesday   *Sibylline Oracles* 4:1–23
    Thursday   Proverbs 8:22–31
    Friday   *Gospel of Mary* [Magdalene] 17.7–18.15
    Saturday   *Odes of Solomon* 33.5–13

Third Week of Easter
    Sunday   *Odes of Solomon* 40
    Monday   *Holy Women of the Syrian Orient*: Martha
    Tuesday   *Holy Women of the Syrian Orient*: Martha
    Wednesday   *Holy Women of the Syrian Orient*: Martha
    Thursday   *Holy Women of the Syrian Orient*: Martha
    Friday   *Holy Women of the Syrian Orient*: Martha
    Saturday   Acts 9:36–42

Fourth Week of Easter
    Sunday   *Acts of John* 82–83
    Monday   *Acts of John* 19–23 passim
    Tuesday   *Acts of John* 24
    Wednesday   Epitaph of Regina
    Thursday   John 11:1–6
    Friday   John 11:17–27
    Saturday   John 11:28–37

Fifth Week of Easter
  Sunday   John 11:38–45
  Monday   Acts 12:11–17
  Tuesday   Mark 16:1–8
  Wednesday *Gospel of Bartholomew* 2.1–12
  Thursday   *Gospel of Bartholomew* 2.13–14
  Friday   *Gospel of Bartholomew* 2.15–22
  Saturday   *Acts of Thomas* 27

Sixth Week of Easter
  Sunday   Matthew 28:1–10
  Monday   Acts 16:16–18
  Tuesday   *Egeria's Travels* 45:1–46:4
  Wednesday *Holy Women of the Syrian Orient:*
         Anahid
  Thursday (Ascension) Hildegaard of Bingen
  Friday   Acts 18:1–4
  Saturday   Acts 18:18–28

Seventh Week of Easter
  Sunday   Hadewijch, *Vision* 13
  Monday   Acts 1:12–14
  Tuesday   Hadewijch, *School of Love* passim
  Wednesday Hadewijch, *School of Love* passim
  Thursday   *The Ecclesiastical Canons*
         of the Apostles 24
  Friday   *Didascalia Apostolorum* 3, 12, 1–13, 1
  Vigil of Pentecost Prayer for the Ordination of a Deaconess,
         Apostolic Constitutions 8.19–20
  Pentecost Sunday Hadewijch, *The Paradoxes of Love*

SOLEMNITIES OF THE LORD DURING ORDINARY TIME
  Trinity Sunday (The Sunday after Pentecost)
    Vigil   Job 19:25–27

    Solemnity Julian of Norwich, *Showings* 54

  Corpus Christi (The Sunday after Trinity Sunday)
    Vigil   John 12:1–8

Solemnity   Julian of Norwich, *Showings*, 60

Sacred Heart (Friday after Corpus Christi)
    Vigil   Hadewijch, *The Madness of Love*

Solemnity   *Odes of Solomon* 8

Christ the King
    (See Thirty-fourth Sunday of the Year)

OTHER MAJOR CELEBRATIONS DURING ORDINARY TIME
    November 1   All Saints   Hadewijch, *Love Alone*
    November 2   All Souls   Dhuoda's Epitaph

SEASON OF THE YEAR
First Week of the Year
    Sunday   (See Baptism of the Lord)
    Monday   *Testaments of the Twelve Patriarchs* 1:5–12
    Tuesday   Judges 4:4–16
    Wednesday   Judges 4:17–22
    Thursday   Judges 5:1, 6–9, 12–15b, 24–31
    Friday   Pseudo-Philo, *Biblical Antiquities* 32:11–18
    Saturday   Pseudo-Philo, *Biblical Antiquities* 33:1–6

Second Week of the Year
    Sunday   *Acts of Paul* 9
    Monday   Jerome, *Life of Paula* 1–2
    Tuesday   Jerome, *Life of Paula* 3
    Wednesday   Jerome, *Life of Paula* 3
    Thursday   Jerome, *Life of Paula* 15–16
    Friday   Jerome, *Life of Paula* 20
    Saturday   Jerome, *Life of Paula* 20–21

Third Week of the Year
    Sunday   John 2:1–11
    Monday   Jerome, *Life of Paula* 21–22
    Tuesday   Jerome, *Life of Paula* 27
    Wednesday   Jerome, *Life of Paula* 28–29

Thursday	Jerome, *Life of Paula* 30–31
Friday	Jerome, *Life of Paula* 32–33
Saturday	Jerome, *Life of Paula* 34–35

Fourth Week of the Year

Sunday	Judith 13:18–20
Monday	Tertullian, *On the Soul* 9
Tuesday	Luke 8:40–42, 49–56
Wednesday	*Sibylline Oracles* 8:480–500
Thursday	1 Samuel 28:5–8, 11–14, 20, 24–25
Friday	Mark 6:14–29
Saturday	Genesis 20:1–18

Fifth Week of the Year

Sunday	Mark 1:29–39
Monday	*Sayings of the Desert Mother Theodora*
Tuesday	*Sayings of the Desert Mother Theodora*
Wednesday	1 Kings 10:1–10, 13
Thursday	Genesis 24:10–28
Friday	Genesis 24:42–49
Saturday	Genesis 24:50–67

Sixth Week of the Year

Sunday	Matthew 26:6–13
Monday	*Holy Women of the Syrian Orient:* Elizabeth
Tuesday	*Apostolic Constitutions* 2.26.6, 8
Wednesday	1 Samuel 25:2–42 passim
Thursday	*Egeria's Travels* 3.1–6
Friday	*Egeria's Travels* 3.6–4.1
Saturday	*Egeria's Travels* 10.7

Seventh Week of the Year

Sunday	Mark 7:24–30
Monday	Genesis 25:19–28
Tuesday	Julian, *Showings* 58
Wednesday	Mechtild of Magdeburg, *The Soul and God*
Thursday	Romans 16:1–16

| Friday | John Chrysostom, *Homily on Romans* 16:1–2 |
| Saturday | John Chrysostom, *Homily on Romans* 16:6–7 |

Eighth Week of the Year
Sunday	Luke 8:19–21
Monday	Julian, *Showings* 53
Tuesday	Epitaphs of Two Women Deacons
Wednesday	Numbers 27:1–8
Thursday	1 Samuel 1:1–8
Friday	1 Samuel 1:9–20
Saturday	1 Samuel 1:21–28

Ninth Week of the Year
Sunday	1 Samuel 2:1–10
Monday	4 Maccabees 14:11–20
Tuesday	4 Maccabees 15:1–13, 16–17
Wednesday	4 Maccabees 15:24–31
Thursday	4 Maccabees 16:1–4, 12–25
Friday	4 Maccabees 17:1–6
Saturday	Epiphanius, *Medicine Box* 48.2.4; 12.4; 13.1; 49.1.3; Eusebius, *Ecclesiastical History* 5.16.17

Tenth Week of the Year
Sunday	Luke 7:11–16a
Monday	Epiphanius, *Medicine Box* 79
Tuesday	1 Kings 17:7–16
Wednesday	1 Kings 17:17–24
Thursday	*Acts of Peter* 6:17
Friday	*Acts of Peter* 6:17
Saturday	1 Kings 21:1–11, 14–16

Eleventh Week of the Year
Sunday	Luke 7:36–50
Monday	Gregory of Nyssa, *Life of Macrina*
Tuesday	Gregory of Nyssa, *Life of Macrina*
Wednesday	Gregory of Nyssa, *Life of Macrina*
Thursday	Gregory of Nyssa, *Life of Macrina*

Friday   Gregory of Nyssa, *Life of Macrina*
Saturday   Gregory of Nyssa, *Life of Macrina*

Twelfth Week of the Year
    Sunday   Proverbs 9:1–6
    Monday   Gregory of Nyssa, *Life of Macrina*
    Tuesday   Gregory of Nyssa, *Life of Macrina*
    Wednesday   Gregory of Nyssa, *Life of Macrina*
    Thursday   Gregory of Nyssa, *Life of Macrina*
    Friday   Gregory of Nyssa, *Life of Macrina*
    Saturday   Gregory of Nyssa, *Life of Macrina*

Thirteenth Week of the Year
    Sunday   Mark 5:25–34
    Monday   Pseudo-Philo, *Biblical Antiquities* 50:4–8
    Tuesday   Genesis 19:15–26
    Wednesday   Genesis 21:5, 8–21
    Thursday   Egeria's Travels 16.1–4
    Friday   Egeria's Travels 17.1–19.4
    Saturday   Judges 16:4–21

Fourteenth Week of the Year
    Sunday   Isaiah 66:10–14
    Monday   Mark 15:40–47
    Tuesday   *Thunder, Perfect Mind* 13, 1–14, 1
    Wednesday   *Thunder, Perfect Mind* 14, 26–15, 16
    Thursday   *Thunder, Perfect Mind* 15, 17–16, 5
    Friday   *Thunder, Perfect Mind* 16, 12–36
    Saturday   *Thunder, Perfect Mind* 20, 27–35; 21, 12–32

Fifteenth Week of the Year
    Sunday   Epitaphs of Sophia, Marin and Rufina
    Monday   Acts 5:1–11
    Tuesday   Exodus 2:1–10
    Wednesday   Exodus 2:15b–22
    Thursday   Exodus 15:19–22
    Friday   Numbers 12:1–16; 20:1
    Saturday   Proverbs 4:5–13

Sixteenth Week of the Year
Sunday	Luke 10:38–42
Monday	Micah 6:1–4, 6–8
Tuesday	Mark 3:31–35
Wednesday	Genesis 18:1–15
Thursday	*Acts of Andrew* 2–5, 7
Friday	*Acts of Andrew* 14
Saturday	*Acts of Andrew* Martyrdom 2.10

Seventeenth Week of the Year
Sunday	*Acts of Thomas* 6–7
Monday	Matthew 13:31–35
Tuesday	Genesis 1:26–2:3
Wednesday	*Sibylline Oracles* 1:1–18
Thursday	*Sibylline Oracles* 3:816–830
Friday	Matthew 13:54–58
Saturday	Song of Solomon 8:1–5

Eighteenth Week of the Year
Sunday	Isaiah 42:14–16
Monday	2 Timothy 1:1–8
Tuesday	Sirach 6:5–17
Wednesday	*Acts of Paul and Thecla* 7–10
Thursday	*Acts of Paul and Thecla* 15–19
Friday	*Acts of Paul and Thecla* 20–22
Saturday	*Acts of Paul and Thecla* 23–25

Nineteenth Week of the Year
Sunday	*Acts of Paul and Thecla* 26–29
Monday	*Acts of Paul and Thecla* 30–33
Tuesday	*Acts of Paul and Thecla* 34–36
Wednesday	*Acts of Paul and Thecla* 37–39
Thursday	*Acts of Paul and Thecla* 40–43
Friday	*Egeria's Travels* 22.1–23.6
Saturday	Proverbs 3:13–18

Twentieth Week of the Year
Sunday	Matthew 15:21–28
Monday	Joshua 2:1–21

Tuesday	Joshua 6:17–25
Wednesday	Ruth 1:1–9
Thursday	Ruth 1:10–22
Friday	Ruth 3:1–13
Saturday	Ruth 4:7–17

Twenty-first Week of the Year

Sunday	2 Corinthians 5:14–17
Monday	*Life of Olympias* 1–4
Tuesday	*Life of Olympias* 5–7
Wednesday	*Life of Olympias* 8–10
Thursday	*Life of Olympias* 10–11
Friday	*Life of Olympias* 12–13
Saturday	*Life of Olympias* 14–16

Twenty-second Week of the Year

Sunday	Matthew 25:1–13
Monday	Epiphanius, *Medicine Box* 49:1–2
Tuesday	Augustine, *Confessions* 9.8
Wednesday	Augustine, *Confessions* 9.8
Thursday	Augustine, *Confessions* 9.9
Friday	Augustine, *Confessions* 9.9
Saturday	Augustine, *Confessions* 9.10

Twenty-third Week of the Year

Sunday	Augustine, *Confessions* 9.10–11
Monday	Augustine, *Confessions* 9.12
Tuesday	Augustine, *Confessions* 9.12–13
Wednesday	Proverbs 6:20–23
Thursday	Genesis 29:4–12
Friday	Genesis 29:13–30
Saturday	Genesis 35:16–21

Twenty-fourth Week of the Year

Sunday	Luke 8:1–3
Monday	Esther 1:5–22 passim
Tuesday	Esther 2:1–11
Wednesday	Esther 2:12–18 passim
Thursday	Esther 2:19–23

Friday	Esther 3:1–4:8 passim
Saturday	Esther 4:9–16

Twenty-fifth Week of the Year

Sunday	Esther D 15:1–16
Monday	Esther 5:3–8
Tuesday	Esther 5:9–14
Wednesday	Esther 6:1–14 passim
Thursday	Esther 7:1–10
Friday	Esther 8:3–10
Saturday	Esther 9:20–32 passim

Twenty-sixth Week of the Year

Sunday	Jerome, *Life of Marcella* 1–2
Monday	Jerome, *Life of Marcella* 3–4
Tuesday	Jerome, *Life of Marcella* 5
Wednesday	Jerome, *Life of Marcella* 6–7
Thursday	Jerome, *Life of Marcella* 8–10
Friday	Jerome, *Life of Marcella* 13–14
Saturday	Job 42:10–17

Twenty-seventh Week of the Year

Sunday	Genesis 2:18–25
Monday	*Life of Adam and Eve* 9–11
Tuesday	*Shepherd of Hermas*, Vision 1.2.2–3; 3.3–4.3
Wednesday	*Shepherd of Hermas*, Vision 3.1.1–6
Thursday	*Shepherd of Hermas*, Vision 3.8.1–10
Friday	*Shepherd of Hermas*, Vision 3.10.1–13.4
Saturday	Luke 11:27–28

Twenty-eighth Week of the Year

Sunday	Dhuoda, *On John 15 to Her Son*
Monday	*Acts of Perpetua and Felicitas* 2–3
Tuesday	*Acts of Perpetua and Felicitas* 4
Wednesday	*Acts of Perpetua and Felicitas* 5–6
Thursday	*Acts of Perpetua and Felicitas* 7–9
Friday	*Acts of Perpetua and Felicitas* 10
Saturday	*Acts of Perpetua and Felicitas* 15

Twenty-ninth Week of the Year
    Sunday   *Acts of Perpetua and Felicitas* 16–17
    Monday   *Acts of Perpetua and Felicitas* 18
    Tuesday   *Acts of Perpetua and Felicitas* 19–20
    Wednesday   *Acts of Perpetua and Felicitas* 21
    Thurday   Judges 11:29–40
    Friday   Pseudo-Philo, *Biblical Antiquities* 40:1–3
    Saturday   Pseudo-Philo, *Biblical Antiquities* 40:4–8

Thirtieth Week of the Year
    Sunday   Luke 13:10–17
    Monday   Luke 15:1–10
    Tuesday   Rudolf, *Life of Leoba*
    Wednesday   Rudolf, *Life of Leoba*
    Thursday   Rudolf, *Life of Leoba*
    Friday   Rudolf, *Life of Leoba*
    Saturday   Rudolf, *Life of Leoba*

Thirty-first Week of the Year
    Sunday   Rudolf, *Life of Leoba*
    Monday   Rudolf, *Life of Leoba*
    Tuesday   Rudolf, *Life of Leoba*
    Wednesday   Rudolf, *Life of Leoba*
    Thursday   Rudolf, *Life of Leoba*
    Friday   Rudolf, *Life of Leoba*
    Saturday   Rudolf, *Life of Leoba*

Thirty-second Week of the Year
    Sunday   Mark 12:38–44
    Monday   *Sayings of the Desert Mother Sarah*
    Tuesday   Jerome, *Letter 77 on Fabiola* 2
    Wednesday   Jerome, *Letter 77 on Fabiola* 3
    Thursday   Jerome, *Letter 77 on Fabiola* 3–5
    Friday   Jerome, *Letter 77 on Fabiola* 6
    Saturday   Jerome, *Letter 77 on Fabiola* 7

Thirty-third Week of the Year
    Sunday   Proverbs 31:13–31
    Monday   Jerome, *Letter 77 on Fabiola* 8–9

Tuesday   Jerome, *Letter 77 on Fabiola* 10
Wednesday   Jerome, *Letter 77 on Fabiola* 11–12
Thursday   Epitaph of Arsinoe
Friday   2 Samuel 13:1–14
Saturday   2 Samuel 13:15–22

Thirty-fourth or Last Week of the Year
Sunday   Solemnity of Christ the King
                           Martyrdom of Potamiaena and Basilides
Monday   Luke 21:1–4
Tuesday   *Martyrdom of Sts. Agape, Irene, Chione and Companions* 1–2
Wednesday   *Martyrdom of Sts. Agape, Irene, Chione and Companions* 3–4
Thursday   *Martyrdom of Sts. Agape, Irene, Chione and Companions* 5
Friday   *Martyrdom of Sts. Agape, Irene, Chione and Companions* 6
Saturday   *Sibylline Oracles* 2:1–31

FIRST SUNDAY OF ADVENT
Revelation 12:1–6

The liturgical year begins with a primordial symbol: a woman giving birth.

A great portent appeared in heaven: a woman clothed with the sun, with the moon under her feet, and on her head a crown of twelve stars. She was pregnant and was crying out in birthpangs, in the agony of giving birth. Then another portent appeared in heaven: a great red dragon, with seven heads and ten horns, and seven diadems on his heads. His tail swept down a third of the stars of heaven and threw them to the earth. Then the dragon stood before the woman who was about to bear a child, so that he might devour her child as soon as it was born. And she gave birth to a son, a male child, who is to rule all the nations with a rod of iron. But her child was snatched away and taken to God and to God's throne; and the woman fled into the wilderness, where she has a place prepared by God, so that there she can be nourished for one thousand two hundred sixty days.

FIRST WEEK OF ADVENT
Monday
1 Enoch 42:1–3

Wisdom, the female Sophia, finding no place to dwell on earth, returns to her heavenly home. The author of John's Prologue employs this theme to interpret Jesus as the one sent by God.

Wisdom could not find a place in which she could dwell,
but a place was found for her in the heavens.

Then Wisdom went out to dwell with the children of the people,
but she found no dwelling place.
Wisdom returned to her place
and she settled permanently among the angels.
Then Iniquity went out of her rooms,
and found whom she did not expect.
And she dwelt with them,
like rain in a desert,
like dew on a thirsty land.

FIRST WEEK OF ADVENT
Tuesday
Sirach 1:1–10

The preacher sings the praises of Wisdom. She is the one who has been "lavished upon all those who love the Lord."

All wisdom is from the Lord,
    and with God it remains forever.
The sand of the sea, the drops of rain,
    and the days of eternity—who can count them?
The height of heaven, the breadth of the earth,
    the abyss, and wisdom—who can search them out?
Wisdom was created before all other things,
    and prudent understanding from eternity.
The root of wisdom—to whom has it been revealed?
Her subtleties—who knows them?
There is but one who is wise,
    greatly to be feared,
    seated upon a throne—the Lord.
It is God who created her;
    saw her and took her measure;
    poured her out upon all works,
    upon all the living according to God's gift;
God lavished her upon those who love the Lord.

FIRST WEEK OF ADVENT
Wednesday
Sirach 4:11–18

Wisdom teaches us about God's ways. She reveals the divine mysteries to those who remain faithful.

Wisdom teaches her children
    and gives help to those who seek her.
Whoever loves her loves life,
    and those who seek her from early morning are filled with joy.
Whoever holds her fast inherits glory,
    and the Lord blesses the place she enters.
Those who serve her minister to the Holy One;
    the Lord loves those who love her.
Those who obey her will judge the nations,
    and all who listen to her will live secure.
If they remain faithful, they will inherit her;
    their descendants will also obtain her.
For at first she will walk with them on tortuous paths;
    she will bring fear and dread upon them,
and will torment them by her discipline
    until she trusts them,
and she will test them with her ordinances.
Then she will come straight back to them again and gladden them,
    and will reveal her secrets to them.

FIRST WEEK OF ADVENT
Thursday
Sirach 6:18–31

The invitation of Jesus to "Come" and to "Shoulder my yoke" (Mt 11:28–30) echoes the words of Sirach. Christians saw in Jesus the manifestation of Wisdom; she alone gave rest and joy to those who searched and found her.

My child, from your youth choose discipline,
    and when you have gray hair you will still find wisdom.
Come to her like one who plows and sows,
    and wait for her good harvest.
For when you cultivate her you will toil but little,
    and soon you will eat of her produce.
She seems very harsh to the undisciplined;
    fools cannot remain with her.
She will be like a heavy stone to test them,
    and they will not delay in casting her aside.
For wisdom is like her name;
    she is not readily perceived by many.
Listen, my child, and accept my judgment;
    do not reject my counsel.
Put your feet into her fetters,
    and your neck into her collar.
Bend your shoulders and carry her,
    and do not fret under her bonds.
Come to her with all your soul,
    and keep her ways with all your might.
Search out and seek, and she will become known to you;
    and when you get hold of her, do not let her go.
For at last you will find the rest she gives,
    and she will be changed into joy for you.
Then her fetters will become for you a strong defense,
    and her collar a glorious robe.

Her yoke is a golden ornament,
  and her bonds a purple cord.
You will wear her like a glorious robe,
  and put her on like a splendid crown.

FIRST WEEK OF ADVENT
Friday
Sirach 24:1–12

*Like the Word of John's Prologue, Wisdom was with God in the
beginning, co-creator with the Most High, who "pitched her tent"
among us.*

Wisdom praises herself,
  and tells of her glory in the midst of her people.
In the assembly of the Most High she opens her mouth,
  and in the presence of God's hosts she tells of her glory:
"I came forth from the mouth of the Most High,
  and covered the earth like a mist.
I dwelt in the highest heavens,
  and my throne was in a pillar of cloud.
Alone I compassed the vault of heaven
  and traversed the depths of the abyss.
Over waves of the sea, over all the earth,
  and over every people and nation I have held sway.
Among all these I sought a resting place;
  in whose territory should I abide?

"Then the Creator of all things gave me a command,
  and my Creator chose the place for my tent.
God said, 'Make your dwelling in Jacob,
  and in Israel receive your inheritance.'
Before the ages, in the beginning, God created me,
  and for all the ages I shall not cease to be.

In the holy tent I ministered before God,
   and so I was established in Zion.
Thus in the beloved city God gave me a resting place,
   and in Jerusalem was my domain.
I took root in an honored people,
   in the portion of the Lord, the Lord's heritage."

FIRST WEEK OF ADVENT
Saturday
Sirach 24:13–14, 19–21

---

*The cry of Wisdom to "Come and eat" the food and drink that will
satisfy became a symbol for eucharist in the early church. The
hunger and thirst expressed in this text also convey our longing in
this season.*

"I grew tall like a cedar in Lebanon,
   and like a cypress on the heights of Hermon.
I grew tall like a palm tree in En-gedi,
   and like rosebushes in Jericho;
like a fair olive tree in the field,
   and like a plane tree beside water I grew tall.

"Come to me, you who desire me,
   and eat your fill of my fruits.
For the memory of me is sweeter than honey,
   and the possession of me sweeter than the honeycomb.
Those who eat of me will hunger for more,
   and those who drink of me will thirst for more."

SECOND SUNDAY OF ADVENT
Genesis 16:1–12, 15–16

Conception and birth are overarching themes of Advent. In this reading we hear of Hagar, the rejected and oppressed woman, who was blessed by God.

Sarai, Abram's wife, bore him no children. She had an Egyptian slave-girl whose name was Hagar, and Sarai said to Abram, "You see that the Lord has prevented me from bearing children; go in to my slave-girl; it may be that I shall obtain children by her." And Abram listened to the voice of Sarai. So, after Abram had lived ten years in the land of Canaan, Sarai, Abram's wife, took Hagar the Egyptian, her slave-girl and gave her to her husband Abram as a wife. He went in to Hagar, and she conceived; and when she saw that she had conceived, she looked with contempt on her mistress. Then Sarai said to Abram, "May the wrong done to me be on you! I gave my slave-girl to your embrace, and when she saw that she had conceived, she looked on me with contempt. May the Lord judge between you and me!" But Abram said to Sarai, "Your slave-girl is in your power; do to her as you please." Then Sarai dealt harshly with her, and she ran away from her.

The angel of the Lord found her by a spring of water in the wilderness, the spring on the way to Shur. And he said, "Hagar, slave-girl of Sarai, where have you come from and where are you going?" She said, "I am running away from my mistress Sarai." The angel of the Lord said to her, "Return to your mistress, and submit to her." The angel of the Lord also said to her, "I will so greatly multiply your offspring that they cannot be counted for multitude." And the angel of the Lord said to her,

"Now you have conceived and shall bear a son;
you shall call him Ishmael,
for the Lord has given heed to your affliction.
He shall be a wild ass of a man,
with his hand against everyone, and everyone's hand against him;
and he shall live at odds with all his kin."

Hagar bore Abram a son; and Abram named his son, whom Hagar

bore, Ishmael [Ish' ma el]. Abram was eighty-six years old when Hagar bore him Ishmael.

**See Gal 4:24–5:1, Second Week of Lent, Saturday,
and Gen 21:5, 8–20, Thirteenth Week of the Year, Wednesday**

SECOND WEEK OF ADVENT
Monday
Martyrdom of Saint Crispina (#1 of 3)

Crispina, from the city of Toura in North Africa, is brought to trial in the city of Tebessa on December 5, 304 CE. The record of her solitary interrogation reveals a courageous and determined woman. For her Advent was an anticipation of Christ's final coming. (This reading could be very effectively read in parts.)

It was the fifth day of December in the ninth consulate of Diocletian [Di o cle' ti an] Augustus and the eighth of Maximian [Max im' i an] Augustus (December 5, 304) in the colony of Tebessa [Te bes' sa]. The proconsul Anullinus [A nul li' nus] sat in judgement on the tribunal in his council-chamber, and the court clerk spoke, "Crispina [Cris pi' na], a lady of Toura, is to be tried at your good pleasure; she has spurned the law of our lords the emperors."

"Bring her in," said the proconsul Anullinus.

When Crispina had come in, the proconsul Anullinus said, "Are you aware of what is commanded by the sacred decree?"

"No," said Crispina, "I do not know what has been commanded."

Anullinus said, "That you should offer sacrifice to all our gods for the welfare of the emperors, in accordance with the law issued by our lords, the reverend Augusti Diocletian and Maximian and the most noble Caesars Constantius [Con stan' ti us] and Maximus [Max' i mus]."

"I have never sacrificed," replied Crispina, "and I shall not do so save to the one true God and to our Lord, Jesus Christ, who was born and died."

"Break with this superstition," said the proconsul Anullinus, "and bow your head to the sacred rites of the gods of Rome."

Crispina replied, "Every day I worship my God almighty. I know of no other God."

"You are a stubborn and insolent woman," said Anullinus, "and you will soon begin to feel the force of our laws against your will."

"Whatever happens," said Crispina, "I shall be glad to suffer it on behalf of the faith which I hold firm."

Anullinus said, "It is merely the folly of your mind that you will not put aside this superstition and worship the sacred gods."

"I worship daily," replied Crispina, "but I worship the living and true God, who is my Lord, and I know no other."

Anullinus said, "I put before you the sacred edict. You must obey it."

"I will obey the edict," replied Crispina, "but the one given by my Lord Jesus Christ."

"I will have you beheaded," said the proconsul Anullinus, "if you do not obey the edicts of our lords the emperors. You will be forced to yield and obey them; all the province of Africa has offered sacrifice, as you are well aware."

"May they never find it easy," replied Crispina, "to make me offer sacrifice to demons: but I sacrifice to the Lord who has made heaven and earth, the sea, and all things that are in them." (Ps 146:6; cf. Acts 4:24)

SECOND WEEK OF ADVENT
Tuesday
Martyrdom of Saint Crispina (#2 of 3)

The trial of the Advent martyr Crispina continues. In the face of intimidating threats, she confirms her resolution to remain in the faith into which she was born.

"So our gods are not acceptable to you!" said Anullinus. "But you shall be forced to show them respect if you want to remain alive for any worship at all!"

"That piety is worthless," replied Crispina, "which forces people to be crushed against their will."

Anullinus said, "But all we ask of your religion is that you bow your head in the sacred temples and offer incense to the gods of Rome."

"I have never done this since I was born," replied Crispina. "I do not know how, nor will I ever do it so long as I live."

"Do so now," said Anullinus, "if you wish to escape unharmed from the sanctions of the law."

"I do not fear anything you say," replied Crispina. "That is nothing. But if I deliberately choose to commit a sacrilege, the God who is in heaven will destroy me at once, and I shall not be found in God on the last day."

"You will not commit sacrilege," said Anullinus, "if you obey the sacred edicts."

Crispina replied, "Perish the gods who have not made heaven and earth! (Jer 10:11) I offer sacrifice to the eternal God who abides for ever. This one is the true God who is to be feared; God has made the sea, the green grass, and the dry earth. But what can humans offer me who are the creatures of God's hand?"

Anullinus said, "Revere the religion of Rome, which is observed by our lords the unconquerable Caesars as well as ourselves."

"I have told you again and again," replied Crispina, "I am prepared to undergo any tortures that you wish to subject me to, rather than defile my soul with idols which are stones and the creations of human hands."

SECOND WEEK OF ADVENT
Wednesday
Martyrdom of Saint Crispina (#3 of 3)

Crispina is first sentenced to have her head shaved, a ritual of humiliation, especially for an upper-class woman as she probably is. Finally the death sentence is pronounced and she is beheaded. She goes to death convinced that she has chosen "security" and life, and that to renounce her faith in God would be to choose ultimate death.

"You utter blasphemy," said Anullinus, "in not honouring what is conducive to your safety." Anullinus then turned to the court notary and added: "Let her be completely disfigured by having her hair cut and her head shaved with a razor till she is bald, that her beauty might first thus be brought to shame."

"Let your gods speak," replied Crispina, "and then I shall believe. If I were not seeking my own security I should not now be on trial before your tribunal."

Anullinus said: "Do you wish to live a long life or die in agony like the rest of your companions?"

Crispina replied: "If I wished to die and to give my soul to destruction in the eternal fire, I should already have surrendered my will to your demons."

Anullinus said: "If you despise the worship of our venerable gods, I shall order your head to be cut off."

"I should thank my God," replied Crispina, "if I obtained this. I should be very happy to lose my head for the sake of my God. For I refuse to sacrifice to these ridiculous deaf and dumb statues."

Anullinus the proconsul said: "And so you absolutely persist in this foolish frame of mind?"

Crispina replied: "My God who is and who abides for ever ordered me to be born; it was God who gave me salvation through the saving waters of baptism; who is at my side, helping me, strengthening the handmaid in all things so that she will not commit sacrilege."

Anullinus said, "Why should we suffer this impious Christian woman any further? Read back the minutes of the trial from the record."

And when they were read, the proconsul Anullinus read the sentence from a tablet, "Seeing that Crispina has persisted in infamous superstition and refuses to offer sacrifice to our gods in accordance with the heavenly decrees of the Augustan law, I have ordered her to be executed with the sword."

Crispina replied, "I bless God who has so deigned to free me from your hands. Thanks be to God!" And making the sign of the cross on her forehead and putting out her neck, she was beheaded for the name of the Lord Jesus Christ, to whom is honour for ever. Amen.

[Alternative ending]

The blessed Crispina suffered in the colony of Tebessa on the fifth day of December, under the proconsul Anullinus, in the reign of our Lord Jesus Christ in the unity of the Holy Spirit for ever. Amen.

SECOND WEEK OF ADVENT
Thursday
Sibylline Oracles Book 3:1–23

In this season of prophets it is good to listen to the voice of the Sibyl, the woman prophet and seer, who proclaims her praises of God the marvelous Creator.

Blessed, heavenly one, who thunders on high, who have the cherubim
as your throne, I entreat you to give a little rest
to me who have prophesied unfailing truth, for my heart is tired within.
But why does my heart shake again? and why is my spirit
lashed by a whip, compelled from within to proclaim
an oracle to all? But I will utter everything again,
as much as God bids me say to people.

Creatures who have the form which God molded in the divine image,
why do you wander in vain, and not walk the straight path
ever mindful of the immortal creator?
There is one God, sole ruler, ineffable, who lives in the sky,
self-begotten, invisible, who sees all things.
No sculptor's hand made God, nor does a cast of gold or ivory reveal
God, by the crafts of humans. But God, eternal, is revealed divinity
as existing now, and formerly and again in the future.
For who, being mortal, is able to see God with eyes?
Or who will be able even to hear only
the name of the great heavenly God who rules the world?

God created everything by a word, heaven and sea,
untiring sun, full moon,
shining stars, strong mother Tethys,
springs and rivers, imperishable fire, days, nights.

SECOND WEEK OF ADVENT
Friday
2 Kings 22:8, 11–20

The prophet Huldah's authentication of the newly discovered book of the law makes it authoritative for the community.

The high priest Hilkiah [Hil ki' ah] said to Shaphan the secretary, "I have found the book of the law in the house of the Lord."

When the king heard the words of the book of the law, he tore his clothes. Then the king commanded the priest Hilkiah, Ahikam [A hi' kam] son of Shaphan, Achbor son of Micaiah [Mi chai' ah], Shaphan the secretary, and the king's servant Asaiah [A sa' i ah], saying, "Go, inquire of the Lord for me, for the people, and for all Judah, concerning the words of this book that has been found; for great is the wrath of the Lord that is kindled against us, because our ancestors did not obey the words of this book, to do according to all that is written concerning us."

So the priest Hilkiah, Ahikam, Achbor, Shaphan, and Asaiah went to the prophet Huldah, the wife of Shallum, son of Tikvah, son of Harhas, keeper of the wardrobe; she resided in Jerusalem in the Second Quarter, where they consulted her. She declared to them, "Thus says the Lord, the God of Israel: Tell the man who sent you to me, Thus says the Lord, I will indeed bring disaster on this place and on its inhabitants—all the words of the book that the king of Judah has read. Because they have abandoned me and have made offerings to other gods, so that they have provoked me to anger with all the work of their hands, therefore my wrath will be kindled against this place, and it will not be quenched. But as to the king of Judah, who sent you to inquire of the Lord, thus shall you say to him, Thus says the Lord, the God of Israel: Regarding the words that you have heard, because your heart was penitent, and you humbled yourself before the Lord, when you heard how I spoke against this place, and against its inhabitants, that they should become a desolation and a curse, and because you have torn your clothes and wept before me, I also have heard you, says the Lord. Therefore, I will gather you to your ancestors, and you shall be gathered to your grave in peace; your eyes shall not see all the disaster that I will bring on this place." They took the message back to the king.

SECOND WEEK OF ADVENT
Saturday
John 16:20–22

Childbirth is often the best analogy for apocalyptic expectation (cf. Rom 8:22; 1 Thess 5:3).

Jesus continued, "Very truly, I tell you, you will weep and mourn, but the world will rejoice; you will have pain, but your pain will turn into joy. When a woman is in labor, she has pain, because her hour has come. But when her child is born, she no longer remembers the anguish because of the joy of having brought a human being into the world. So you have pain now; but I will see you again, and your hearts will rejoice, and no one will take your joy from you."

THIRD SUNDAY OF ADVENT
Luke 1:26–38

Two exceptional pregnancies—of a virgin and an elderly woman—demonstrate that every new stirring of life is an unpredictable gift and demands a faith-filled response.

In the sixth month the angel Gabriel was sent by God to a town in Galilee called Nazareth, to a virgin engaged to a man whose name was Joseph, of the house of David. The virgin's name was Mary. And he came to her and said, "Greetings, favored one! The Lord is with you." But she was much perplexed by his words and pondered what sort of greeting this might be. The angel said to her, "Do not be afraid, Mary, for you have found favor with God. And now, you will conceive in your womb and bear a son, and you will name him Jesus. He will be great, and will be called the Son of the Most High, and the Lord God will give to him the throne of his ancestor David. He will reign over the house of

Jacob forever, and of his kingdom there will be no end." Mary said to the angel, "How can this be, since I am a virgin?" The angel said to her, "The Holy Spirit will come upon you, and the power of the Most High will overshadow you; therefore the child to be born will be holy; he will be called Son of God. And now, your relative Elizabeth in her old age has also conceived a son; and this is the sixth month for her who was said to be barren. For nothing will be impossible with God." Then Mary said, "Here am I, the servant of the Lord; let it be with me according to your word." Then the angel departed from her.

THIRD WEEK OF ADVENT
Monday
Hadewijch, *To Learn Mary's Humility*

The mystical reflections of Hadewijch set the mystery of Mary's life in the context which best celebrates her role and ours as those who long to bear God's life to others.

David said that when he remembered
    God, he was moved
And his spirit swooned away.
    He indeed was called strong in work,
    But Mary wrought a work of greater strength.
Truly David bore the largest share of that great work
Save for Mary, who received him totally.
As God and as Infant.
There can we first perceive
The genuine work of Love.

It was by deep longing
That this mystery happened to her,
That this noble Love was released
    To this noble woman
    Of high praise
In overflowing measure,

Because she wished nothing else and owned nothing else,
She wholly possessed him of whom every Jewish woman had read.

THIRD WEEK OF ADVENT
Tuesday
Testaments of the Three Patriarchs 5:9–6:8

Sarah interprets the meaning of the revelation to Abraham, and demonstrates that she, too, is gifted with the insight of faith, a primary Advent virtue.

Then Abraham arose and opened the door for Isaac. Isaac entered, hung upon his neck, and began to cry in a loud voice. Then Abraham's heart was moved, and he too cried with him in a loud voice. When the Commander-in-chief [Michael, the Archangel] saw them crying he too cried. Then Sarah, who was in her tent, heard their crying and came running to them. She found them embracing and crying. And Sarah said with tears, "My lord Abraham, what are you crying about? Tell me, my lord. Did this brother who is staying as our guest today bring you news about your nephew Lot, that he has died? Is it for this that you mourn thus?" Then the Commander-in-chief answered and said to her, "No, sister Sarah, it is not as you say. Rather, your son Isaac, it appears, had a dream and came to us crying, and when we saw him our hearts were likewise moved, and we cried."

When Sarah heard the Commander-in-chief's distinction of speech, she immediately realized that the speaker was an angel of the Lord. Then Sarah beckoned Abraham to come to the door and step outside, and she said to him, "My lord Abraham, do you know who this man is?" Abraham said, "I do not know." Sarah said, "You must know, my lord, the three heavenly men who stayed as guests in our tent beside the oak of Mamre when you slaughtered the unblemished calf and set a table for them. After the meat had been eaten, the calf got up again and exultantly suckled its mother. Do you not know, my lord Abraham, that they gave us Isaac, the very fruit of my womb, as was promised to us? For this man is one of those three holy men." Then Abraham said, "O Sarah, you have spoken truly. Glory and blessing from our God! For I too, late this evening, when I was washing his feet in the vessel which has the wash basin, said in my heart, 'These feet are those of one of the three men that I washed previously.' And later when his tears fell into the basin they became precious stones." And Abraham took them out of his bosom and gave them to Sarah and said, "If you do not believe me, look at them." Sarah took them and knelt down and embraced him and said, "Glory be to God who shows us wonders. And now know, my lord Abraham, that a revelation of something is among us, whether it be evil or good."

THIRD WEEK OF ADVENT
Wednesday
Genesis 38:13–18, 24–27

Tamar is the first woman named in the genealogy of Matthew's gospel (Mt 1:3). Left childless by the two wicked sons of Judah and by the delay of her father-in-law to give her his young son as a husband, Tamar had the courage to pursue her legal right to children and she gave birth to twins whose father was Judah.

When Tamar was told, "Your father-in-law is going up to Timnah to shear his sheep," she put off her widow's garments, put on a veil, wrapped herself up, and sat down at the entrance to Enaim, which is on the road to Timnah. She saw that Shelah was grown up, yet she had not been given to him in marriage. When Judah saw her, he thought her to be a prostitute, for she had covered her face. He went over to her at the road side, and said, "Come, let me come in to you," for he did not know that she was his daughter-in-law. She said, "What will you give me?" He answered, "I will send you a kid from the flock." And she said, "Only if you give me a pledge, until you send it . . . your signet and your cord, and the staff that is in your hand." So he gave them to her, and she conceived by him. About three months later Judah was told, "Your daughter-in-law Tamar . . . is pregnant as a result of whoredom." And Judah said, "Bring her out, and let her be burned." As she was being brought out, she sent word to her father-in-law, "It was the owner of these who made me pregnant." And she said, "Take note, please, whose these are, the signet and the cord and the staff." Then Judah acknowledged them and said, "She is more in the right than I. . . ." When the time of her delivery came, there were twins in her womb.

THIRD WEEK OF ADVENT
Thursday
Acts 21:8-14

An intriguing glimpse of the gift of prophecy among women is tucked into this narrative of Paul's journey. The narrative also provides a counterpoint to Mary's "Fiat": his to death and hers to life.

We came to Caesarea; and we went into the house of Philip the evangelist, one of the seven, and stayed with him. He had four unmarried daughters who had the gift of prophecy. While we were staying for several days, a prophet named Agabus [Ag′ a bus] came down from Judea. He came to us and took Paul's belt, bound his own feet and hands with it, and said, "Thus says the Holy Spirit, 'This is the way the Jews in Jerusalem will bind the man who owns this belt and will hand him over to the Gentiles.' " When we heard this, we and the people there urged him not to go up to Jerusalem. Then Paul answered, "What are you doing, weeping and breaking my heart? For I am ready not only to be bound but even to die in Jerusalem for the name of the Lord Jesus." Since he would not be persuaded, we remained silent except to say, "The Lord's will be done."

THIRD WEEK OF ADVENT
Friday
Hippolytus, *Refutation of All Heresies* 8.19

Hippolytus in early third-century Rome gives a hostile account of the powerful charismatic leadership of two women prophets, Maximilla and Priscilla in eastern Asia Minor. Through his ridicule we can see what influential leaders they were.

Some who are Phrygians by birth have been led astray by certain women, Priscilla and Maximilla [Max i mil' la], whom they consider prophets. They say that the Paraclete Spirit entered into them and previous to them they likewise consider Montanus [Mon ta' nus] a prophet. Since they have innumerable books of theirs, these people are deceived, neither exercising good judgment about their sayings, nor listening to those capable of judging but they are swept away by uncritical faith in them. They affirm that through them they have learned more than from law, prophets, and Gospels. They value these mere women above the Apostles and every spiritual gift, so that some of them dare to say that in them something greater than Christ has happened. With the Church they believe that God is the Father of all and Creator of all things, and they believe everything the Gospel says about Christ. But they introduce new fasts and feasts and the eating of dried foods and cabbages, claiming to have been thus taught by the women.

FOURTH SUNDAY OF ADVENT
Luke 1:39–56

In the midst of an intimate visit, the conversation of Mary and Elizabeth erupts into the praise of God.

In those days Mary set out and went with haste to a Judean town in the hill country, where she entered the house of Zechariah [Zech a ri' ah] and greeted Elizabeth. When Elizabeth heard Mary's greeting, the child leaped in her womb. And Elizabeth was filled with the Holy Spirit and exclaimed with a loud cry, "Blessed are you among women, and blessed is the fruit of your womb. And why has this happened to me, that the mother of my Lord comes to me? For as soon as I heard the sound of your greeting, the child in my womb leaped for joy. And blessed is she who believed that there would be a fulfillment of what was spoken to her by the Lord." And Mary said,

> "My soul magnifies the Lord,
> and my spirit rejoices in God my Savior
> who has looked with favor on me, a lowly serving maid.
> From this day all generations will call me blessed.
> The Mighty One has done great things for me;
> holy the name of the Lord,
> whose mercy is on the God-fearing
> from generation to generation.
> The arm of the Lord is filled with strength,
> scattering the proudhearted.
> God hurled the mighty from their thrones,
> lifting up the lowly.
> God filled the hungry with good things,
> sending the rich away empty.
> God has come to the help of Israel, the Lord's servant,
> remembering mercy,
> the mercy promised to our forebears,
> to Abraham and his children forever."

And Mary remained with her about three months and then returned to her home.

DECEMBER 17
Sirach 51:12b–20

Wisdom, always a female figure in Jewish tradition, is the one who gives access to God to those who search for her. The theme of searching and longing for wisdom is captured in the O Antiphon of today.

> I thank you and praise you,
>> and I bless the name of the Lord.
>
> While I was still young, before I went on my travels,
>> I sought wisdom openly in my prayer.
>
> Before the temple I asked for her,
>> and I will search for her until the end.
>
> From the first blossom to the ripening grape
>> my heart delighted in her;
>
> my foot walked on the straight path;
>> from my youth I followed her steps.
>
> I inclined my ear a little and received her,
>> and I found for myself much instruction.
>
> I made progress in her;
>> to the one who gives wisdom I will give glory.
>
> For I resolved to live according to wisdom,
>> and I was zealous for the good,
>> and I shall never be disappointed.
>
> My soul grappled with wisdom,
>> and in my conduct I was strict;
>
> I spread out my hands to the heavens,
>> and lamented my ignorance of her.
>
> I directed my soul to her,
>> and in purity I found her.
>
> With her I gained understanding from the first;
>> therefore I will never be forsaken.

DECEMBER 18
1 Samuel 4:4–22

The ark of the covenant, Israel's symbol of Immanuel, God-with-us, is captured in battle. This story also reflects the truth that women, though often not engaged in violence, suffer its consequences.

The people sent to Shiloh, and brought from there the ark of the covenant of the Lord of hosts, who is enthroned on the cherubim. The two sons of Eli, Hophni and Phinehas [Phin' e has], were there with the ark of the covenant of God.

When the ark of the covenant of the Lord came into the camp, all Israel gave a mighty shout, so that the earth resounded. When the Philistines [Phi lis' tines] heard the noise of the shouting, they said, "What does this great shouting in the camp of the Hebrews mean?" When they learned that the ark of the Lord had come to the camp, the Philistines were afraid; for they said, "Gods have come into the camp." They also said, "Woe to us! For nothing like this has happened before. Woe to us! Who can deliver us from the power of these mighty gods? These are the gods who struck the Egyptians with every sort of plague in the wilderness. Take courage, and be men, O Philistines, in order not to become slaves to the Hebrews as they have been to you; be men and fight."

So the Philistines fought; Israel was defeated, and they fled, everyone to his home. There was a very great slaughter, for there fell of Israel thirty thousand foot soldiers. The ark of God was captured; and the two sons of Eli, Hophni and Phinehas, died.

A man of Benjamin ran from the battle line, and came to Shiloh the same day, with his clothes torn and with earth upon his head. When he arrived Eli was sitting upon his seat by the road watching, for his heart trembled for the ark of God. When the man came into the city and told the news, all the city cried out. When Eli heard the sound of the outcry, he said, "What is this uproar?" Then the man came quickly and told Eli. Now Eli was ninety-eight years old and his eyes were set, so that he could not see. The man said to Eli, "I have just come from the battle; I fled from the battle today." He said, "How did it go, my son?" The messenger replied, "Israel has fled before the Philistines, and there has also been a great slaughter among the troops; your two sons also, Hophni and Phinehas, are dead, and the ark of God has been captured." When he mentioned the ark of God, Eli fell over backward from his seat by the side of the gate and his neck was broken and he died, for he was an old man, and heavy. He had judged Israel forty years.

Now his daughter-in-law, the wife of Phinehas, was pregnant, about to give birth. When she heard the news that the ark of God was captured, and that her father-in-law and her husband were dead, she bowed and gave birth; for her labor pains overwhelmed her. As she was about to die, the women attending her said to her, "Do not be afraid, for you have borne a son." But she did not answer or give heed. She named the child Ichabod [Ich' a bod], meaning, "The glory has departed from Israel," because the ark of God had been captured and because of her father-in-law and her husband. She said, "The glory has departed from Israel, for the ark of God has been captured."

DECEMBER 19
Romans 8:35–39

The Savior for whom we long is the liberator sent by God. The real mystery of Advent is the mystery of freedom in Christ.

Who will separate us from the love of Christ? Will hardship, or distress, or persecution, or famine, or nakedness, or peril, or sword? As it is written,

> "For your sake we are being killed all day long;
> we are accounted as sheep to be slaughtered."

Now in all these things we are more than conquerors through him who loved us. For I am convinced that neither death, nor life, nor angels, nor rulers, nor things present, nor things to come, nor powers, nor height, nor depth, nor anything else in all creation, will be able to separate us from the love of God in Christ Jesus our Lord.

DECEMBER 20
Isaiah 54:7-8

God's mercy is presented here in maternal terms, specifically as RAHAMIM—"womb-love."

For a brief moment I abandoned you,
   but with great compassion I will gather you.
In overflowing wrath for a moment
   I hid my face from you,
but with everlasting love I will have compassion on you,
   says the Lord, your Redeemer.

DECEMBER 21
Zephaniah 3:14-18

The anticipation of human liberation is cause for great rejoicing.

Sing aloud, O daughter Zion;
   shout, O Israel!
Rejoice and exult with all your heart,
   O daughter Jerusalem!
The Lord has taken away the judgments against you,
   God has turned away your enemies.
The king of Israel, the Lord, is in your midst;
   you shall fear disaster no more.
On that day it shall be said to Jerusalem:
Do not fear, O Zion;
   do not let your hands grow weak.
The Lord, your God, is in your midst,
   a warrior who gives victory;
God will rejoice over you with gladness,
   the Lord will renew you in God's love;

the Lord will exult over you with loud singing
  as on a day of festival.
I will remove disaster from you,
  so that you will not bear reproach for it.

DECEMBER 22
Galatians 4:4–7

---

*Our adoption as children of God through Christ is effected through
a woman.*

When the fullness of time had come, God sent the Son, born of a
woman, born under the law, in order to redeem those who were under
the law, so that we might receive adoption as children. And because you
are children, God has sent the Spirit of the Son into our hearts, crying,
"Abba!" So you are no longer a slave but a child, and if a child then also
an heir, through God.

DECEMBER 23
Matthew 1:18–23

---

*Like the other women in Matthew's genealogy, Tamar, Rahab,
Ruth, and Bathsheba (1:3–6), Mary's maternity is surrounded by
unusual circumstances.*

Now the birth of Jesus the Messiah took place in this way. When his
mother Mary had been engaged to Joseph, but before they lived together,
she was found to be with child from the Holy Spirit. Her husband Joseph,
being a righteous man and unwilling to expose her to public disgrace,
planned to dismiss her quietly. But just when he had resolved to do this,
an angel of the Lord appeared to him in a dream and said, "Joseph, son of

David, do not be afraid to take Mary as your wife, for the child conceived in her is from the Holy Spirit. She will bear a son, and you are to name him Jesus, for he will save his people from their sins." All this took place to fulfill what had been spoken by the Lord through the prophet:

> "Look, the virgin shall conceive
> and bear a son,
> and they shall name him Emmanuel" (Is 7:14),

which means, "God is with us."

VIGIL OF CHRISTMAS
Hildegard of Bingen

Perhaps Hildegard's vision of the feminine aspect of Jesus can save us from sentimentality in this season and refocus our faith on the mystery of Christ's humanity.

During the celebration on the eve of our Lord's Nativity, around the hour of the divine sacrifice, I entered a trance and saw something like a sun of marvelous brightness in the heaven, and in the middle of the sun the likeness of a virgin whose appearance was exceedingly beautiful in form and desirable to see. She was seated on a throne. Her hair was loosened over her shoulders, and on her head was a crown of the most splendid gold. In her right hand was a golden chalice. She was emerging from the sun which surrounded her on all sides. From the virgin herself emanated a splendor of great brilliance, which seemed at first to fill the place of our dwelling. Then gradually expanding after some period of time, it seemed to fill the whole earth.

Now next to that same sun there appeared a great cloud, extremely dark and horrible to see. When I gazed at the cloud, it rushed abruptly against the sun, darkened it, and cut off its splendor from the earth for some time. I saw this happen very often, moreover, so that the world was by turns darkened by the cloud and again illuminated by the sun. Whenever it happened that the cloud approached the sun and obstructed its light from the earth, the virgin who was enthroned within the sun seemed to be weeping copiously, as if grieving greatly because of the darkening of the world. I beheld this vision throughout that day without interruption, and all the following night, for I remained ever wakeful in prayer.

On the holy day of Christmas, now, when the solemnities of the masses were being celebrated, I asked the holy angel of God who appeared to me what sort of vision that was and what significance it had. He replied to me concerning that virgin, for I especially desired to know who she was, and he said: "That virgin whom you see is the sacred humanity of the Lord Jesus."

CHRISTMAS
Mass at Midnight
The Sibylline Oracles Book 8:456–479

The Sibyl retells the Incarnation story.

In the last times God changed the earth and, coming late
as a new light, God rose from the womb of the Virgin Mary.
Coming from heaven, God put on a mortal form.
First, then, Gabriel was revealed in his strong and holy person.
Second, the archangel also addressed the maiden in speech:
"Receive God, Virgin, in your immaculate bosom." Thus speaking, he
breathed in the grace of God, even to one who was always a maiden.
Fear and, at the same time, wonder seized her as she listened.
She stood trembling. Her mind fluttered
while her heart was shaken by the unfamiliar things she heard.
But again she rejoiced, and her heart was healed by the voice.
The maiden laughed and reddened her cheek,
rejoicing with joy and enchanted in heart with awe.
Courage also came over her. A word flew to her womb.
In time it was made flesh and came to life in the womb,
and was fashioned in mortal form and became a boy
by virgin birth. For this is a great wonder to humans,
but nothing is a great wonder for God.

The joyful earth fluttered to the child at its birth.
The heavenly throne laughed and the world rejoiced.
A wondrous, new-shining star was venerated by Magi.
The newborn child was revealed in a manger to those who obey God:
cowherds and goatherds and shepherds of sheep.
And Bethlehem was said to be the divinely named homeland of
    the word.

CHRISTMAS DAY
Luke 2:1–14

The birth of Jesus according to the flesh.

In those days a decree went out from Emperor Augustus that all the world should be registered. This was the first registration and was taken while Quirinius [Qui rin' i us] was governor of Syria. All went to their own towns to be registered. Joseph also went from the town of Nazareth in Galilee to Judea, to the city of David called Bethlehem, because he was descended from the house and family of David. He went to be registered with Mary, to whom he was engaged and who was expecting a child. While they were there, the time came for her to deliver her child. And she gave birth to her firstborn son and wrapped him in bands of cloth, and laid him in a manger, because there was no place for them in the inn.

In that region there were shepherds living in the fields, keeping watch over their flock by night. Then an angel of the Lord stood before them, and the glory of the Lord shone around them, and they were terrified. But the angel said to them, "Do not be afraid; for see—I am bringing you good news of great joy for all the people: to you is born a Savior, who is the Messiah, the Lord. This will be a sign for you: you will find a child wrapped in bands of cloth and lying in a manger." And suddenly there was with the angel a multitude of the heavenly host, praising God and saying,

"Glory to God in the highest heaven,
    and on earth peace among those whom God favors!"

SUNDAY IN THE OCTAVE OF CHRISTMAS —FEAST OF THE HOLY FAMILY
Julian of Norwich, *Showings* 59

The great mystic Julian contemplates motherhood in God.

Jesus is our true Mother in nature by our first creation, and he is our true Mother in grace by his taking our created nature. All the lovely works and all the sweet loving offices of beloved motherhood are appropriated to the second person, for in him we have this godly will, whole and safe forever, both in nature and in grace, from his own goodness proper to him.

I understand three ways of contemplating motherhood in God. The first is the foundation of our nature's creation; the second is his taking of our nature, where the motherhood of grace begins; the third is the motherhood at work. And in that, by the same grace, everything is penetrated, in length and in breadth, in height and in depth without end; and it is all one love.

DECEMBER 26
Second Day in the Octave of Christmas
Julian of Norwich, *Showings* 49

As the liturgical calendar developed, comites Christi, *friends of Christ, were assigned to the Christmas Octave, for example, Stephen, John, the Holy Innocents. In this reading Julian enlarges our understanding of the Christmas mystery by imaging salvation as a wide circle of friendship.*

I saw very truly that all our endless friendship, our place, our life and our being are in God. For that same endless goodness which protects us when we sin so that we do not perish, that same endless goodness constantly draws into us a peace, opposing our wrath and our perverse falling, and makes us see our need with true fear, and urgently to beseech God that we may have forgiveness, with a grace-given desire for our salvation. For we cannot be blessedly saved until we are truly in peace and in love, for that is our salvation.

DECEMBER 27
Third Day in the Octave of Christmas
Exodus 1:15–22

On the eve of the Feast of the Holy Innocents this reading invites reflection on all victimized children. Note in the story that the midwives have names and Pharaoh does not. Their cleverness carries out God's designs—sometimes subversion of authority is the only way to obey God.

The king of Egypt said to the Hebrew midwives, one of whom was named Shiphrah [Shiph' rah] and the other Puah [Pu' ah], "When you act as midwives to the Hebrew women, and see them on the birthstool, if it is a boy, kill him; but if it is a girl, she shall live." But the midwives feared God; they did not do as the king of Egypt commanded them, but they let the boys live. So the king of Egypt summoned the midwives and said to them, "Why have you done this, and allowed the boys to live?" The midwives said to Pharaoh, "Because the Hebrew women are not like the Egyptian women; for they are vigorous and give birth before the midwife comes to them." So God dealt well with the midwives; and the people multiplied and became very strong. And because the midwives feared God, God gave them families. Then Pharaoh commanded all his people, "Every boy that is born to the Hebrews you shall throw into the Nile, but you shall let every girl live."

DECEMBER 28
Fourth Day in the Octave of Christmas
Luke 2:15-19

Like all mothers, Mary ponders the mysterious birth, identity and fate of her child.

When the angels had left and gone into heaven, the shepherds said to one another, "Let us go now to Bethlehem and see this thing that has taken place, which the Lord has made known to us." So they went with haste and found Mary and Joseph, and the child lying in the manger. When they saw this, they made known what had been told them about this child; and all who heard it were amazed at what the shepherds told them. But Mary treasured all these words and pondered them in her heart.

DECEMBER 29
Fifth Day in the Octave of Christmas
Luke 2:22-35

All parents hope their children will turn out well, but parenting often entails suffering.

When the time came for the couple's purification according to the law of Moses, they brought Jesus up to Jerusalem to present him to the Lord [as it is written in the law of the Lord, "Every firstborn male shall be designated as holy to the Lord" (Ex 13:2)], and they offered a sacrifice according to what is stated in the law of the Lord, "A pair of turtledoves or two young pigeons" (Lev 12:8).

Now there was a man in Jerusalem whose name was Simeon; this man was righteous and devout, looking forward to the consolation of Israel, and the Holy Spirit rested on him. It had been revealed to him by the Holy Spirit that he would not see death before he had seen the Lord's Messiah. Guided by the Spirit, Simeon came into the temple; and when the parents brought in the child Jesus, to do for him what was customary under the law, Simeon took him in his arms and praised God, saying,

"Master, now you are dismissing your servant in peace,
    according to your word;
for my eyes have seen your salvation,
    which you have prepared in the presence of all peoples,
a light for revelation to the Gentiles
    and for glory to your people Israel."

And the child's father and mother were amazed at what was being said about him. Then Simeon blessed them and said to his mother Mary, "This child is destined for the falling and the rising of many in Israel, and to be a sign that will be opposed so that the inner thoughts of many will be revealed—and a sword will pierce your own soul, too."

DECEMBER 30
Sixth Day in the Octave of Christmas
Luke 2:36–40

The faithfulness of the prophet Anna is matched by her wisdom in recognizing the significance of this child.

There was also there a prophet, Anna, the daughter of Phanuel [Pha' nu el], of the tribe of Asher. She was of a great age, having lived with her husband seven years after her marriage, then as a widow to the age of eighty-four. She never left the temple but worshiped there with fasting and prayer night and day. When the child was brought to the temple, she began to praise God and to speak about the child to all who were looking for the redemption of Jerusalem.

When they had finished everything required by the law of the Lord, they returned to Galilee, to their own town of Nazareth. The child grew and became strong, filled with wisdom; and the favor of God was upon him.

DECEMBER 31
Seventh Day in the Octave of Christmas
Luke 2:41–52

A first sword pierces the heart of Jesus' mother.

Now every year the parents of Jesus went to Jerusalem for the festival of the Passover. And when he was twelve years old, they went up as usual for the festival. When the festival was ended and they started to return, the boy Jesus stayed behind in Jerusalem, but his parents did not know it. Assuming that he was in the group of travelers, they went a day's journey. Then they started to look for him among their relatives and friends. When they did not find him, they returned to Jerusalem to search for him. After three days they found him in the temple, sitting among the teachers, listening to them and asking them questions. And all who heard him were amazed at his understanding and his answers. When his parents saw him they were astonished; and his mother said to him, "Child, why have you treated us like this? Look, your father and I have been searching for you in great anxiety." He said to them, "Why were you searching for me? Did you not know that I must be in my Father's house?" But they did not understand what he said to them. Then he went down with them and came to Nazareth, and was obedient to them. His mother treasured all these things in her heart.

And Jesus increased in wisdom and in years, and in divine and human favor.

JANUARY 1
Solemnity of Mary, Mother of God
Epiphanius, *Medicine Box* 78.23

A fourth century Christian writer ridicules a local custom he has heard about, whereby women assemble to celebrate their own kind of liturgy in honor of Mary. We know nothing more about this custom except what Epiphanius tells us.

It is related that some women in Arabia, who come from the region of Thrace, put forward this silly idea: they prepare a kind of cake in the name of the ever-Virgin, assemble together, and in the name of the holy Virgin they attempt to undertake a deed that is irreverent and blasphemous beyond measure—in her name they function as priests for women. Now all this is godless and irreverent, a degeneration from the proclamation of the Holy Spirit, all of it a diabolic device and the teaching of an unclean spirit. In their regard the saying is fulfilled: "Some will separate themselves from the sound teaching, clinging to myths and demonic teachings" [1 Tim 4:1].

SECOND SUNDAY AFTER CHRISTMAS
Clement of Alexandria, *Who Is the Rich One Who Can Be Saved?* 37

In a treatise on the economic challenge of the gospel, Clement slips in a surprising reference to the femininity of God.

What more is necessary? See the mysteries of love, and then you will see a vision of the Father's bosom, whom the only-begotten God revealed (John 1:18). God is love itself and has been revealed to us through love. The unspeakable aspect of God is Father, the aspect that feels with us is Mother. By loving, the Father became feminine, and the great sign of this is what is born of God, for the fruit that is born of love is love.

JANUARY 2
Hosea 11:1–9

God's love for Israel is a mother's love, which rears with compassion and overwhelms with affection.

When Israel was a child, I loved him,
    and out of Egypt I called my son.
The more I called them,
    the more they went from me;
they kept sacrificing to the Baals,
    and offering incense to idols.

Yet it was I who taught Ephraim [E′ phra im] to walk,
    I took them up in my arms;
    but they did not know that I healed them.
I led them with cords of human kindness,
    with bands of love.
I was to them like those
    who lift infants to their cheeks.
    I bent down to them and fed them.

They shall return to the land of Egypt,
    and Assyria [As syr′ i a] shall be their king,
    because they have refused to return to me.
The sword rages in their cities,
    it consumes their oracle-priests,
    and devours because of their schemes.
My people are bent on turning away from me.
    To the Most High they call,
    but God does not raise them up at all.

How can I give you up, Ephraim?
  How can I hand you over, O Israel?
How can I make you like Admah?
  How can I treat you like Zeboiim [Ze boi′ im]?
My heart recoils within me;
  my compassion grows warm and tender.
I will not execute my fierce anger;
  I will not again destroy Ephraim;
for I am God and no mortal,
  the Holy One in your midst,
  and I will not come in wrath.

JANUARY 3
Protoevangelium of James 4.1–9 (#1 of 3)

This apocryphal text recounts Joachim and Anna longing for a child and their joy at the conception of Mary.

And behold an angel of the Lord came to her (Luke 2:9; Acts 12:7) and said: "Anna, Anna, the Lord has heard your prayer. You shall conceive and bear and your offspring shall be spoken of in the whole world." And Anna said: "As the Lord my God lives, if I bear a child, whether male or female, I will bring it as a gift to the Lord my God, and this child shall serve God all the days of its life" (1 Sam 2:11; 1:28).

And behold there came two messengers, who said to her: "Behold Joachim [Jo′ a chim] your husband is coming with his flocks; for an angel of the Lord came down to him and said to him: 'Joachim, Joachim, the Lord God has heard your prayer. Go down; behold, your wife Anna has conceived.'" And Joachim went down and called his herdsmen and said: "Bring me ten lambs without blemish and without spot; they shall belong to the Lord my God. And bring me twelve tender calves for the priests and elders, and a hundred kids for the whole people." And behold Joachim came with his flocks, and Anna stood at the gate and saw Joachim coming and ran immediately and hung on his neck, saying: "Now I know that the Lord God has greatly blessed me; for behold the widow is no longer a widow, and I, who was childless, have conceived."

JANUARY 4
Protoevangelium of James 5.1–6.1 (#2 of 3)

Mary's birth is told in language reminiscent of Luke. Anna, too, "magnifies God" and the child Mary grew strong day by day.

And Joachim rested the first day in his house.

But the next day he offered his gifts, saying in himself: "If the Lord God is gracious to me the frontlet of the priest (Exod 28:36–38) will make it clear to me."

And Joachim offered his gifts, and observed the priest's frontlet when he went up to the altar of the Lord; and he saw no sin in himself. And Joachim said: "Now I know that the Lord God is gracious to me and has forgiven all my sins." And he went down from the temple of the Lord justified, and went to his house.

And her months were fulfilled as the angel had said; in the ninth month Anna brought forth. And she said to the midwife: "What have I brought forth?" And she said: "A female." And Anna said: "My soul is magnified this day." And she lay down. And when the days were fulfilled, Anna purified herself from her childbed and gave suck to the child, and called her Mary.

Day by day the child waxed strong; when she was six months old, her mother stood her on the ground to see if she could stand. And she walked twice seven steps and came to her bosom. And she took her up, saying: "As the Lord my God lives, you shall walk no more upon this ground until I take you into the temple of the Lord." And she made a sanctuary in her bedchamber, and did not permit anything common or unclean to pass through it. And she summoned the undefiled daughters of the Hebrews, and they cared for her amusement.

JANUARY 5
Protoevangelium of James 6.2 (#3 of 3)

A charming account of Mary's first birthday party when she was blessed by the priests of the chief priests in the presence of all the people.

On the child's first birthday Joachim made a great feast, and invited the chief priests and the priests and the scribes and the elders and the whole people of Israel. And Joachim brought the child to the priests, and they blessed her, saying: "O God of our ancestors, bless this child and give her a name renowned for ever among all generations." And all the people said: "So be it, so be it, Amen." And they brought her to the chief priests, and they blessed her, saying: "O God of the heavenly heights, look upon this child and bless her with a supreme and unsurpassable blessing." And her mother carried her into the sanctuary of her bed-chamber and gave her suck. And Anna sang this song to the Lord God (1 Sam 2:1):

> "I will sing praises to the Lord my God,
> for God has visited me and taken away from me the reproach of
>   my enemies.
> And the Lord gave me the fruit of righteousness, unique and
>   manifold before God.
> Who will proclaim to the children of Reubel [Reuben] that Anna
>   gives suck?
> Hearken, hearken, you twelve tribes of Israel: Anna gives suck."

And she laid the child down to rest in the bedchamber with its sanctuary, and went out and served them. When the feast was ended, they went down rejoicing and glorifying the God of Israel.

EPIPHANY
Sibylline Oracles Book 2:1–5, 32–55

The Sibyl prophesies concerning the end time. Her images echo the traditional Epiphany vision of the convergence of all peoples in the holy city (Is 60).

When indeed God stopped my most perfectly wise song
as I played many things, God also again placed in my breast
a delightful utterance of wondrous words.
I will speak the following with my whole person in ecstasy
for I do not know what I say, but God bids me utter each thing.

Every harbor, every port will be free for people
as it was before, and shamelessness will perish.
And then again God will perform a great sign,
for a star will shine like a resplendent crown,
resplendent, gleaming from the radiant heaven
for no small number of days. For then God will show from heaven a
    crown to people who strive in contest.

Then again there will be a great contest for entry
to the heavenly city. It will be universal for all
people, holding the glory of immortality.
Then every people will strive for the immortal prizes
of most noble victory. For no one there can shamelessly
buy a crown for silver.

For holy Christ will make just awards to these
and crown the worthy. But to martyrs he will give
an immortal treasure, to those who pursue the contest even to death.
He will give an imperishable prize from the treasure
to virgins who run well and to all
who perform justice and to diverse nations
who live piously and acknowledge one God,
who love marriage and refrain from adultery.
He will give rich gifts and eternal hope to these also.

For every soul of mortals is a gracious gift of God
and it is not lawful for people to defile it with any grievous things.

SUNDAY AFTER JANUARY 6
Baptism of the Lord
Wisdom of Solomon 7:21–28

---

*It is the same Spirit of wisdom which filled Jesus at his baptism
which makes us, too, the friends of God and prophets in our world.*

I learned both what is secret and what is manifest,
for wisdom, the fashioner of all things, taught me.
There is in her a spirit that is intelligent, holy,
unique, manifold, subtle,
mobile, clear, unpolluted,
distinct, invulnerable, loving the good, keen,
irresistible, beneficent, humane,
steadfast, sure, free from anxiety,
all-powerful, overseeing all,
and penetrating through all spirits
that are intelligent, pure, and altogether subtle.
For wisdom is more mobile than any motion;
because of her pureness she pervades and penetrates all things.
For she is a breath of the power of God,
and a pure emanation of the glory of the Almighty;
therefore nothing defiled gains entrance into her.
For she is a reflection of eternal light,
a spotless mirror of the working of God,
and an image of God's goodness.
Although she is but one, she can do all things,
and while remaining in herself, she renews all things;
in every generation she passes into holy souls
and makes them friends of God, and prophets;
for God loves nothing so much as the person who lives with wisdom.

JANUARY 7 OR MONDAY AFTER EPIPHANY
Acts of Peter 7:20

The compassion of Jesus toward the widow in Naim (Lk 7:11–17) is imitated by Peter in his cure of this old and blind widow.

Peter went in and saw one of the old people, a widow that was blind, and her daughter giving her a hand and leading her to Marcellus' house. And Peter said to her, "Mother, come here; from this day onward Jesus gives you his right hand, through whom we have light unapproachable which no darkness hides; and he says to you through me, 'Open your eyes and see, and walk on your own.'" And at once the widow saw Peter laying his hand on her.

JANUARY 8 OR TUESDAY AFTER EPIPHANY
Acts of Peter 7:21

Peter cures many aged widows of their blindness and they, in turn, reveal to the crowd the mysteries of God.

When the ninth hour was fully come they stood up to pray. And now suddenly some of the old blind widows, who still sat there unknown to Peter and had not stood up, called out and said to Peter, "We sit here together, Peter, hoping in Christ Jesus and believing in him. So as you have now made one of us to see, we beg you, sir Peter, let us also share his mercy and goodness." And Peter said to them, "If there is in you the faith which is in Christ, if it is established in you, then see with your mind what you do not see with your eyes; and though your ears be closed, yet let them open in your mind within you. These eyes shall again be closed, that see nothing but men and cattle and dumb animals and stones and sticks; but only the inner eyes see Jesus Christ. Yet now, Lord, let your sweet and holy name assist these women; touch their eyes, for you are able, that they may see with their own eyesight."

And when prayer was made by all, the room in which they were shone as if with lightning, such as shines in the clouds. Yet it was not such light as is seen by day but, ineffable, invisible, such as no one could describe, a light that shone on us so brightly that we were senseless with bewilderment, and called upon the Lord and said, "Have mercy on us your servants, Lord. Let your gift to us, Lord, be such as we can endure." And as we lay there, there stood there only those widows, which were blind. But the bright light which appeared to us entered into their eyes and made them see.

Then Peter said to them, "Tell us what you saw." And they said, "We saw an old man, who had such a presence as we cannot describe to you"; but others said, "We saw a growing lad"; and others said, "We saw a boy who gently touched our eyes, and so our eyes were opened." So Peter praised the Lord, saying, "You alone are God the Lord, to whom praise is due. How many lips should we need to give thanks to you in accordance with your mercy? So, brothers and sisters, as I told you a little while ago, God is greater than our thoughts, as we have learnt from the aged widows, how they have seen the Lord in a variety of forms."

JANUARY 9 OR WEDNESDAY AFTER EPIPHANY
Galatians 3:23–28

This fundamental text affirming the equality of all the baptized in Christ Jesus has yet to be realized.

Now before faith came, we were imprisoned and guarded under the law until faith would be revealed. Therefore the law was our disciplinarian until Christ came, so that we might be justified by faith. But now that faith has come, we are no longer subject to a disciplinarian, for in Christ Jesus you are all children of God through faith. As many of you as were baptized into Christ have clothed yourselves with Christ. There is no longer Jew or Greek, there is no longer slave or free, there is no longer male and female; for all of you are one in Christ Jesus. And if you belong to Christ, then you are Abraham and Sarah's offspring, heirs according to the promise.

JANUARY 10 OR THURSDAY AFTER EPIPHANY
2 Samuel 6:12–23

For David, religious devotion takes priority over cultural expectations; but Michal expects more dignified behavior of her king. Her "insolence" is costly.

David went and brought up the ark of God from the house of Obededom [O bed e' dom] to the city of David with rejoicing; and when those who bore the ark of the Lord had gone six paces, he sacrificed an ox and a fatling. David danced before the Lord with all his might; David was girded with a linen ephod. So David and all the house of Israel brought up the ark of the Lord with shouting, and with the sound of the trumpet.

As the ark of the Lord came into the city of David, Michal daughter of Saul looked out of the window, and saw King David leaping and dancing before the Lord; and she despised him in her heart.

They brought in the ark of the Lord, and set it in its place, inside the tent that David had pitched for it; and David offered burnt offerings and offerings of well-being before the Lord. When David had finished offering the burnt offerings and the offerings of well-being, he blessed the people in the name of the Lord of hosts, and distributed food among all the people, the whole multitude of Israel, both men and women, to each a cake of bread, a portion of meat, and a cake of raisins. Then all the people went back to their homes.

David returned to bless his household. But Michal the daughter of Saul came out to meet David, and said, "How the king of Israel honored himself today, uncovering himself today before the eyes of his servants' maids, as any vulgar fellow might shamelessly uncover himself." David said to Michal, "It was before the Lord, who chose me in place of your father and all his household, to appoint me as prince over Israel, the people of the Lord, that I have danced before the Lord. I will make myself yet more contemptible than this, and I will be abased in my own eyes; but by the maids of whom you have spoken, by them I shall be held in honor." And Michal the daughter of Saul had no child to the day of her death.

JANUARY 11 OR FRIDAY AFTER EPIPHANY
2 Samuel 11:1-17, 26-27

The culture does not permit Bathsheba to refuse the king, and thus she becomes an accomplice in royal adultery and, indirectly, in murder.

In the spring of the year, the time when kings go out to battle, David sent Joab with his officers and all Israel with him; they ravaged the Ammonites [Am' mon ites], and besieged Rabbah. But David remained at Jerusalem.

It happened, late one afternoon, when David rose from his couch and was walking about on the roof of the king's house, that he saw from the roof a woman bathing; the woman was very beautiful. David sent someone to inquire about the woman. It was reported, "This is Bathsheba [Bath she' ba] daughter of Eliam [E li' am], the wife of Uriah [U ri' ah] the Hittite." So David sent messengers to get her, and she came to him, and he lay with her. (Now she was purifying herself after her period.) Then she returned to her house. The woman conceived; and she sent and told David, "I am pregnant."

So David sent word to Joab, "Send me Uriah the Hittite." And Joab sent Uriah to David. When Uriah came to him, David asked how Joab and the people fared, and how the war was going. Then David said to Uriah, "Go down to your house, and wash your feet." Uriah went out of the king's house, and there followed him a present from the king. But Uriah slept at the entrance of the king's house with all the servants of his lord, and did not go down to his house. When they told David, "Uriah did not go down to his house," David said to Uriah, "You have just come from a journey. Why did you not go down to your house?" Uriah said to

David, "The ark and Israel and Judah remain in booths; and my lord Joab and the servants of my lord are camping in the open field; shall I then go to my house, to eat and to drink, and to lie with my wife? As you live, and as your soul lives, I will not do such a thing." Then David said to Uriah, "Remain here today also, and tomorrow I will send you back." So Uriah remained in Jerusalem that day. On the next day, David invited him to eat and drink in his presence and made him drunk; and in the evening he went out to lie on his couch with the servants of his lord, but he did not go down to his house.

In the morning David wrote a letter to Joab, and sent it by the hand of Uriah. In the letter he wrote, "Set Uriah in the forefront of the hardest fighting, and then draw back from him, so that he may be struck down and die." As Joab was besieging the city, he assigned Uriah to the place where he knew there were valiant warriors. The men of the city came out and fought with Joab; and some of the servants of David among the people fell. Uriah the Hittite was killed as well. Then Joab sent and told David all the news about the fighting.

When the wife of Uriah heard that her husband was dead, she made lamentation for him. When the mourning was over, David sent and brought her to his house, and she became his wife, and bore him a son.

See Matthew 1:6

JANUARY 12 OR SATURDAY AFTER EPIPHANY
2 Kings 11:1-4, 9-16, 20

Two women, Athaliah and Jehosheba, are pitted against each other for control of the kingdom.

Now when Athaliah [Ath a li' ah], Ahaziah's [A ha zi' ah's] mother, saw that her son was dead, she set about to destroy all the royal family. But Jehosheba [Je hosh' e ba], King Joram's daughter and Ahaziah's sister, took Joash son of Ahaziah, and stole him away from among the king's children who were about to be killed; she put him and his nurse in a bedroom. Thus she hid him from Athaliah, so that he was not killed; he remained with her six years, hidden in the house of the Lord, while Athaliah reigned over the land.

But in the seventh year Jehoiada [Je hoi' a da] summoned the captains of the Carites and of the guards and had them come to him in the house of the Lord. He made a covenant with them and put them under oath in the house of the Lord; then he showed them the king's son.

The captains did according to all that the priest Jehoiada [Je hoi' a da] commanded; each brought him men who were to go off duty on the sabbath, with those who were to come on duty on the sabbath, and came to the priest Jehoiada. The priest delivered to the captains the spears and shields that had been King David's, which were in the house of the Lord; the guards stood, every man with his weapons in his hand, from the south side of the house to the north side of the house, around the altar and the house, to guard the king on every side. Then he brought out the king's son, put the crown on him, and gave him the covenant; they proclaimed him king, and anointed him; they clapped their hands and shouted, "Long live the king!"

When Athaliah heard the noise of the guard and of the people, she went into the house of the Lord to the people; when she looked, there was the king standing by the pillar, according to custom, with the captains and the trumpeters beside the king, and all the people of the land rejoicing and blowing trumpets. Athaliah tore her clothes and cried, "Treason! Treason!" Then the priest Jehoiada commanded the captains who were set over the army, "Bring her out between the ranks, and kill with the sword anyone who follows her." For the priest said, "Let her not be killed in the house of the Lord." So they laid hands on her; she went through the horses' entrance to the king's house and there she was put to death. So all the people of the land rejoiced; and the city was quiet after Athaliah had been killed with the sword at the king's house.

ASH WEDNESDAY
Joseph and Aseneth 21:11–21

Inspiring narratives grew up around Genesis 41:45, which records that Pharaoh gave to Joseph as his wife, Aseneth, the daughter of Potiphera, a priest of On. One such narrative, recorded here, sets the tone for the celebration of Ash Wednesday. Assured that God had heard her prayer for forgiveness, Aseneth offered a psalm of thanksgiving which closely parallels David's prayer for mercy in Psalm 51.

[This reading could be proclaimed antiphonally.]

Aseneth [As' e neth] began to confess to the Lord God and gave thanks, praying, for all the good things of which she was deemed worthy by the Lord:

> I have sinned, Lord, I have sinned,
> before you I have sinned much,
> I, Aseneth, daughter of Pentephres [Pen' te phres], priest of
> Heliopolis [He li op' o lis],
> who is an overseer of everything.

> I have sinned, Lord, I have sinned;
> before you I have sinned much.
> I was prospering in my father's house,
> and was a boastful and arrogant virgin.

> I have sinned, Lord, I have sinned;
> before you I have sinned much.
> And I have worshiped strange gods who were without number,
> and eaten bread from their sacrifices.

> I have sinned, Lord, I have sinned;
> before you I have sinned much.
> Bread of strangulation I have eaten,
> and a cup of insidiousness I have drunk from the table of death.

I have sinned, Lord, I have sinned;
  before you I have sinned much.
And I did not know the Lord the God of Heaven,
and I did not trust in the Most High God of life.

I have sinned, Lord, I have sinned;
  before you I have sinned much.
For I trusted in the richness of my glory and in my beauty,
and I was boastful and arrogant.

I have sinned, Lord, I have sinned;
  before you I have sinned much.
And I despised every person on earth,
and there was no one who achieved something before me.

I have sinned, Lord, I have sinned;
  before you I have sinned much.
And I had come to hate all who had asked my hand in marriage,
and despised them and scorned them.

I have sinned, Lord, I have sinned;
  before you I have sinned much.

THURSDAY AFTER ASH WEDNESDAY
Wisdom of Solomon 6:12–19

Wisdom's initiative and our desire meet in the discipline of the Lenten season.

Wisdom is radiant and unfading,
and she is easily discerned by those who love her,
and is found by those who seek her.
She hastens to make herself known to those who desire her.
One who rises early to seek her will have no difficulty,
for she will be found sitting at the gate.

To fix one's thought on her is perfect understanding
and one who is vigilant on her account will soon be free from care,
because she goes about seeking those worthy of her,
and she graciously appears to them in their paths,
and meets them in every thought.

The beginning of wisdom is the most sincere desire for instruction,
and concern for instruction is love of her,
and love of her is the keeping of her laws,
and giving heed to her laws is assurance of immortality,
and immortality brings one near to God.

FRIDAY AFTER ASH WEDNESDAY
Wisdom of Solomon 7:7–14b

Wisdom purifies our hearts and reconciles us with God.

I prayed and understanding was given me;
I called on God and the spirit of wisdom came to me.
I preferred her to scepters and thrones,
and accounted wealth as nothing in comparison with her.
Neither did I liken to her any priceless gem,
because all gold is but a little sand in her sight,
and silver will be accounted as clay before her.
I loved her more than health and beauty,
and I chose to have her rather than light,
because her radiance never ceases.
All good things came to me along with her,
and in her hands uncounted wealth.
I rejoiced in them all, because wisdom leads them;
but I did not know that she was their mother.
I learned without guile and I impart without grudging;
I do not hide her wealth,
for it is an unfailing treasure for mortals;
those who get it obtain friendship with God.

SATURDAY AFTER ASH WEDNESDAY
James 3:13–18

The Wisdom tradition, treasured by the early church, invites us not only to correct our behavior but to change our hearts.

Who is wise and understanding among you? Show by your good life that your works are done with gentleness born of wisdom [Sophia]. But if you have bitter envy and selfish ambition in your hearts, do not be boastful and false to the truth. Such wisdom does not come down from above, but is earthly, unspiritual, devilish. For where there is envy and selfish ambition, there will also be disorder and wickedness of every kind. But the wisdom [Sophia] from above is first pure, then peaceable, gentle, willing to yield, full of mercy and good fruits, without a trace of partiality or hypocrisy. And a harvest of righteousness is sown in peace for those who make peace.

FIRST SUNDAY OF LENT
Mechtild of Magdeburg, "True Sorrow"

Mechtild's natural images match well the parables of Jesus which call us to examine the soil of our lives in which God's word has been planted.

Lord, my earthly nature is stood before my eyes
like a barren field
which hath few good plants grown in it.
Alas, sweetest Jesus and Christ,
now send me the sweet rain of thy humanity
and the hot sun of thy living Godhead
and the gentle dew of the holy Spirit
that I may wail and cry out the aches of my heart.

FIRST WEEK OF LENT
Monday
Catherine of Siena, *Dialogue*

As we begin our Lenten journey, Catherine reminds us, in strong words, of the primacy of love in our attempts to "turn away from sin and believe the good news."

I have ordained every exercise of vocal and mental prayer to bring souls to perfect love for me and their neighbors, and to keep them in this love.

So they offend me more by abandoning charity for their neighbor for a particular exercise or for spiritual quiet than if they had abandoned the exercise for their neighbor. For in charity for their neighbors they find me, but in their own pleasure, where they are seeking me, they will be deprived of me. Why? Because by not helping they are by that very fact diminishing their charity for their neighbors. When their charity for their neighbors is diminished, so is my love for them. And when my love is diminished, so is consolation. So, those who want to gain, lose, and those who are willing to lose, gain. In other words, those who are willing to lose their own consolation for their neighbors' welfare receive and gain me and their neighbors, if they help and serve them lovingly. And so they enjoy the graciousness of my charity at all times.

FIRST WEEK OF LENT
Tuesday
Hadewijch, *Letters*, 151, 163

Hadewijch's reflection on love is really a statement about our call to communion with one another: to move out of autonomy into relationship, out of fear into love.

It seems to me that the commandment of love that God spoke to Moses is the weightiest I know in Scripture: "You shall love your Lord your God with all your heart, with all your soul, and with all your strength" (Deut 6:5). These words you shall never forget, sleeping or waking. If you sleep, you must dream of them; if you are awake, you must think of them, and recite them, and carry them into effect. These words you shall write on the threshold, and on the lintel, and on the wall, and in all the places where you shall be, that you may not forget what you must do there (See Deut 6:6–9).

In other words, God commands that we nevermore forget Love, either sleeping or waking, in any manner, with all that we are, with heart, with soul, with mind, with strength, and with our thoughts. God gave this commandment to Moses and in the Gospel (Matt 22:37; Mark 12:30; Luke 10:27), that in this way we should live wholly for Love. Woe indeed! How dare we then give Love short measure in anything? Alas, is it not fearful robbery (Is 61:8) that we spare anything for Love, or hold back anything? Alas! Think about this, and work without neglect to promote Love above all things.

FIRST WEEK OF LENT
Wednesday
Philippians 4:1–9

The conflict between Euodia and Syntyche, leaders in the church at Philippi, disturbs the whole church. Paul urges them to reconciliation, and reflects on the ideals of Christian harmony.

My brothers and sisters, whom I love and long for, my joy and crown, stand firm in the Lord in this way, my beloved.

I urge Euodia [Eu o' di a] and I urge Syntyche [Syn' ty che] to be of the same mind in the Lord. Yes, and I ask you also, my loyal companion, help these women, for they have struggled beside me in the work of the gospel, together with Clement and the rest of my co-workers, whose names are in the book of life.

Rejoice in the Lord always; again I will say, Rejoice. Let your gentleness be known to everyone. The Lord is near. Do not worry about anything, but in everything by prayer and supplication with thanksgiving let your requests be made known to God. And the peace of God, which surpasses all understanding, will guard your hearts and your minds in Christ Jesus.

Finally, beloved, whatever is true, whatever is honorable, whatever is just, whatever is pure, whatever is pleasing, whatever is commendable, if there is any excellence and if there is anything worthy of praise, think about these things. Keep on doing the things that you have learned and received and heard and seen in me, and the God of peace will be with you.

FIRST WEEK OF LENT
Thursday
Esther (Greek) C 14:18b, 3–5, 12–15a

The courage and faith of Esther are remembered each year during the Jewish feast of Purim. Her prayer of petition ranks among the great prayers of Hebrew women.

Queen Esther, seized with deadly anxiety, fled to the Lord. She prayed to the Lord God of Israel, and said: "O my Lord, you only are our king; help me, who am alone and have no helper but you, for my life is in my hand. Ever since I was born I have heard in the tribe of my family that you, O Lord, took Israel out of all the nations, and our ancestors from among all their forebears, for an everlasting inheritance, and that you did for them all that you promised. Remember, O Lord; make yourself known in this time of our affliction, and give me courage, O King of the gods and Master of all dominion! Put eloquent speech in my mouth before the lion, and turn his heart to hate the man who is fighting against us, so that there may be an end of him and those who agree with him. But save us by your hand, and help me, who am alone and have no helper but you, O Lord. You have knowledge of all things.

FIRST WEEK OF LENT
Friday
Joseph and Aseneth 11:3–14 (#1 of 2)

According to tradition, Joseph in his fidelity to God refused to take an idolatrous woman as his wife (Gen 41:45), but prayed for her conversion. Aseneth's great love for Joseph impelled her to give up her idols, to turn from her selfish conceit, and, as a sign of repentance, to undertake a week of fasting and weeping. At the end of the fast Aseneth turned to God in this prayer.

Aseneth [As' e neth] said in her heart without opening her mouth:

I have heard many saying
that the God of the Hebrews is a true God,
and a living God, and a merciful God,
and compassionate and long-suffering and pitiful and gentle,
and does not count the sin of a humble person,
nor expose the lawless deeds of afflicted persons at the time of their
        affliction.
Therefore I will take courage too and turn to God,
and take refuge with God,
and confess all my sins to God,
and pour out my supplication before God.
Who knows, maybe God will see my humiliation
and have mercy on me.
Perhaps God will see this desolation of mine
and have compassion on me,
or see my orphanage
and protect me,
because God is the parent of the orphans,
and a protector of the persecuted,
and of the afflicted a helper.
I will take courage and cry to God.

FIRST WEEK OF LENT
Saturday
Joseph and Aseneth 11:19–12:4 (#2 of 2)

Aseneth confessed her sins and prayed for acceptance. Afterward an angel came to her to assure her that she was reborn and fed her a piece of honeycomb.

Aseneth rose again from the wall where she sat and straightened up on her knees and spread her hand eastward and looked with her eyes up toward heaven, and opened her mouth to God, and said:

Lord God of the ages,
who created all things and gave life to them,
who gave breath of life to your whole creation,
who brought the invisible things out into the light,
who made the things that are and the ones that have an
      appearance from non-appearing and non-being,
who lifted up the heaven
and founded it on a firmament upon the back of the winds,
who founded the earth upon the waters,
who put big stones on the abyss of the water,
and the stones will not be submerged,
but they are like oak leaves floating on top of the water,
and they are living stones
and hear your voice, Lord,
and keep your commandments which you have commanded
      to them,
and never transgress your ordinances,
but are doing your will to the end.
For you, Lord, spoke and they were brought to life,
because your word, Lord, is life for all your creatures.
With you I take refuge, Lord,
to you I will pour out my supplication,
to you I will confess my sins,

and to you I will reveal my lawless deeds.
Spare me, Lord,
because I have sinned much before you.

SECOND SUNDAY OF LENT
Mechtild of Magdeburg, "Praise of God"

---

*Mechtild's litany of stunning images serves as an appropriate coun-
terpoint to the disciples' prosaic response in today's gospel of the
Transfiguration.*

> O burning mountain, O chosen sun,
> O perfect moon, O fathomless well,
> O unattainable height, O clearness beyond measure,
> O wisdom without end, O mercy without limit,
> O strength beyond resistance, O crown of all majesty,
> The humblest you created sings your praise.

SECOND WEEK OF LENT
Monday
Isaiah 46:3–4

---

*God's lament over an unfaithful people is voiced in the tone of
mother-love.*

> Listen to me, O house of Jacob,
>   all the remnant of the house of Israel,
> who have been borne by me from your birth,
>   carried from the womb;
> even to your old age I am God,
>   even when you turn gray, I will carry you.

I have made, and I will bear;
I will carry and will save.

SECOND WEEK OF LENT
Tuesday
Acts of Peter, Berlin Coptic Papyrus 8502

Peter, calling on the power of the risen Jesus, restores his own daughter to full health. During the season of Lent, stories of healings give courage to all who long for wholeness.

On the first day of the week, which is the Lord's day, a crowd collected, and they brought many sick people to Peter for him to heal them. (See Mark 6:55; Matt 4:24; Acts 5:16, etc.) But one of the crowd ventured to say to Peter, "Look, Peter, before our eyes you have made many who were blind to see, and the deaf to hear and the lame to walk, and you have helped them walk and given them strength. (See Matt 11:5) Why have you not helped your virgin daughter, who has grown up beautiful and has believed on the name of God? For she is quite paralysed on one side, and she lies there stretched out in the corner helpless. We see the people you have healed; but your own daughter you have neglected."

But Peter smiled and said to him, "My son, it is evident to God alone why her body is not well. You must know, then, that God is not weak or powerless to grant this gift to my daughter. But to convince your soul and increase the faith of those who are here"—he looked then towards his daughter, and spoke to her: "Rise up from your place without any help but Jesus' alone and walk naturally before them all and come to me." And she rose up and went to him; but the crowd rejoiced at what had happened (See Mark 2:10–12). Then Peter said to them, "Look, your heart is convinced that God is not powerless in all the things which we ask."

SECOND WEEK OF LENT
Wednesday
Matthew 20:17–28

It is James and John in the gospel of Mark who ask for privilege, but Matthew puts the request on the lips of their mother because the ambition of her sons is an embarrassment to Matthew's community.

While Jesus was going up to Jerusalem, he took the twelve disciples aside by themselves, and said to them on the way, "See, we are going up to Jerusalem, and the Child of Humanity will be handed over to the chief priests and scribes, and they will condemn him to death; then they will hand him over to the Gentiles to be mocked and flogged and crucified; and on the third day he will be raised."

Then the mother of the sons of Zebedee came to him with her sons, and kneeling before him, she asked a favor of him. And he said to her, "What do you want?" She said to him, "Declare that these two sons of mine will sit, one at your right hand and one at your left, in your kingdom." But Jesus answered, "You do not know what you are asking. Are you able to drink the cup that I am about to drink?" They said to him, "We are able." He said to them, "You will indeed drink my cup, but to sit at my right hand and at my left, this is not mine to grant, but it is for those for whom it has been prepared by my Father."

When the ten heard it, they were angry with the two brothers. But Jesus called them to him and said, "You know that the rulers of the Gentiles lord it over them, and their great ones are tyrants over them. It will not be so among you; but whoever wishes to be great among you must be your servant, and whoever wishes to be first among you must be your slave; just as the Child of Humanity came not to be served but to serve, and to give his life as a ransom for many."

See Mark 10:35–45

SECOND WEEK OF LENT
Thursday
Socrates, *Church History* 1.17 (#1 of 2)

The fifth century Christian historian, Socrates Scholasticus, records the work of Helena, mother of the emperor Constantine, to discover the true cross in Jerusalem. The miraculous power attributed to the cross of Jesus is in keeping with contemporary belief in the perceptible power of holy persons and things.

Helena [Hel' e na], the emperor's mother, being divinely directed by dreams, went to Jerusalem. She sought carefully the sepulchre of Christ, from which he arose after his burial; and after much difficulty, by God's help she discovered it. What the cause of the difficulty was I will explain in a few words. Those who embraced the Christian faith, after the period of his passion, greatly venerated this tomb; but those who hated Christianity, having covered the spot with a mound of earth, erected on it a temple to Venus, and set up her image there, not caring for the memory of the place. This succeeded for a long time; and it became known to the emperor's mother. Accordingly having caused the statue to be thrown down, the earth to be removed, and the ground entirely cleared, she found three crosses in the sepulchre: one of these was that blessed cross on which Christ had hung, the other two were those on which the two thieves that were crucified with him had died. With these was also found the tablet of Pilate, on which he had inscribed in various characters, that the Christ who was crucified was king of the Jews. Since, however, it was doubtful which cross they were in search of, the emperor's mother was not a little distressed; but from this trouble the bishop of Jerusalem, Macarius [Ma ca' ri us], shortly relieved her. And he solved the doubt by faith, for he sought a sign from God and obtained it. The sign was this: a certain woman of the neighborhood, who had been long afflicted with disease, was now just at the point of death; the bishop therefore arranged it so that each of the crosses should be brought to the dying woman, believing that she would be healed on touching the precious cross. Nor was he disappointed in his expectation: for the two crosses having been applied which were not the Lord's, the woman still continued in a dying state; but when the third, which was the true cross, touched her, she was immediately healed, and recovered her former strength. In this manner then was the genuine cross discovered.

SECOND WEEK OF LENT
Friday
Socrates, *Church History* 1.17 (#2 of 2)

Helena, mother of Constantine, erected the first great churches at the holy places in Jerusalem.

The emperor's mother erected over the place of the sepulchre a magnificent church, and named it *New Jerusalem*, having built it facing that old and deserted city. There she left a portion of the cross, enclosed in a silver case, as a memorial to those who might wish to see it: the other part she sent to the emperor. He supplied all materials for the construction of the churches, and wrote to Macarius [Ma ca' ri us] the bishop to expedite these edifices. When the emperor's mother had completed the *New Jerusalem*, she reared another church not at all inferior, over the cave at Bethlehem where Christ was born according to the flesh: nor did she stop here, but built a third on the mount of his Ascension. So devoutly was she affected in these matters, that she would pray in the company of women; and inviting the virgins enrolled in the register of the churches to a repast, serving them herself, she brought the dishes to table. She was also very munificent to the churches and to the poor; and having lived a life of piety, she died when about eighty years old. Her remains were conveyed to New Rome [Constantinople], the capital, and deposited in the imperial sepulchres.

SECOND WEEK OF LENT
Saturday
Galatians 4:24–5:1

Paul draws on the figures of the matriarchs, Sarah and Hagar, to illustrate his concept of freedom. At the same time, he reinforces both patriarchal oppression of the rejected woman and women's collusion in such oppression. Not a bad meditation for Lent.

Now this is an allegory: these women are two covenants. One woman, in fact, is Hagar, from Mount Sinai, bearing children for slavery. Now Hagar is Mount Sinai in Arabia and corresponds to the present Jerusalem, for she is in slavery with her children. But the other woman corresponds to the Jerusalem above; she is free, and she is our mother. For it is written,

> "Rejoice, you childless one, you who bear no children,
>   burst into song and shout, you who endure no birthpangs;
> for the children of the desolate woman are more numerous
>   than the children of the one who is married."

Now you, my friends, are children of the promise, like Isaac. But just as at that time the child who was born according to the flesh persecuted the child who was born according to the Spirit, so it is now also. But what does the scripture say? "Drive out the slave and her child; for the child of the slave will not share the inheritance with the child of the free woman." So then, friends, we are children, not of the slave but of the free woman. For freedom Christ has set us free. Stand firm, therefore, and do not submit again to a yoke of slavery.

THIRD SUNDAY OF LENT
John 4:5–30, 39–42

The Samaritan woman encounters Jesus at the well, first as stranger, then as prophet, Messiah, and Savior of the world. She cannot keep this revelation to herself but undertakes the mission of inviting others into relationship with Jesus.

Jesus came to a Samaritan city called Sychar, near the plot of ground that Jacob had given to his son Joseph. Jacob's well was there, and Jesus, tired out by his journey, was sitting by the well. It was about noon.

A Samaritan woman came to draw water, and Jesus said to her, "Give me a drink." (His disciples had gone to the city to buy food.) The Samaritan woman said to him, "How is it that you, a Jew, ask a drink of me, a woman of Samaria?" (Jews do not share things in common with Samaritans.) Jesus answered her, "If you knew the gift of God, and who it is that is saying to you, 'Give me a drink,' you would have asked him, and he would have given you living water." The woman said to him, "Sir, you have no bucket, and the well is deep. Where do you get that living water? Are you greater than our ancestor Jacob, who gave us the well, and with his sons and his flocks drank from it?" Jesus said to her, "Everyone who drinks of this water will be thirsty again, but those who drink of the water that I will give them will never be thirsty. The water that I will give will become in them a spring of water gushing up to eternal life." The woman said to him, "Sir, give me this water, so that I may never be thirsty or have to keep coming here to draw water."

Jesus said to her, "Go, call your husband, and come back." The woman answered him, "I have no husband." Jesus said to her, "You are right in saying, 'I have no husband'; for you have had five husbands, and the one you have now is not your husband. What you have said is true!" The woman said to him, "Sir, I see that you are a prophet. Our ancestors worshiped on this mountain, but you say that the place where people must worship is in Jerusalem." Jesus said to her, "Woman, believe me, the hour is coming when you will worship God neither on this mountain nor in Jerusalem. You worship what you do not know; we worship what we know, for salvation is from the Jews. But the hour is coming, and is now here, when the true worshipers will worship God in spirit and truth, for God seeks such as these for worship. God is spirit, and those who worship God must worship in spirit and truth. The woman said to him, "I know that Messiah is coming" (who is called Christ). "When he comes, he will proclaim all things to us." Jesus said to her, "I am he, the one who is speaking to you."

Just then his disciples came. They were astonished that he was speaking with a woman, but no one said, "What do you want?" or "Why are you speaking with her?" Then the woman left her water jar and went back to the city. She said to the people, "Come and see a man who told me everything I have ever done! He cannot be the Messiah, can he?" They left the city and were on their way to him.

Many Samaritans from that city believed in him because of the woman's testimony, "He told me everything I have ever done." So when the Samaritans came to him, they asked him to stay with them; and he stayed there two days. And many more believed because of his word. They said to the woman, "It is no longer because of what you said that we believe, for we have heard for ourselves, and we know that this is truly the Savior of the world."

THIRD WEEK OF LENT
Monday
Testament of Job 21:1–22:3 (#1 of 4)

Sitis, the wife of Job, demonstrates her faithfulness, courage, and ingenuity.

Job speaks . . .
I spent forty-eight years on the dung heap outside the city under the plague so that I saw with my own eyes, my children, my first wife carrying water into the house of a certain nobleman as a maidservant so she might get bread and bring it to me. I was stunned. And I said, "The gall of these city fathers! How can they treat my wife like a female slave?" After this I regained my senses.

After eleven years they kept even bread itself from me, barely allowing her to have her own food. And as she did get it, she would divide it between herself and me, saying with pain, "Woe is me! Soon he will not even get enough bread." She would not hesitate to go out into the market to beg bread from the bread sellers so she might bring it to me so I could eat.

THIRD WEEK OF LENT
Tuesday
Testament of Job 23:1–24:10 (#2 of 4)

Job's wife, Sitis, is tempted by the devil, and cries out to Job to protest against God.

When Satan knew that Sitis begged bread from the bread sellers, he disguised himself as a bread seller. It happened by chance that my wife went to him and begged bread, thinking he was a man. And Satan said to her, "Pay the price and take what you like." But she answered him and said, "Where would I get money? Are you unaware of the evils that have befallen us? If you have any pity on me, show mercy; but if not, you shall see!"

And he answered her, saying, "Unless you deserved the evils, you would not have received them in return. Now then if you have no money at hand, offer me the hair of your head and take three loaves of bread. Perhaps you will be able to live for three more days." Then she said to herself, "What good is the hair of my head compared to my hungry husband?" And so, showing disdain for her hair, she said to him, "Go ahead, take it."

Then he took scissors, sheared off the hair of her head, and gave her three loaves, while all were looking on. When she got the loaves, she came and brought them to me. Satan followed her along the road, walking stealthily, and leading her heart astray.

At once my wife drew near. Crying out with tears she said to me, "Job, Job! How long will you sit on the dung heap outside the city thinking, 'Only a little longer!' and awaiting the hope of your salvation?

As for me, I am a vagabond and a maidservant going round from place to place. Your memorial has been wiped away from the earth—my sons and the daughters of my womb for whom I toiled with hardships in vain. And here you sit in worm-infested rottenness, passing the night in the open air. And I for my part am a wretch immersed in labor by day and in pain by night, just so I might provide a loaf of bread and bring it to you. Any more I barely receive my own food, and I divide that between you and me—wondering in my heart that it is not bad enough for you to be ill, but neither do you get your fill of bread.

"So I ventured unashamedly to go into the market, even if I was pierced in my heart to do so, and the bread seller said, 'Give money, and you shall receive,' But I also showed him our straits and then heard from him, 'If you have no money, woman, pay with the hair of your head and take three loaves. Perhaps you will live for three more days.' Being remiss, I said to him, 'Go ahead, cut my hair.' So, he arose and cut my hair disgracefully in the market, while the crowd stood by and marveled."

THIRD WEEK OF LENT
Wednesday
Testament of Job 39:1–40:14 (#3 of 4)

Sitis, the wife of Job, laments her children and dies praising God.

While I was saying these things to them, my wife Sitis arrived in tattered garments, fleeing from the servitude of the official she served, since he had forbidden her to leave lest the fellow kings see her and seize her. When she came, she threw herself at their feet and said weeping, "Do you remember me, Eliphas [El′ i phas]—you and your two friends —what sort of person I used to be among you and how I used to dress? But now look at my debut and my attire!"

Then, when they had made a great lamentation and were doubly exhausted, they fell silent so that Eliphas seized his purple robe, tore it off, and threw it about my wife.

But she began to beg them, saying, "I plead with you, order your soldiers to dig through the ruins of the house that fell on my children so that at least their bones might be preserved as a memorial since we cannot because of the expense. Let us see them, even if it is only their bones. Have I the womb of cattle or of a wild animal that my ten children have died and I have not arranged the burial of a single one of them?"

And they left to dig, but I forbade it, saying, "Do not trouble yourselves in vain. For you will not find my children, since they were taken up into heaven by the Creator their King."

Then again they answered me and said, "Who then will not say you are demented and mad when you say, 'My children have been taken up into heaven!' Tell us the truth now!"

And I replied to them and said, "Lift me up so I can stand erect." And they lifted me up, supporting my arms on each side. And then when I had stood up, I sang praises to God. And after the prayer I said to them, "Look up with your eyes to the east and see my children crowned with the splendor of the heavenly one."

And when she saw that, Sitis my wife fell to the ground worshiping and said, "Now I know that I have a memorial with the Lord. So I shall arise and return to the city and nap awhile and then refresh myself before the duties of my servitude." And when she left for the city she went to the cow shed of her oxen, which had been confiscated by the rulers whom she served. And she lay down near a certain manger and died in good spirits.

When her domineering ruler sought her but could not find her, he went when it was evening into the folds of the herds and found her sprawled out dead. And all who saw cried out in an uproar of lament over her, and the sound reached through the whole city. When they rushed in to discover what had happened, they found her dead and the living animals standing about weeping over her.

And so bearing her in procession, they attended to her burial, locating her near the house that had collapsed on her children. And the poor of the city made a great lamentation, saying, "Look! This is Sitis, the woman of pride and splendor! She was not even considered worthy of a decent burial!"

So then you will find in "The Miscellanies [Mis' cel la nies]" the lament made for her.

THIRD WEEK OF LENT
Thursday
Testament of Job 46:1–51:4 (#4 of 4)

The daughters of Job receive their inheritance and sing magnificent hymns to God.

And they brought forth the estate for distribution among the seven males only. For he did not present any of the goods to the females. They were grieved and said to their father, "Our father, sir, are we not also your children? Why then did you not give us some of your goods?"

But Job said to the females, "Do not be troubled, my daughters: I have not forgotten you. I have already designated for you an inheritance better than that of your seven brothers."

Then when he had called his daughter who was named Hemera [He′ mer a] he said to her, "Take the signet ring, go to the vault, and bring the three golden boxes, so that I may give you your inheritance." So she left and brought them back.

And he opened them and brought out three multicolored cords whose appearance was such that no one could describe, since they were not from earth but from heaven, shimmering with fiery sparks like the rays of the sun. And he gave each one a cord, saying, "Place these about your breast, so it may go well with you all the days of your life."

Then the other daughter, named Kasia [Ka′ si a], said to him, "Father, is this the inheritance which you said was better than that of our brothers? Who has any use for these unusual cords? We cannot gain a living from them, can we?"

And their father said to them, "Not only shall you gain a living from these, but these cords will lead you into the better world, to live in the heavens. Are you then ignorant, my children, of the value of these strings? The Lord considered me worthy of these in the day in which he wished to show me mercy and to rid my body of the plagues and the worms. Calling me, he furnished me with these three cords and said, 'Arise, gird your loins. I shall question you, and you answer me.'

"So I took them and put them on. And immediately from that time the worms disappeared from my body and the plagues, too. And then my body got strength through the Lord as if I actually had not suffered a thing. I also forgot the pains in my heart. And the Lord spoke to me in power, showing me things present and things to come.

"Now then, my children, since you have these objects you will not have to face the enemy at all, but neither will you have worries of him in your mind, since it is a protective amulet of God. Rise then, gird yourselves with them before I die in order that you may be able to see those who are coming for my soul, in order that you may marvel over the creatures of God."

Thus when the one called Hemera arose, she wrapped around her her own string just as her father said. And she took on another heart—no longer minded toward earthly things—but she spoke ecstatically in the angelic dialect, sending up a hymn to God in accord with the hymnic style of the angels. And as she spoke ecstatically, she allowed "The Spirit" to be inscribed on her garment.

Then Kasia bound hers on and had her heart changed so that she no longer regarded worldly things. And her mouth took on the dialect of the archons and she praised God for the creation of the heights.

Then the other one also, named Amaltheia's [Am al the' i a's] Horn, bound on her cord. And her mouth spoke ecstatically in the dialect of those on high, since her heart also was changed, keeping aloof from worldly things. For she spoke in the dialect of the cherubim, glorifying the Master of virtues by exhibiting their splendor.

After the three had stopped singing hymns, while the Lord was present as was I, Nereus [Ne' re us], the brother of Job, and while the holy angel also was present I sat near Job on the couch. And I heard the magnificent things, while each one made explanation to the other. And I wrote out a complete book of most of the contents of hymns that issued from the three daughters of my brother, so that these things would be preserved. For these are the magnificent things of God.

THIRD WEEK OF LENT
Friday
Holy Women of the Syrian Orient: Ruhm (#1 of 2)

A Syrian martyr of the sixth century CE, Ruhm goes to death willingly for Christ "who died for our sakes."

Blessed Ruhm proclaimed, "The king has sent a message to me that I should deny Christ and so save my life. But I have sent reply to him, saying that, if I were to deny Christ I would die, but if I do not deny him, then I shall live. Far be it from me, my fellow women, far be it from me that I should deny Christ my God, for it is in him that I have faith; in his name was I baptized myself and I had my daughters baptized as well; his cross do I venerate, and for his sake I and my daughters will die, just as he died for our sakes.

"My gold that belongs to the earth I leave for the earth: let anyone who wants to take my gold do so, let anyone who wants to take my silver and jewelry take them. Of my own free will I leave everything behind, in order to go and receive a substitute for it from my Lord.

"Blessed are you, my fellow women, if you listen to my words; blessed are you, fellow women, if you recognize the truth, for whose sake I am going to die—both I and my daughters. Blessed are you, my fellow women, if you love Christ. Blessed am I and blessed are my daughters, for what a blessed state it is into which we are going!"

THIRD WEEK OF LENT
Saturday
Holy Women of the Syrian Orient: Ruhm (#2 of 2)

Ruhm was known as a quiet noblewoman, outstanding for decorum; her final act of life includes a stripping off of the obligatory veil and an assertive walk into martyrdom.

"Henceforth there shall be peace and quiet for the people of Christ: the blood of my brothers and sisters who have been killed for Christ's sake shall act as a wall for this town if it holds fast to Christ my Lord. With my face uncovered I leave your town where I have lived as though in a temporary tabernacle, to go with my daughters to another city where I have betrothed them.

"Pray for me, my fellow women, that Christ my Lord may receive me, and forgive me for remaining in this life for three days after the death of the father of my daughters."

After the blessed Ruhm had finished, a wail went up from all the women of the town, and the wicked king, together with those with him outside the town to whom it reached, were shaken by it.

When the men sent by the king to fetch the blessed woman arrived back, they told him all that the glorious Ruhm had uttered, and how the women were raising lamentations for her. The king wanted to put them to death for having allowed her to speak at such length and thus lead the town astray through her sorcery.

FOURTH SUNDAY OF LENT
Martyrs of Lyon and Vienne 16–19

Only the fourth century church historian Eusebius has preserved this stirring account of the death of a group of martyrs in Gaul in the summer of 177 CE. The slave woman Blandina proved to be the most heroic of them all.

The blessed martyrs underwent torments beyond all description; and Satan strove to have some word of blasphemy escape their lips.

All the wrath of the mob, the prefect, and the soldiers fell with overwhelming force on the deacons Sanctus of Vienne [Vi enne'], on Maturus [Ma tu' rus] who was, though newly baptized, a noble athlete, on Attalus [At' ta lus] whose family came from Pergamum [Per' ga mum], who had always been a pillar and ground of the community there, and on Blandina [Blan di' na], through whom Christ proved that the things that men think cheap, ugly, and contemptuous are deemed worthy of glory before God, by reason of her love for him which was not merely vaunted in appearance but demonstrated in achievement.

All of us were in terror; and Blandina's earthly mistress, who was herself among the martyrs in the conflict, was in agony lest because of her bodily weakness she would not be able to make a bold confession of her faith. Yet Blandina was filled with such power that even those who were taking turns to torture her in every way from dawn to dusk were weary and exhausted. They themselves admitted that they were beaten, that there was nothing further they could do to her, and they were surprised that she was still breathing, for her entire body was broken and torn. They testified that even one kind of torture was enough to release her soul, let alone the many they applied with such intensity. Instead, this blessed woman like a noble athlete got renewed strength with her confession of faith: her admission, "I am a Christian; we do nothing to be ashamed of" brought her refreshment, rest, and insensibility to her present pain.

FOURTH WEEK OF LENT
Monday
Sayings of the Desert Mother Syncletica (#1 of 6)

Amma [Mother] Syncletica was a wise desert monastic woman of Egypt in the fifth century CE. A good number of her sayings to her disciples, as well as those of other Desert Mothers, are preserved in the form of aphorisms.

Amma Syncletica [Syn clet' i ca] said, "In the beginning there are a great many battles and a good deal of suffering for those who are advancing towards God and afterwards, ineffable joy. It is like those who wish to light a fire; at first they are choked by the smoke and cry, and by this means obtain what they seek (as it is said: 'Our God is a consuming fire' [Heb 12:24]): so we also must kindle the fire in ourselves through tears and hard work."

She also said, "Just as the most bitter medicine drives out poisonous creatures so prayer joined to fasting drives evil thoughts away."

She also said, "Do not let yourself be seduced by the delights of the riches of the world, as though they contained something useful on account of vain pleasure. Worldly people esteem the culinary art, but you, through fasting and thanks to cheap food, go beyond their abundance of food. It is written: 'The one who is sated loathes honey' (Prov 27:7). Do not fill yourself with bread and you will not desire wine."

She was asked if poverty is a perfect good. She said, "For those who are capable of it, it is a perfect good. Those who can sustain it receive suffering in the body but rest in the soul, for just as one washes coarse clothes by trampling them underfoot and turning them about in all directions, even so the strong soul becomes much more stable thanks to voluntary poverty."

FOURTH WEEK OF LENT
Tuesday
Sayings of the Desert Mother Syncletica (#2 of 6)

Amma Syncletica was a wise desert monastic woman of Egypt in the fifth century CE. A good number of her sayings were preserved by her disciples.

Amma Syncletica said, "Many are the wiles of the devil. If he is not able to disturb the soul by means of poverty, he suggests riches as an attraction. If he has not won the victory by insults and disgrace, he suggests praise and glory. Overcome by health, he makes the body ill. Not having been able to seduce it through pleasures, he tries to overthrow it by involuntary sufferings. He joins to this, very severe illness to disturb the fainthearted in their love of God. But he also destroys the body by very violent fevers and weighs it down with intolerable thirst. If, being a sinner, you undergo all these things, remind yourself of the punishment to come, the everlasting fire and the sufferings inflicted by justice, and do not be discouraged here and now. Rejoice that God visits you and keep this blessed saying on your lips: 'The Lord has chastened me sorely but has not given me over unto death' (Ps 118:18). You were iron, but fire has burnt the rust off you. If you are righteous and fall ill, you will go from strength to strength. Are you gold? You will pass through fire purged. Have you been given a thorn in the flesh (2 Cor 12:1)? Exult, and see who else was treated like that; it is an honour to have the same sufferings as Paul. Are you being tried by fever? Are you being taught by cold? Indeed Scripture says: 'We went through fire and water; yet thou hast brought us forth to a spacious place' (Ps 66:12). You have drawn the first lot? Expect the second. By virtue offer holy words in a loud voice. For it is said: 'I am afflicted and in pain' (Ps 69:29). By this share of wretchedness you will be made perfect. For it says: 'The Lord hears when I call' (Ps 4:3). So open your mouth wider to be taught by these exercises of the soul, seeing what we are under the eyes of our enemy."

FOURTH WEEK OF LENT
Wednesday
Sayings of the Desert Mother Syncletica (#3 of 6)

Amma Syncletica was a wise desert monastic woman of Egypt in the fifth century CE. Some of her sayings use practical images of sailing and building.

Amma Syncletica said, "When you have to fast, do not pretend illness. For those who do not fast often fall into real sicknesses. If you have begun to act well, do not turn back through constraint of the enemy, for through your endurance, the enemy is destroyed. Those who put out to sea at first sail with a favourable wind; then the sails spread, but later the winds become adverse. Then the ship is tossed by the waves and is no longer controlled by the rudder. But when in a little while there is calm, and the tempest dies down, then the ship sails on again. So it is with us, when we are driven by the spirits who are against us; we hold to the cross as our sail and so we can set a safe course."

She also said, "Those who have endured the labours and dangers of the sea and then amass material riches, even when they have gained much desire to gain yet more and they consider what they have at present as nothing and reach out for what they have not got. We, who have nothing of that which we desire, wish to acquire everything through the fear of God."

Syncletica said, "Imitate the publican, and you will not be condemned with the Pharisee. Choose the meekness of Moses and you will find your heart which is a rock changed into a spring of water."

She also said, "It is dangerous for anyone to teach who has not first been trained in the 'practical' life. For someone who owns a ruined house and receives guests there does them harm because of the dilapidation of his or her dwelling. It is the same in the case of someone who has not first built an interior dwelling; that one causes loss to those who come. By words one may convert them to salvation, but by evil behaviour, one injures them."

FOURTH WEEK OF LENT
Thursday
Sayings of the Desert Mother Syncletica (#4 of 6)

Amma Syncletica was a wise desert monastic woman of Egypt in the fifth century CE. Her asceticism stresses the need for balance.

Amma Syncletica said, "There is an asceticism which is determined by the enemy and his disciples practice it. So how are we to distinguish between the divine and royal *asceticism* and the demonic tyranny? Clearly through its quality of *balance*. Always use a single rule of fasting. Do not fast four or five days and break it the following day with any amount of food. In truth lack of proportion always corrupts. While you are young and healthy, fast, for old age with its weakness will come. As long as you can, lay up treasure, so that when you cannot, you will be at peace."

She also said, "As long as we are in the monastery, obedience is preferable to asceticism. The one teaches pride, the other humility."

Syncletica said, "We must direct our souls with discernment. As long as we are in the monastery, we must not seek our own will, nor follow our personal opinion, but obey our elders in the faith."

She also said, "It is written, 'Be wise as serpents and innocent as doves' (Matt 10:16). Being like serpents means not ignoring attacks and wiles of the devil. Like is quickly known to like. The simplicity of the dove denotes purity of action."

Amma Syncletica said, "There are many who live in the mountains and behave as if they were in the town, and they are wasting their time. It is possible to be a solitary in one's mind while living in a crowd, and it is possible for one who is a solitary to live in the crowd of one's own thoughts."

She also said, "In the world, if we commit an offence, even an involuntary one, we are thrown into prison; let us likewise cast ourselves into prison because of our sins, so that voluntary remembrance may anticipate the punishment that is to come."

FOURTH WEEK OF LENT
Friday
Sayings of the Desert Mother Syncletica (#5 of 6)

Amma Syncletica was a wise woman of the desert in Egypt in the fifth century CE. A good number of her sayings use nautical images. Perhaps she grew up near the great seaport of Alexandria.

Amma Syncletica said, "Just as it is impossible to be at the same moment both a plant and a seed, so it is impossible for us to be surrounded by worldly honour and at the same time to bear heavenly fruit."

She also said, "My children, we all want to be saved, but because of our habit of negligence, we swerve away from salvation."

She also said, "We must arm ourselves in every way against the demons. For they attack us from outside, and they also stir us up from within; and the soul is then like a ship when great waves break over it, and at the same time it sinks because the hold is too full. We are just like that: we lose as much by the exterior faults we commit as by the thoughts inside us. So we must watch for the attacks that come from outside us, and also repel the interior onslaughts of our thoughts."

She also said, "Here below we are not exempt from temptations. For Scripture says, 'Let those who think that they stand take heed lest they fall' (1 Cor 10:12). We sail on in darkness. The psalmist calls our life a sea and the sea is either full of rocks, or very rough, or else it is calm. We [desert monastics] are like those who sail on a calm sea, and others are like those on a rough sea. We always set our course by the sun of justice, but it can often happen that others are saved in tempest and darkness, for they keep watch as they ought, while we go to the bottom through negligence, although we are on a calm sea, because we have let go of the guidance of justice."

She also said, "Just as one cannot build a ship unless one has some nails, so it is impossible to be saved without humility."

FOURTH WEEK OF LENT
Saturday
Sayings of the Desert Mother Syncletica (#6 of 6)

Amma Syncletica was a wise woman of the desert in Egypt in the fifth century CE. The images she used helped to make her sayings clear as well as easy to remember.

Amma Syncletica said, "If you find yourself in a monastery do not go to another place, for that will harm you a great deal. Just as the bird who abandons the eggs she was sitting on prevents them from hatching so the monk or the nun grows cold and their faith dies, when they go from one place to another."

She also said, "If illness weighs us down, let us not be sorrowful as though, because of the illness and the prostration of our bodies we could not sing, for all these things are for our good, for the purification of our desires. Truly fasting and sleeping on the ground are set before us because of our sensuality. If illness then weakens this sensuality the reason for these practices is superfluous. For this is the great asceticism: to control oneself in illness and to sing hymns of thanksgiving to God."

Syncletica said, "It is good not to get angry, but if this should happen, the Apostle does not allow you a whole day for this passion, for he says: 'Let not the sun go down' (Eph 4:25). Will you wait till all your time is ended? Why hate the one who has grieved you? It is not that one who has done the wrong, but the devil. Hate sickness but not the sick person."

She also said, "Those who are great athletes must contend against stronger enemies." [Cf. 1 Cor 9:24–27]

She also said, "Just as a treasure that is exposed loses its value, so a virtue which is known vanishes, just as wax melts when it is near fire, so the soul is destroyed by praise and loses all the results of its labour."

She also said, "There is grief that is useful, and there is grief that is destructive. The first sort consists in weeping over one's own faults and weeping over the weakness of one's neighbours, in order not to destroy one's purpose, and attach oneself to the perfect good. But there is also grief that comes from the enemy, full of mockery, which some call *accidie** [ac ci' di e]. This spirit must be cast out, mainly by prayer and psalmody."

FIFTH SUNDAY OF LENT
John 8:2-11

Though the law (Deut 22:22) required that both woman and man be stoned, the man seems to have escaped judgment in this instance, prompting the conjecture that Jesus wrote on the ground: "Where's the man?"

Early in the morning Jesus came again to the temple. All the people came to him and he sat down and began to teach them. The scribes and the Pharisees brought a woman who had been caught in adultery; and making her stand before all of them, they said to him, "Teacher, this woman was caught in the very act of committing adultery. Now in the law Moses commanded us to stone such women. Now what do you say?" They said this to test him, so that they might have some charge to bring

---

* sadness, spiritual torpor, sloth; Cassian (360–435) depicts it as a state of restlessness and inability either to work or to pray.

against him. Jesus bent down and wrote with his finger on the ground. When they kept on questioning him, he straightened up and said to them, "Let anyone among you who is without sin be the first to throw a stone at her." And once again he bent down and wrote on the ground. When they heard it, they went away, one by one, beginning with the elders; and Jesus was left alone with the woman standing before him. Jesus straightened up and said to her, "Woman, where are they? Has no one condemned you?" She said, "No one, sir." And Jesus said, "Neither do I condemn you. Go your way, and from now on do not sin again."

FIFTH WEEK OF LENT
Monday
Daniel 13:1-9, 15-17, 19-27 (#1 of 3)

Susanna refuses to collaborate in the wickedness of the elders.

There was a man living in Babylon whose name was Joakim [Jo' a kim]. He married the daughter of Hilkiah [Hil ki' ah], named Susanna, a very beautiful woman and one who feared the Lord. Her parents were righteous, and had trained their daughter according to the law of Moses. Joakim was very rich, and had a fine garden adjoining his house; the Jews used to come to him because he was the most honored of them all.

That year two elders from the people were appointed as judges. Concerning them the Lord had said: "Wickedness came forth from Babylon, from elders who were judges, who were supposed to govern the people." These men were frequently at Joakim's house, and all who had a case to be tried came to them there.

When the people left at noon, Susanna would go into her husband's garden to walk. Every day the two elders used to see her, going in and walking about, and they began to lust for her. They suppressed their consciences and turned away their eyes from looking to Heaven or remembering their duty to administer justice.

Once, while they were watching for an opportune day, she went in as before with only two maids, and wished to bathe in the garden, for it was a hot day. No one was there except the two elders, who had hidden themselves and were watching her. She said to her maids, "Bring me olive oil and ointments and shut the garden doors so that I can bathe."

When the maids had gone out, the two elders got up and ran to her. They said, "Look, the garden doors are shut, and no one can see us. We are burning with desire for you; so give your consent, and lie with us. If you refuse, we will testify against you that a young man was with you, and this was why you sent your maids away."

Susanna groaned and said, "I am completely trapped. For if I do this, it will mean death for me; if I do not, I cannot escape your hands. I choose not to do it; I will fall into your hands, rather than sin in the sight of the Lord."

Then Susanna cried out with a loud voice, and the two elders shouted against her. And one of them ran and opened the garden doors. When the people in the house heard the shouting in the garden, they rushed in at the side door to see what had happened to her. And when the elders told their story, the servants felt very much ashamed, for nothing like this had ever been said about Susanna.

FIFTH WEEK OF LENT
Tuesday
Daniel 13:28–30, 33–43 (#2 of 3)

Despite the testimony of her accusers, Susanna trusts in the Lord.

The next day, when the people gathered at the house of her husband Joakim [Jo' a kim], the two elders came, full of their wicked plot to have Susanna put to death. In the presence of the people they said, "Send for Susanna daughter of Hilkiah, the wife of Joakim." So they sent for her. And she came with her parents, her children, and all her relatives. Those who were with her and all who saw her were weeping.

Then the two elders stood up before the people and laid their hands on her head. Through her tears she looked up toward Heaven, for her heart trusted in the Lord. The elders said, "While we were walking in the garden alone, this woman came in with two maids, shut the garden doors, and dismissed the maids. Then a young man, who was hiding there, came to her and lay with her. We were in a corner of the garden, and when we saw this wickedness we ran to them. Although we saw them embracing, we could not hold the man, because he was stronger than we, and he opened the doors and got away. We did, however, seize this woman and asked who the young man was, but she would not tell us. These things we testify."

Because they were elders of the people and judges, the assembly believed them and condemned her to death.

Then Susanna cried out with a loud voice, and said, "O eternal God, you know what is secret and are aware of all things before they come to be; you know that these men have given false evidence against me. And now I am to die though I have done none of the wicked things that they have charged against me."

FIFTH WEEK OF LENT
Wednesday
Daniel 13:44–60, 62–63 (#3 of 3)

According to the law of Deuteronomy (19:15) the testimony of two witnesses was required for a valid trial. Here, the witnesses conspire against Susanna but their testimony does not agree and they are put to death. Susanna's innocence is vindicated.

The Lord heard Susanna's cry. Just as she was being led off to execution, God stirred up the holy spirit of a young lad named Daniel, and he shouted with a loud voice, "I want no part in shedding this woman's blood!"

All the people turned to him and asked, "What is this you are saying?" Taking his stand among them he said, "Are you such fools, O Israelites, as to condemn a daughter of Israel without examination and without learning the facts? Return to court, for these men have given false evidence against her."

So all the people hurried back. And the rest of the elders said to him, "Come, sit among us and inform us, for God has given you the standing of an elder." Daniel said to them, "Separate them far from each other, and I will examine them."

When they were separated from each other, he summoned one of them and said to him, "You old relic of wicked days, your sins have now come home, which you have committed in the past, pronouncing unjust judgments, condemning the innocent and acquitting the guilty, though the Lord said, 'You shall not put an innocent and righteous person to death.' Now then, if you really saw this woman, tell me this: Under what tree did you see them being intimate with each other?" He answered, "Under a mastic tree." And Daniel said, "Very well! This lie has cost you your head, for the angel of God has received the sentence from God and will immediately cut you in two."

Then, putting him to one side, he ordered them to bring the other. And he said to him, "You offspring of Canaan and not of Judah, beauty has beguiled you and lust has perverted your heart. This is how you have been treating the daughters of Israel, and they were intimate with you through fear; but a daughter of Judah would not tolerate your wickedness. Now then, tell me: Under what tree did you catch them being intimate with each other?" He answered, "Under an evergreen oak." Daniel said to him, "Very well! This lie has cost you also your head, for the angel of God is waiting with sword to split you in two, so as to destroy you both."

Then the whole assembly raised a great shout and blessed God, who saves those who hope in God. Acting in accord with the law of Moses, they put the elders to death. Thus innocent blood was spared that day.

Hilkiah and his wife praised God for their daughter Susanna, and so did her husband Joakim and all her relatives, because she was found innocent of a shameful deed.

FIFTH WEEK OF LENT
Thursday
2 Kings 4:1–7

Faced with homelessness and hunger, a widow finds that her situation is reversed through Elisha's intervention. Not only is her need relieved but she is empowered to provide for herself and her children.

Now the wife of a member of the company of prophets cried to Elisha [E li' sha], "Your servant my husband is dead; and you know that your servant feared the Lord, but a creditor has come to take my two children as slaves." Elisha said to her, "What shall I do for you? Tell me, what do you have in the house?" She answered, "Your servant has nothing in the house, except a jar of oil." He said, "Go outside, borrow vessels from all your neighbors, empty vessels and not just a few. Then go in, and shut the door behind you and your children, and start pouring into all these vessels; when each is full, set it aside." So she left him and shut the door behind her and her children; they kept bringing vessels to her, and she kept pouring. When the vessels were full, she said to her son, "Bring me another vessel." But he said to her, "There are no more." Then the oil stopped flowing. She came and told Elisha, and he said, "Go sell the oil and pay your debts, and you and your children can live on the rest."

FIFTH WEEK OF LENT
Friday
2 Kings 4:8–17

The Shunammite woman's hospitality finds its reward in the miraculous conception of her child.

One day Elisha [E li' sha] was passing through Shunem, where a wealthy woman lived, who urged him to have a meal. So whenever he passed that way, he would stop there for a meal. She said to her husband, "Look, I am sure that this man who regularly passes our way is a holy man of God. Let us make a small roof chamber with walls, and put there for him a bed, a table, a chair, and a lamp, so that he can stay there whenever he comes to us."

One day when he came there, he went up to the chamber and lay down there. He said to his servant Gehazi [Ge ha' zi], "Call the Shunammite [Shu' nam ite] woman." When he had called her, she stood before him. He said to the servant, "Say to her, Since you have taken all this trouble for us, what may be done for you? Would you have a word spoken on your behalf to the king or to the commander of the army?" She answered, "I live among my own people." He said, "What then may be done for her?" Gehazi answered, "Well, she has no son, and her husband is old." He said, "Call her." When he had called her, she stood at the door. He said, "At this season, in due time, you shall embrace a son." She replied, "No, Elisha, do not deceive your servant."

The woman conceived and bore a son at that season, in due time, as Elisha had declared to her.

FIFTH WEEK OF LENT
Saturday
2 Kings 4:18-37

Disconsolate at the death of her child, the Shunammite woman's faith is sorely tested. Yet Elisha restores the child to life. Note the juxtaposition in yesterday's reading and today's of a miraculous conception and the raising to life.

When the Shunammite's [Shu' nam ite's] promised child was older, he went out one day to his father among the reapers. He complained to his father, "Oh, my head, my head!" The father said to his servant, "Carry him to his mother." He carried him and brought him to his mother; the child sat on her lap until noon, and he died. She went up and laid him on the bed of Elisha [E li' sha], closed the door on him, and left. Then she called to her husband, and said, "Send me one of the servants and one of the donkeys, so that I may quickly go to Elisha and come back again." He said, "Why go to him today? It is neither new moon nor sabbath." She said, "It will be all right." Then she saddled the donkey and said to her servant, "Urge the animal on; do not hold back for me unless I tell you." So she set out, and came to Elisha at Mount Carmel.

When Elisha saw her coming, he said to Gehazi [Ge ha' zi] his servant, "Look, there is the Shunammite woman; run at once to meet her, and say to her, Are you all right? Is your husband all right? Is the child all right?" She answered, "It is all right." When she came to Elisha at the mountain, she caught hold of his feet. Gehazi approached to push her away. But Elisha said, "Let her alone, for she is in bitter distress; the

Lord has hidden it from me and has not told me." Then she said, "Did I ask you for a son? Did I not say, Do not mislead me?" He said to Gehazi, "Gird up your loins, and take my staff in your hand, and go. If you meet anyone, give no greeting, and if anyone greets you, do not answer; and lay my staff on the face of the child." Then the mother of the child said, "As the Lord lives, and as you yourself live, I will not leave without you." So he rose up and followed her. Gehazi went on ahead and laid the staff on the face of the child, but there was no sound or sign of life. He came back to meet Elisha and told him, "The child has not awakened."

When Elisha came into the house, he saw the child lying dead on his bed. So he went in and closed the door on the two of them, and prayed to the Lord. Then he got up on the bed and lay upon the child, putting his mouth upon his mouth, his eyes upon his eyes, and his hands upon his hands and while he lay bent over him, the flesh of the child became warm. He got down, walked once to and fro in the room, then got up again and bent over him; the child sneezed seven times, and the child opened his eyes. Elisha summoned Gehazi and said, "Call the Shunammite woman." So he called her. When she came to him, he said, "Take your son." She came, and fell at his feet, bowing to the ground; then she took her son and left.

PASSION SUNDAY (PALM SUNDAY)
Mark 14:3–9

A woman without name recognizes "the anointed one" and, with great insight and generosity, she prepares his body for burial.

While Jesus was at Bethany in the house of Simon the leper, as he sat at the table, a woman came with an alabaster jar of very costly ointment of nard, and she broke open the jar and poured the ointment on his head. But some were there who said to one another in anger, "Why was the ointment wasted in this way? For the ointment could have been sold for more than three hundred denarii, and the money given to the poor." And they scolded her. But Jesus said, "Let her alone; why do you trouble her? She has performed a good service for me. For you always have the poor with you, and you can show kindness to them whenever you wish; but you will not always have me. She has done what she could; she has anointed my body beforehand for its burial. Truly I tell you, wherever the good news is proclaimed in the whole world, what she has done will be told in remembrance of her."

See Matthew 26:6–13
John 12:1–8

MONDAY OF HOLY WEEK
Matthew 27:15–26

Pilate ignores the dream of his wife to his shame.

Now at the festival the governor was accustomed to release a prisoner for the crowd, anyone whom they wanted. At that time they had a notorious prisoner, called Jesus Barabbas [Ba rab' bas]. So after they had gathered, Pilate said to them, "Whom do you want me to release for you, Jesus Barabbas or Jesus who is called the Messiah?" For he realized that it was out of jealousy that they had handed him over. While he was sitting on the judgment seat, his wife sent word to him, "Have nothing to do with that innocent man, for today I have suffered a great deal because of a dream about him." Now the chief priests and the elders persuaded the crowds to ask for Barabbas and to have Jesus killed. The governor again said to them, "Which of the two do you want me to release for you?" And they said, "Barabbas." Pilate said to them, "Then what should I do with Jesus who is called the Messiah?" All of them said, "Let him be crucified!" Then he asked, "Why, what evil has he done?" But they shouted all the more, "Let him be crucified!"

So when Pilate saw that he could do nothing, but rather that a riot was beginning, he took some water and washed his hands before the crowd, saying, "I am innocent of this man's blood; see to it yourselves." Then the people as a whole answered, "His blood be on us and on our children!" So he released Barabbas for them; and after flogging Jesus, he handed him over to be crucified.

TUESDAY OF HOLY WEEK
Luke 23:26–31

The compassion of the women is reciprocated by Jesus, for them and for their world.

As they led Jesus away, they seized a man, Simon of Cyrene, who was coming from the country, and they laid the cross on him, and made him carry it behind Jesus. A great number of the people followed him, and among them were women who were beating their breasts and wailing for him. But Jesus turned to them and said, "Daughters of Jerusalem, do not weep for me, but weep for yourselves and for your children. For the days are surely coming when they will say, 'Blessed are the barren, and the wombs that never bore, and the breasts that never nursed.' Then they will begin to say to the mountains, 'Fall on us;' and to the hills, 'Cover us.' For if they do this when the wood is green, what will happen when it is dry?"

WEDNESDAY OF HOLY WEEK
Mark 14:66–72

Peter fears that the servant-girl will unmask him, and so denies the Lord.

While Peter was below in the courtyard, one of the servant-girls of the high priest came by. When she saw Peter warming himself, she stared at him and said, "You also were with Jesus, the man from Nazareth." But he denied it, saying, "I do not know or understand what you are talking about." And he went out into the forecourt. Then the cock crowed. And the servant-girl, on seeing him, began again to say to the bystanders, "This man is one of them." But again he denied it. Then after a little while the bystanders again said to Peter, "Certainly you are one of them; for you are a Galilean." But he began to curse, and he swore an oath, "I do not know this man you are talking about." At that moment the cock crowed for the second time. Then Peter remembered that Jesus had said to him, "Before the cock crows twice, you will deny me three times." And he broke down and wept.

See Matthew 26:69–75
Luke 22:54–62
John 18:15–18, 25–27

MASS OF THE LORD'S SUPPER
John 19:25–27

Before all others Mary can say of Jesus: "This is my body, this is my blood."

Standing near the cross of Jesus were his mother, and his mother's sister, Mary the wife of Clopas, and Mary Magdalene. When Jesus saw his mother and the disciple whom he loved standing beside her, he said to his mother, "Woman, here is your son." Then he said to the disciple, "Here is your mother." And from that hour the disciple took her into his own home.

GOOD FRIDAY
Martyrs of Lyon and Vienne 40–42

The martyrs Maturus, Sanctus, Blandina, and Attalus are led into the amphitheatre of Lyon to be tortured and killed. In Blandina, her companions see the crucified Christ.

Though their spirits endured much throughout the long contest, they were in the end sacrificed, after being made all the day long a spectacle to the world to replace the varied entertainment of the gladiatorial combat. Blandina [Blan di′ na] was hung on a post and exposed as bait for the wild animals that were let loose on her. She seemed to hang there in the form of a cross, and by her fervent prayer she aroused intense enthusiasm in those who were undergoing their ordeal, for in their torment with their physical eyes they saw in the person of their sister him who was crucified for them that he might convince all who believe in him that all who suffer for Christ's glory will have eternal fellowship in the living God.

But none of the animals had touched her, and so she was taken for another ordeal: and thus for her victory in further contests she would make irreversible the condemnation of the crooked serpent, and tiny, weak, and insignificant as she was, she would give inspiration to her brothers, for she had put on Christ, that mighty and invincible athlete, and had overcome the Adversary in many contests, and through her conflict had won the crown of immortality.

HOLY SATURDAY MEDITATION
Martyrs of Lyon and Vienne 53–56

The fifteen year old boy Ponticus and the slave woman Blandina are the last of their group to die. Even the executioners bear witness to Blandina's superior courage. All are amazed that a slave woman could prove to be the most heroic of the martyrs.

Finally, on the last day of the gladiatorial games, they brought back Blandina [Blan di′ na] again, this time with a boy of fifteen named Ponticus [Pon′ ti cus]. Every day they had been brought in to watch the torture of the others, while attempts were made to force them to swear by the pagan idols. And because they persevered and contemned their persecutors, the crowd grew angry with them, so that they had little pity for the child's age and no respect for the woman. Instead, they subjected them to every atrocity and led them through every torture in turn, constantly trying to force them to swear, but to no avail.

Ponticus, after being encouraged by his sister in Christ so that even the pagans realized that she was urging him on and strengthening him, and after nobly enduring every torment, gave up his spirit. The blessed Blandina was last of all: like a noble mother encouraging her children (2 Macc 7:20–23), she sent them before her in triumph to the King, and then, after duplicating in her own body all her children's sufferings, she hastened to rejoin them, rejoicing and glorying in her death as though she had been invited to a bridal banquet instead of being a victim of the beasts. After the scourges, the animals, and the hot griddle, she was at last tossed into a net and exposed to a bull. After being tossed a good deal by the animal, she no longer perceived what was happening because of the hope and possession of all she believed in and because of her intimacy with Christ. Thus she too was offered in sacrifice, while the pagans themselves admitted that no woman had ever suffered so much in their experience.

EASTER VIGIL
Luke 24:1–12

Among the first to be witnesses, women are among the last to be believed.

On the first day of the week, at early dawn, some women came to the tomb, taking the spices that they had prepared. They found the stone rolled away from the tomb, but when they went in, they did not find the body. While they were perplexed about this, suddenly two men in dazzling clothes stood beside them. The women were terrified and bowed their faces to the ground, but the men said to them, "Why do you look for the living among the dead? He is not here, but has risen. Remember how he told you, while he was still in Galilee, that the Child of Humanity must be handed over to sinners, and be crucified, and on the third day rise again." Then they remembered his words, and returning from the tomb, they told all this to the eleven and to all the rest. Now it was Mary Magdalene, Joanna, Mary the mother of James, and the other women with them who told this to the apostles. But these words seemed to them an idle tale, and they did not believe them. But Peter got up and ran to the tomb; stooping and looking in, he saw the linen cloths by themselves; then he went home, amazed at what had happened.

EASTER SUNDAY
John 20:1–2, 11–18

An empty tomb story turns into a joyous encounter between the risen Christ and his faithful disciple, Mary Magdalene, who is then commissioned as "apostle of the apostles."

Early on the first day of the week while it was still dark, Mary Magdalene came to the tomb and saw that the stone had been removed from the tomb. So she ran and went to Simon Peter and the other disciple, the one whom Jesus loved, and said to them, "They have taken the Lord out of the tomb, and we do not know where they have laid him."

Mary stood weeping outside the tomb. As she wept, she bent over to look into the tomb; and she saw two angels in white, sitting where the body of Jesus had been lying, one at the head and the other at the feet. They said to her, "Woman, why are you weeping?" She said to them, "They have taken away my Lord, and I do not know where they have laid him." When she had said this, she turned around and saw Jesus standing there, but she did not know that it was Jesus. Jesus said to her, "Woman, why are you weeping? Whom are you looking for?" Supposing him to be the gardener, she said to him, "Sir, if you have carried him away, tell me where you have laid him, and I will take him away." Jesus said to her, "Mary!" She turned and said to him in Hebrew, "Rabbouni!" (which means Teacher). Jesus said to her, "Do not hold on to me, because I have not yet ascended to the Father. But go to my brothers and sisters and say to them, 'I am ascending to my Father and your Father, to my God and your God.'" Mary Magdalene went and announced to the disciples, "I have seen the Lord," and she told them that he had said these things to her.

OCTAVE OF EASTER
Monday
Gospel of Mary [Magdalene] 9.6–10.16

Mary Magdalene strengthens frightened disciples and instructs them in the mysteries of God revealed to her by the risen Lord.

The disciples of Jesus were grieved. They wept greatly, saying, "How shall we go to the Gentiles and preach the gospel of the kingdom of the Child of Humanity? If they did not spare him, how will they spare us?" Then Mary stood up, greeted them all, and said to her brothers, "Do not weep and do not grieve nor be irresolute, for the Savior's grace will be entirely with you and will protect you. But rather let us praise the Savior's greatness, for he has prepared us and made us into adult people." When Mary said this, she turned their hearts to the Good, and they began to discuss the words of the Savior.

Peter said to Mary, "Sister, we know that the Savior loved you more than the rest of women. Tell us the words of the Savior which you remember—which you know but we do not nor have we heard them." Mary answered and said, "What is hidden from you I will proclaim to you." And she began to speak to them these words: "I," she said, "I saw the Lord in a vision and I said to him, 'Lord, I saw you today in a vision.' He answered and said to me, 'Blessed are you, that you did not waver at the sight of me. For where the mind is, there is the treasure.' "

See John 20:1–2, 11–20

OCTAVE OF EASTER
Tuesday
Song of Solomon 3:1-4

Mary Magdalene sought Jesus at the tomb, then heard him call her name and saw him standing before her. Her pain and joy find their echo in this song of separated lovers. [This reading is assigned in the Roman lectionary to the feast of Mary Magdalene and may be read through her eyes.]

Upon my bed at night
I sought him whom my soul loves;
I sought him, but found him not;
  I called him, but he gave no answer.
I will rise now and go about the city,
  in the streets and in the squares;
I will seek him whom my soul loves.
  I sought him, but found him not.
The sentinels found me,
  as they went about in the city.
"Have you seen him whom my soul loves?"
Scarcely had I passed them,
  when I found him whom my soul loves.
I held him, and would not let him go
  until I brought him into my mother's house,
  and into the chamber of her that conceived me.

OCTAVE OF EASTER
Wednesday
Gertrude, *Spiritual Exercises*

What is recorded of Gertrude of Helfta's intimacy with God is eminently true of Mary Magdalene's relationship with Christ.

Carried away one day by the excess of her love, she said to the Lord: "Would, O Lord, that I might have a fire that could liquefy my soul so that I could pour it totally out like a libation unto thee!" The Lord answered: "Thy will is such a fire."

OCTAVE OF EASTER
Thursday
Matthew 27:55-61

These women who followed Jesus during his life remained with him at his death.

Many women were also there, looking on from a distance; they had followed Jesus from Galilee and had provided for him. Among them were Mary Magdalene, and Mary the mother of James and Joseph, and the mother of the sons of Zebedee [Zeb' e dee].

When it was evening, there came a rich man from Arimathea, named Joseph, who was also a disciple of Jesus. He went to Pilate and asked for the body of Jesus; then Pilate ordered it to be given to him. So Joseph took the body and wrapped it in a clean linen cloth and laid it in his own new tomb, which he had hewn in the rock. He then rolled a great stone to the door of the tomb and went away. Mary Magdalene and the other Mary were there, sitting opposite the tomb.

OCTAVE OF EASTER
Friday
Apocalypse of Elijah 4:1–6

A Christian author describes the martyrdom of Tabitha (Dorcas, Acts 9:36). After Peter raised her in Acts 9:36, there was no subsequent report of her death. Therefore Christians assumed she was still alive and would serve as witness until the final days. "Shameless One" personifies evil, another name for Satan.

The virgin, whose name is Tabitha [Tab′ i tha], will hear that the shameless one has revealed himself in the holy places. And she will put on her garment of fine linen. And she will pursue him up to Judea, scolding him up to Jerusalem, saying, "O shameless one, O child of lawlessness, O you who have been hostile to all the saints."

Then the shameless one will be angry at the virgin. He will pursue her up to the regions of the sunset. He will suck her blood in the evening. And he will cast her upon the temple, and she will become a healing for the people. She will rise up at dawn. And she will live and scold him, saying, "O shameless one, you have no power against my soul or my body, because I live in the Lord always. And also my blood which you have cast upon the temple has become a healing for the people."

OCTAVE OF EASTER
Saturday
Mark 16:9–13

From the beginning it has not been unusual for women's experience of God to be discounted.

Now after Jesus rose early on the first day of the week, he appeared first to Mary Magdalene, from whom he had cast out seven demons. She went out and told those who had been with him, while they were mourning and weeping. But when they heard that he was alive and had been seen by her, they would not believe it.

After this he appeared in another form to two of them, as they were walking into the country. And they went back and told the rest, but they did not believe them.

See Matthew 28:1–10
John 20:18

SECOND SUNDAY OF EASTER
Odes of Solomon 19.1–7

The image of a nursing child provides the author of this Ode with rich symbolism to portray how God communicates goodness and nourishment to the believer.

A cup of milk was offered to me,
and I drank it in the sweetness of the Lord's kindness.

The Son is the cup,
and the Father is he who was milked;
and the Holy Spirit is she who milked him;

Because his breasts were full,
and it was undesirable that his milk should be released without purpose.

The Holy Spirit opened her bosom,
and mixed the milk of the two breasts of the Father.

Then she gave the mixture to the generation without their knowing,
and those who have received it are in the perfection of the right hand.

The womb of the Virgin took it,
and she received conception and gave birth.
So the Virgin became a mother with great mercies.

SECOND WEEK OF EASTER
Monday
Julian of Norwich, *Showings* 59

Julian presents a fresh image of paschal blessings.

We have all this bliss by mercy and grace, and this kind of bliss we never could have had and known, unless that property of goodness which is in God had been opposed, through which we have this bliss. For wickedness has been suffered to rise in opposition to that goodness; and the goodness of mercy and grace opposed that wickedness, and turned everything to goodness and honor for all who will be saved. For this is that property in God which opposes good to evil. So Jesus Christ, who opposes good to evil, is our true Mother. We have our being from him, where the foundation of motherhood begins, with all the sweet protection of love which endlessly follows. As truly as God is our Father, so truly is God our Mother.

SECOND WEEK OF EASTER
Tuesday
Acts 16:11–15

Lydia, a successful business woman and one of the first converts of Macedonia, offers her house to Paul and his companions as the center for a new house church.

We set sail from Troas and took a straight course to Samothrace [Sam' o thrace], the following day to Neapolis [Ne ap' o lis], and from there to Philippi [Phil' ip pi], which is a leading city of the district of Macedonia [Mac e do' ni a] and a Roman colony. We remained in this city for some days. On the sabbath day we went outside the gate by the river, where we supposed there was a place of prayer; and we sat down and spoke to the women who had gathered there. A certain woman named Lydia [Lyd' i a], a worshiper of God, was listening to us; she was from the city of Thyatira [Thy a ti' ra] and a dealer in purple cloth. The Lord opened her heart to listen eagerly to what was said by Paul. When she and her household were baptized, she urged us, saying, "If you have judged me to be faithful to the Lord, come and stay at my home." And she prevailed upon us.

SECOND WEEK OF EASTER
Wednesday
Sibylline Oracles Book 4:1–23

The Sibyl, prophet and seer, proclaims the sovereignty of the God who called her to prophesy.

People of boastful Asia and Europe, give ear
to the unfailing truths that I am about to prophesy
through my honey-voiced mouth from our shrine.
I am not an oracle-monger of false Phoebus, whom vain
people called a god, and falsely described as a seer,
but of the great God, whom no human hands fashioned
in the likeness of speechless idols of polished stone.
For God does not have a house, a stone set up as a temple,
dumb and toothless, a bane which brings many woes to humans,
but one which it is not possible to see from earth nor to measure
with mortal eyes, since it was not fashioned by mortal hand.
God sees all at once but is seen by no one.
Dark night is God's, and day, sun and
stars, moon and fish-filled sea,
and land and rivers and source of perennial springs,
things created for life, also showers which engender
the fruit of the soil, and trees, both vine and olive.
God it is who drove a whip through my heart within,
to narrate accurately to people what now is,
and what will yet be, from the first generation

until the tenth comes. For God will prove everything
by accomplishing it. But you, people, listen to the Sibyl in all things
as she pours forth true speech from her holy mouth.

SECOND WEEK OF EASTER
Thursday
Proverbs 8:22–31

---

*In the Sophia tradition, Wisdom is the co-creator, present and active
from the beginning. She is the model for Jesus as Word in John's
gospel.*

The Lord created me at the beginning of God's work,
   the first of God's acts of long ago.
Ages ago I was set up,
   at the first, before the beginning of the earth.
When there were no depths I was brought forth,
   when there were no springs abounding with water.
Before the mountains had been shaped,
   before the hills, I was brought forth—
when God had not yet made earth and fields,
   or the world's first bits of soil.
When God established the heavens, I was there,
   when God drew a circle on the face of the deep,
when God made firm the skies above,
   when God established the fountains of the deep,
when God assigned to the sea its limit,
   so that the waters might not transgress God's command,
when God marked out the foundations of the earth,
   then I was beside God, like a skilled artisan;
and I was daily God's delight,
   rejoicing before God always,
rejoicing in God's inhabited world
   and delighting in the human race.

See John 1:1–18

SECOND WEEK OF EASTER
Friday
Gospel of Mary [Magdalene] 17.7–18.15

*This reading from the gnostic Gospel of Mary highlights the impor-
tance of the traditions about Mary Magdalene in gnostic circles.
The memory of her leadership and preeminence compares with that
of Peter.*

When Mary had spoken to the disciples about the risen Lord, she
fell silent, since it was to this point that the Savior had spoken with her.
But Andrew answered and said to the brothers, "Say what you wish to say
about what she has said. I at least do not believe that the Savior said this.
For certainly these teachings are strange ideas." Peter answered and
spoke concerning these same things. He questioned them about the Savior: "Did he really speak privately with a woman and not openly to us?
Are we to turn about and all listen to her? Did he prefer her to us?"
    Then Mary wept and said to Peter, "My brother Peter, what do you
think? Do you think that I thought this up myself in my heart, or that I am
lying about the Savior?" Levi answered and said to Peter, "Peter, you
have always been hot-tempered. Now I see you contending against the
woman like the adversaries. But if the Savior made her worthy, who are
you indeed to reject her? Surely the Savior knows her very well. That is
why he loved her more than us."

SECOND WEEK OF EASTER
Saturday
Odes of Solomon 33.5–13

*The prophetic voice of "the perfect Virgin," one image of the
church, warns believers against corruption. Echoing the call of Wisdom, she invites all to hear and be saved.*

The perfect Virgin stood
who was preaching and summoning and saying:

O you sons of men and women, return,
and you their daughters, come.

And abandon the ways of that Corrupter,
and approach me.

I will enter into you,
and bring you forth from destruction,
and make you wise in the ways of truth.

Be not corrupted
nor perish.

Hear me and be saved,
for I am proclaiming unto you the grace of God.

And through me you will be saved and become blessed.
I am your judge;

They who have put me on will not be rejected,
but they will possess incorruption in the new world.

My elect ones have walked with me,
and my ways I shall make known to them who seek me;
and I shall promise them my name.

Hallelujah.

THIRD SUNDAY OF EASTER
Odes of Solomon 40

*In this early Christian hymn, honey from the honeycomb and milk
from the breast symbolize the abundance of hope in God felt by the
author of this Ode.*

As honey drips from the honeycomb of bees,
and milk flows from the woman who loves her children,
so also is my hope upon you, O my God.

As a spring gushes forth its water,
so my heart gushes forth the praise of the Lord,
and my lips bring forth praise to God.

My tongue becomes sweet by God's anthems,
and my members are anointed by odes.

My face rejoices in God's exultation,
and my spirit exults in God's love,
and my nature shines in God.

And they who are afraid will trust in God,
in whom salvation will be established.

And the possession is immortal life,
and those who receive it are incorruptible.
Hallelujah.

THIRD WEEK OF EASTER
Monday
Holy Women of the Syrian Orient: Martha (#1 of 5)

In the middle of the fourth century CE, in what is now Iraq and western Iran, Syrian Christians and Greek-speaking Christians who were prisoners of war, were persecuted by the Zoroastrian authorities. In this account of a young Martha, the authorities are as much angered by her vow of virginity as by her faith, since such a vow was abhorrent to Zoroastrian mores. Evidently some young Christian women of the period took such a vow at the time of adult baptism and became known as "daughters of the covenant."

Now the glorious Posi had a daughter called Martha who was a "daughter of the covenant." She too was accused, and at the third hour on the Sunday of the great feast of the Resurrection she was arrested. They brought the blessed Martha, daughter of the glorious Posi, into the presence of the chief Mobed, who then went in to inform the king about her. The king bade him to go out and interrogate her, saying, "If she abandons her religion and renounces Christianity, well and good; if not, she should be married off. If, however she fails to follow either of these courses, she should be handed over to be put to death."

So the chief Mobed went out and started to interrogate the glorious Martha as follows: "What are you?" To which the blessed Martha replied derisively, "I am a woman, as you can see." Those who happened to be there in the presence of the chief Mobed blushed and bent down their heads when they heard the wise Martha's reply to his question. The Mobed's face became green with anger and shame, but he controlled his feelings and said, "Reply to my question." To which the wise Martha said, "I did reply to the question I was asked."

The Mobed then said, "What did I ask you, and what reply did you give?" Martha said, "Your honor asked, 'what are you?' and I replied, 'I am a woman as you can see.'"

THIRD WEEK OF EASTER
Tuesday
Holy Women of the Syrian Orient: Martha (#2 of 5)

The interrogation of Martha continues. Reference to Christians as the "betrothed of Christ" is a favorite and consistent theme in Syriac theology.

The betrothed of Christ, Martha, then said, "So how can your authority order me to marry a man to whom I am not betrothed when I am already betrothed to someone else?"

To which the Mobed said, "Are you really betrothed, then?" And the blessed Martha replied, "I am in truth betrothed." "To whom?" asked the Mobed. "Is not your honor aware of him?" said the glorious Martha. "Where is he?" asked the Mobed. Wise in our Lord, she replied, "He has set out on a long journey on business; but he is close by and is on the point of coming back." "What is his name?" inquired the Mobed. "Jesus," replied the blessed Martha.

Still not understanding, the Mobed went on, "What country has he gone to? In what city is he now?" The splendid Martha replied, "He has gone off to heaven, and he is now in Jerusalem on high."

At this point the Mobed realized that she was speaking of our Lord Jesus Christ, whereupon he said, "Didn't I say at the very beginning that this was a stubborn people, not open to persuasion? I will spatter you from head to toe with blood, and then your fiancé can come along to find you turned into dust and rubbish: let him marry you then."

The courageous Martha replied, "He will indeed come in glory, riding on the chariot of the clouds, accompanied by the angels and powers of heaven, and all that is appropriate for his wedding feast; he will shake from the dust the bodies of all those who are betrothed to him, wash them in the dew of heaven, anoint them with the oil of gladness, and clothe them in the garment of righteousness, which consists of glorious light; he will place on their fingers rings as the surety of his grace, while on their heads he will put a crown of splendor, that is to say, unfading glory. He will allow them to sit on his chariot, the glorious cloud, and will raise them up into the air, bringing them into the heavenly bridal chamber that has been set up in a place not made by hands, but built in Jerusalem the free city on high."

THIRD WEEK OF EASTER
Wednesday
Holy Women of the Syrian Orient: Martha (#3 of 5)

Martha's prayer before her martyrdom echoes many of the prayers of the eucharistic liturgy.

They led the chaste virgin Martha off on the Sunday of the great feast of Christ's resurrection, at midday. As they were getting ready the place where she was to be put to death, she fell down on her face and, as she knelt before God facing east, she said, "I thank you, Jesus Christ, my Lord, my King and my Betrothed, for preserving my virginity sealed up with the imprint of the seal-ring of your promise, and for preserving my faith in the glorious Trinity—the faith in which I was born, in which my parents brought me up, and in which I was baptized. For this confession, for which my father Posi was also crowned, I give you thanks, O Lamb of God who takes away the sin of the world, for whose sake the bishops, our shepherds, have been sacrificed, as have the head pastors, the priests, and along with them the members of the holy covenant; and slaughtered too have been the sheep—Guhshtazad [Guhsh' ta zad] and Posi my father. And now it is the turn of me, the young lamb who has been fattened up on the pastures of your promises and by the springs of your declarations: here I am being sacrificed before you. At your hands, Jesus, the true High Priest, may I be offered up as a pure, holy, and acceptable offering before the glorious Trinity of the hidden Being, in whose name you taught us to be instructed and baptized. Visit, Lord, your persecuted people; preserve them in true faith in the midst of their enemies, and may they be found to be like pure gold in the furnace of persecution that has been erected against your people; may they be strengthened in the worship of your majesty, fearlessly worshipping and confessing Father, Son, and Holy Spirit, now and always and for eternal ages, amen."

THIRD WEEK OF EASTER
Thursday
Holy Women of the Syrian Orient: Martha (#4 of 5)

Martha continues her preparation for death with a remarkable freedom of spirit and courage.

The moment she had finished her prayer, while no one was near at hand, she rushed off and stretched herself on the ground above the pit they had dug for her. When the officer approached to tie her up, she said, "Do not tie me up, for I am gladly accepting immolation for the sake of my Lord." When she saw the knife being brandished by the officer, she laughed and said, "Now I can say, not like Isaac, 'Here is the fire and the wood, but where is the lamb for the burnt offering?' but rather I can say, 'Here is the lamb and the knife, but where is the wood and the fire?' But I *do* have wood and fire, for the wood is the cross of Jesus my Lord, and I *do* have fire too—the fire that Christ left on earth, just as he said, 'I came to cast fire on earth: I only wish it had already caught alight!' "

The thousands of spectators who stood by were astounded at the chaste girl's courage, and everyone gave praise to the God who encourages those who fear God in this way.

The officer then approached and slaughtered her like a lamb, while she entrusted her soul to Christ.

THIRD WEEK OF EASTER
Friday
Holy Women of the Syrian Orient: Martha (#5 of 5)

Martha's martyrdom is commemorated by the community.

The blessed Martha was crowned on the Sunday of the great feast of the Resurrection.

The blessed woman who had helped prepare Martha and her father for burial used to keep their memorial each year in her home, close by where the priests and clergy lived. This she did all her life, and after her death her house passed to her brother's son. He too diligently kept their memorial, following that blessed woman's custom. When this nephew died, he left behind him two sons, and sometime after his death they had a quarrel over the saint's bones: one of them wanted to divide them up between himself and his brother, because the house of the blessed woman had fallen to his share. The matter came to the knowledge of Sawmay, bishop of Karka, of blessed memory, and he persuaded the two of them to take away the bones; whereupon he presented them to the people of the church of Karka, to serve as a fair memento, and to be a valued treasure in the Church of Christ. This was done by the holy bishop Sawmay in the eighth year of king Barharan [Bar' ha ran], son of Yazdgard [Yazd' gard], eighty-nine years after their crowning. This was what happened to Posi and his daughter.

THIRD WEEK OF EASTER
Saturday
Acts 9:36–42

Tabitha was much loved by the women among whom she exercised her ministry.

Now in Joppa there was a disciple whose name was Tabitha [Tab' i tha], which in Greek is Dorcas. She was devoted to good works and acts of charity. At that time she became ill and died. When they had washed her, they laid her in a room upstairs. Since Lydda was near Joppa, the disciples, who heard that Peter was there, sent two men to him with the request, "Please come to us without delay." So Peter got up and went with them; and when he arrived, they took him to the room upstairs. All the widows stood beside him, weeping and showing tunics and other clothing that Dorcas had made while she was with them. Peter put all of them outside, and then he knelt down and prayed. He turned to the body and said, "Tabitha, get up." Then she opened her eyes, and seeing Peter, she sat up. He gave her his hand and helped her up. Then calling the saints and widows, he showed her to be alive. This became known throughout Joppa, and many believed in the Lord.

FOURTH SUNDAY OF EASTER
Acts of John 82–83

Drusiana, after she was raised from the dead by the power of the Apostle John, prays to the risen Christ and, in turn, raises Fortunatus from the dead.

After she had been raised Drusiana [Dru si an' a] made no delay, but rejoicing in spirit and soul she went up to the body of Fortunatus [For tu na' tus] and said, "O God of all ages, Jesus Christ, God of truth, who suffered me to see wonders and signs and did grant me to become partaker of your name, who revealed yourself to me with your many-formed countenance and had mercy on me in every way; who by your great goodness protected me when I suffered violence from my former consort Andronicus [An dro ni' cus]; who gave me your servant Andronicus as my brother; who kept me, your handmaid, pure until this day; who has raised me up from death through thy servant John, and when I was raised has shown me the man who fell as now unfallen; who has given me perfect rest in you, and relieved me of the secret madness; whom I have loved and embraced; I entreat you, O Christ, do not refuse your Drusiana's petition that you raise up Fortunatus, for all that he strove to become my betrayer."

And she grasped the dead man's hand, and said, "Rise up, Fortunatus, in the name of our Lord Jesus Christ." And Fortunatus rose up, and saw John in the sepulchre and Andronicus and Drusiana, now raised from the dead, and Callimachus, now a believer, and the rest of the people glorifying God.

FOURTH WEEK OF EASTER
Monday
Acts of John 19–23 passim

The power of Christ, working through the apostle John, raises Cleopatra from her mortal illness and all the Ephesians marvel at the wondrous deed in their midst.

As we approached the city Lycomedes [Ly co' me des] met us, a wealthy man who was praetor of the Ephesians; and he fell at John's feet and entreated him, saying, "Is your name John? The God whom you preach has sent you to help my wife who has been paralyzed for the past seven days and is lying there unable to be cured. But glorify your God by healing her, and have pity upon us. For while I was considering with myself what conclusion to draw from this, someone came to me and said, 'Lycomedes, enough of this thought which besets you, for it is harmful. Do not submit to it! For I have had compassion on my servant Cleopatra [Cle o pa' tra] and have sent from Miletus [Mi le' tus] a man named John, who will raise her up and restore her to you in good health.' Do not delay then, servant of God who has revealed you to me; come quickly to my wife, who is only just breathing."

But when Lycomedes came with John into the house in which the woman was lying, he grasped his feet again and said, "See, my Lord, this faded beauty; look at her youth; look at the famous flower-like grace of my poor wife, at which all Ephesus was amazed!"

And Lycomedes, still speaking to Cleopatra, approached her bed and lamented with a loud voice.

And while John was crying aloud the city of the Ephesians came running together to the house of Lycomedes, supposing him dead. But John, seeing the great crowd that had come together, said to the Lord, "You yourself have said, O Christ, 'Ask, and it shall be given you.' (Matt 7:7 and parallels) We therefore ask of you, O King, not gold or silver, not substance or possessions, nor any of the perishable things upon earth, but two souls, through whom you will convert those who are present to your way and to your teaching, to your confidence, to your excellent promise; for some of them shall be saved when they learn your power through the resurrection of these who are lifeless. So now grant hope in you. I am going, then, to Cleopatra and say, 'Arise in the name of Jesus Christ.' "

And he went to her and touched her face and said, "Cleopatra, God speaks, whom every ruler fears. Arise, he says, and be not an excuse for many who wish to disbelieve, and an affliction to souls who are able to hope and be saved." And Cleopatra cried out at once with a loud voice, "I arise, Master, save your handmaid."

When Cleopatra had arisen after seven days of mortal sickness, the city of the Ephesians was stirred at that amazing sight.

FOURTH WEEK OF EASTER
Tuesday
Acts of John 24

With the power of God at work in her, Cleopatra raises her husband from the dead.

After she had been raised, Cleopatra asked about her husband Lycomedes [Ly co' me des]. But John said to her, "Cleopatra, keep your soul unmoved and unwavering, and then you shall have your husband standing here with you, if you are not disturbed nor shaken by what has happened, but have come to believe in my God, who through me shall give him back to you alive. Come then with me to your other bedroom, and you shall see him dead indeed, but rising again through the power of God." And when Cleopatra came with John into her bedroom and saw Lycomedes dead on her account, she lost her voice, and ground her teeth and bit her tongue, and closed her eyes, raining down tears; and she quietly attended to the Apostle.

But John had pity upon Cleopatra when he saw her neither raging nor distraught, and called upon the perfect and condescending mercy, and said, "Lord Jesus Christ, you see her distress, you see her need, you see Cleopatra crying out her soul in silence; for she contains within her the intolerable raging of her sorrow; and I know that for Lycomedes' sake she will follow him to death." And she quietly said to John, "That is in my mind, Master, and nothing else." Then the Apostle went up to the couch on which Lycomedes lay, and taking Cleopatra's hand he said, "Cleopatra, because of the crowd that is present, and because of your relatives who have come here also, speak with a loud voice to your husband and say, 'Rise up and glorify the name of God, since to the dead God gives back the dead.' " And she went near and spoke to her husband as she was instructed, and immediately raised him up. And he arose and fell to the ground and kissed John's feet; but John lifted him up and said, "It is not my feet, man, that you should kiss, but those of God in whose power you both have been raised up."

FOURTH WEEK OF EASTER
Wednesday
Epitaph of Regina, Jewish Woman Praised for Her Piety and Observance of Jewish Law

---

This funerary inscription from second century Rome testifies not only to marital love but also to belief in the resurrection.

Here lies Regina, sheltered by such a tomb, set up by her husband, set up as fitting gesture for his love. Beyond twenty years she spent with him still another year, four months and eight days. She will live again, see light again, for she can hope that she will rise in the new age, as promised by our true faith to the worthy and the pious, for she has merited a place in the holy land. This your piety has obtained for you, this your pure life, this your love of your people, this your observance of the Law, your conjugal devotion, for the glory of your marriage was dear to you. On all these things rests your hope for the future. In this hope your grieving husband seeks comfort.

FOURTH WEEK OF EASTER
Thursday
John 11:1-6 (#1 of 4)

Martha, Mary, and Lazarus are loved deeply by Jesus—an unusual pattern of equal relationships and intimacy between unrelated men and women in Jesus' day.

Now a certain man was ill, Lazarus of Bethany, the village of Mary and her sister Martha. Mary was the one who anointed the Lord with perfume and wiped his feet with her hair; her brother Lazarus was ill. So the sisters sent a message to Jesus, "Lord, he whom you love is ill." But when Jesus heard it, he said, "This illness does not lead to death; rather it is for God's glory, so that the Son of God may be glorified through it." Accordingly, though Jesus loved Martha and her sister and Lazarus, after having heard that Lazarus was ill, he stayed two days longer in the place where he was.

FOURTH WEEK OF EASTER
Friday
John 11:17-27 (#2 of 4)

The dialogue between Jesus and Martha culminates in one of the four great confessions of faith in John's gospel, closely paralleling Peter's confession of faith in the synoptic gospels.

When Jesus arrived at Bethany, he found that Lazarus had already been in the tomb four days. Now Bethany was near Jerusalem, some two miles away, and many of the Jews had come to Martha and Mary to console them about their brother. When Martha heard that Jesus was coming, she went and met him, while Mary stayed at home. Martha said to Jesus, "Lord, if you had been here, my brother would not have died.

But even now I know that God will give you whatever you ask." Jesus said to her, "Your brother will rise again." Martha said to him, "I know that he will rise again in the resurrection on the last day." Jesus said to her, "I am the resurrection and the life. Those who believe in me, even though they die, will live, and everyone who lives and believes in me will never die. Do you believe this?" She said to him, "Yes, Lord, I believe that you are the Messiah, the Son of God, the one coming into the world."

See Mark 8:29

FOURTH WEEK OF EASTER
Saturday
John 11:28–37 (#3 of 4)

Mary's grief stirs Jesus' grief. Often women's freedom in expressing what most deeply moves them frees men to do the same.

Martha called her sister Mary, and told her privately, "The Teacher is here and is calling for you." And when she heard it, she got up quickly and went to him. Now Jesus had not yet come to the village, but was still at the place where Martha had met him. The Jews who were with her in the house, consoling her, saw Mary get up quickly and go out. They followed her because they thought that she was going to the tomb to weep there. When Mary came where Jesus was and saw him, she knelt at his feet and said to him, "Lord, if you had been here, my brother would not have died." When Jesus saw her weeping, and the Jews who came with her also weeping, he was greatly disturbed in spirit and deeply moved. He said, "Where have you laid him?" They said to him, "Lord, come and see." Jesus began to weep. So the Jews said, "See how he loved him!" But some of them said, "Could not he who opened the eyes of the blind man have kept this man from dying?"

FIFTH SUNDAY OF EASTER
John 11:38–45 (#4 of 4)

Jesus engages the community in the act of liberation. It is our role to unbind one another.

Then Jesus, again greatly disturbed, came to the tomb. It was a cave, and a stone was lying against it. Jesus said, "Take away the stone." Martha, the sister of the dead man, said to him, "Lord, already there is a stench because he has been dead four days." Jesus said to her, "Did I not tell you that if you believed, you would see the glory of God?" So they took away the stone. And Jesus looked upward and said, "Father, I thank you for having heard me. I knew that you always hear me, but I have said this for the sake of the crowd standing here, so that they may believe that you sent me." When he had said this, he cried with a loud voice, "Lazarus, come out!" The dead man came out, his hands and feet bound with strips of cloth, and his face wrapped in a cloth. Jesus said to them, "Unbind him, and let him go."

Many of the Jews therefore, who had come with Mary and had seen what Jesus did, believed in him.

FIFTH WEEK OF EASTER
Monday
Acts 12:11–17

The house of Mary mentioned in this text was no doubt an early house-church for the gathering of the community. In this reading, Rhoda's testimony is dismissed by the assembly, perhaps an echo of the incredulity of Luke's male disciples who refused to believe the testimony of the women from the tomb.

Peter came to himself and said, "Now I am sure that the Lord has sent his angel and rescued me from the hands of Herod and from all that the Jewish people were expecting."

As soon as he realized this, he went to the house of Mary, the mother of John whose other name was Mark, where many had gathered and were praying. When he knocked at the outer gate, a maid named Rhoda came to answer. On recognizing Peter's voice, she was so over-joyed that, instead of opening the gate, she ran in and announced that Peter was standing at the gate. They said to her, "You are out of your mind!" But she insisted that it was so. They said, "It is his angel." Mean-while Peter continued knocking; and when they opened the gate, they saw him and were amazed. He motioned to them with his hand to be silent, and described for them how the Lord had brought him out of the prison. And he added, "Tell this to James and to the believers." Then he left and went to another place.

See Luke 24:10–11

FIFTH WEEK OF EASTER
Tuesday
Mark 16:1–8

While this gospel passage suggests that the women were afraid to tell their experience of Jesus, the very fact that we read the story proves that they were not!

When the sabbath was over, Mary Magdalene, and Mary the mother of James, and Salome [Sa lo' me] bought spices, so that they might go and anoint Jesus. And very early on the first day of the week, when the sun had risen, they went to the tomb. They had been saying to one another, "Who will roll away the stone for us from the entrance to the tomb?" When they looked up, they saw that the stone, which was very large, had already been rolled back. As they entered the tomb, they saw a young man, dressed in a white robe, sitting on the right side; and they were alarmed. But he said to them, "Do not be alarmed; you are looking for Jesus of Nazareth, who was crucified. He has been raised; he is not here. Look, there is the place they laid him. But go, tell his disciples and Peter that he is going ahead of you to Galilee; there you will see him, just as he told you." So they went out and fled from the tomb, for terror and amazement had seized them; and they said nothing to anyone, for they were afraid.

FIFTH WEEK OF EASTER
Wednesday
Gospel of Bartholomew 2.1–12 (#1 of 3)

Despite Mary's reluctance, the apostles urge her to lead them in prayer and to reveal to them the mystery of Jesus' conception. Mary's response is in the tradition of mystagogical catechesis during the great fifty days.

Now the apostles were with Mary. And Bartholomew [Bar thol' o mew] came to Peter and Andrew and John, and said to them: Let us ask Mary, her who is highly favoured, how she conceived the incomprehensible, or how she carried him who cannot be carried, or how she bore so much greatness. But they hesitated to ask her. Therefore, Bartholomew said to Peter: Father Peter, do you as the chief one go to her and ask her. But Peter said to John: You are a chaste youth and blameless; you must ask her. And as they all were doubtful and pondered the matter to and fro, Bartholomew came to her with a cheerful countenance and said: You who are highly favoured, tabernacle of the Most High, unblemished, we, all the apostles, ask you, but they have sent me to you. Tell us how you conceived the incomprehensible, or how you carried him who cannot be carried, or how you bore so much greatness. But Mary answered: Do not ask me concerning this mystery. If I begin to tell you, fire will come out of my mouth and consume the whole earth. But they asked her still more urgently. And since she did not wish to deny the apostles a hearing, she said: Let us stand up in prayer. And the apostles stood behind Mary. And she said to Peter: Peter, chief of the apostles, the greatest pillar, do you stand behind me? Did not our Lord say: The head of the man is Christ, but the head of the woman is the man? Therefore stand in front of me to pray. But they said to her: In you the Lord set his tabernacle and was pleased to be contained by you. Therefore, you now have more right than we to lead in the prayer. But she answered them: You are shining stars, as the prophet said: I lifted up my eyes to the hills, from which comes my help (Ps 120:1 LXX). You, then, are the hills and you must pray. The apostles said to her: You ought to pray as the mother of the heavenly king. Mary said to them: In your likeness God formed the sparrows and sent them to the four corners of the world. But they answered her: The One whom the seven heavens scarcely contain was pleased to be contained in you.

FIFTH WEEK OF EASTER
Thursday
Gospel of Bartholomew 2.13–14 (#2 of 3)

Mary leads the apostles in prayer and extols the God who worked miracles in her. At the apostles' pleading, she prepares to share with them the ineffable mystery of the "Word made flesh" in her.

Then Mary stood up before the apostles and spread out her hands to heaven and began to pray thus: O God exceeding great and all-wise, king of the ages, indescribable, ineffable, who did create the breadths of the heavens by thy word and arrange the vault of heaven in harmony, who did give form to disorderly matter and did bring together that which was separated, who did part the gloom of the darkness from the light, who did make the waters to flow from the same source, before whom the beings of the air tremble and the creatures of the earth fear, who did give to the earth its place and did not wish it to perish, in bestowing upon it abundant rain and caring for the nourishment of all things, the eternal Word (Logos) of the Father. The seven heavens could scarcely contain you, but you were pleased to be contained in me, without causing me pain, you who are the perfect Word (Logos) of the Father, through whom everything was created. Glorify your exceedingly great name, and allow me to speak before your holy apostles. And when she had ended the prayer, she began to say to them: Let us sit down on the ground. Come, Peter, chief of the apostles, sit on my right hand and put your left hand under my shoulder. And you, Andrew, do the same on my left hand. And you, chaste John, hold my breast. And you, Bartholomew, place your knees on my shoulders and press close my back so that, when I begin to speak, my limbs are not loosed.

FIFTH WEEK OF EASTER
Friday
Gospel of Bartholomew 2.15–22 (#3 of 3)

Mary begins to recount to the apostles the moment of the annunciation but its awesome mystery can neither be fathomed nor told.

And when the apostles had sat down, Mary began: When I lived in the temple of God and received my food from the hand of an angel, one day there appeared to me one in the form of an angel; but his face was indescribable and in his hand he had neither bread nor cup, as had the angel who came to me before. And immediately the veil of the temple was rent and there was a violent earthquake, and I fell to the earth, for I could not bear the sight of him. But he took me with his hand and raised me up. And I looked toward heaven; and there came a cloud of dew on my face and sprinkled me from head to foot, and he wiped me with his robe. Then he said to me: Hail, you who are highly favoured, the chosen vessel. And then he struck the right side of his garment and there came forth an exceedingly large loaf, and he placed it upon the altar of the temple, and first ate of it himself and then gave to me also. And again he struck his garment, on the left side, and I looked and saw a cup full of wine. And he placed it upon the altar of the temple, and drank from it first himself and gave it also to me. And I looked and saw that the bread did not diminish and the cup was full as before. Then he said: Three years more, and I will send my word and you shall conceive my son, and through him the whole world shall be saved. But you will bring salvation to the world. Peace be with you, favoured one, and my peace shall be with you for ever. And when he had said this, he vanished from my eyes and the temple was as before.

As she was saying this, fire came from her mouth, and the world was on the point of being burned up. Then came Jesus quickly and said to Mary: Say no more, or today my whole creation will come to an end. And the apostles were seized with fear lest God should be angry with them.

FIFTH WEEK OF EASTER
Saturday
Acts of Thomas 27

In this baptismal prayer of invocation, the apostle Thomas, while proclaiming the gospel in India, calls down the presence of God on the king of India and his brother as they are sealed with the holy oil. He invokes God as "compassionate mother," woman "revealer of hidden mysteries," and as Sophia "Mother of the seven houses."

The apostle took the oil and pouring it on their heads anointed and chrismed them, and began to say:

Come, holy name of Christ *that is above every name* (Phil 2:9);
Come, power of the Most High and perfect compassion;
Come, thou highest gift;
Come, compassionate mother;
Come, fellowship of the male;
Come, woman who reveals the hidden mysteries;
Come, mother of the seven houses, that your rest may be in the
    eighth house;
Come, elder messenger of the five members, understanding,
    thought, prudence, consideration, reasoning,
Communicate with these young men!
Come, Holy Spirit, and purify their reins and their heart
And give them the added seal in the name of Father and Son and
    Holy Spirit.

And when they had been sealed there appeared to them a young man carrying a blazing torch, so that the very lamps were darkened at the onset of its light. And going out he vanished from their sight. But the apostle said to the Lord: "Beyond our comprehension, Lord, is your light, and we are not able to bear it; for it is greater than our sight." But when dawn came and it was light, he broke bread and made them partakers in the eucharist of Christ. And they rejoiced and were glad. And many others also, believing, were added to the faithful and came into the refuge of the Saviour.

SIXTH SUNDAY OF EASTER
Matthew 28:1–10

How often in our lives are revelations from God cause for both fear and joy.

After the sabbath, as the first day of the week was dawning, Mary Magdalene and the other Mary went to see the tomb. And suddenly there was a great earthquake; for an angel of the Lord, descending from heaven, came and rolled back the stone and sat on it. His appearance was like lightning, and his clothing white as snow. For fear of him the guards shook and became like dead men. But the angel said to the women, "Do not be afraid; I know that you are looking for Jesus who was crucified. He is not here; for he has been raised, as he said. Come, see the place where he lay. Then go quickly and tell his disciples. 'He has been raised from the dead, and indeed he is going ahead of you to Galilee; there you will see him.' This is my message for you." So they left the tomb quickly with fear and great joy, and ran to tell his disciples. Suddenly Jesus met them and said, "Greetings!" And they came to him, took hold of his feet, and worshiped him. Then Jesus said to them, "Do not be afraid; go and tell my brothers and sisters to go to Galilee; there they will see me."

SIXTH WEEK OF EASTER
Monday
Acts 16:16–18

A slave girl recognizes the power of God at work in the disciples.

One day, as we were going to the place of prayer, we met a slave girl who had a spirit of divination and brought her owners a great deal of money by fortune-telling. While she followed Paul and us, she would cry out, "These men are slaves of the Most High God, who proclaim to you a way of salvation." She kept doing this for many days. But Paul, very much annoyed, turned and said to the spirit, "I order you in the name of Jesus Christ to come out of her." And it came out that very hour.

SIXTH WEEK OF EASTER
Tuesday
Egeria's Travels 45.1–46.4

Egeria's reminiscences to her sisters have provided a wealth of price-less information about late fourth century liturgical practice in Jerusalem.

I feel I should add something about the way they instruct those who are to be baptized at Easter. Names must be given in before the first day of Lent. Then, on the second day of Lent, one by one those seeking baptism are brought up, men coming with their fathers and women with their mothers. As they come in one by one, the bishop asks their neighbours questions about them. He asks the men and the women the same questions.

Now, ladies and loving sisters, I want to write something which will save you from thinking all this is done without due explanation. They have here the custom that those who are preparing for baptism during the season of the Lenten fast go to be exorcised by the clergy first thing in the morning, directly after the morning dismissal in the Anastasis [An a sta' sis] [church of the resurrection]. As soon as that has taken place, the bishop's chair is placed in the Great Church, and all those to be baptized, the men and the women, sit around him in a circle. There is a place where the fathers and mothers stand, and any of the people who want to listen (the faithful, of course) can come in and sit down. During the forty days he goes through the whole Bible, beginning with Genesis, and first relating the literal meaning of each passage, then interpreting its spiritual meaning. He also teaches them at this time all about the resurrection and the faith. And this is called *catechesis*. After five weeks' teaching they receive the Creed, whose content he explains article by article in the same way as he explained the Scriptures, first literally and then spiritually. Thus all the people in these parts are able to follow the Scriptures when they are read in church, since there has been teaching on all the Scriptures from six to nine in the morning all through Lent, three hours' catechesis a day. At ordinary services when the bishop sits and preaches, ladies and sisters, the faithful utter exclamations, but when they come and hear him explaining the catechesis, their exclamations are far louder, God is my witness; and when it is related and interpreted like this they ask questions on each point.

SIXTH WEEK OF EASTER
Wednesday
Holy Women of the Syrian Orient: Anahid

Anahid was a Persian martyr of the fifth century, CE. She and many other women of the period were killed in a purge by Zoroastrian authorities; the crimes for which they died were largely related to the "ceremony of consecrating the bread." There is also some evidence that the ordinary people considered Anahid an apparition of the goddess of the same name.

While Anahid [A' na hid] was in prison, held under close guard, during the middle of the night she was giving praise and thanks to God, making use of the psalms of David, and saying, "I will confess you, O Lord, with all my heart, and before kings will I sing of your name. I will worship you in your holy temple and give thanks to your name for your grace and truth, for you have answered me on the day I called upon you, and you have given my soul great strength." (Ps 138:1–3) With these and other such words she spent the night praising God until the morning.

When morning came, the nobles assembled in the presence of Adurfrazgard [A dur' fraz gard] and sent for the holy woman. Since she could not walk because of the fetters, they had to carry her into their presence. Once she had been set down in front of them, they urged her to abandon the doctrines she clung to. Some of them used threats, others cajoled her, while one of them, a close relative of hers, went up to her and said, "My daughter Anahid, what is the matter with you, what has happened to you that you act differently from everyone else? If they have eliminated your father Adurhormizd [A dur' hor mizd] the Christian, and he has met a bad end, what demon has got hold of you? Why should Ahriman [Ah' ri man] be battling with you like this? Even if you do not revert to Magianism [Ma' gi an ism], at least say, 'I am not a Christian,' and then I can save you and carry you off to somewhere where there are Christians, and you can live there in Christianity all the rest of your life."

The wise woman replied, "You silly and senseless man, how can I deny God in whom we live and move and have our being (Acts 17:28)— we and all created things? Where can I go to where God is not there, what place is there that is not filled with God and God is there? Furthermore, our Lord Christ said that 'those who deny me before others, I will deny before my Father in heaven' (Matt 10:33). As it is, I have already renounced your gods—which are not gods—and I continue to do so; and I have confessed him and will continue to confess him right up to death."

FEAST OF THE ASCENSION
Hildegard of Bingen

*Hildegard's mystical images in this poem comment eloquently on
the holy tension of our life in Christ.*

O most beautiful form,
O sweetest fragrance of desirable delights,
we sigh for you always in our sorrowful banishment!
When may we see you and remain with you?

But we dwell in the world,
and you dwell in our mind;
we embrace you in our heart
as if we had you here with us.

You, bravest lion, have burst through the heavens.
You have destroyed death, and are building life
in the golden city.

Grant us society in that city,
and let us dwell in you. . . .

SIXTH WEEK OF EASTER
Friday
Acts 18:1-4

*From this text and others like it, we know there were missionary
couples who participated in the ministry of the gospel.*

Paul left Athens and went to Corinth. There he found a Jew named
Aquila, a native of Pontus, who had recently come from Italy with his

wife Priscilla, because Claudius had ordered all Jews to leave Rome. Paul went to see them, and, because he was of the same trade, he stayed with them, and they worked together—by trade they were tentmakers. Every sabbath he would argue in the synagogue and would try to convince Jews and Greeks.

See Romans 16:7, 15

SIXTH WEEK OF EASTER
Saturday
Acts 18:18–28

A husband and wife team up in the ministry of the gospel. Sometime companions and co-workers of Paul, they are here depicted as catechists. It is interesting to note that here and in many references to them Priscilla's name appears first, clear evidence of Priscilla's importance and ministerial equality.

After staying in Corinth for a considerable time, Paul said farewell to the believers and sailed for Syria, accompanied by Priscilla [Pri scil' la] and Aquila [Aq' ui la]. At Cenchreae [Cen' chre ae] he had his hair cut, for he was under a vow. When they reached Ephesus, he left them there, but first he himself went into the synagogue and had a discussion with the Jews. When they asked him to stay longer, he declined; but on taking leave of them he said, "I will return to you, if God wills." Then he set sail from Ephesus.

Now there came to Ephesus a Jew named Apollos, a native of Alexandria. He was an eloquent man, well-versed in the scriptures. He had been instructed in the Way of the Lord; and he spoke with burning enthusiasm and taught accurately the things concerning Jesus, though he knew only the baptism of John. He began to speak boldly in the synagogue; but when Priscilla and Aquila heard him, they took him aside and explained the Way of God to him more accurately. And when he wished to cross over to Achaia [A cha'i a], the believers encouraged him and wrote to the disciples to welcome him. On his arrival he greatly helped those who through grace had become believers, for he powerfully refuted the Jews in public, showing by the scriptures that the Messiah is Jesus.

SEVENTH SUNDAY OF EASTER
Hadewijch, *Vision* 13

Hadewijch's vision contains a glimpse into a surprising, new understanding of the "new heaven" of the book of Revelation.

On the Sunday before Pentecost, before dawn, I was raised up in spirit to God, who made Love known to me; until that hour, she had ever been hidden from me. There I saw and heard how the songs of praise resounded, which come from the silent love humility conceals; humility imagines, and says, and swears that it does not love, and that it gives honor and right to neither God nor human in love or service of veritable virtue. There I saw and heard how the songs of praise resounded and adorned the Love of all loves. In this hour was revealed to me *a new heaven* (Apoc 21:1), which never appeared to me before, and the Allelujah song of the Seraphim [Ser' a phim]. And one Seraph cried with a loud voice and said: "See here the new secret heaven, which is closed to all those who never were God's mother with perfect motherhood, who never wandered with him in Egypt or on all the ways, who never presented him where the sword of prophecy pierced their soul (Luke 2:35), who never reared that Child to manhood and who, at the end, were not at his grave: for them it shall remain eternally hidden!"

SEVENTH WEEK OF EASTER
Monday
Acts 1:12–14

After the resurrection, women and men were gathered together in prayer, awaiting the outpouring of the Spirit of God.

The apostles returned to Jerusalem from the mount called Olivet, which is near Jerusalem, a sabbath day's journey away. When they had entered the city, they went to the room upstairs where they were staying, Peter, and John, and James, and Andrew, Philip and Thomas, Bartholomew and Matthew, James son of Alphaeus, and Simon the Zealot, and Judas son of James. All these were constantly devoting themselves to prayer, together with certain women, including Mary the mother of Jesus, as well as his brothers and sisters.

SEVENTH WEEK OF EASTER
Tuesday
Hadewijch, *School of Love* passim (#1 of 2)

What kind of love is required of those who follow the Risen One? Hadewijch describes both its scope and its depth.

The most joyous season of the year,
When all the birds sing clearly,
And the nightingale publicly
    Makes its joy known to us,
Is the time of greatest sadness
    For the heart noble Love has wounded.

At all times when the arrow strikes,
It increases the wound and brings torment.

All who love know well
    That these must ever be one:
Sweetness or pain, or both together,
    Tempestuous before the countenance of Love.

Here the soul that loves Love cannot defend itself;
    We must sustain her kingdom and her power,
However we fear to go to ruin in love;
    This is unknown to aliens;
So the higher the palace of desire is,
    The deeper yawns the abyss.

But there are few who, for the sake of all love, love all,
And fewer still long for Love with love.
All too late, therefore, shall they attain
    That kingdom and that sublime mystery,
And that knowledge Love imparts
To those who go to school to her.

SEVENTH WEEK OF EASTER
Wednesday
Hadewijch, *School of Love* passim (#2 of 2)

Hadewijch continues her instruction on the mystical delights and pains of Love.

It is a great pity that we thus stray,
And that high wisdom remains hidden from us
Which Love entrusted to the masters
    Who give lessons on true Love;
In the school of Love the highest lesson
    Is how one can content Love.

But they who early leave off,
And then nevertheless jubilate

And feast their Beloved
   For a brief while with salutations—
Provided they live in concord with the virtues—
   Can still master the course of study.

But they who wish to enjoy the Beloved here on earth,
And dance with feelings of delight,
And dwell in this with pleasure,
   I say to them in advance:
They must truly adorn themselves with virtues,
   Or the course of study is a loss to them.

But those who arrange their lives with truth in Love
And are then enlightened by clear reason,
Love will place in her school:
   They shall be masters
And receive Love's highest gifts,
   Which wound beyond cure.

In those whom Love thus blesses with her wounds,
And to whom she shows the vastness knowable in her,
Longing keeps the wounds open and undressed,
   Because Love stormily inflames them;
If these souls shudder at remaining unhealed,
   That fails to surprise us.

Anyone who had thus waded through Love's depths,
Now with deep hunger, now with full satiety,
Neither withering nor blossoming can harm,
   And no season can help:
In the deepest waters, on the highest gradients,
   Love's being remains unalterable.

SEVENTH WEEK OF EASTER
Thursday
Ecclesiastical Canons of the Apostles 24

An interesting glimpse of early arguments for and against the ordination of women.

Andrew said: It would be very good, my brethren, if we established ministries for the women. Peter said: Having given commandment and directions concerning all these things, we have come thus far. Now we will give careful teaching concerning the oblation of the Body and Blood. John said: You have forgotten, my brethren, that our Teacher, when he asked for the bread and the cup, and blessed them, saying: "This is my Body and my Blood," did not permit these (the women) to stand with us. Martha said (concerning Mary): I saw her laughing between her teeth exultingly. Mary said: I did not really laugh, only I remembered the words of our Lord and I exulted; for you know that he told us before, when he was teaching: "The weak shall be saved through the strong." Cephas said: We ought to remember several things, for it does not befit women that they should stand up for prayer, but that they should sit down on the ground. James said: How then with regard to the women can we fix any ministry, except that they strengthen and keep vigil for those women who are in want?

SEVENTH WEEK OF EASTER
Friday
Didascalia Apostolorum 3.12.1–13.1

While the reading assigned yesterday (Seventh Week of Easter, Thursday) debates the issue of ordination, today's reading demonstrates the presence and ministry of deaconesses in the early church.

Wherefore, O bishop, appoint workers of righteousness as helpers who may cooperate with you unto salvation. Those that please you out of all the people you shall choose and appoint as deacons, a man for the performance of most things that are required, but a woman for the ministry of women. For there are houses where you cannot send a deacon to the women, on account of the heathen, but you may send a deaconess. Also, because in many other matters the office of a woman deacon is required. In the first place, when women go down into the water, those who go down into the water ought to be anointed by a deaconess with the oil of anointing; and where there is no woman at hand, and especially no deaconess, he who baptizes must of necessity anoint her who is being baptized. But where there is a woman, and especially a deaconess, it is not fitting that women should be seen by men: but with imposition of the hand you anoint the head only. As of old the priests and kings were anointed in Israel, do you in like manner, with imposition of the hand, anoint the head of those who receive baptism, whether of men or of women; and afterwards—whether you yourself baptize, or command the deacons or presbyters to baptize—let a woman deacon, as we have already said, anoint the women.

But let a man pronounce over them the invocation of the divine Names in the water. And when she who is being baptized has come up from the water, let the deaconess receive her, and teach and instruct her how the seal of baptism ought to be kept unbroken in purity and holiness. For this cause we say that the ministry of a woman deacon is especially needful and important. For our Lord and Savior also was ministered unto by women ministers, Mary Magdalene, and Mary the daughter of James and mother of Joses, and the mother of the sons of Zebedee, with other women besides (Matt 27:56; Mark 15:40; Luke 8:2-3). And you also have need of the ministry of a deaconess for many things; for a deaconess is required to go into the houses of the heathen where there are believing women, and to visit those who are sick, and to minister to them in that of which they have need, and to bathe those who have begun to recover from sickness.

Let the deacons imitate the bishops in their conversation: nay let them even be laboring more than he. Let them not love filthy lucre; but let them be diligent in the ministry. And in proportion to the number of the congregation of the people of the Church, so let deacons be, that they may be able to take knowledge of each severally and refresh all; so that for the aged women who are infirm, and for the brethren and sisters who are in sickness—for every one they may provide the ministry which is proper for each.

But let a woman rather be devoted to the ministry of women, and a male deacon to the ministry of men. And let them be ready to obey and to submit to the command of the bishops. And let them labor and toil in every place where they are sent to minister or to speak of some matter to any one.

VIGIL OF PENTECOST
Prayer for the Ordination of a Deaconess
Apostolic Constitutions 8.19–20

This fourth century Syrian church document gives the ordination and consecration prayers for the many orders of the clergy in the church of its day. Alongside the deacons, deaconesses were ordained for ministry, especially to women. One of the more famous deaconesses of the early church was Olympias (see 21st Week of the Year).

O bishop, lay hands on her, surrounded by the presbyters, deacons, and deaconesses, and say: "Eternal God of our Lord Jesus Christ, creator of man and woman, who filled with the Spirit Miriam, Deborah, Hannah, and Huldah, who did not disdain to have your only son born of a woman, who in the Tabernacle of testimony and in the Temple established women guardians of the gates (Exod 38:8; 1 Sam 2:22), now look upon your servant selected for ministry and give her the Holy Spirit, and cleanse her from all impurity of flesh and spirit so that she may worthily fulfill the work designated to her, to your glory and the praise of your Christ, with whom be glory and worship to you and the Holy Spirit forever. Amen."

PENTECOST
Hadewijch, *The Paradoxes of Love*

Hadewijch's "Paradoxes of Love" are an excellent meditation on the gifts of the Spirit. Hadewijch challenges our way of viewing reality with the creative chaos of God's ways.

What is sweetest in Love is her tempestuousness;
Her deepest abyss is her most beautiful form;
To lose one's way in her is to touch her close at hand;
To die of hunger for her is to feed and taste;
Her despair is assurance;
Her sorest wounding is all curing;
To waste away for her sake is to be in repose;
Her hiding is finding at all hours;
To languish for her sake is to be in good health;
Her concealment reveals what can be known of her;
Her retentions are her gifts;
Wordlessness is her most beautiful utterance;
Imprisonment by her is total release;
Her sorest blow is her sweetest consolation;
Her ruthless robbery is great profit;
Her withdrawal is approach;
Her deepest silence is her sublime song;
Her greatest wrath is her dearest thanks;
Her greatest threat is pure fidelity;
Her sadness is the alleviation of all pain.

We can say yet more about Love:
Her wealth is her lack of everything;
Her truest fidelity brings about our fall;
Her highest being drowns us in the depths;
Her great wealth bestows pauperism;
Her largesse proves to be our bankruptcy;
Her tender care enlarges our wounds;
Association with her brings death over and over;

Her table is hunger; her knowledge is error;
Seduction is the custom of her school;
Encounters with her are cruel storms;
Rest in her is the unreachable;
Her revelation is the total hiding of herself;
Her gifts, besides, are thieveries;
Her promises are all seductions;
Her adornments are all undressing;
Her truth is all deception;
To many her assurance appears to lie—
This is the witness that can be truly borne
At any moment by me and many others
To whom Love has often shown
Wonders by which we were mocked,
Imagining we possessed what she kept back for herself.
After she first played these tricks on me,
And I considered all her methods,
I went to work in a wholly different way:
By her threats and her promises
I was no longer deceived.

    I will belong to her, whatever she may be,
Gracious or merciless; to me it is all one!

TRINITY SUNDAY
Vigil
Job 19:25–27

Any image we have of God, any title we employ, is only a metaphor for the God we can never name or know completely. As Job teaches, only in death will we see God face to face.

For I know that my Redeemer lives,
    and that at the last my Redeemer will stand upon the earth;

and after my skin has been thus destroyed,
  then in my flesh I shall see God,
whom I shall see on my side,
  and my eyes shall behold, and not another.
My heart faints within me!

TRINITY SUNDAY
Solemnity
Julian of Norwich, *Showings* 54

The powerful mystical vision of Julian of Norwich gives us fresh words with which to reflect on the mystery of the triune God.

I saw no difference between God and our substance, but, as it were, all God; and still my understanding accepted that our substance is in God, that is to say that God is God, and our substance is a creature in God. For the almighty truth of the Trinity is our Father, for he made us and keeps us in him. And the deep wisdom of the Trinity is our Mother, in whom we are enclosed. And the high goodness of the Trinity is our Lord, and in him we are enclosed and he in us. We are enclosed in the Father, and we are enclosed in the Son, and we are enclosed in the Holy Spirit. And the Father is enclosed in us, the Son is enclosed in us, and the Holy Spirit is enclosed in us, almighty, all wisdom and all goodness, one God, one Lord.

CORPUS CHRISTI
Vigil
John 12:1–8

On this eve of Corpus Christi, Mary's anointing of Jesus' body suggests that we not be too quick to spiritualize the feast. Care for Jesus' body in our world today is equally sacramental.

Six days before the Passover Jesus came to Bethany, the home of Lazarus, whom he had raised from the dead. There the friends of Jesus gave a dinner for him. Martha served, and Lazarus was one of those at table with Jesus. Mary took a pound of costly perfume made of pure nard, anointed Jesus' feet, and wiped them with her hair. The house was filled with the fragrance of the perfume. But Judas Iscariot [Is car' i ot], one of his disciples (the one who was about to betray him), said, "Why was this perfume not sold for three hundred denarii and the money given to the poor?" (He said this not because he cared about the poor, but because he was a thief; he kept the common purse and used to steal what was put into it.) Jesus said, "Leave her alone. She bought it so that she might keep it for the day of my burial. You always have the poor with you, but you do not always have me."

CORPUS CHRISTI
Solemnity
Julian of Norwich, *Showings* 60

Julian of Norwich provides a novel approach to this feast by reflecting on the maternal image of Jesus our mother, our nourishment, our life.

The mother can give her child to suck of her milk, but our precious Mother Jesus can feed us with himself, and does, most courteously and most tenderly, with the blessed sacrament, which is the precious food of true life; and with all the sweet sacraments he sustains us most mercifully and graciously, and so he meant in these blessed words, where he said: I am the one whom Holy Church preaches and teaches to you. That is to say: All the health and the life of the sacraments, all the power and the grace of my word, all the goodness which is ordained in Holy Church for you, I am the one.

The mother can lay her child tenderly to her breast, but our tender Mother Jesus can lead us easily into his blessed breast through his sweet open side, and show us there a part of the godhead and of the joys of heaven, with inner certainty of endless bliss.

SACRED HEART
Vigil
Hadewijch, *The Madness of Love*

Hadewijch describes the madness of love which is revealed in the pierced Heart of Christ.

The madness of love
Is a rich fief;
Anyone who recognized this
Would not ask Love for anything else:
I can unite opposites
And reverse the paradox.
I am declaring the truth about this:
The madness of love makes bitter what was sweet,
It makes the stranger a kinsman,
And it makes the smallest the proudest.

The madness of love makes the strong weak
And the sick healthy.
It makes the sturdy one a cripple
And heals those who were wounded.
It instructs the ignorant person
About *the broad way*
Whereon many (Matt 7:13) inevitably lose themselves;
It teaches them everything
That can be learned
In high Love's school.

In high Love's school
Is learned the madness of Love;
For it causes delirium
In a person formerly of good understanding.
To one who at first had misfortune,
It now gives success;
It makes that one lord of all the property

Of which Love herself is Lady.
I am convinced of this,
And I will not change my mind.

To souls who have not reached such love,
I give this good counsel:
If they cannot do more,
Let them beg Love for amnesty,
And serve with faith,
According to the counsel of noble Love,
And think: "It can happen,
Love's power is so great!"
Only after death
Is one beyond cure.

High-minded are they
Who become so fully ruled by Love
That they can read
In Love's power her judgments on them.

SACRED HEART
Solemnity
Odes of Solomon 8

Christ, in this Ode, invites Christians to partake of the milk of his breasts. This image of Christ as Mother finds a central place in medieval Christian mysticism.

Open, open your hearts to the exultation of the Lord,
and let your love abound from the heart to the lips,

In order to bring forth fruits to the Lord, a holy life;
and to speak with watchfulness in God's light.

Stand and be established,
you who once were brought low.

You who were in silence, speak,
for your mouth has been opened.

You who were despised, from henceforth be raised,
for your Righteousness has been raised;

For the right hand of the Lord is with you,
and God will be your Helper.

And peace was prepared for you,
before what may be your war.

Christ Speaks

Hear the word of truth,
and receive the knowledge of the Most High.

Your flesh may not understand that which I am about to say to you;
nor your garment that which I am about to declare to you.

Keep my mystery, you who are kept by it;
keep my faith, you who are kept by it.

And understand my knowledge, you who know me in truth;
love me with affection, you who love;

for I turn not my face from my own,
because I know them.

And before they had existed,
I recognized them;
and imprinted a seal on their faces.

I fashioned their members,
and my own breasts I prepared for them,
that they might drink my holy milk and live by it.

I am pleased by them,
and am not ashamed by them.

For my work are they,
and the power of my thoughts.

Therefore who can stand against my work?
Or who is not subject to them?

I willed and fashioned mind and heart;
and they are my own.
And upon my right hand I have set my elect ones.

And my righteousness goes before them;
and they will not be deprived of my name;
for it is with them.

Hallelujah.

SOLEMNITY OF CHRIST THE KING
(Thirty-Fourth Sunday of the Year)
Martyrdom of Potamiaena and Basilides

This story of two third century Alexandrian martyrs tells how the power of a woman's heroic example and her appearance in a dream converted one of her guards.

Seventh among the disciples of Origen [O' ri gen] should be numbered Basilides [Ba si li' des], who had led the famous Potamiaena [Po ta mi ae' na] to execution. Even today she is much in honour among her own people. Boundless were her sufferings, until at last after tortures terrible and horrifying to describe she was consumed by fire with her mother Marcella [Mar cel' la].

The story goes that her judge, a man named Aquila [A' qui la], subjected her entire body to cruel torments, and then threatened to hand her over to his gladiators to assault her physically. For a moment the girl reflected, and then when asked what her decision was, she gave some answer which impressed them as being contrary to their religion.

No sooner had she uttered the word and received the sentence of condemnation, when a man named Basilides, who was one of those in the armed services, seized the condemned girl and led her off to execution. The crowd then tried to annoy her and to insult her with vulgar remarks; but Basilides, showing her the utmost pity and kindness, prevented them and drove them off. The girl welcomed the sympathy shown her and urged the man to be of good heart: when she went to her Lord she would pray for him, and it would not be long before she would pay him back for all he had done for her.

After she had said this she nobly endured the end: boiling pitch was slowly poured drop by drop over different parts of her body, from her toes to the top of her head. Such was the struggle that this magnificent young woman endured.

Not long afterwards Basilides for one reason or another was asked by his fellow soldiers to take an oath; but he insisted that he was not at all allowed to do so, since he was a Christian and made no secret of it. For a while they thought at first that he was joking; but then when he persistently assured them it was so, he was brought before the magistrate, and when he admitted the situation he was put into prison. His brothers and sisters in the Lord came to visit him, and when they questioned him about this strange and sudden turn, he is said to have replied that three days after her martyrdom Potamiaena appeared to him at night and put a crown on his head; she said she had requested grace for him from the Lord and had obtained her prayer, and that she would welcome him before long.

At this, his brothers and sisters shared with him the Seal of the Lord (baptism), and on the next day he was beheaded, eminent in his witness for the Lord. Indeed, in accordance with what has been said, many others in Alexandria are reported to have gone over to the word of Christ in a body, after Potamiaena had appeared to them in sleep and called their names. But this must now suffice.

NOVEMBER 1—SOLEMNITY OF ALL SAINTS
Hadewijch, *Love Alone*, Poem 45

Hadewijch voices the longing and the fidelity that makes saints of sinners and makes our common search for God a holy one.

No matter what the time of year,
Nothing exists anywhere in the world
That can give me delight
    Except: *verus amor!* (true love)
O Love! In fidelity (since you are all
My soul's joy, my heart's goal),
Pity distress; look upon struggle;
    Hear: *cordis clamor!* (call of the heart)

However I cry out and complain of my woe,
May Love do with me according to her pleasure;
I wish to give her, throughout my life,
    Laus et honor (praise and honor)
Alas, Love, if the eyes of fidelity but saw you!
For by mentioning fidelity I become valiant;
For when I first glimpsed your high summits,
    Your: *traxit odor.* (fragrance drew)

O Love! Indeed you have never deceived
For you showed me in my youth
What I request (for it is in your power)—
    Be *medicina!* (medicine)
O Love! since all things are in your disposition,
Give me for Love's sake what most delights me;
For you are the mother of all virtues,
    Lady and *regina.* (queen)

O dearest Love, true and pure,
Why do you not see how I suffer,
And be in my smarting bitterness
    condimentum. (condiment/relish)

Amid hardships I go in quest of adventure.
All other things, apart from you, are bitter to me;
Give me fully, Love, your sublime nature,
  Sacramentum. (sacrament)

Whether I am in plenty or in want,
Let all, Love, be according to your counsel;
Your blows show me the grace I owe
  Redemptori. (to the Redeemer)
Whether I wade the deep or climb the summits,
Or find myself in hunger or in satiety,
All I wish, Love, is fully to content you,
  Unde mori. Amen, Amen. (therefore I die)

NOVEMBER 2—FEAST OF ALL SOULS
Dhuoda's Epitaph

The epitaph of Dhuoda, a learned lay woman of the Carolingian period, relies upon our ancient tradition of calling on the many names of God in prayer. The epitaph challenges us to broaden our images of God, in union with the souls of Christians of ages before us.

Dhuoda's body, formed of earth,
Lies buried in this tomb.
  Immense King, receive her!
Here the earth has received in its bowels
The all too fragile clay which belonged to it.
  Benign King, grant her pardon!
Under and over her are the opaque depths
Of the grave, bathed in her wounds.
  O King, forgive her sins!
O you of all ages and sexes who come
And go here, I beg you, say this:
  Great Hagios, unlock her chains!

Detained by dire death in the depths
Of the tomb, she has ended her earthly life.
   O King, pardon her sins!
As that dark serpent wishes to capture
Her soul, pray against him this prayer:
   Clement God, come to her aid!
No one should leave her without having read.
I urge all that they may pray, saying this:
   Almus, give her rest!
And command, Benign One, that she be given
Eternal light with the saints in the end.
   And may she receive Amen* after her death!

* See Revelation 3:14

FIRST SUNDAY OF THE YEAR
(See Baptism of the Lord, p. 66)

FIRST WEEK OF THE YEAR
Monday
Testaments of the Twelve Patriarchs 1:5–12

The patriarch Naphtali describes his birth from Jacob's wife, Bilhah, and enumerates the women who played a part in his ancestry. Though the scriptures are filled with genealogies tracing the patrilineal ancestry, this text highlights the women. (See Matthew's genealogy of Jesus which mentions five women.)

Naphtali [Naph' ta li] began to say to his sons, "Listen, my children, sons of Naphtali, hear your father's words. I was born from Bilhah; Rachel acted by trickery, giving Bilhah to Jacob in place of herself, and she bore me on the knees of Rachel, for which reason she called me Naphtali. Rachel loved me because I was born in her lap; while I was tender in appearance she would kiss me and say, 'May I see a brother of yours, like you, from my own womb!' Thus Joseph was like me in every way, in keeping with Rachel's prayer. But my mother was Bilhah, daughter of Rotheos, Deborah's brother, nurse of Rebecca; she was born the very day on which Rachel was born. Rotheos was of Abraham's tribe, a Chaldean, one who honored God, free and well-born, but he was taken captive and bought by Laban who gave him Aina, his servant girl, as a wife. She bore a daughter and called her Zelpha from the name of the village in which he had been taken captive. After that she bore Bilhah, saying, 'My daughter is ever eager for new things: No sooner had she been born than she hurried to start sucking.' "

FIRST WEEK OF THE YEAR
Tuesday
Judges 4:4–16 (#1 of 3)

Deborah, the rabbis say, cared for the lamps of the tabernacle. How significant since she was a prophet and became a light to her people! The Israelites chose her as judge and eventually followed her into battle.

At that time Deborah, a prophet, wife of Lappidoth [Lap′ pi doth], was judging Israel. She used to sit under the palm of Deborah between Ramah and Bethel in the hill country of Ephraim [E′ phra im] and the Israelites came up to her for judgment. She sent and summoned Barak son of Abinoam [A bin′ o am] from Kedesh in Naphtali [Naph′ ta li], and said to him, "The Lord, the God of Israel, commands you, 'Go, take position at Mount Tabor, bringing ten thousand from the tribe of Naphtali and the tribe of Zebulun [Zeb′ u lun]. I will draw out Sisera [Sis′ er a], the general of Jabin's army, to meet you by the Wadi Kishon with his chariots and his troops; and I will give him into your hand.' " Barak said to her, "If you will go with me, I will go; but if you will not go with me, I will not go." And she said, "I will surely go with you; nevertheless, the road on which you are going will not lead to your glory, for the Lord will sell Sisera into the hand of a woman." Then Deborah got up and went with Barak to Kedesh. Barak summoned Zebulun and Naphtali to Kedesh; and ten thousand warriors went up behind him; and Deborah went up with him.

Now Heber the Kenite had separated from the other Kenites, that is, the descendants of Hobab the father-in-law of Moses, and had encamped as far away as Elon-bezaanannim [E'lon-be za a nan'nim], which is near Kedesh.

When Sisera was told that Barak son of Abinoam had gone up to Mount Tabor, Sisera called out all his chariots, nine hundred chariots of iron, and all the troops who were with him, from Harosheth-ha-goiim [Ha ro' sheth-ha-goi im] to the Wadi Kishon. Then Deborah said to Barak, "Up! For this is the day on which the Lord has given Sisera into your hand. The Lord is indeed going out before you." So Barak went down from Mount Tabor with ten thousand warriors following him. And the Lord threw Sisera and all his chariots and all his army into a panic before Barak; Sisera got down from his chariot and fled away on foot while Barak pursued the chariots and the army to Harosheth-ha-goiim. All the army of Sisera fell by the sword; no one was left.

FIRST WEEK OF THE YEAR
Wednesday
Judges 4:17–22 (#2 of 3)

Jael, another woman in the time of Deborah, is remembered for her bravery in killing the enemy, Sisera. Nevertheless, the violence of the act we choose not to emulate.

Sisera had fled away on foot to the tent of Jael wife of Heber the Kenite; for there was peace between King Jabin of Hazor and the clan of Heber the Kenite. Jael came out to meet Sisera, and said to him, "Turn aside, my lord, turn aside to me; have no fear." So he turned aside to her into the tent, and she covered him with a rug. Then he said to her,

"Please give me a little water to drink; for I am thirsty." So she opened a skin of milk and gave him a drink and covered him. He said to her, "Stand at the entrance of the tent, and if anybody comes and asks you, 'Is anyone here?' say, 'No.'" But Jael wife of Heber took a tent peg, and took a hammer in her hand, and went softly to him and drove the peg into his temple, until it went down into the ground—he was lying fast asleep from weariness—and he died. Then, as Barak came in pursuit of Sisera, Jael went out to meet him, and said to him, "Come, and I will show you the man whom you are seeking." So he went into her tent; and there was Sisera lying dead, with the tent peg in his temple.

FIRST WEEK OF THE YEAR
Thursday
Judges 5:1, 6–9, 12–15b, 24–31 (#3 of 3)

This victory song of Deborah is the oldest text in the Hebrew Bible. Its bloodthirsty tone testifies to the level of violence common in ancient Israel, a society in which the struggle to survive often necessitated violence against one's enemies.

Deborah and Barak son of Abinoam sang on that day, saying:

"In the days of Shamgar son of Anath,
  in the days of Jael, caravans ceased
  and travelers kept to the byways.
The peasantry prospered in Israel,
  they grew fat on plunder,
because you arose, Deborah,
  arose as a mother in Israel.
When new gods were chosen,
  then war was in the gates.
Was shield or spear to be seen
  among forty thousand in Israel?
My heart goes out to the commanders of Israel
  who offered themselves willingly among the people.
Bless the Lord.

"Awake, awake, Deborah!
 Awake, awake, utter a song!
Arise, Barak, lead away your captives,
 O son of Abinoam.
Then down marched the remnant of the noble;
 the people of the Lord marched down for God against the
   mighty.
From Ephraim they set out into the valley,
 following you, Benjamin, with your kin;
from Machir marched down the commanders,
 and from Zebulun those who bear the marshal's staff;
the chiefs of Issachar came with Deborah,
 and Issachar faithful to Barak;
  into the valley they rushed out at his heels.

"Most blessed of women be Jael,
 the wife of Heber the Kenite,
 of tent-dwelling women most blessed.
He asked water and she gave him milk,
 she brought him curds in a lordly bowl.
She put her hand to the tent peg
 and her right hand to the workmen's mallet;
she struck Sisera a blow,
 she crushed his head,
 she shattered and pierced his temple.
He sank, he fell,
 he lay still at her feet;
at her feet he sank, he fell;
 where he sank, there he fell dead.

"Out of the window she peered,
 the mother of Sisera gazed through the lattice;
'Why is his chariot so long in coming?
 Why tarry the hoofbeats of his chariots?'
Her wisest ladies make answer,
 indeed, she answers the question herself:
'Are they not finding and dividing the spoil?—
 A girl or two for every man;

spoil of dyed stuffs for Sisera,
  spoil of dyed stuffs embroidered,
  two pieces of dyed work embroidered for my neck as spoil?'

"So perish all your enemies, O Lord!
  But may your friends be like the sun as it rises in its might."

FIRST WEEK OF THE YEAR
Friday
Pseudo-Philo, *Biblical Antiquities*
32:11–18 (#1 of 2)

This story praises the judge and prophetess Deborah. It recalls the tradition recounted in Judges 4 and 5 in which the combined efforts of two women, Deborah and Jael, win victory for the Israelite tribes.

In these days Sisera [Sis′ er a] arose to enslave us. We cried out to our Lord, and God commanded the stars and said, "Depart from your positions and burn up my enemies so that they may know my power." The stars came down and attacked their camp and guarded us without any strain. So we will not cease singing praise, nor will our mouth be silent in telling God's wonders, because God has remembered both recent and ancient promises and shown saving power to us. So Jael is glorified among women (Judg 5:24), because she alone has made straight the way to success by killing Sisera with her own hands. But you, Deborah, sing praises, and let the grace of the holy spirit awaken in you, and begin to praise the works of the Lord, because there will not again arise such a day on which the stars will band together and attack the enemies of Israel as was commanded them. From this hour, if Israel falls into distress, it will call upon those witnesses along with these servants, and they will form a delegation to the Most High, and God will remember that day and send the saving power of the covenant. You, Deborah, begin to tell what you saw in the field, how the people were walking about and going forth in safety and the stars fought for them. Rejoice, earth, over those dwelling in you, because the knowledge of the Lord that builds a tower among you is present. Then I will cease my hymn, for the time is readied for God's just judgments. For I will sing a hymn to God in the renewal of creation. When Deborah made an end to her words, she along with the people went up to Shiloh, and they offered sacrifices and holocausts, and they sang to the accompaniment of the trumpets. When they were singing and the sacrifices had been offered, Deborah said, "This will be as a testimony of trumpets between the stars and their Lord." Deborah came down from there and judged Israel forty years (Judg 5:31).

FIRST WEEK OF THE YEAR
Saturday
Pseudo-Philo, *Biblical Antiquities* 33:1–6 (#2 of 2)

The death of Deborah is recounted. She is remembered with reverence as "the holy one who exercised leadership in the house of Jacob."

When the days of her death drew near, Deborah sent and gathered all the people and said to them, "Listen now, my people. Behold I am warning you as a woman of God and am enlightening you as one from the female race; and obey me like your mother and heed my words as people who will also die. Behold I am going today on the way of all flesh, on which you also will come. Only direct your heart to the Lord your God during the time of your life, because after your death you cannot repent of those things in which you live. For then death is sealed up and brought to an end, and the measure and the time and the years have returned their deposit. For even if you seek to do evil in hell after your death, you cannot, because the desire for sinning will cease and the evil impulse will lose its power, because even hell will not restore what has been received and deposited to it unless it be demanded by the one who has made the deposit to it. Now therefore, my sons and daughters, obey my voice; while you have the time of life and the light of the Law, make straight your ways." And while Deborah was saying these words, all the people raised up their voice together and wept and said, "Behold now,

Mother, you will die, and to whom do you commend your sons and daughters whom you are leaving? Pray therefore for us, and after your departure your soul will be mindful of us forever." And Deborah answered and said to the people, "While people are still alive they can pray for themselves and for their sons and daughters but after their end they cannot pray or be mindful of anyone. Therefore do not hope in your ancestors. For they will not profit you at all unless you be found like them. But then you will be like the stars of the heaven, which now have been revealed among you." And Deborah died and slept with her ancestors and was buried in the city of her ancestors. And the people mourned for her seventy days, and while they were mourning for her, they said these words as a lamentation:

"Behold there has perished a mother from Israel,
and the holy one who exercised leadership in the house of Jacob.
She firmed up the fence about her generation,
and her generation will grieve over her."

And after her death the land had rest for seven years.

SECOND SUNDAY OF THE YEAR
Acts of Paul 9

Myrta, in this text, is both woman prophet and presider.

The Spirit came upon Myrta, so that she said: "Brothers and sisters why are you alarmed at the sight of this sign? Paul, the servant of the Lord, will save many in Rome, and will nourish many with the word, so that there is no number to count them, and he will become manifest above all the faithful, and greatly will the glory come upon him, so that there will be great grace in Rome." And immediately, when the Spirit that was in Myrta was at peace, each one took of the bread and feasted according to custom amid the singing of psalms of David and of hymns. And Paul too enjoyed himself.

SECOND WEEK OF THE YEAR
Monday
Jerome, *Life of Paula* 1-2 (#1 of 12)

Paula, Roman aristocrat and Jerome's faithful companion in the monastic life at Bethlehem, has died. The grief for an old friend is evident in his language.

If all the members of my body were to be converted into tongues, and if each of my limbs were to be gifted with a human voice, I could still do no justice to the virtues of the holy and venerable Paula. Noble in family, she was nobler still in holiness; rich formerly in this world's goods, she is now more distinguished by the poverty that she has embraced for Christ. Of the stock of the Gracchi [Grac' chi] and descended from the Scipios [Sci' pi os], the heir and representative of that Paulus whose name she bore, the true and legitimate daughter of that Marita Papyria [Pa py' ri a] who was mother to Africanus [Af ri ca'nus], she yet preferred Bethlehem to Rome, and left her palace glittering with gold to dwell in a mud cabin. We do not grieve that we have lost this perfect woman; rather we thank God that we have had her, nay that we have her still. For all live unto God, and they who return unto the Lord are still to be reckoned members of his family. We have lost her, it is true, but the heavenly mansions have gained her; for as long as she was in the body she was absent from the Lord and would constantly complain with tears: "Woe is me that I sojourn in Mesech [Me' sech], that I dwell in the tents of Kedar [Ke' dar]; my soul hath been this long time a pilgrim." It was no wonder that she sobbed out that even she was in darkness (for this is the meaning of the word Kedar) seeing that, according to the apostle, "the world lieth in the power of the evil one"; and that, "as its darkness is, so is its light"; and that "the light shineth in darkness and the darkness comprehended it not." And when the pain which she bore with such wonderful patience darted through her, as if she saw the heavens opened she would say: "Oh that I had wings like a dove! for then would I fly away and be at rest."

I call Jesus and his saints, yes and the particular angel who was the guardian and the companion of this admirable woman to bear witness that these are no words of adulation and flattery but sworn testimony every one of them borne to her character. They are, indeed, inadequate to the virtues of one whose praises are sung by the whole world, who is admired by bishops, regretted by bands of virgins, and wept for by crowds of monks and poor. Would you know all her virtues, reader, in short? She has left those dependent on her poor, but not so poor as she was herself. In dealing thus with her relatives and the men and women of her small household—her brothers and sisters rather than her servants—she has done nothing strange: for she has left her daughter Eustochium [Eu sto' chi um]—a virgin consecrated to Christ for whose comfort this sketch is made—far from her noble family and rich only in faith and grace.

SECOND WEEK OF THE YEAR
Tuesday
Jerome, *Life of Paula* 3 (#2 of 12)

Jerome describes Paula's background. She belonged to one of the oldest aristocratic families of Rome, yet was more outstanding for her holiness.

Let me then begin my narrative. Others may go back a long way even to Paula's cradle and, if I may say so, to her swaddling-clothes, and may speak of her mother Blaesilla [Blae sil'la] and her father Rogatus [Ro ga' tus]. Of these the former was a descendant of the Scipios and the Gracchi; whilst the latter came of a line distinguished in Greece down to the present day. He was said, indeed, to have in his veins the blood of Agamemnon [A ga mem' non] who destroyed Troy after ten years' siege. But I shall praise only what belongs to herself, what wells forth from the pure spring of her holy mind. When in the gospel the apostles ask their Lord and Saviour what he will give to those who have left all for his sake, he tells them that they shall receive an hundredfold now in this time and in the world to come eternal life. From which we see that it is not the possession of riches that is praiseworthy but the rejection of them for Christ's sake; that, instead of glorying in our privileges, we should make them of small account as compared with God's faith. Truly the Saviour has now in this present time made good his promise to his servants and handmaidens. For one who despised the glory of a single city is to-day famous throughout the world; and one who while she lived at Rome was known by no one outside it has by hiding herself at Bethlehem become the admiration of all lands, Roman and barbarian. For what race is there which does not send pilgrims to the holy places? And who could there find a greater marvel than Paula? As among many jewels the most precious shines most brightly, and as the sun with its beams obscures and puts out the paler stars; so by her lowliness she surpassed all others in virtue and influence and, while she was least among all, was greater than all. The more she cast herself down, the more she was lifted up by Christ. She was hidden and yet she was not hidden. By shunning glory she earned glory; for glory follows virtue as its shadow; and deserting those who seek it, it seeks those who despise it.

SECOND WEEK OF THE YEAR
Wednesday
Jerome, *Life of Paula* 3 (#3 of 12)

Jerome describes Paula's marriage and widowhood, as well as her early practice of charity.

Being then of such parentage, Paula married Toxotius [Tox o' ti us] in whose veins ran the noble blood of Aeneas [Ae ne' as] and the Julii [Ju' li i]. Accordingly his daughter, Christ's virgin Eustochium [Eu sto' chi um], is called Julia, as he Julius. "A name from great Iulus [Iu' lus] handed down." I speak of these things not as of importance to those who have them, but as worthy of remark in those who despise them. People of the world look up to persons who are rich in such privileges. We on the other hand praise those who for the Saviour's sake despise them; and strangely depreciating all who keep them, we eulogize those who are unwilling to do so. Thus nobly born, Paula through her fruitfulness and her chastity won approval from all, from her husband first, then from her relatives, and lastly from the whole city. She bore five children; Blaesilla [Blae sil' la], for whose death I consoled her while at Rome; Paulina [Pau li' na], who has left the reverend and admirable Pammachius [Pam ma' chi us] to inherit both her vows and property, to whom also I addressed a little book on her death; Eustochium, who is now in the holy places, a precious necklace of virginity and of the church; Rufina [Ru fi' na], whose untimely end overcame the affectionate heart of her mother; and Toxotius [Tox o' ti us], after whom she had no more children. You can thus see that it was not her wish to fulfill a wife's duty, but that she only complied with her husband's longing to have male offspring.

When he died, her grief was so great that she nearly died herself: yet so completely did she then give herself to the service of the Lord, that it might have seemed that she had desired his death.

In what terms shall I speak of her distinguished, and noble, and formerly wealthy house; all the riches of which she spent upon the poor? How can I describe the great consideration she showed to all and her far reaching kindness even to those whom she had never seen? What poor man as he lay dying, was not wrapped in blankets given by her? What bedridden person was not supported with money from her purse? She would seek out such with the greatest diligence throughout the city, and would think it a misfortune were any hungry or sick person to be supported by another's food. So lavish was her charity that she robbed her children; and when her relatives remonstrated with her for doing so, she declared that she was leaving to them a better inheritance in the mercy of Christ.

SECOND WEEK OF THE YEAR
Thursday
Jerome, *Life of Paula* 15–16 (#4 of 12)

Paula, who was one of the wealthiest women of her day, was remarkable for her simplicity and humility.

I am now free to describe at greater length the virtue which was her peculiar charm; and in setting this forth I call God to witness that I am no flatterer. I add nothing. I exaggerate nothing. On the contrary, I tone down much that I may not appear to relate incredibilities. My carping critics must not insinuate that I am drawing on my imagination or decking Paula, like Aesop's [Ae' sop's] crow, with the fine feathers of other birds. Humility is the first of Christian graces, and hers was so pronounced that one who had never seen her, and who on account of her celebrity had desired to see her, would have believed that he or she saw not her but the lowest of her maids. When she was surrounded by companies of virgins she was always the least remarkable in dress, in speech, in gesture, and in gait. No mind could be more considerate than hers, or none kinder towards the lowly. She did not court the powerful; at the same time, if the proud and the vainglorious sought her, she did not turn from them with disdain. If she saw a poor man, she supported him: and if she saw a rich one, she urged him to do good. Her liberality alone knew no bounds. Indeed so anxious was she to turn no needy person away that she borrowed money at interest and often contracted new loans to pay off old ones. I was wrong, I admit; but when I saw her so profuse in giving, I reproved her alleging the apostle's words: "I do not mean that there should be relief for others and pressure on you, but a fair balance between your present abundance and their need, so that their abundance may be for your need" (2 Cor 8:13–14). I quoted from the gospel the Saviour's words: "Whosoever has two coats, must share with anyone who has none" (Luke 3:11); and I warned her that she might not always have means to do as she would wish. Other arguments I adduced to the same purpose; but with admirable modesty and brevity she overruled them all. "God is my witness," she said, "that what I do I do for his sake. My prayer is that I may die a beggar not leaving a penny to my daughter and indebted to strangers for my winding sheet." She then concluded with these words: "I, if I beg, shall find many to give to me; but if this beggar does not obtain help from me who by borrowing can give it to him, he will die; and if he dies, of whom will his soul be required?" I wished her to be more careful in managing her concerns, but she with a faith more glowing than mine clave to the Saviour with her whole heart and, poor in spirit, followed the Lord in his poverty, giving back to him what she had received and becoming poor for his sake. She obtained her wish at last and died leaving her daughter overwhelmed with a mass of debt. This Eustochium [Eu sto' chi um] still owes and indeed cannot hope to pay off by her own exertions; only the mercy of Christ can free her from it.

Many married ladies make it a habit to confer gifts upon their own trumpeters, and while they are extremely profuse to a few, withhold all help from the many. From this fault Paula was altogether free. She gave her money to each according as each had need, not ministering to self-indulgence but relieving want. No poor person went away from her empty handed. And all this she was enabled to do not by the greatness of her wealth but by her careful management of it.

SECOND WEEK OF THE YEAR
Friday
Jerome, *Life of Paula* 20 (#5 of 12)

Life in Paula's monastery at Bethlehem was simple and austere but Paula knew how to be an effective spiritual leader.

I shall now describe the order of her monastery and the method by which she turned the continence of saintly souls to her own profit. She gave earthly things that she might receive heavenly things; she forwent things temporal that she might in their stead obtain things eternal. Besides establishing a monastery for men, the charge of which she left to men, she divided into three companies and monasteries the numerous virgins whom she had gathered out of different provinces, some of whom are of noble birth while others belonged to the middle or lower classes. But, although they worked and had their meals separately from each other, these three companies met together for psalm-singing and prayer. After the chanting of the Alleluia—the signal by which they were summoned to the Collect—no one was permitted to remain behind. But either first or among the first Paula used to await the arrival of the rest, urging them to diligence rather by her own modest example than by motives of fear. At dawn, at the third, sixth, and ninth hours, at evening, and at midnight they recited the psalter each in turn. No sister was allowed to be ignorant of the psalms, and all had every day to learn a certain portion of the holy scriptures. On the Lord's day only they proceeded to the church beside which they lived, each company following its own mother-superior. Returning home in the same order, they then devoted themselves to their allotted tasks, and made garments either for themselves or else for others. All the sisters were clothed alike. Linen was not used except for drying the hands. So strictly did Paula separate them from men that she would not allow even eunuchs to approach them; lest she should give occasion to slanderous tongues (always ready to cavil at the religious) to console themselves for their own misdoing. When a sister was backward in coming to the recitation of the psalms or showed herself remiss in her work, Paula used to approach her in different ways. Was she quick-tempered? Paula coaxed her. Was she phlegmatic? Paula chided her, copying the example of the apostle who said: "What do you prefer? Am I to come to you with a stick or with love in a spirit of gentleness?" (1 Cor 4:21). Apart from food and raiment she allowed no one to have anything she could call her own, for Paul had said, "If we have food and clothing, let us be content with these" (1 Tim 6:8). She was afraid lest the custom of having more should breed covetousness in them, an appetite which no wealth can satisfy, for the more it has the more it requires, and neither opulence nor indigence is able to diminish it. When the sisters quarreled one with another she reconciled them with soothing words.

SECOND WEEK OF THE YEAR
Saturday
Jerome, *Life of Paula* 20–21 (#6 of 12)

As with so many of us, Paula's charity toward others was not matched by gentleness with herself.

When she saw a sister verbose and talkative or forward and taking pleasure in quarrels, and when she found after frequent admonitions that the offender showed no signs of improvement, she placed her among the lowest of the sisters and outside their society, ordering her to pray at the door of the refectory instead of with the rest, and commanding her to take her food by herself, in the hope that where rebuke had failed, shame might bring about a reformation. The sin of theft she loathed as if it were sacrilege; and that which among those of the world is counted little or nothing, she declared to be in a monastery a crime of the deepest dye. How shall I describe her kindness and attention towards the sick or the wonderful care and devotion with which she nursed them? When others were sick, she freely gave them every indulgence, and even allowed them to eat meat. When she fell ill herself, she made no concessions to her own weakness, and seemed unfairly to change in her own case to harshness, the kindness which she was always ready to show others.

No young girl of sound and vigorous constitution could have delivered herself up to a regimen so rigid as that imposed upon herself by Paula, whose physical powers age had impaired and enfeebled. I admit that in this she was too determined, refusing to spare herself or to listen to advice. I will relate what I know to be a fact. In the extreme heat of the month of July she was once attacked by a violent fever and we despaired of her life. However, by God's mercy she rallied, and the doctors urged upon her the necessity of taking a little light wine to accelerate her recovery, saying that if she continued to drink water they feared that she might become dropsical. I, on my side, secretly appealed to the blessed pope Epiphanius [Ep i pha' ni us] to admonish, nay even to compel her, to take the wine. But she, with her usual sagacity and quickness, at once perceived the stratagem, and with a smile let him see that the advice he was giving her was after all not his but mine. Not to waste more words, the blessed prelate after many exhortations left her chamber; and, when I asked him what he had accomplished, replied, "Only this: that old as I am, I have been almost persuaded to drink no more wine." I relate this story not because I approve of persons rashly taking upon themselves burdens beyond their strength (for does not the scripture say: "Burden not thyself above thy power"?) but because I wish from this quality of perseverance in her to show the passion of her mind and the yearning of her believing soul; both of which made her sing in David's words, "My soul thirsts for you, my flesh longs for you" (Ps 63:1).

THIRD SUNDAY OF THE YEAR
John 2:1–11

Jesus' first sign is prompted by Mary's sensitivity.

On the third day there was a wedding in Cana of Galilee, and the mother of Jesus was there. Jesus and his disciples had also been invited to the wedding. When the wine gave out, the mother of Jesus said to him, "They have no wine." And Jesus said to her, "Woman, what concern is that to you and to me? My hour has not yet come." His mother said to the servants, "Do whatever he tells you." Now standing there were six stone water jars for the Jewish rites of purification, each holding twenty or thirty gallons. Jesus said to them, "Fill the jars with water." And they filled them up to the brim. He said to them, "Now draw some out, and take it to the chief steward." So they took it. When the steward tasted the water that had become wine, and did not know where it came from (though the servants who had drawn the water knew), the steward called the bride-groom and said to him, "Everyone serves the good wine first, and then the inferior wine after the guests have become drunk. But you have kept the good wine until now." Jesus did this, the first of his signs, in Cana of Galilee, and revealed his glory; and his disciples believed in him.

THIRD WEEK OF THE YEAR
Monday
Jerome, *Life of Paula* 21–22 (#7 of 12)

Paula knew the sorrow of seeing her husband and children die. Despite her deep faith, she suffered very human grief and loss at their deaths.

While unyielding in her contempt for food, Paula was easily moved to sorrow and felt crushed by the deaths of her kinsfolk, especially those of her children. When one after another her husband and her daughters fell asleep, on each occasion the shock of their loss endangered her life. And although she signed her mouth and her breast with the sign of the cross, and endeavoured thus to alleviate a mother's grief, her feelings over-powered her and her maternal instincts were too much for her confiding mind. Thus while her intellect retained its mastery she was overcome by sheer physical weakness. On one occasion a sickness seized her and clung to her so long that it brought anxiety to us and danger to herself. Yet even then she was full of joy and repeated every moment the apostle's words: "O wretched one that I am! who shall deliver me from the body of this death?" (Rom 7:24) The careful reader may say that my words are an invective rather than an eulogy. I call that Jesus whom she served and whom I desire to serve to be my witness that so far from unduly eulogizing her or depreciating her, I tell the truth about her as one Christian writing of another; that I am writing a memoir and not a panegyric, and that what were faults in her might well be virtues in others less saintly. I speak thus of her faults to satisfy my own feelings and the passionate regret of us her brothers and sisters, who all of us love her still and all of us deplore her loss. However, she has finished her course, she has kept the faith, and now she enjoys the crown of righteousness. She follows the Lamb whithersoever he goes. She is filled now because once she was hungry.

THIRD WEEK OF THE YEAR
Tuesday
Jerome, *Life of Paula* 27 (#8 of 12)

Paula had a keen mind, was an avid biblical scholar, and even learned Hebrew more easily than Jerome. Though living in Jerusalem she remained deeply attached to her family in Rome.

No mind was ever more docile than was hers. She was slow to speak and swift to hear, remembering the precept, "Keep silence and hearken, O Israel" (Deut 6:4). The holy scriptures she knew by heart, and said of the history contained in them that it was the foundation of the truth; but though she loved even this, she still preferred to seek for the underlying spiritual meaning and made this the keystone of the spiritual building raised within her soul. She asked leave that she and her daughter might read over the old and new testaments under my guidance. Out of modesty I at first refused compliance, but as she persisted in her demand and frequently urged me to consent to it, I at last did so and taught her what I had learned not from myself—for self-confidence is the worst of teachers —but from the church's most famous writers. Wherever I stuck fast and honestly confessed myself at fault, she would by no means rest content but would force me by fresh questions to point out to her which of many different solutions seemed to me the most probable. I will mention here another fact which to those who are envious may well seem incredible. While I myself beginning as a young man have with much toil and effort partially acquired the Hebrew tongue and study it now unceasingly lest if I leave it, it also may leave me; Paula, on making up her mind that she too would learn it, succeeded so well that she could chant the psalms in Hebrew and could speak the language without a trace of the pronunciation peculiar to Latin. The same accomplishment can be seen to this day in her daughter Eustochium [Eu sto' chi um], who always kept close to her mother's side, obeyed all her commands, never slept apart from her, never walked abroad or took a meal without her, never had a penny that she could call her own, rejoiced when her mother gave to the poor her little patrimony, and fully believed that in filial affection she had the best heritage and the truest riches. I must not pass over in silence the joy which Paula felt when she heard her little granddaughter and namesake, the child of Laeta [Lae' ta] and Toxotius [Tox o' ti us], in her cradle sing "alleluia" and falter out the words "grandmother" and "aunt." One wish alone made her long to see her native land again; that she might know her son and his wife and child to have renounced the world and to be serving Christ. And it has been granted to her in part. For while her granddaughter is destined to take the veil, her daughter-in-law has vowed herself to perpetual chastity, and by faith and alms emulates the example that her mother has set her. She strives to exhibit at Rome the virtues which Paula set forth in all their fulness at Jerusalem.

THIRD WEEK OF THE YEAR
Wednesday
Jerome, *Life of Paula* 28–29 (#9 of 12)

Paula dies as she had lived, in prayer and praise. The status and numbers of those who came to be present for her death and funeral witness to the extent of her reputation.

Who could tell the tale of Paula's dying with dry eyes? She fell into a most serious illness and thus gained what she most desired, power to leave us and to be joined more fully to the Lord. Eustochium's affection for her mother, always true and tried, in this time of sickness approved itself still more to all. She sat by Paula's bedside, she fanned her, she supported her head, she arranged her pillows, she chafed her feet, she rubbed her stomach, she smoothed down the bedclothes, she heated hot water, she brought towels. In fact she anticipated the servants in all their duties, and when one of them did anything she regarded it as so much taken away from her own gain. How unceasingly she prayed, how copiously she wept, how constantly she ran to and fro between her prostrate mother and the cave of the Lord! imploring God that she might not be deprived of a companion so dear, that if Paula was to die she might herself no longer live, and that one bier might carry to burial her and her mother. Alas for the frailty and perishableness of human nature!

Paula's intelligence showed her that her death was near. Her body and limbs grew cold and only in her holy breast did the warm beat of the living soul continue. Yet, as though she were leaving strangers to go home to her own people, she whispered the verses of the psalmist: "Lord, I have loved the habitation of your house and the place where your honour dwells" (Ps 26:8), and "How amiable are your tabernacles, O Lord of hosts! My soul longs and faints for the courts of the Lord" (Ps 84:2–3), and "I had rather be an outcast in the house of my God than to dwell in the tents of wickedness" (Ps 84:11). When I asked her why she remained silent, refusing to answer my call, and whether she was in pain, she replied in Greek that she had no suffering and that all things were to her eyes calm and tranquil. After this she said no more but closed her eyes and kept repeating the verses just quoted, down to the moment in which she breathed out her soul, but in a tone so low that we could scarcely hear what she said. Raising her finger also to her mouth she made the sign of the cross upon her lips. Then her breath failed her and she gasped for death; yet even when her soul was eager to break free, she turned the death-rattle (which comes at last to all) into the praise of the Lord. The bishop of Jerusalem and some from other cities were present, also a great number of the lower clergy, both priests and levites. The entire monastery was filled with virgins and monks. As soon as Paula heard the bridegroom saying: "Rise up, my love, my fair one, my dove, and come away: for, lo, the winter is past, the rain is over and gone," she answered joyfully "The flowers appear on the earth; the time to cut them has come" (Song 2:10–12) and "I believe that I shall see the good things of the Lord in the land of the living" (Ps 27:13).

THIRD WEEK OF THE YEAR
Thursday
Jerome, *Life of Paula* 30–31 (#10 of 12)

Paula's funeral was a major event in Palestine. She who had been one of the richest persons in the empire died in debt, having given away everything to charity.

No weeping or lamentation followed her death, such as are the customs of the world; but all present united in chanting the psalms in their several tongues. The bishops lifted up the dead woman with their own hands, placed her upon a bier, and carrying her on their shoulders to the church in the cave of the Saviour, laid her down in the centre of it. Other bishops meantime carried torches and tapers in the procession, and yet others led the singing of the choirs. The whole population of the cities of Palestine came to her funeral. Not a single monk lurked in the desert or lingered in his cell. Not a single virgin remained shut up in the seclusion of her chamber. To each and all it would have seemed sacrilege to have withheld the last tokens of respect from a woman so saintly. As in the case of Dorcas (Acts 9:39), the widows and the poor showed the garments Paula had given them; while the destitute cried aloud that they had lost in her a mother and a nurse. Strange to say, the paleness of death had not altered her expression; only a certain solemnity and seriousness had overspread her features. You would have thought her not dead but asleep.

One after another they chanted the psalms, now in Greek, now in Latin, now in Syriac; and this not merely for the three days which elapsed before she was buried beneath the church and close to the cave of the Lord, but throughout the remainder of the week. All who were assembled felt that it was their own funeral at which they were assisting, and shed tears as if they themselves had died. Paula's daughter, the revered virgin Eustochium [Eu sto'chi um], "as a child that is weaned of her mother," could not be torn away from her parent. She kissed her eyes, pressed her lips upon her brow, embraced her frame, and wished for nothing better than to be buried with her.

Jesus is witness that Paula has left not a single penny to her daughter, but on the contrary a large mass of debt; and, worse even than this, a crowd of brothers and sisters whom it is hard for her to support but whom it would be undutiful to cast off. Could there be a more splendid instance of self-renunciation than that of this noble lady who in the fervour of her faith gave away so much of her wealth that she reduced herself to the last degree of poverty? Others may boast, if they will, of money spent in charity, or large sums heaped up in God's treasury, of votive offerings hung up with cords of gold. None of them has given more to the poor than Paula, for Paula has kept nothing for herself. But now she enjoys the true riches and those good things which eye hath not seen nor ear heard, neither have they entered into the human heart (1 Cor 2:9). If we mourn, it is for ourselves and not for her; yet even so, if we persist in weeping for one who reigns with Christ, we shall seem to envy her her glory.

THIRD WEEK OF THE YEAR
Friday
Jerome, *Life of Paula* 32–33 (#11 of 12)

Jerome and Paula had been close friends for over twenty years. Jerome conveys his expressions of grief at his personal loss to Eustochium, Paula's daughter. His words reveal the depth of their friendship.

Be not fearful, Eustochium [Eu sto' chi um], you are endowed with a splendid heritage. The Lord is your portion; and, to increase your joy, your mother has now after a long martyrdom won her crown. It is not only the shedding of blood that is accounted a confession: the spotless service of a devout mind is itself a daily martyrdom. Like Abraham, your mother heard the words: "Go out of your country, and from your kindred, to a land that I will show you" (Gen 12:1) and not only that, but the Lord's command given through Jeremiah: "Flee out of the midst of Babylon, and deliver every one your soul" (Jer 51:6). To the day of her death she never returned to Chaldaea [Chal dae' a], or regretted the fleshpots of Egypt or its strong-smelling meats. Accompanied by her virgin bands she became a fellow-citizen of the Saviour; and now that she has ascended from her little Bethlehem to the heavenly realms she can say to the true Naomi: "Your people shall be my people and your God my God" (Ruth 1:16).

I have spent the labour of two nights in dictating for you this treatise; and in doing so I have felt a grief as deep as your own. I say in "dictating" for I have not been able to write it myself. As often as I have taken up my pen and have tried to fulfil my promise, my fingers have stiffened, my hand has fallen, and my power over it has vanished. The rudeness of the diction, devoid as it is of all elegance or charm, bears witness to the feeling of the writer.

THIRD WEEK OF THE YEAR
Saturday
Jerome, *Life of Paula* 34–35 (#12 of 12)

The aging Jerome has lost his best friend. He gives the text of the two inscriptions he had set up at her burial place in the cave of Bethlehem. Unfortunately, both have since disappeared.

Now, Paula, farewell, and aid with your prayers the old age of your votary. Your faith and your works unite you to Christ; thus standing in his presence you will the more readily gain what you ask. In this letter I have built to your memory a monument more lasting than bronze, which no lapse of time will be able to destroy. And I have cut an inscription on your tomb, which I here subjoin; that, wherever my narrative may go, the reader may learn that you are buried at Bethlehem and not uncommemorated there.

The Inscription on Paula's Tomb
Within this tomb a child of Scipio [Scip' i o] lies,
A daughter of the far-famed Pauline house,
A scion of the Gracchi, of the stock
Of Agamemnon's [Ag a mem' non] self, illustrious:
Here rests the lady Paula, well-beloved
Of both her parents, with Eustochium [Eu sto' chi um]

For daughter; she the first of Roman dames
Who hardship chose and Bethlehem for Christ.

In front of the cavern there is another inscription as follows:

Seest thou here hollowed in the rock a grave,
'Tis Paula's tomb; high heaven has her soul.
Who Rome and friends, riches and home forsook,
Here in this lonely spot to find her rest.
For here Christ's manger was, and here the kings
To him, both God and man, their off'rings made.

The holy and blessed Paula fell asleep on the seventh day before the Kalends [Ka' lends] of February, on the third day of the week, after the sun had set. She was buried on the fifth day before the same Kalends, in the sixth consulship of the Emperor Honorius [Ho no' ri us] and the first of Aristaenetus [A ris tae ne' tus] (January 26, 404). She lived in the vows of religion five years at Rome and twenty years at Bethlehem. The whole duration of her life was fifty-six years eight months and twenty-one days.

FOURTH SUNDAY OF THE YEAR
Judith 13:18-20

For her acts of heroism, Judith is praised before God and all the people.

Uzziah [Uz zi' ah] said to Judith, "O daughter, you are blessed by the Most High God above all other women on earth; and blessed be the Lord God, who created the heavens and the earth, who has guided you to cut off the head of the leader of our enemies. Your praise will never depart from the hearts of those who remember the power of God. May God grant this to be a perpetual honor to you, and may God reward you with blessings, because you risked your own life when our nation was brought low, and you averted our ruin, walking in the straight path before our God." And all the people said, "Amen. Amen."

FOURTH WEEK OF THE YEAR
Monday
Tertullian, *On the Soul* 9

Tertullian records the visions of a woman in the early church of Carthage. Her vision of a soul is proof for him of its existence.

We have now amongst us a sister whose lot it has been to be favoured with gifts of revelation, which she experiences in the Spirit by ecstatic vision amidst the sacred rites of the Lord's Day in the church. She converses with angels, and sometimes even with the Lord. She both sees and hears mysterious communications. Some people's hearts she discerns, and she obtains directions for healing for such as need them. Whether it be in the reading of the Scriptures, or in the chanting of psalms, or in the preaching of sermons, or in the offering up of prayers, in all these religious services matter and opportunity are afforded her of seeing visions. Perchance, while this sister of ours was in the Spirit, we had discoursed on some topic about the soul.

After the people are dismissed at the conclusion of the sacred services, she is in the regular habit of reporting to us whatever things she may have seen in vision; for all her communications are examined with the most scrupulous care, in order that their truth may be probed. "Amongst other things," she says, "there was shown to me a soul in bodily shape, and a spirit appeared to me; not, however, a void and empty illusion, but such as would offer itself to be even grasped by the hand, clear and transparent and of an ethereal colour, and in form resembling that of a human being in every respect." This was her vision, and for her witness, there was God; and the apostle is a fitting surety that there were to be spiritual gifts in the Church.

FOURTH WEEK OF THE YEAR
Tuesday
Luke 8:40–42, 49–56

Jesus directs his healing ministry to a little girl.

When Jesus arrived, the crowd welcomed him, for they were all waiting for him. Just then there came a man named Jairus, a leader of the synagogue. He fell at Jesus' feet and begged him to come to his house, for he had an only daughter, about twelve years old, who was dying.

As he went, the crowd pressed in on him. Then someone came from the leader's house to say, "Your daughter is dead; do not trouble the teacher any longer." When Jesus heard this, he replied, "Do not fear. Only believe, and she will be saved." When he came to the house, he did not allow anyone to enter with him, except Peter, John, and James, and the child's father and mother. They were all weeping and wailing for her; but he said, "Do not weep; for she is not dead but sleeping." And they laughed at him, knowing that she was dead. But he took her by the hand and called out, "Child, get up!" Her spirit returned, and she got up at once. Then he directed them to give her something to eat. Her parents were astounded; but he ordered them to tell no one what had happened.

See Matthew 9:18–19, 23–26
Mark 5:21–24, 35–43

FOURTH WEEK OF THE YEAR
Wednesday
Sibylline Oracles Book 8:480–500

The Sibylline prophet echoes the sayings of Jesus and exhortations of Paul.

Be humble in heart, hate bitter power,
and, above all, love your neighbor as yourself,

and love God from the soul and serve God.
Therefore we are also of the holy heavenly race
of Christ, and are called brothers and sisters.
Having a remembrance of joy in worship,
we walk the paths of piety and truth.
Rejoicing with holy minds and glad spirit,
abundant love and hands that bring good gifts
with gracious psalms and songs appropriate to God,
we are bidden to sing your praises as imperishable and pure from all
        deceit,
God, wise begetter of all.

FOURTH WEEK OF THE YEAR
Thursday
1 Samuel 28:5–8, 11–14, 20, 24–25

---

*Saul had driven the mediums and the wizards from the land, so it
was in secret that he consulted the medium of Endor.*

When Saul saw the army of the Philistines, he was afraid, and his
heart trembled greatly. When Saul inquired of the Lord, the Lord did not
answer him, not by dreams, or by Urim, or by prophets. Then Saul said to
his servants, "Seek out for me a woman who is a medium, so that I may
go to her and inquire of her." His servants said to him, "There is a
medium at Endor." So Saul disguised himself and put on other clothes
and went there, he and two men with him. They came to the woman by
night. And he said, "Consult a spirit for me, and bring up for me the one
whom I name to you. . . ." Then the woman said, "Whom shall I bring
up for you?" He answered, "Bring up Samuel for me." When the
woman saw Samuel, she cried out with a loud voice; and the woman said
to Saul, "Why have you deceived me? You are Saul!" The king said to
her, "Have no fear; what do you see?" The woman said to Saul, "I see a
divine being coming up out of the ground." He said to her, "What is his
appearance?" She said, "An old man is coming up; he is wrapped in a
robe." So Saul knew that it was Samuel, and he bowed with his face to the

ground, and did obeisance. . . . Saul fell full length on the ground, filled with fear because of the words of Samuel; and there was no strength in him, for he had eaten nothing all day and all night. . . . Now the woman had a fatted calf in the house. She quickly slaughtered it, and she took flour, kneaded it, and baked unleavened cakes. She put them before Saul and his servants, and they ate.

FOURTH WEEK OF THE YEAR
Friday
Mark 6:14–29

Two women, one a conniver and the other an accomplice, partici-pate in the violence caused by an oppressive regime in which royal alliances are more important than life itself.

King Herod heard of the preaching and miracles, for Jesus' name had become known. Some were saying, "John the baptizer has been raised from the dead; and for this reason these powers are at work in him." But others said, "It is Elijah." And others said, "It is a prophet, like one of the prophets of old." But when Herod heard of it, he said, "John, whom I beheaded, has been raised."

For Herod himself had sent men who arrested John, bound him, and put him in prison on account of Herodias, his brother Philip's wife, because Herod had married her. For John had been telling Herod, "It is not lawful for you to have your brother's wife." And Herodias had a grudge against him, and wanted to kill him. But she could not, for Herod feared John, knowing that he was a righteous and holy man, and he protected him. When he heard him, he was greatly perplexed, and yet he liked to listen to him. But an opportunity came when Herod on his birthday gave a banquet for his courtiers and officers and for the leaders of Galilee. When the daughter of Herodias came in and danced, she pleased Herod and his guests; and the king said to the girl, "Ask me for whatever you wish, and I will give it." And he solemnly swore to her, "Whatever you ask me, I will give you, even half of my kingdom." She went out and said to her mother, "What should I ask for?" She replied, "The head of

John the Baptist on a platter." The king was deeply grieved; yet out of regard for his oaths and for the guests, he did not want to refuse her. Immediately the king sent a soldier of the guard with orders to bring John's head. He went and beheaded him in the prison, brought his head on a platter, and gave it to the girl. Then the girl gave it to her mother. When his disciples heard about it, they came and took his body, and laid it in a tomb.

See Matthew 14:1–2

FOURTH WEEK OF THE YEAR
Saturday
Genesis 20:1–18

Three separate "versions" of this tradition appear in Genesis (12:10–20; 20:1–18; 26:1–11). In each case the life of the patriarchs (Abraham or Isaac) is deemed more precious than his wife's honor (Sarah or Rebekah).

Abraham journeyed toward the region of the Negeb, and settled between Kadesh and Shur. While residing in Gerar as an alien, Abraham said of his wife Sarah, "She is my sister." And King Abimelech [A bim' e lech] of Gerar sent and took Sarah. But God came to Abimelech in a dream by night, and said to him. "You are about to die because of the woman whom you have taken; for she is a married woman." Now Abimelech had not approached her; so he said, "Lord, will you destroy an innocent people? Did he not himself say to me, 'She is my sister'? And she herself said, 'He is my brother.' I did this in the integrity of my heart and the innocence of my hands." Then God said to him in the dream, "Yes, I know that you did this in the integrity of your heart. Furthermore it was I who kept you from sinning against me. Therefore I did not let you touch her. Now then, return the man's wife for he is a prophet, and he will pray for you and you shall live. But if you do not restore her, know that you shall surely die, you and all that are yours."

So Abimelech rose early in the morning, and called all his servants and told them all these things; and the men were very much afraid. Then

Abimelech called Abraham, and said to him, "What have you done to us? How have I sinned against you, that you have brought such great guilt on me and my kingdom? You have done things to me that ought not to be done." And Abimelech said to Abraham, "What were you thinking of, that you did this thing?" Abraham said, "I did it because I thought, There is no fear of God at all in this place, and they will kill me because of my wife. Besides, she is indeed my sister, the daughter of my father but not the daughter of my mother; and she became my wife. And when God caused me to wander from my father's house, I said to her, 'This is the kindness you must do me: at every place to which we come, say of me, He is my brother.' " Then Abimelech took sheep and oxen, and male and female slaves, and gave them to Abraham, and restored his wife Sarah to him. Abimelech said, "My land is before you; settle where it pleases you." To Sarah he said, "Look, I have given your brother a thousand pieces of silver; it is your exoneration before all who are with you; you are completely vindicated." Then Abraham prayed to God; and God healed Abimelech, and also healed his wife and female slaves so that they bore children. For the Lord had closed fast all the wombs of the house of Abimelech because of Sarah, Abraham's wife.

See Genesis 12:10–20
Genesis 26:1–11

FIFTH SUNDAY OF THE YEAR
Mark 1:29–39

Jesus' healing of Simon's mother-in-law is the first of a large number of healings; her cure is instantaneous and she immediately resumes her social obligations.

Jesus entered the house of Simon and Andrew, with James and John. Now Simon's mother-in-law was in bed with a fever, and they told him about her at once. He came and took her by the hand and lifted her up. Then the fever left her, and she began to serve them.

That evening, at sundown, they brought to him all who were sick or possessed with demons. And the whole city was gathered around the door. And he cured many who were sick with various diseases, and cast out many demons; and he would not permit the demons to speak, because they knew him.

In the morning, while it was still very dark, he got up and went out to a deserted place, and there he prayed. And Simon and his companions hunted for him, and when they found him, they said, "Everyone is searching for you." He answered, "Let us go on to the neighboring towns, so that I may proclaim the message there also; for that is what I came out to do." And he went throughout Galilee, proclaiming the message in their synagogues and casting out demons.

See Luke 4:38-44
Matthew 8:14-15

FIFTH WEEK OF THE YEAR
Monday
Sayings of the Desert Mother Theodora (#1 of 2)

Amma Theodora was one of the famous hermits or nuns of the fifth century Egyptian desert. These sayings show her wisdom about illness and temptation.

Amma Theodora [The o do' ra] said, "Let us strive to enter by the narrow gate. Just as the trees, if they have not stood before the winter's storms, cannot bear fruit, so it is with us; this present age is a storm and it is only through many trials and temptations that we can obtain an inheritance in the kingdom of heaven."

She also said, "It is good to live in peace, for the wise person practises perpetual prayer. It is truly a great thing for a virgin or a monk to live in peace, especially for the younger ones. However, you should realize that as soon as you intend to live in peace, at once evil comes and weighs down your soul through *accidie* [ac ci' di e],* faintheartedness, and evil

---

* sadness, spiritual torpor, sloth; Cassian (360–435) depicts it as a state of restlessness and inability either to work or to pray.

thoughts. It also attacks your body through sickness, debility, weakening of the knees, and all the members. It dissipates the strength of soul and body, so that one believes one is ill and no longer able to pray. But if we are vigilant, all these temptations fall away. There was, in fact, a nun who was seized by cold and fever every time she began to pray, and she suffered from headaches, too. In this condition, she said to herself, 'I am ill, and near to death; so now I will get up before I die and pray.' By reasoning in this way, she did violence to herself and prayed. When she had finished, the fever abated also. So, by reasoning in this way, the sister resisted, and prayed and was able to conquer her thoughts."

The same Amma Theodora said, "A devout woman happened to be insulted by someone, and she said to her, 'I could say as much to you, but the commandment of God keeps my mouth shut.' " Again she said this, "A Christian discussing the body with a Manichean expressed herself in these words, 'Give the body discipline and you will see that the body is for the one who made it.' "

FIFTH WEEK OF THE YEAR
Tuesday
Sayings of the Desert Mother Theodora (#2 of 2)

Amma Theodora was one of the famous hermits or nuns of the fifth century Egyptian desert. Here we see especially the value of humility.

Amma Theodora said that a teacher ought to be a stranger to the desire for domination, vain-glory, and pride; one should not be able to fool her by flattery, nor blind her by gifts, nor conquer her by the stomach, nor dominate her by anger; but she should be patient, gentle and humble as far as possible; she must be tested and without partisanship, full of concern, and a lover of souls.

She also said that neither asceticism nor vigils nor any kind of suffering are able to save, only true humility can do that. There was an anchorite who was able to banish the demons; and she asked them, "What makes you go away? Is it fasting?" They replied, "We do not eat or drink." "Is it vigils?" They replied, "We do not sleep." "Is it separation from the world?" "We live in the deserts." "What power sends you away then?" They said, "Nothing can overcome us, but only humility." Do you see how humility is victorious over the demons?

The same amma was asked about the conversations one hears. "If one is habitually listening to worldly speech, how can one yet live for God alone, as you suggest?" She said, "Just as when you are sitting at table and there are many courses, you take some but without pleasure, so when worldly conversations come your way, have your heart turned towards God, and thanks to this disposition, you will hear them without pleasure, and they will not do you any harm."

An old person questioned Amma Theodora saying, "At the resurrection of the dead, how shall we rise?" She said, "As pledge, as example, and as prototype we have Christ who died for us and is risen, Christ our God."

FIFTH WEEK OF THE YEAR
Wednesday
1 Kings 10:1–10, 13

The queen of Sheba, whose wealth and power were legendary, came from a great distance to visit King Solomon whose wisdom was equally the subject of legends.

When the queen of Sheba heard of the fame of Solomon (fame due to the name of the Lord), she came to test him with hard questions. She came to Jerusalem with a very great retinue, with camels bearing spices, and very much gold, and precious stones; and when she came to Solomon, she told him all that was on her mind. Solomon answered all her questions; there was nothing hidden from the king that he could not explain to her. When the queen of Sheba had observed all the wisdom of Solomon, the house that he had built, the food of his table, the seating of his officials, and the attendance of his servants, their clothing, his valets, and his burnt offerings that he offered at the house of the Lord, there was no more spirit in her.

So she said to the king, "The report was true that I heard in my own land of your accomplishments and of your wisdom, but I did not believe the reports until I came and my own eyes had seen it. Not even half had been told me; your wisdom and prosperity far surpass the report that I had heard. Happy are your wives! Happy are these your servants, who continually attend you and hear your wisdom! Blessed be the Lord your God, who has delighted in you and set you on the throne of Israel! Because the Lord loved Israel forever, the Lord has made you king to execute justice and righteousness." Then she gave the king one hundred twenty talents of gold, a great quantity of spices, and precious stones; never again did spices come in such quantity as that which the queen of Sheba gave to King Solomon.

Meanwhile King Solomon gave to the queen of Sheba every desire that she expressed, as well as what he gave her out of Solomon's royal bounty. Then she returned to her own land, with her servants.

FIFTH WEEK OF THE YEAR
Thursday
Genesis 24:10–28 (#1 of 3)

According to the custom of endogamous marriage, Abraham sends his servant in search of a wife for his son Isaac among his kinsfolk in Haran. With the help of a sign from God Rebekah is chosen.

Abraham's servant took ten of his master's camels and departed, taking all kinds of choice gifts from his master; and he set out and went to Aram-naharaim [A'ram-na ha' ra im] (Mesopotamia), to the city of Nahor. He made the camels kneel down outside the city by the well of water; it was toward evening, the time when women go out to draw water. And he said, "O Lord, God of my master Abraham, please grant me success today and show steadfast love to my master Abraham. I am standing here by the spring of water, and the daughters of the townspeople are coming out to draw water. Let the girl to whom I shall say, 'Please offer your jar that I may drink,' and who shall say, 'Drink, and I will water your camels'

—let her be the one whom you have appointed for your servant Isaac. By this I shall know that you have shown steadfast love to my master."

Before he had finished speaking, there was Rebekah, who was born to Bethuel [Be thu' el] son of Milcah, the wife of Nahor, Abraham's brother, coming out with her water jar on her shoulder. The girl was very fair to look upon, a virgin, whom no man had known. She went down to the spring, filled her jar, and came up. Then the servant ran to meet her and said, "Please let me sip a little water from your jar." "Drink, my lord," she said, and quickly lowered her jar upon her hand and gave him a drink. When she had finished giving him a drink, she said, "I will draw for your camels also, until they have finished drinking." So she quickly emptied her jar into the trough and ran again to the well to draw, and she drew for all his camels. The man gazed at her in silence to learn whether or not the Lord had made his journey successful.

When the camels had finished drinking, the man took a gold nosering weighing a half shekel, and two bracelets for her arms weighing ten gold shekels, and said, "Tell me whose daughter you are. Is there room in your father's house for us to spend the night?" She said to him, "I am the daughter of Bethuel son of Milcah, whom she bore to Nahor." She added, "We have plenty of straw and fodder and a place to spend the night." The man bowed his head and worshiped the Lord and said, "Blessed be the Lord, the God of my master Abraham, who has not forsaken steadfast love and faithfulness toward my master. As for me, the Lord has led me on the way to the house of my master's kin."

Then the girl ran and told her mother's household about these things.

FIFTH WEEK OF THE YEAR
Friday
Genesis 24:42–49 (#2 of 3)

The servant of Abraham recognizes in Rebekah the signs of a generous and industrious woman and recounts to Laban, her brother, all that the Lord had revealed to him.

"I came today to the spring, and said, 'O Lord, the God of my master Abraham, if now you will only make successful the way I am going! I am standing here by the spring of water; let the young woman who comes out to draw, to whom I shall say, "Please give me a little water from your jar to drink," and who will say to me, "Drink, and I will draw for your camels also"—let her be the woman whom the Lord has appointed for my master's son.'

"Before I had finished speaking in my heart, there was Rebekah coming out with her water jar on her shoulder, and she went down to the spring, and drew. I said to her, 'Please let me drink.' She quickly let down her jar from her shoulder, and said, 'Drink, and I will also water your camels.' So I drank, and she also watered the camels. Then I asked her, 'Whose daughter are you?' She said, 'The daughter of Bethuel, Nahor's son, whom Milcah bore to him.' So I put the ring on her nose, and the bracelets on her arms. Then I bowed my head and worshiped the Lord, and blessed the Lord, the God of my master Abraham, who had led me the right way to obtain the daughter of my master's kinsman for his son. Now then, if you will deal loyally and truly with my master, tell me; and if not, tell me so that I may turn either to the right hand or to the left."

FIFTH WEEK OF THE YEAR
Saturday
Genesis 24:50–67 (#3 of 3)

In accordance with ancient custom, Rebekah must give consent to the marriage arranged by her brother, especially since she was being asked to leave her homeland. Having agreed to the marriage, Rebekah receives a solemn blessing as she journeys toward the Negeb.

Laban and Bethuel answered, "The thing comes from the Lord; we cannot speak to you anything bad or good. Look, Rebekah is before you, take her and go, and let her be the wife of your master's son, as the Lord has spoken."

When Abraham's servant heard their words, he bowed himself to the ground before the Lord. And the servant brought out jewelry of silver and of gold, and garments, and gave them to Rebekah; he also gave to her brother and to their mother costly ornaments. Then he and the men who were with him ate and drank, and they spent the night there. When they rose in the morning, he said, "Send me back to my master." Her brother and her mother said, "Let the girl remain with us a while, at least ten days; after that she may go." But he said to them, "Do not delay me, since the Lord has made my journey successful; let me go that I may go to my master." They said, "We will call the girl, and ask her." And they called Rebekah, and said to her, "Will you go with this man?" She said, "I will." So they sent away their sister Rebekah and her nurse along with Abraham's servant and his men. And they blessed Rebekah and said to her,

> "May you, our sister, become thousands of myriads;
> may your offspring gain possession
> of the gates of their foes."

Then Rebekah and her maids rose up, mounted the camels, and followed the man; thus, the servant took Rebekah, and went his way.

Now Isaac had come from Beer-lahai-roi [Be er-la' hai roi], and was settled in the Negeb. Isaac went out in the evening to walk in the field; and looking up, he saw camels coming. And Rebekah looked up, and when she saw Isaac, she slipped quickly from the camel, and said to the servant, "Who is the man over there, walking in the field to meet us?" The servant said, "It is my master." So she took her veil and covered herself. And the servant told Isaac all the things that he had done. Then Isaac brought her into his mother Sarah's tent. He took Rebekah, and she became his wife; and he loved her. So Isaac was comforted after his mother's death.

SIXTH SUNDAY OF THE YEAR
Matthew 26:6–13

Jesus was very clear that the good news of this woman's deed should not be forgotten. Why, then, has her name been erased from memory, especially when we remember even the name of the betrayer?

Now while Jesus was at Bethany in the house of Simon the leper, a woman came to him with an alabaster jar of very costly ointment, and she poured it on his head as he sat at table. But when the disciples saw it, they were angry and said, "Why this waste? For this ointment could have been sold for a large sum, and the money given to the poor." But Jesus, aware of this, said to them, "Why do you trouble the woman? She has performed a good service for me. For you always have the poor with you, but you will not always have me. By pouring this ointment on my body she has prepared me for burial. Truly I tell you, wherever this good news is proclaimed in the whole world, what she has done will be told in remembrance of her."

SIXTH WEEK OF THE YEAR
Monday
Holy Women of the Syrian Orient: Elizabeth

One of the martyrs of Najran and obviously a leader in the persecuted church of the Arabian peninsula, Elizabeth suffered a violent death. She was buried by two male relatives who risked their lives to honor her memory.

The sister of the holy bishop and martyr Paul was a deaconess named Elizabeth. She was in hiding in a house where the Christians had forcibly concealed her. On learning that the church was in flames, with the "members of the covenant" and the bones of her brother inside it, she dashed out of the house where the Christians had hidden her and went straight to the church, crying out, "I shall go to Christ with you, my brother, and with all the rest of you." This was what she was crying out as she reached the courtyard of the church, and when the people saw her there, they seized her, saying, "She has escaped from the fire, she has vanquished the fire by sorcery and got out!" But she assured them, "I haven't left the church—far be it; rather, I have come from outside in order to enter it and to be burnt along with the bones of my brother and with the priests, his companions. I want to be burnt in the church where I have ministered, together with my brother's bones." She was about forty-seven years old.

SIXTH WEEK OF THE YEAR
Tuesday
Apostolic Constitutions 2.26.6, 8

This theological description of the relationships among church officers in the fourth century Syrian church gives us a glimpse of the honor given to widows, but especially of the position of deaconesses among the clergy.

Let the deaconess be honored by you as a representative of the Holy Spirit and do not do or say anything without the deacon; just as the Paraclete does and says nothing alone, but glorifies Christ by waiting for his will. Just as we cannot believe in Christ without the teaching of the Spirit, so let no woman approach the deacon or the bishop without the deaconess. Let the widows and orphans be honored among you as representatives of the altar of burnt-offering; and let the virgins be honored as representatives of the altar of incense, and even the incense itself.

SIXTH WEEK OF THE YEAR
Wednesday
1 Samuel 25:2–42 passim

Abigail, though unappreciated by her surly husband, intervenes to prevent violence which he has provoked by his stupidity. Her wisdom is rewarded with good fortune.

There was a man in Maon, whose property was in Carmel. The man was very rich. Now the name of the man was Nabal, and the name of his wife was Abigail. The woman was clever and beautiful, but the man was surly and mean.

David said to ten of his young men, "Go up to Carmel, and go to Nabal, and greet him in my name. Thus you shall salute him: 'Peace be to you, and peace be to your house, and peace be to all that you have. I hear that you have shearers; now your shepherds have been with us, and we did them no harm, and they missed nothing, all the time they were in Carmel. Therefore let my young men find favor in your sight; for we have come on a feast day. Please give whatever you have at hand to your servants and to your son David.'" Nabal answered David's servants, "Shall I take my bread and my water and the meat that I have butchered for my shearers, and give it to men who come from I do not know where?" So David's young men turned away, and came back and told him all this. David said to his men, "Every man strap on his sword!" And every one of them strapped on his sword; David also strapped on his sword.

But one of Nabal's young men told Abigail, Nabal's wife. Then Abigail hurried and took two hundred loaves, two skins of wine, five sheep ready dressed, five measures of parched grain, one hundred clusters of raisins, and two hundred cakes of figs. She loaded them on donkeys and said to her young men, "Go on ahead of me; I am coming after you." But she did not tell her husband Nabal. As she rode on the donkey and came down under cover of the mountain, David and his men came down toward her; and she met them. When Abigail saw David, she hurried and alighted from the donkey, fell at his feet and said, "Upon me alone, my lord, be the guilt; please let your servant speak in your ear. My lord, do not take seriously this ill-natured fellow, Nabal; for as his name is, so is he; Nabal is his name, and folly is with him; but I, your servant, did not see your young men, whom you sent. And now let this present that your servant has brought to you be given to the young men who follow you. For the Lord will certainly make you a sure house, because you are fighting the battles of the Lord; and evil shall not be found in you so long as you live. If anyone should rise up to pursue you and to seek your life, your life shall be bound in the bundle of the living under the care of the Lord your God. When the Lord has done to you according to all the good spoken concerning you, and has appointed you prince over Israel, then remember your servant."

David said to Abigail, "Blessed be the Lord, the God of Israel, who sent you to meet me today! Blessed be your good sense, and blessed be you, who have kept me today from bloodguilt and from avenging myself by my own hand!" Then David received from her hand what she had brought him; he said to her, "Go up to your house in peace; see, I have heeded your voice, and I have granted your petition."

About ten days later the Lord struck Nabal, and he died. When David heard that Nabal was dead, he said, "Blessed be the Lord who has judged the case of Nabal's insult to me." Then David sent and wooed Abigail, to make her his wife. When David's servants came to Abigail at Carmel, they said to her, "David has sent us to you to take you to him as his wife." Abigail got up hurriedly and rode away on a donkey; her five maids attended her. She went after the messengers of David and became his wife.

SIXTH WEEK OF THE YEAR
Thursday
Egeria's Travels 3.1–6 (#1 of 2)

A late fourth century Spanish nun, an intrepid pilgrim, writes back to the nuns in her monastery about her visit to Sinai. Such extensive and perilous travel was virtually unknown for women in her day.

Late on Saturday we arrived at the Mount of God. There is a church there with a presbyter; that is where we spent the night, and, pretty early on Sunday, we set off with the presbyter and monks who lived there to climb each of the mountains.

They are hard to climb. You do not go round and round them, spiralling up gently, but straight at each one as if you were going up a wall, and then straight down to the foot, till you reach the foot of the central mountain, Sinai itself. Here then, impelled by Christ our God and assisted by the prayers of the holy men who accompanied us, we made the great effort of the climb. It was quite impossible to ride up, but though I had to go on foot I was not conscious of the effort—in fact I hardly noticed it because, by God's will, I was seeing my hopes coming true.

So at ten o'clock we arrived on the summit of Sinai, the Mount of God where the Law was given, and the place where God's glory came down on the day when the mountain was smoking (Exod 19:18). The church which is now there is not impressive for its size (there is too little room on the summit), but it has a grace all its own.

All there is on the actual summit of the central mountain is the church and the cave of holy Moses. No one lives there. So when the whole passage had been read to us from the Book of Moses (on the very spot!), we made the Offering* in the usual way and received Communion.

SIXTH WEEK OF THE YEAR
Friday
Egeria's Travels 3.6–4.1 (#2 of 2)

Through her vivid description, Egeria's sisters are able vicariously to participate in her pilgrimage.

As we were coming out of church the presbyters of the place gave us "blessings," some fruits which grow on the mountain itself. For although Sinai, the holy Mount, is too stony even for bushes to grow on it, there is a little soil around the foot of the mountains, and in this, the holy monks are always busy planting shrubs, and setting out orchards or vegetable-beds round their cells. It may look as if they gather fruit which is growing in the mountain soil, but in fact everything is the result of their own hard work.

I want you to be quite clear about these mountains, reverend ladies my sisters, which surrounded us as we stood beside the church looking down from the summit of the mountain in the middle. They had been almost too much for us to climb and I really do not think I have ever seen any that were higher. From there we were able to see Egypt and Palestine, the Red Sea and the Parthenian [Par the' ni an] Sea (the part that takes you to Alexandria), as well as the vast lands of the Saracens [Sar' a cens]—all unbelievably far below us.

We had been looking forward to all this so much that we had been eager to make the climb. Now that we had done all we wanted, we began the descent.

---

* ("The Offering" is Egeria's normal word for the second part of the Eucharist. No doubt the reading from the Book of Moses occurred in the first part.)

SIXTH WEEK OF THE YEAR
Saturday
Egeria's Travels 10.7

Egeria is clearly a pilgrim and not a tourist.

It was always our practice when we managed to reach one of the places we wanted to see to have first a prayer, then a reading from the book, then to say an appropriate psalm and another prayer. By God's grace we always followed this practice whenever we were able to reach a place we wanted to see.

SEVENTH SUNDAY OF THE YEAR
Mark 7:24–30

The Syrophoenician woman signifies by her physical behavior that Jesus is superior. She engages him in repartee as an equal, and "bests" him in the debate.

Jesus set out and went away to the region of Tyre. He entered a house and did not want anyone to know he was there. Yet he could not escape notice, but a woman whose little daughter had an unclean spirit immediately heard about him, and she came and bowed down at his feet. Now the woman was a Gentile, of Syrophoenician [Sy ro phoe nic' i an] origin. She begged him to cast the demon out of her daughter. He said to her, "Let the children be fed first, for it is not fair to take the children's food and throw it to the dogs." But she answered him, "Sir, even the dogs under the table eat the children's crumbs." Then he said to her, "For saying that, you may go—the demon has left your daughter." So she went home, found the child lying on the bed, and the demon gone.

See Matthew 15:21–28

SEVENTH WEEK OF THE YEAR
Monday
Genesis 25:19–28

A woman's intuitive relationship with the life in her womb conveys the ominous struggle played out in the rivalry between Esau (the Edomites) and Jacob (the Israelites).

These are the descendants of Isaac, Abraham's son: Abraham was the father of Isaac, and Isaac was forty years old when he married Rebekah, daughter of Bethuel [Be thu' el] the Aramean [A ra me' an] of Paddan-aram [Pad dan-a ram'], sister of Laban the Aramean [A ra me' an]. Isaac prayed to the Lord for his wife, because she was barren; and the Lord granted his prayer, and his wife Rebekah conceived. The children struggled together within her; and she said, "If it is to be this way, why do I live?" So she went to inquire of the Lord. And the Lord said to her,

"Two nations are in your womb,
   and two peoples born of you shall be divided;
the one shall be stronger than the other,
   the elder shall serve the younger."

When her time to give birth was at hand, there were twins in her womb. The first came out red, all his body like a hairy mantle; so they named him Esau. Afterward his brother came out, with his hand gripping Esau's heel; so he was named Jacob. Isaac was sixty years old when she bore them.

When the boys grew up, Esau was a skillful hunter, a man of the field, while Jacob was a quiet man, living in tents. Isaac loved Esau, because he was fond of game; but Rebekah loved Jacob.

SEVENTH WEEK OF THE YEAR
Tuesday
Julian of Norwich, *Showings* 58

Julian reimages the nature of the Trinity and the redeeming work of Christ within us.

As to the first, I saw and understood that the high might of the Trinity is our Father, and the deep wisdom of the Trinity is our Mother, and the great love of the Trinity is our Lord; and all these we have in nature and in our substantial creation. And, furthermore, I saw that the second person, who is our Mother, substantially the same beloved person, has now become our mother sensually, because we are double by God's creating, that is to say, substantial and sensual. Our substance is the higher part, which we have in our Father, God almighty; and the second person of the Trinity is our Mother in nature, in our substantial creation, in whom we are founded and rooted, and he is our Mother of mercy in taking our sensuality. And so our Mother is working on us in various ways, in whom our parts are kept undivided; for in our Mother Christ we profit and increase, and in mercy he reforms and restores us, and by the power of his Passion, his Death and his Resurrection he unites us to our substance.

SEVENTH WEEK OF THE YEAR
Wednesday
Mechtild of Magdeburg, *The Soul and God*

Mechtild's imagery of the prayer of desire provides words for what is often inarticulate longing in us.

Your glory pours into my soul
Like sunlight against gold.
When may I rest with You, Lord?

My joys are manifold.
You garment Yourself in my soul,
And my soul is clothed in You;
That a parting must befall
Fills my heart with sorest rue.
If You loved me more I could
Surely go from here, and be
Where through all eternity
I might love You as I would.
I sang to You and still
It is not as I will.
But if You sang to me
Imperfectness would flee.

"When I glow
You must shine,
When I flow
You must be laved.
When you sigh
You draw my heart, God's heart, into yourself.
When you weep for me
I take you in my arms.
But when you love
We two shall be as one.
When we are one at last, then none
Can ever make us part again,
Unending, wishless rapture
Shall dwell between us twain."

Lord, thus I languish on,
In haste and in desire,
In hunger and in growth,
Until that gracious hour
When from Your Godly mouth
Flows out the chosen word,
That none has ever heard,
Save for the soul that cast
The husk of earth at last,
And to Your mouth she lays her ear,
To her the finds of love grow clear.

SEVENTH WEEK OF THE YEAR
Thursday
Romans 16:1–16

Paul commends to the Romans the bearer of his letter, a woman named Phoebe, church deacon and benefactor. As deacon, she exercised leadership in the church. As benefactor, she is of high social status and influence, besides being wealthy. The long list of greetings that Paul sends to those he knows in Rome includes nine women, some of whom are partners in ministry (Prisca, Mary, Tryphaena, Tryphosa, and Persis and one who is called apostle Junia).

I commend to you our sister Phoebe, a deacon of the church at Cenchrae [Cen' chrae], so that you may welcome her in the Lord as is fitting for the saints, and help her in whatever she may require from you, for she has been a benefactor of many and of myself as well.

Greet Prisca and Aquila [A qui' la], who work with me in Christ Jesus, and who risked their necks for my life, to whom not only I give thanks, but also all the churches of the Gentiles. Greet also the church in their house. Greet my beloved Epaenetus [E pae' ne tus], who was the first convert in Asia for Christ. Greet Mary, who has worked very hard among you. Greet Andronicus [An dro' ni cus] and Junia [Ju' ni a], my relatives who were in prison with me; they are prominent among the apostles, and they were in Christ before I was. Greet Ampliatus [Am pli a' tus], my beloved in the Lord. Greet Urbanus [Ur ba' nus], our co-worker in Christ, and my beloved Stachys [Sta' chys]. Greet Apelles [A pel' les], who is approved in Christ. Greet those who belong to the family of Aristobulus [Ar is to bu' lus]. Greet my relative Herodion [He ro' di on]. Greet those in the Lord who belong to the family of Narcissus [Nar cis' sus]. Greet those workers in the Lord, Tryphaena [Try phae' na] and Tryphosa [Try pho' sa]. Greet the beloved Persis [Per' sis], who has worked hard in the Lord. Greet Rufus [Ru' fus], chosen in the Lord; and greet his mother—a mother to me also. Greet Asyncritus [A syn'cri tus], Phlegon [Phle' gon], Hermes [Her' mes], Patrobas [Pat' ro bus], Hermas, and the brothers and sisters who are with them. Greet Philologus [Phi lol' o gus], Julia, Nereus [Ne' re us] and his sister, and Olympas [O lym' pas], and all the saints who are with them. Greet one another with a holy kiss. All the churches of Christ greet you.

SEVENTH WEEK OF THE YEAR
Friday
John Chrysostom, *Homily on Romans* 16:1–2
(#1 of 2)

John Chrysostom, famous fourth to fifth century preacher, arch-bishop of Constantinople, and friend of the deaconess Olympias, has some surprising things to say about the women of whom Paul speaks in Romans 16, here especially Phoebe and Priscilla, wife of Aquila.

"I recommend to you our sister Phoebe, who is a deacon of the church of Cenchreae" [Cen' chre ae] (one of the seaports of Corinth). See in how many ways he dignifies her. He has placed her before all the others and called her sister. It is no small thing to be called Paul's sister. But he gives her even greater importance by calling her deacon. "May you receive her in the Lord in a way worthy of the holy ones, and assist her with whatever need she has, for she has been a patroness to many including myself." Paul praises this blessed woman, and how can she not be blessed who enjoys such praise from Paul, for she was able to help the one who has helped the world. Let us then both men and women imitate this holy woman, as well as her who comes next with her husband. "Greet Priscilla [Pri scil' la] and Aquila [A qui' la], my co-workers in Christ Jesus who have risked their necks for me, whom not only I thank, but all the churches of the Gentiles, and the church that is in their house." See these noble women, in no way hindered by nature in the pursuit of virtue. But this is quite right, for "in Christ Jesus there is no male and female" (Gal 3:28). For she was so good as to make their house a church, opening it to believers and strangers alike. These married people were quite distin-guished, even though their occupation was not, for they were tentmakers.

SEVENTH WEEK OF THE YEAR
Saturday
John Chrysostom, *Homily on Romans* 16:6–7 (#2 of 2)

Chrysostom continues his commentary on the women in Paul's life. Based on a grammatical uncertainty, through the middle ages and into modern times Junia was thought to be a man because she was called an apostle. Chrysostom clearly believed her to be a woman.

"Greet Mary, who has labored much among you." What is this? Again a woman is crowned with praise and proclaimed, again we men are shamed. Rather, we are not only shamed, but honored. We are honored because there are such women among us and shamed because they leave us so far behind. But if we learn with what they were adorned, we will be able to overtake them. With what were they adorned? Listen, both men and women: not with jewelry, servants, and finery, but with their labor on behalf of the truth. "She has labored much" means that besides teaching, she also ministered in other ways involving risk, money, and travel. In those days the women were more ardent than lions, taking up with the apostles the labor of preaching the word. They traveled with them and performed all other ministries with them. Even with Christ there were women who followed, ministering to the Teacher from their possessions (Luke 8:3).

"Greet Andronicus [An dro ni' cus] and Junia [Ju' ni a], my relatives [or people from the same land] who were prisoners with me, who are noteworthy among the apostles." It is already great to be apostles, but to be noteworthy among the apostles is high praise. They are noteworthy for their labors and their righteousness. What wisdom must this woman have had, to be called an apostle!

EIGHTH SUNDAY OF THE YEAR
Luke 8:19-21

Jesus extends to all disciples the closeness of family relationships, an inclusiveness which is also our task.

Then Jesus' mother and his brothers came to him, but they could not reach him because of the crowd. And he was told, "Your mother and your brothers and sisters are standing outside, wanting to see you." But he said to them, "My mother and my brothers and sisters are those who hear the word of God and do it."

EIGHTH WEEK OF THE YEAR
Monday
Julian of Norwich, *Showings* 53

Julian describes God's creative love for us, and our union with God, in whom we are inextricably "knitted" and held.

In this endless love we are led and protected by God, and we never shall be lost; for God wants us to know that the soul is a life, which life of goodness and grace will last in heaven without end, loving God, thanking God, praising God. And just as we were to be without end, so we were treasured and hidden in God, known and loved from without beginning. Therefore God wants us to know that the noblest thing ever made is humankind, and the fullest substance and the highest power is the blessed soul of Christ. And, furthermore, God wants us to know that this beloved soul was preciously knitted in its making, by a knot so subtle and so mighty that it is united in God. In this uniting it is made endlessly holy. Furthermore, God wants us to know that all the souls which will be saved in heaven without end are knit in this knot, and united in this union, and made holy in this holiness.

EIGHTH WEEK OF THE YEAR
Tuesday
Epitaphs of Two Christian Women Deacons

These two funerary inscriptions, from different centuries and different continents (Delphi, Greece, fifth century CE and Archelais, Asia Minor, sixth century CE), testify to the diaconal ministry of women in the early church. The curse levied against intruders in the first inscription is a commonplace in such inscriptions, but here Christianized.

Epitaph of the deaconess Athanasia [Ath a na' si a]
The most pious deaconess Athanasia
having lived a blameless life modestly
having been ordained a deaconess by the most holy bishop,
Pantamianos [Pan ta mi an' os], made this monument, in
    which lie her remains.
If any other dares to open this monument, in which the
deaconess has been deposited, he will have the portion of
Judas, the betrayer of our Lord, Jesus Christ.
No less so those clerics who may be present at this time,
    and assent [to the removal of] the aforementioned
    deaconess. . . .

Epitaph of Maria the deacon
Here lies Maria the deacon, of pious and holy memory, who according to the saying of the apostle raised children, practiced hospitality, washed the feet of the saints, and distributed her bread to the oppressed. Remember her, Lord, when you come into your kingdom.

EIGHTH WEEK OF THE YEAR
Wednesday
Numbers 27:1–8

In an unusual change of inheritance custom, the daughters of Zelophehad inherit their father's land and the right to ensure the continuance of the patrilineal line.

Then the daughters of Zelophehad [Ze lo' phe had] came forward. Zelophehad was son of Hepher, son of Gilead [Gil' e ad], son of Machir, son of Manasseh [Ma nas' seh], son of Joseph, a member of the Manassite [Ma nas' site] clans. The names of his daughters were: Mahlah, Noah, Hoglah, Milcah, and Tirzah. They stood before Moses, Eleazar [El e a' zar] the priest, the leaders, and all the congregation, at the entrance of the tent of meeting, and they said, "Our father died in the wilderness; he was not among the company of those who gathered themselves together against the Lord in the company of Korah, but died for his own sin; and he had no sons. Why should the name of our father be taken away from his clan because he had no son? Give to us a possession among our father's brothers."

Moses brought their case before the Lord. And the Lord spoke to Moses, saying: The daughters of Zelophehad are right in what they are saying; you shall indeed let them possess an inheritance among their father's brothers and pass the inheritance of their father on to them. You shall also say to the Israelites, "If a man dies, and has no son, then you shall pass his inheritance on to his daughter."

EIGHTH WEEK OF THE YEAR
Thursday
1 Samuel 1:1–8 (#1 of 4)

In so many societies, a woman's worth is determined by reproductive capacity. Contrary to cultural expectations Elkanah continues to love his childless wife.

There was a certain man of Ramathaim [Ra ma tha' im], a Zuphite [Zuph' ite] from the hill country of Ephraim [E' phra im], whose name was Elkanah [El ka' nah] son of Jeroham [Je ro' ham] son of Elihu [E li' hu] son of Tohu son of Zuph, an Ephraimite. He had two wives; the name of the one was Hannah, and the name of the other Peninnah [Pe nin' nah]. Peninnah had children, but Hannah had no children.

Now this man used to go up year by year from his town to worship and to sacrifice to the Lord of Hosts at Shiloh, where the two sons of Eli, Hophni and Phinehas [Phin' e has], were priests of the Lord. On the day when Elkanah sacrificed, he would give portions to his wife Peninnah and to all her sons and daughters; but to Hannah he gave a double portion, because he loved her, though the Lord had closed her womb. Her rival used to provoke her severely, to irritate her, because the Lord had closed her womb. So it went on year by year; as often as Hannah went up to the house of the Lord, Phinehas used to provoke her. Therefore Hannah wept and would not eat. Her husband Elkanah said to her, "Hannah, why do you weep? Why do you not eat? Why is your heart sad? Am I not more to you than ten sons?"

EIGHTH WEEK OF THE YEAR
Friday
1 Samuel 1:9–20 (#2 of 4)

Just as the disciples were thought drunk in their exuberance (Acts 2:15), so too Hannah in her sorrow. Are we squeamish about strong emotion?

After they had eaten and drunk at Shiloh, Hannah rose and presented herself before the Lord. Now Eli the priest was sitting on the seat beside the doorpost of the temple of the Lord. Hannah was deeply distressed and prayed to the Lord, and wept bitterly. She made this vow: "O Lord of hosts, if only you will look on the misery of your servant, and remember me, and not forget your servant, but will give to your servant a male child, then I will set him before you as a nazirite until the day of his death. He shall drink neither wine nor intoxicants, and no razor shall touch his head."
As she continued praying before the Lord, Eli observed her mouth. Hannah was praying silently; only her lips moved, but her voice was not heard; therefore Eli thought she was drunk. So Eli said to her, "How long will you make a drunken spectacle of yourself? Put away your wine." But Hannah answered, "No, my lord, I am a woman deeply troubled; I have drunk neither wine nor strong drink, but I have been pouring out my soul before the Lord. Do not regard your servant as a worthless woman, for I have been speaking out of my great anxiety and vexation all this time." Then Eli answered, "Go in peace; the God of Israel grant the petition you have made." And she said, "Let your servant find favor in your sight." Then the woman went to her quarters, ate and drank with her husband, and her countenance was sad no longer. They rose early in the morning and worshiped before the Lord; then they went back to their house at Ramah. Elkanah knew his wife Hannah, and the Lord remembered her. In due time Hannah conceived and bore a son. She named him Samuel, for she said, "I have asked him of the Lord."

EIGHTH WEEK OF THE YEAR
Saturday
1 Samuel 1:21–28 (#3 of 4)

This reading provides an unusual glimpse of a mother's authority to decide the destiny of her son.

The man Elkanah and all his household went up to offer to the Lord the yearly sacrifice, and to pay his vow. But Hannah did not go up, for she said to her husband, "As soon as the child is weaned, I will bring him, that he may appear in the presence of the Lord, and remain there forever; I will offer him as a nazirite for all time." Her husband Elkanah said to her, "Do what seems best to you, wait until you have weaned him; only—may the Lord establish his word." So the woman remained and her son, until she weaned him. When she had weaned him, she took him up with her, along with a three-year-old bull, an ephah of flour, and a skin of wine. She brought him to the house of the Lord at Shiloh; and the child was young. Then they slaughtered the bull, and they brought the child to Eli. And she said, "Oh, my lord! As you live, my lord, I am the woman who was standing here in your presence, praying to the Lord. For this child I prayed; and the Lord has granted me the petition that I made to him. Therefore I have lent him to the Lord; as long as he lives, he is given to the Lord."

She left him there for the Lord.

NINTH SUNDAY OF THE YEAR
1 Samuel 2:1–10 (#4 of 4)

Hannah's prayer will find an echo, centuries later, in Mary's song.

Hannah prayed and said,
"My heart exults in the Lord;
    my strength is exalted in my God.

My mouth derides my enemies,
    because I rejoice in my victory.

"There is no Holy One like the Lord,
    no one besides you;
    there is no Rock like our God.
Talk no more so very proudly,
    let not arrogance come from your mouth;
for the Lord is a God of knowledge,
    and by God actions are weighed.
The bows of the mighty are broken,
    but the feeble gird on strength.
Those who were full have hired themselves out for bread,
    but those who were hungry are fat with spoil.
The barren has borne seven,
    but she who has many children is forlorn.
The Lord kills and brings to life;
    brings down to Sheol and raises up.
The Lord makes poor and makes rich;
    brings low, also exalts.
The Lord raises up the poor from the dust;
    lifts the needy from the ash heap,
to make them sit with princes
    and inherit a seat of honor.
For the pillars of the earth are the Lord's,
    and on them the Lord has set the world.

"The Lord will guard the feet of the faithful ones,
    but the wicked shall be cut off in darkness;
    for not by might does one prevail.
The Lord! The Lord's adversaries shall be shattered;
    the Most High will thunder in heaven.
The Lord will judge the ends of the earth;
    will give strength to the king,
    and exalt the power of the anointed."

NINTH WEEK OF THE YEAR
Monday
4 Maccabees 14:11–20 (#1 of 5)

What pain could be greater than that of a mother made to witness
the torture and death of her children? And yet this nameless woman
does not waver in her faith and fidelity to God.

Do not count it amazing that in Judas Maccabeus [Mac ca be′ us]
and his brothers, reason triumphed over tortures, when a woman's mind
scorned still more manifold torments; for the mother of the seven youths
endured the agonies inflicted on every one of her children. Consider how
tangled is the web of a mother's love for her children so that her whole
feeling is the profoundest inward affection for them. Even animals not
possessed of reason have an affection and love for their young similar to
that of human beings. Among the winged creatures, the tame ones shield
their young by nesting under the roofs of houses, while those that build
their nests on the peaks of mountains and in the clefts of rocks and in the
holes or tops of trees hatch their young and ward off the intruders. But if
they cannot ward them off, they flutter around about the nestlings in the
pangs of love and call to them in their own speech and assist their offspring in whatever way they can. But what need is there to demonstrate
the affection of irrational animals for their young when even the bees
fend off intruders at the season of making the honeycomb and pierce with
their sting like a sword those who molest their young, and defend them to
the death? But not even her affection for her young causes the mother of
the youths, whose soul was like Abraham's, to waver.

NINTH WEEK OF THE YEAR
Tuesday
4 Maccabees 15:1–13, 16, 17 (#2 of 5)

The mother of the seven Maccabean martyrs is remembered in this song of praise as one "who alone among women brought perfect piety to birth."

O reason that was lord over the passions of the sons! O piety that was dearer to the mother than her sons! When two options lay before her, namely piety or the instant deliverance of her seven sons according to the tyrant's promise, she loved piety better, which preserves to eternal life according to God's word. How can I possibly express the deep love of parents for their children? On the tender nature of the child, we impress a wonderful likeness of soul and form. No mother ever loved her children more than the mother of the seven sons, who in seven childbirths implanted in herself a profound affection for them; and because of the many pains she suffered in each case, was constrained to feel her bond of love with them; but on account of her fear of God, she discounted the immediate safety of her children. Indeed, because of her sons' moral heroism and their willing obedience to the Law, she cherished an even greater love for them. For they were just, and temperate, and brave, and magnanimous, and so filled with love for each other and for their mother that in obedience they kept the Law even unto death. Nevertheless, although all the many promptings of maternal love pulled the mother toward the bond of affection for them, in not a single case did their varied tortures avail to sway her reason, but each child and all of them together did the mother urge on to death for piety's sake. O sacred nature, parental love, filial affection, nurture, and unconquerable maternal affections. O mother, sorely tried now by pains sharper than the pains of birth! O woman who alone among women brought perfect piety to birth!

NINTH WEEK OF THE YEAR
Wednesday
4 Maccabees 15:24–31 (#3 of 5)

The praises of this valiant woman can be sung for thousands of other women whose bravery and faith have gone unheralded.

Although she saw the destruction of her seven children and the endlessly varied series of tortures, that noble mother of the Maccabees disregarded all of it because of her faith in God. In the council chamber of her own heart, so to speak, she saw clever advocates, nature and parenthood and maternal love and the torment of her children—a mother holding two votes in regard to her children, one to consign them to death and the other to preserve them alive; but she did not decide on the safe course that would preserve her sons for a little while, but like a true daughter of God-fearing Abraham called to mind Abraham's unflinching bravery. O mother of the nation, champion of the Law, defender of true religion, and winner of the prize in the inward contest of the heart! More noble in fortitude and stronger than heroes in endurance! Like the ark of Noah, carrying the universe in the worldwide cataclysm and stoutly enduring the waves (Gen 6:5–8:22), so did you, guardian of the Law, buffeted on every side in the flood of the passions and by the mighty gales of your sons' torments, so did you by your perseverance nobly weather the storms that assailed you for religion's sake.

NINTH WEEK OF THE YEAR
Thursday
4 Maccabees 16:1–4, 12–25 (#4 of 5)

Mother of seven martyred sons, she is praised in Jewish tradition as "mother," "soldier," "elder," "brave woman."

If then, indeed, a woman of advanced years, the mother of seven sons, held out while looking upon her children being tortured to death, we must concede that devout reason is sovereign over the passions. I have therefore demonstrated that not only men have conquered human passions, but that a woman also despised the greatest torments. Not so wild were the lions around Daniel (Dan 6), not so blazing hot in its greedy flame was the furnace of Mishael [Mish' a el] (Dan 3) as the natural mother's love that burned in her when she saw her seven sons so indiscriminately tortured. But by pious reason, the mother quenched all these fiery emotions.

But the holy and God-fearing mother lamented none of them, nor urged any of them to avoid death, nor grieved over them in the moment of their death. Rather, as though she had a mind of adamant and were this time to bring her brood of sons to birth into immortal life, she encouraged them and pleaded with them to die for piety's sake. Mother, soldier of God in piety's cause, elder and woman! By your brave endurance, you have overcome even the tyrant and in deeds, as in words, have proven yourself strong. When you were seized along with your sons, you stood watching Eleazar [El e a' zar] under torture and said to your children in the Hebrew tongue, "My children, noble is the struggle, and since you have been summoned to it to bear witness for our nation, fight zealously for our ancestral Law. Shameful was it indeed that this old man should endure agonies for piety's sake, while you young men were terrified of torments. Remember, that it is for God's sake you were given a share in the world and the benefit of life, and, accordingly, you owe it to God to endure all hardship for God's sake, for whom our father Abraham ventured boldly to sacrifice his son Isaac, the father of our nation; and Isaac, seeing his father's hand, with knife in it, fall down against him, did not flinch (Gen 22:10). Daniel also, the righteous one, was thrown to the lions and Hananiah [Han a ni' ah] and Azariah [Az a ri' ah] and Mishael [Mish' a el] were cast into the fiery furnace, and all endured for the sake of God. Therefore, you who have the same faith in God must not be dismayed. For it would be unreasonable for you who know true religion not to withstand hardships."

With these words the mother of the seven exhorted each one and persuaded them to die rather than transgress the commandment of God, and they knew full well themselves that those who die for the sake of God live unto God (Ex 3:6; Mk 12:26f).

NINTH WEEK OF THE YEAR
Friday
4 Maccabees 17:1–6 (#5 of 5)

The mother of seven martyred sons herself meets death, the way to victory. "Not so majestic stands the moon in heaven as you stand. . . ."

Some of the guards declared that when she, too, was about to be seized and put to death, she threw herself into the fire so that no one would touch her body (2 Macc 7:41). O mother with the seven sons, who broke down the violence of the tyrant and thwarted his wicked devices and exhibited the nobility of faith! Nobly set like a roof upon the pillars of your children, you sustained, without yielding, the earthquake of the tortures. Be of good cheer, therefore, mother of holy soul, whose hope of endurance is secure with God. Not so majestic stands the moon in heaven as you stand, lighting the way to piety for your seven starlike sons (Test Job 39:9–40:5), honored by God and firmly set with them in heaven.

NINTH WEEK OF THE YEAR
Saturday
Epiphanius, *Medicine Box* 48.2.4; 12.4; 13.1; 49.1.3; Eusebius, *Ecclesiastical History* 5.16.17

These prophetic oracles of the second century Montanist prophets, Maximilla and Priscilla, as preserved in these fourth century sources, are actual quotations attributed to the prophets themselves during prophetic ecstasy.

"After me, there will be no more prophet, but the consummation. Listen not to me; but to Christ who speaks through me. The Lord has sent me as partisan, informer, and interpreter of this burden of the covenant and of the promise; I am compelled, whether willingly or unwillingly, to learn the knowledge of God."

"In a vision, Christ came to me in the form of a woman in a bright garment, endowed me with wisdom and revealed to me that this place is holy, and it is here that Jerusalem is to descend from heaven."

"I am driven like a wolf from the sheep. I am not a wolf. I am Word and Spirit and Power."

TENTH SUNDAY OF THE YEAR
Luke 7:11-16a

A widow was vulnerable in a patriarchal society and even more so if she lost her only son. Jesus had compassion on the widow of Nain and, transgressing the laws of ritual purity, restored her child to life—the first person Jesus raised from the dead.

Jesus went to a town called Nain, and his disciples and a large crowd went with him. As he approached the gate of the town, a man who had died was being carried out. He was his mother's only son, and she was a widow; and with her was a large crowd from the town. When the Lord saw her, he had compassion for her and said to her, "Do not weep." Then he came forward and touched the bier, and the bearers stood still. And he said, "Young man, I say to you, rise!" The dead man sat up and began to speak, and Jesus gave him to his mother. Fear seized all of them; and they glorified God, saying, "A great prophet has risen among us!"

See 1 Kings 17:17-24

TENTH WEEK OF THE YEAR
Monday
Epiphanius, *Medicine Box* 79

A fourth century Christian writer tells, in more detail, a story also reported elsewhere more briefly [see reading for Octave of Christmas], about women in Arabia who conduct their own liturgical service in honor of Mary. The author's ridicule betrays his threatened feelings. We know nothing more about this custom.

There is a heresy taken up in Arabia from Thrace and the upper parts of Scythia [Scyth' i a] that has come to our attention. It is quite a ridiculous joke to those who know better, for it will be thought of as silly rather than intelligent, just like others similar to it. Because of an insulting attitude regarding Mary, some sow harmful fantasies in human minds by many conjectures; so too these who incline to the opposite extreme are seized by such consummate foolhardiness. Thus what is sung about by some outside (i.e., pagan) philosophers is fulfilled in them, namely, "opposite extremes are just as bad." The harm is equal in both these heresies, of those who disparage the holy Virgin, and of those who glorify her beyond what is proper. Are not those who teach this merely women? The female sex is easily mistaken, fallible, and poor in intelligence. It is apparent that through women the devil has vomited this forth. Just as the teaching associated with Quintilla [Quin til' la], Maximilla [Max i mil' la], and Priscilla [Pri scil' la] was utterly ridiculous, so also is this one. For some women prepare a certain kind of little cake with four indentations, cover it with a fine linen veil on a solemn day of the year, and on certain days they set forth bread and offer it in the name of Mary. They all partake of the bread; this is part of what we refuted in the letter written to Arabia. But now we shall clearly set forth everything about it and the refutations against it, and beseeching God, we will give an explanation to the best of our ability, so that by cutting of the roots of this idol-making heresy we may be able, in God, to destroy such madness.

TENTH WEEK OF THE YEAR
Tuesday
1 Kings 17:7–16 (#1 of 2)

Jesus reminded his hearers that in the midst of famine Elijah was sent to this Phoenician widow rather than to a widow of Israel to secure food (Lk 4:25–26). Her faith and acceptance of the prophet stand in stark contrast to Israel's rejection of the prophets, and she was rewarded with two miracles.

The Wadi Cherith [Che' rith] dried up because there was no rain in the land. Then the word of the Lord came to Elijah, saying, "Go now to Zarephath [Zar' e phath], which belongs to Sidon, and live there; for I have commanded a widow there to feed you." So he set out and went to Zarephath. When he came to the gate of the town, a widow was there gathering sticks; he called to her and said, "Bring me a little water in a vessel, so that I may drink." As she was going to bring it, he called to her and said, "Bring me a morsel of bread in your hand." But she said, "As the Lord your God lives, I have nothing baked, only a handful of meal in a jar, and a little oil in a jug; I am now gathering a couple of sticks, so that I may go home and prepare it for myself and my son, that we may eat it, and die." Elijah said to her, "Do not be afraid; go and do as you have said; but first make me a little cake of it and bring it to me, and afterwards make something for yourself and your son. For thus says the Lord, the God of Israel: The jar of meal will not be emptied and the jug of oil will not fail until the day that the Lord sends rain on the earth." She went and did as Elijah said, so that she as well as he and her household ate for many days. The jar of meal was not emptied; neither did the jug of oil fail, according to the word of the Lord that he spoke by Elijah.

TENTH WEEK OF THE YEAR
Wednesday
1 Kings 17:17–24 (#2 of 2)

Through the intervention of Elijah, God's compassion is extended to a widow who is bold enough to question God's way.

The son of the woman, the mistress of the house where Elijah was staying, became ill; his illness was so severe that there was no breath left in him. She then said to Elijah, "What have you against me, O man of God? You have come to me to bring my sin to remembrance, and to cause the death of my son!" But he said to her, "Give me your son." He took him from her bosom, carried him up into the upper chamber where he was lodging, and laid him on his own bed. He cried out to the Lord, "O Lord, my God, have you brought calamity even upon the widow with whom I am staying, by killing her son?" Then he stretched himself upon the child three times, and cried out to the Lord, "O Lord my God, let this child's life come into him again." The Lord listened to the voice of Elijah; the life of the child came into him again, and he revived. Elijah took the child, brought him down from the upper chamber into the house, and gave him to his mother; then Elijah said, "See, your son is alive." So the woman said to Elijah, "Now I know that you are a man of God, and that the word of the Lord in your mouth is truth."

TENTH WEEK OF THE YEAR
Thursday
Acts of Peter 6:17 (#1 of 2)

Eubula, a wealthy and independent woman, is challenged by Peter to leave possessions behind and to devote herself wholeheartedly to the Lord Jesus Christ.

Peter stayed in Judea with a woman named Eubula [Eu bu' la], a woman of some distinction in this world, who possessed much gold and pearls of no little value. Simon [Magus] stole into her house with two others like himself; though none of the household saw these two, but only Simon; and by means of a spell they took away all the woman's gold and disappeared. But Eubula discovering this crime began to torture her household, saying, "You took advantage of the visit of this godly man and have robbed me, because you saw him coming in to me to do honor to a simple woman; but his name is 'the power of the Lord.'"

Peter came to Eubula and found her sitting and lamenting with her clothes torn and her hair in disorder. He said to her, "Eubula, rise up from your bed and compose your face, put up your hair and put on a dress that becomes you, and pray to the Lord Jesus Christ who judges every soul. In him you must be saved, if indeed you repent with all your heart of your former sins. And receive power from him; for now the Lord says to you through me, 'All that you have lost you shall find.' And when you have received them, be sure that you find yourself, so as to renounce this present world and seek for everlasting refreshment."

See Mark 8:36

TENTH WEEK OF THE YEAR
Friday
Acts of Peter 6:17 (#2 of 2)

Unlike the rich young man of the gospel tradition (Mk 10:17–31),
Eubula forsakes her wealth in favor of a life dedicated to the Lord.

Peter left Eubula and went with two of her stewards, and came to Agrippinus [Ag rip pi' nus] and said to him, "Make sure that you take not of these men. For tomorrow two young men will come to you, wishing to sell you a young satyr in gold set with stones, which belongs to the mistress of these men. So you are to take it as if to inspect it and to admire its workmanship. Afterwards these men will come in; then God shall bring the rest to the proof." And on the next day the lady's stewards came about the ninth hour, and also those young men, wishing to sell Agrippinus the golden satyr; and at once they were seized, and word was sent to the lady. But she, in great distress of mind, went to the magistrate, and loudly declared what had happened to her. And when the magistrate Pompeius [Pom pe' ius] saw her so distressed, whereas she had never before come out in public, he immediately rose up from the bench and went to the guardroom and ordered them to be produced and examined. And they, under torture, confessed that they were acting as Simon's [Magus] agents—"who gave us money to do it." And when tortured further they confessed that all that Eubula had lost had been put underground in a cave outside the gate, and more besides. When Pompeius heard this, he got up to go to the gate, having those two men bound with two chains each. And there!—Simon came in at the gate, looking for them because they had been so long; and he saw a great crowd coming, and those men held fast in chains. At once he realized what had happened and took to flight, and has not been seen in Judea until this day. But Eubula having recovered all her property gave it for the care of the poor; she believed in the Lord Jesus Christ and was strengthened in the faith; and despising and renouncing this world she gave alms to the widows and orphans and clothed the poor; and after a long time she gained her repose. Now these things were done in Judea; and so he came to be expelled from there, who is called the messenger of Satan.

TENTH WEEK OF THE YEAR
Saturday
1 Kings 21:1–11, 14–16

Jezebel will stop at nothing to satisfy herself or to prop up her husband's regime

Naboth the Jezreelite [Jez' re el ite] had a vineyard in Jezreel [Jez' re el], beside the palace of King Ahab of Samaria. And Ahab said to Naboth, "Give me your vineyard, so that I may have it for a vegetable garden, because it is near my house; I will give you a better vineyard for it; or, if it seems good to you, I will give you its value in money." But Naboth said to Ahab, "The Lord forbid that I should give you my ancestral inheritance." Ahab went home resentful and sullen because of what Naboth the

Jezreelite had said to him; for he had said, "I will not give you my ancestral inheritance." He lay down on his bed, turned away his face, and would not eat.

His wife Jezebel [Jez' e bel] came to him and said, "Why are you so depressed that you will not eat?" He said to her, "Because I spoke to Naboth the Jezreelite and said to him, 'Give me your vineyard for money; or else, if you prefer, I will give you another vineyard for it'; but he answered, 'I will not give you my vineyard.'" His wife Jezebel said to him, "Do you now govern Israel? Get up, eat some food, and be cheerful; I will give you the vineyard of Naboth, the Jezreelite."

So she wrote letters in Ahab's name and sealed them with his seal; she sent the letters to the elders and the nobles who lived with Naboth in his city. She wrote in the letters, "Proclaim a fast, and seat Naboth at the head of the assembly; seat two scoundrels opposite him, and have them bring a charge against him, saying, 'You have cursed God and the king.' Then take him out, and stone him to death." The men of his city, the elders and the nobles who lived in his city, did as Jezebel had sent word to them, just as it was written in the letters that she had sent to them. Then they sent to Jezebel, saying, "Naboth has been stoned; he is dead."

As soon as Jezebel heard that Naboth had been stoned and was dead, Jezebel said to Ahab, "Go, take possession of the vineyard of Naboth the Jezreelite, which he refused to give you for money; for Naboth is not alive, but dead." As soon as Ahab heard that Naboth was dead, Ahab set out to go down to the vineyard of Naboth the Jezreelite, to take possession of it.

ELEVENTH SUNDAY OF THE YEAR
Luke 7:36–50

This is a story which contrasts religious self-righteousness and generous, self-giving love. Of the woman with ointment who crashes Simon's dinner party, Jesus declares: her great love proves that her sins have been forgiven. This woman should not be confused with the report about Mary Magdalene in Luke 8:1–3.

One of the Pharisees asked Jesus to eat with him, and he went into the Pharisee's house and took his place at the table. And a woman in the city, who was a sinner, having learned that he was eating in the Pharisee's house, brought an alabaster jar of ointment. She stood behind him at his feet, weeping, and began to bathe his feet with her tears and to dry them with her hair. Then she continued kissing his feet and anointing them with the ointment. Now when the Pharisee who had invited him saw it, he said to himself, "If this man were a prophet, he would have known who and what kind of woman this is who is touching him—that she is a sinner." Jesus spoke up and said to him, "Simon, I have something to say to you." "Teacher," he replied, "speak." "A certain creditor had two debtors; one owed five hundred denarii, and the other fifty. When they could not pay, he canceled the debts for both of them. Now which of them will love him more?" Simon answered, "I suppose the one for whom he canceled the greater debt." And Jesus said to him, "You have judged rightly." Then turning toward the woman, he said to Simon, "Do you see this woman? I entered your house; you gave me no water for my feet, but she has bathed my feet with her tears and dried them with her hair. You gave me no kiss, but from the time I came in, she has not stopped kissing my feet. You did not anoint my head with oil, but she has anointed my feet with ointment. Therefore, I tell you, her sins, which were many, have been forgiven; hence she has shown great love. But the one to whom little is forgiven, loves little." Then he said to her, "Your sins are forgiven." But those who were at the table with him began to say among themselves, "Who is this who even forgives sins?" And he said to the woman, "Your faith has saved you; go in peace."

ELEVENTH WEEK OF THE YEAR
Monday
Gregory of Nyssa, *Life of Macrina* (#1 of 12)

Gregory writes to a friend after the death of his elder sister, Macrina, to give an account of her holy life and how much she meant to him. Here he recounts Macrina's childhood under the patronage of St. Thecla. (See readings for 18th and 19th Weeks of the Year.)

We did not have to rely on hearsay since experience was our teacher, and the details of our story did not depend on the testimony of others. The maiden we spoke of was no stranger to my family so that I did not have to learn the wondrous facts about her from others; we were born of the same parents, she being, as it were, an offering of first fruits, the earliest flowering of our mother's womb.

The maiden's name was Macrina [Ma cri'na]. She had been given this name by her parents in memory of a remarkable Macrina earlier in the family, our father's mother, who had distinguished herself in the confession of Christ at the time of the persecutions. This was her official name which her acquaintances used, but she had been given another secretly in connection with a vision which occurred before she came into the light at birth. Her mother was extremely virtuous, following the will of God in all things. However, since she was an orphan and flowering in the springtime of her beauty, and the fame of her loveliness had attracted many suitors, there was danger that, if she were not joined to someone by choice, she might suffer some unwished-for violence, because some of the suitors, maddened by her beauty, were preparing to carry her off. For this reason, she chose a man well known and recommended for the dignity of his life, and thus she acquired a guardian for her own life. In her first pregnancy, she became Macrina's mother. When the time came in which she was to be freed from her pain by giving birth to the child, she fell asleep and seemed to be holding in her hands the child still in her womb, and a person of greater than human shape and form appeared to be addressing the infant by the name of Thecla. (There was a Thecla of much fame among virgins.) After doing this and invoking her as a witness three times, he disappeared from sight and gave ease to her pain so that, as she awoke from her sleep, she saw the dream realized. This, then, was her secret name. It seems to me that the one who appeared was not so much indicating how the child should be named, but foretelling the life of the child and intimating that she would choose a life similar to that of her namesake.

ELEVENTH WEEK OF THE YEAR
Tuesday
Gregory of Nyssa, *Life of Macrina* (#2 of 12)

Macrina's early education was centered on scripture. The marriage planned for her by her father was thwarted by the tragic death of her betrothed.

So the child grew, nursed chiefly by her mother, although she had a nurse of her own. Upon leaving infancy, she was quick to learn what children learn, and to whatever learning the judgment of her parents directed her, the little one's nature responded brilliantly. Her mother was eager to have the child given instruction, but not in the secular curriculum, which meant, for the most part, teaching the youngsters through poetry. Instead of this, whatever of inspired scripture was adaptable to the early years, this was the child's subject matter, especially the Wisdom of Solomon and, beyond this, whatever leads us to a moral life. She was especially well versed in the Psalms, going through each part of the psalter at the proper time; when she got up or did her daily tasks or rested, when she sat down to eat or rose from the table, when she went to bed or rose from it for prayer, she had the psalter with her at all times, like a good and faithful traveling companion.

Growing up with these and similar pursuits and becoming extraordinarily skilled in the working of wool, she came to her twelfth year in which the flowering of youth begins especially to shine forth. Here, it is worth marveling at how the young girl's beauty did not escape notice, although it had been concealed. Nor did there seem to be anything in all that country comparable to her beauty and her loveliness, so that the hand of the painters could not reproduce its perfection, and the art that devises all things and dares the greatest things, even to the fashioning of planets through imitation, was not powerful enough to imitate the excellence of her form. Consequently, a great stream of suitors for her hand crowded round her parents. Her father (he was wise and considered outstanding in his judgment of what was good) singled out from the rest a young man in the family known for his moderation, who had recently finished school, and he decided to give his daughter to him when she came of age. During this period, the young man showed great promise and brought to the girl's father (as a cherished bridal gift, as it were) his reputation as an orator, displaying his rhetorical skill in lawsuits in defense of the wronged. But envy cut short this bright promise by snatching him from life in his piteous youth.

ELEVENTH WEEK OF THE YEAR
Wednesday
Gregory of Nyssa, *Life of Macrina* (#3 of 12)

Macrina resolves not to marry, but to remain with her mother in order to assist her.

The girl was not unaware of what her father had decided, and when the young man's death broke off what had been planned for her, she called her father's decision a marriage on the grounds that what had been decided had actually taken place and she determined to spend the rest of her life by herself; and her decision was more firmly fixed than her age would have warranted. When her parents talked of marriage (many men wanted to marry her on account of the reputation of her beauty), she used to say that it was out of place and unlawful not to accept once and for all a marriage determined for her by her father and to be forced to look to another, since marriage is by nature unique, as are birth and death. She insisted that the young man joined to her by her parent's decision was not dead, but living in God because of the hope of the resurrection, merely off on a journey and not a dead body, and it was out of place, she maintained, for a bride not to keep faith with an absent husband. Thrusting aside the arguments of those trying to persuade her, she settled upon a safeguard for her noble decision, namely, a resolve never to be separated for a moment from her mother, so that her mother often used to say to her that the rest of her children she had carried in her womb for a fixed time, but this daughter she always bore, encompassing her in her womb at all times and under all circumstances. Certainly, the companionship of her daughter was not burdensome or disadvantageous for the mother, because the care she received from her daughter surpassed that of many of her maidservants and there was an exchange of kindly offices between them. The older woman cared for the young woman's soul and the daughter for her mother's body, fulfilling in all things every desirable service, often even making bread for her mother with her own hands. Not that this was her principal concern, but when she had anointed her hands with mystic services, thinking that it was in keeping with her way of life, in the remaining time she furnished food for her mother from her own labor, and, in addition, she shared her mother's worries. Her mother had four sons and five daughters and was paying taxes to three governors because her property was scattered over that many provinces.

ELEVENTH WEEK OF THE YEAR
Thursday
Gregory of Nyssa, *Life of Macrina* (#4 of 12)

Macrina converts her brother Basil the Great and her mother to a life of "philosophy," that is, to asceticism and contemplation.

In a variety of ways, her mother was distracted by worries. (By this time her father had left this life.) In all of these affairs, Macrina was a sharer of her mother's toils, taking on part of her cares and lightening the heaviness of her griefs. In addition, under her mother's direction, she kept her life blameless and witnessed in everything by her, and, at the same time, because of her own life, she provided her mother with an impressive leadership to the same goal; I speak of the goal of philosophy, drawing her on little by little to the immaterial and simpler life. After the mother had skillfully arranged what seemed best for each of Macrina's sisters, her brother, the distinguished Basil [the Great], came home from school where he had had practice in rhetoric for a long time. He was excessively puffed up by his rhetorical abilities and disdainful of all great reputations, and considered himself better than the leading men in the district, but Macrina took him over and lured him so quickly to the goal of philosophy that he withdrew from the worldly show and began to look down upon acclaim through oratory and went over to this life full of labors for one's own hand to perform, providing for himself, through his complete poverty, a mode of living that would, without impediment, lead to virtue. But his life and the outstanding activities, through which he became famous everywhere under the sun and eclipsed in reputation all those conspicuous in virtue, would make a long treatise and take much time, and my attention must be turned back to the subject at hand. When there was no longer any necessity for them to continue their rather worldly way of life, Macrina persuaded her mother to give up her customary mode of living and her more ostentatious existence and the services of her maids, to which she had long been accustomed, and to put herself on a level with the many by entering into a common life with her maids, making them her sisters and equals, rather than her slaves and underlings.

ELEVENTH WEEK OF THE YEAR
Friday
Gregory of Nyssa, *Life of Macrina* (#5 of 12)

Macrina had already been the strongest person in the family, directing her brother Basil, her mother and likewise her youngest brother Peter to the contemplative life. This reading recounts the blessing given Macrina and Peter by their mother on her deathbed.

Macrina had a brother who was a great help towards this fine goal of life; he was named Peter and he was the youngest of us, the last offspring of our parents called at once both son and orphan, for, as he came into the light of life, his father departed from it. His eldest sister, the subject of our story, took him almost immediately from his nurse's breast and reared him herself and led him to all the higher education, exercising him from babyhood in sacred learning so as not to give him leisure to incline his soul to vanities. So, scorning extraneous instructions and having nature as an adequate teacher of all good learning, and always looking to his sister and making her the focal point of every good, he became so virtuous that he was no less esteemed than the great Basil for the excellent qualities of his later life. But then, he was above all a co-worker with his sister and mother in every phase of their angelic existence. Once, when there was a terrible famine and many people came pouring in to our region because of the fame of its prosperity, he furnished so much nourishment through his foresight that the large numbers going to and fro made the hermitage seem like a city.

At this time, our mother, having come to a rich old age, went to God, taking her departure from life in the arms of these two of her children. Worth recording is the blessing she gave to each of her children, suitably remembering each of the absent ones so that none would be without a blessing, and, through prayer, entrusting especially to God the two who were with her. As they were sitting beside her bed, she touched each of them with her hand and said to God in her last words: "To you, O Lord, I offer the first and tenth fruit of my pains. The first fruit, my eldest daughter here, and this my tenth, my last-born son. Both have been dedicated to you by law and are your votive offering. May sanctification, therefore, come to this first and tenth." And she indicated specifically her daughter and her son. Having finished her blessing, she ended her life, instructing her children to place her body in our father's tomb. These two, having fulfilled her command, attained to a higher level of philosophy, always struggling in their individual lives and eclipsing their early successes by their later ones.

ELEVENTH WEEK OF THE YEAR
Saturday
Gregory of Nyssa, *Life of Macrina* (#6 of 12)

Macrina shows her courage in the face of many family deaths, especially that of her brother Basil the Great, who died unexpectedly before the age of fifty.

At this time, Basil, distinguished among the holy, was made bishop of Caesarea [Caes a re' a]. He led his brother [Gregory of Nyssa, the narrator] to the holy vocation of the priesthood, and consecrated him in the mystical services himself. Eight years later, Basil, renowned throughout the entire world, left the mortal world and went to God, and his death was a common source of grief for his country and the world. When Macrina heard the report of his distant death, she was greatly disturbed by such a loss. (How could this fail to touch her when even the enemies of truth were affected by it?) But, just as they say gold is tested in many furnaces, something similar happened in her case. When her lofty understanding had been tried by the different attacks of grief, the genuine and undebased quality of her soul was revealed in every way; previously, by the departure of her other brother, then, by the separation from her mother, and in the third instance, when Basil, the common honor of the family, departed from human life. She remained like an undefeated athlete, in no way overcome by the onslaught of misfortunes.

TWELFTH SUNDAY OF THE YEAR
Proverbs 9:1-6

Wisdom loves to throw a dinner party.

Wisdom has built her house,
    she has hewn her seven pillars.
She has slaughtered her animals, she has mixed her wine,
    she has also set her table.
She has sent out her servant girls, she calls
    from the highest places in the town,
"You that are simple, turn in here!"
    To those without sense she says,
"Come, eat of my bread
    and drink of the wine I have mixed.
Lay aside immaturity, and live,
    and walk in the way of insight."

TWELFTH WEEK OF THE YEAR
Monday
Gregory of Nyssa, *Life of Macrina* (#7 of 12)

Gregory visits his sister Macrina after eight years, only to find her dying. Even so, he is deeply impressed by her spiritual freedom and by her ability to lift his spirits as well.

About nine months after this disaster [the death of their brother, Basil the Great], there was a synod of bishops in the city of Antioch, in which I participated. And when each of us was leaving to return to his own diocese before the year was out, I, Gregory, thought often of visiting Macrina. For a long time had elapsed during which the circumstances of my trials had prevented our coming together, since I was exiled time and again by the leaders of heresy. When I counted up the time during which these troubles prevented our coming face to face, it added up to almost eight years. As I made my way (rumor had announced my presence beforehand to the community), a line of men streamed toward us. It was customary for them to welcome guests by coming out to meet them. However, a group of women from the convent waited modestly at the entrance of the church for us.

An attendant led me to the house where the superior was and opened the door, and I entered that sacred place. She was already very ill, but she was not resting on a couch or bed, but upon the ground; there was a board covered with a coarse cloth, and another board supported her head. When she saw me standing at the door, she raised herself on her elbow; her strength was already so wasted by fever that she was not able to come towards me, but she fixed her hands on the floor and, stretching as far forward as she could, she paid me the honor of a bow. I ran to her and, lifting her bowed head, I put her back in her accustomed reclining position. But she stretched out her hand to God and said, "You have granted me this favor, O God, and have not deprived me of my desire, since you have impelled your servant to visit your handmaid." And in order not to disturb me, she tried to cover up her groans and to conceal somehow the difficulty she had in breathing, and, through it all, she adjusted herself to the brighter side. She initiated suitable topics of conversation and gave me an opportunity to speak by asking me questions. As we spoke, we recalled the memory of the great Basil and my soul was afflicted and my face fell and tears poured from my eyes. But she was so far from being downcast by our sorrow that she made the mentioning of the saint a starting point towards the higher philosophy. She rehearsed such arguments, explaining the human situation through natural principles and disclosing the divine plan hidden in misfortune, and she spoke of certain aspects of the future life as if she was inspired by the Holy Spirit, so that my soul almost seemed to be lifted up out of its human sphere by what she said and, under the direction of her discourse, take its stand in the heavenly sanctuaries.

TWELFTH WEEK OF THE YEAR
Tuesday
Gregory of Nyssa, *Life of Macrina* (#8 of 12)

Macrina, on her deathbed, shares with her brother her recollections of her life and of their family.

When the conversation was finished, she said, "Now, brother, it is time for you to rest your body awhile because the trip must have been tiring." For me, just seeing her and hearing her noble words was truly a great source of relaxation, but, since it was pleasing and desirable to her, in order to seem obedient to her as my teacher in all things, I found a pleasant resting place in one of the gardens nearby and rested in the shade of the vine-clad trees. However, I was unable to enjoy myself because my soul was overwhelmed by the anticipation of sorrows. Guessing, I know not how, that we were dejected by the grief that was to come, Macrina sent a message bidding us to cheer up and to be more hopeful about her condition for she perceived a turn for the better. This was not said to deceive us, but was actually the truth, although we did not recognize it at the time.

Reassured by this message, we began to enjoy what was put before us and the offerings were varied and pleasurable since the great lady was very thoughtful also in such matters. When we returned to her presence (for she did not allow us to idle away the time by ourselves), she took up the story of her life from infancy as if she were putting it all into a monograph. She told what she remembered of our parents' life, both what happened before my birth and afterwards. What she concentrated on in her story was thanksgiving to God, for what she stressed in the life of our parents was not so much their being outstanding among their contemporaries because of their prosperity, but their having been enhanced by divine favor. Our father's parents had been deprived of their possessions because of the confession of Christ; our mother's grandfather was killed by the anger of the emperor and all his property handed over to other masters. Nevertheless, their life was so exalted on account of their faith that no one had a greater reputation among the people of that time. Later, when their property was divided nine ways in accordance with the number of the children, the share of each had been so bountifully increased that the children lived more prosperously than their parents. Macrina did not accept the amount that was assigned to her in the equal distribution, but gave it all into the hands of the priest in accordance with the divine command. By divine dispensation, her existence was such that she never stopped using her hands in the service of God, nor did she look to people for help or any opportunity for living a life of comfort. She never turned away anyone who asked for something, nor did she look for benefactors, but God, in blessing her, secretly made her little resources of activity grow as seeds, as it were, into a full-flowering harvest.

TWELFTH WEEK OF THE YEAR
Wednesday
Gregory of Nyssa, *Life of Macrina* (#9 of 12)

While her brother Gregory keeps vigil, the dying Macrina prays her final prayer.

As she went, I kept wishing that the day might be lengthened so that we could continue to enjoy the sweetness of her words. But the sound of the choir was calling us to vespers and, having sent me off to the church, the Superior withdrew to God in prayer and the night was devoted to it. When dawn came, it was clear to me that this day was to be the last for her in the life of the flesh, for the fever had consumed all her natural strength. When she saw our concern about her weakness, she tried to rouse us from our downcast hopes by dispersing again with her beautiful words the grief of our souls with her last slight and labored breathing. At this point, especially, my soul was in conflict because of what it was confronted by.

The day was almost over and the sun was beginning to set, but the zeal in her did not decline. Indeed, as she neared her end and saw the beauty of the Bridegroom more clearly, she rushed with greater impulse towards the One she desired, no longer speaking to those of us who were present, but to that very One toward whom she looked with steadfast eyes. Her couch was turned to the East and, stopping her conversation with us, for the rest of the time she addressed herself to God in prayer.

She said, "O Lord, You have freed us from the fear of death; You have made the end of life here the beginning of a true life for us. For a time, You give rest to our bodies in sleep and You awaken us again with the last trumpet. O God everlasting, towards whom I have directed myself from my mother's womb, whom my soul has loved with all its strength, to whom I have dedicated my body and my soul from my infancy up to now, prepare for me a shining angel to lead me to the place of refreshment where is the water of relaxation near the bosom of the holy ones. You who broke the flaming sword and compassionately gave Paradise back to the man crucified with You, remember me also in Your kingdom, for I, too, have been crucified with You, having nailed my flesh through fear of You and having feared Your judgments. Let the terrible abyss not separate me from Your chosen ones; let the Slanderer not stand in my way or my sins be discovered before Your eyes if I have fallen and sinned in word or deed or thought because of the weakness of our nature. Do You who have power on earth to forgive sins forgive me so that I may be refreshed and may be found before You once I have put off my body, having no fault in the form of my soul, but blameless and spotless may my soul be taken into Your hands as an offering before Your face." As she said this, she made the sign of the cross upon her eyes and mouth and heart, and little by little, as the fever dried up her tongue, she was no longer able to speak clearly; her voice gave out and only from the trembling of her lips and the motion of her hands did we know that she was continuing to pray.

TWELFTH WEEK OF THE YEAR
Thursday
Gregory of Nyssa, *Life of Macrina* (#10 of 12)

With the end of the evening prayer, Macrina's life ends. Gregory carries out the family duty, usually done by a child of the deceased, to close her eyes with his own hand, as she had requested.

Evening came on and the lamp was brought in. Macrina directed her eyes toward the beam of light and made it clear that she was eager to say the nocturnal prayer and, although her voice failed her, with her heart and the movement of her hands, she fulfilled her desire and moved her lips in keeping with the impulse within her. When she had completed the thanksgiving and indicated that the prayer was over by making the sign of the cross, she breathed a deep breath and with the prayer her life came to an end. From then on, she was without breath and movement, and I recalled an injunction she had given me when I arrived, saying that she wanted my hands to be placed upon her eyes and the customary care of the body to be taken by me. So I placed my hand, deadened by grief, upon her holy face so as not to seem to disregard her request. Actually her eyes required no attention; it was as if she was asleep with her eyelids becomingly lowered; her lips were set naturally and her hands rested naturally on her breast and the whole position of her body was so spontaneously harmonious that there was no need for any arranging hand.

My soul was disquieted for two reasons, because of what I saw and because I heard the weeping of the virgins. Until now, they had controlled themselves and kept in check the grief in their souls and they had choked down the impulse to cry out for fear of her, as if they were afraid of the reproach of her voice already silent; lest, contrary to her order, a sound should break forth from them and their teacher be troubled by it. But when their suffering could no longer be controlled in silence (their grief was affecting their souls like a consuming fire within them), suddenly, a bitter, unrestrained cry broke forth, so that my reason no longer maintained itself, but, like a mountain stream overflowing, it was overwhelmed below the surface by my suffering and, disregarding the tasks at hand, I gave myself over wholly to lamentation.

TWELFTH WEEK OF THE YEAR
Friday
Gregory of Nyssa, *Life of Macrina* (#11 of 12)

Gregory and two of Macrina's disciples prepare her body for burial. Her poverty was such that there was no good dress to bury her in, but Gregory had acquired a fine linen dress for her funeral. He and the deaconess Lampadium from Macrina's monastery divide her cross and ring.

Among Macrina's followers there was a woman outstanding for her wealth and birth and the beauty of her body, and admired in her youth for her other attributes. She had been married to a distinguished man and, after having been with him for a short time, she was released from marriage while still quite young. She made Macrina the guardian and director of her widowhood, and, spending much of her time with the women, she learned from them the life of virtue. The woman's name was Vetiana [Ve ti a' na], whose father was Araxius [A rax' i us], one of the senators. I told her that now, at least, it was suitable to put brighter raiment on the body and to adorn with shining ornament that pure and unsullied flesh. She replied that it was necessary to learn what decisions had been made by the holy one about these matters, for it would not be right for us to do anything to her contrary to what would be pleasing to her. But what was dear and pleasing to God was also desirable to her.

There was a certain woman, a deaconess in charge of a group of the women, whose name was Lampadium [Lam pa' di um], and she said she knew exactly what Macrina had decided about her burial. When I asked her about it (for she happened to be present at our discussion) she replied weeping, "For the holy one, the pure life was what she sought as adornment; for her, this was both the ornament of her life and the shroud of death. She had so little concern for dress that she owned nothing during her lifetime and stored none away for the present situation, so that, even if we desired it, there is nothing more to use than what is already here." I said, "Is there nothing in the storage closets to decorate the funeral bier?" "What closets?" she replied. "You have everything she possessed in your hands. Look at her dress, look at the covering of her head, her worn sandals. This is her wealth, this is her property. There is nothing beyond what you see put aside in hidden places or made secure in treasure houses. She recognized one storage place for private wealth: the treasury of heaven. There she deposited everything and left nothing behind on earth." I said to her, "What if I brought some of the things I had got ready for the funeral? Would this be against her wish?" She replied that she did not think it would be. "For," she said, "if she were alive, she would accept such a gift from you for two reasons: on account of your priesthood, which she always honored, and, on account of your kinship, she would not have thought that what belonged to her brother was not also hers. It was for this reason that she ordered her body to be prepared by your hands."

When this was decided upon and it was necessary for the sacred body to be dressed in fine linen, we divided the various tasks among us. I told one of my attendants to bring in the robe. Vetiana, whom I have mentioned before, was arranging that holy head with her own hands when she put her hand on her neck and said looking at me, "See the necklace the holy one wore." And, at the same time, she unfastened the chain, stretched out her hand, and showed me an iron cross and a ring of the same material. Both of these worn on a thin chain were always on her heart. And I said, "Let us make this a common possession. You take the protection of the cross, and the ring will be enough for me," for on the seal of the ring a cross was carved. Gazing at it, the woman said to me, "You have made a good choice, for the ring is hollowed out and in it is hidden a piece of the wood of life. And thus the seal of the cross on the outside testifies by its form to what is inside."

TWELFTH WEEK OF THE YEAR
Saturday
Gregory of Nyssa, *Life of Macrina* (#12 of 12)

The witness of a grateful father, as well as other stories to which Gregory alludes, demonstrates that, already in her lifetime, Macrina was believed to have performed miraculous deeds for the benefit of others.

When everything was accomplished and it was necessary to go back, I fell upon the tomb and kissed the dust and retraced my steps, downcast and tearful, thinking of the good of which my life had been deprived. Along the way, a certain distinguished military man in charge of a garrison of soldiers in a district of Pontus [Pon' tus], called Sebastopolis [Se bas to' po lis], told me the story of a miracle connected with Macrina [Ma cri'na] and, adding only this to my story, I shall come to an end. When I had stopped crying and we stood talking, he said to me, "Hear what a great and substantial good has been removed from human life," and, speaking thus, he began his tale:

"It happened that my wife and I were eager to visit the monastery of virtue (for that is what I think that place should be called) in which the blessed soul spent her life. There was with us our little girl who was suffering from an eye ailment resulting from an infectious sickness. As we entered the monastery, we separated, my wife and I, for I went to the men's quarters where your brother Peter was superior, and she went to the women's quarters to be with the holy one. We were getting ready to leave, but a kindly remonstrance came to us from both quarters. Your brother urged me to remain and share the monastic table. The blessed one would not let my wife go, and said she would not give up my daughter, whom she was holding in her arms, until she had given them a meal and offered them the wealth of philosophy. She kissed the child as one might expect and put her lips on her eyes and, when she noticed the diseased pupil, she said, "If you do me the favor of remaining for dinner, I will give you a return in keeping with this honor. I have some medicine which is especially effective in curing eye diseases.

"When the feasting was over and grace said (the great Peter, having entertained and cheered us with special graciousness, and the great Macrina, having said goodbye to my wife with every courtesy), we started the journey home bright and happy. My wife was telling everything in order, as if going through a treatise, and when she came to the point at which the medicine was promised, interrupting the narrative she said, 'What have we done? How did we forget the promise, the medicine for the eyes?' I was annoyed at our thoughtlessness and quickly sent one of my men back to ask for the medicine, when the child, who happened to be in her nurse's arms, looked at her mother, and the mother, fixing her gaze on the child's eyes, said, 'Stop being upset by our carelessness.' She said this in a loud voice, joyfully and fearfully. 'Nothing of what was promised to us has been omitted, but the true medicine that heals diseases has already worked; nothing at all is left of the disease of the eyes.' As she said this, she took our child and put her in my arms and I, also, then comprehended the miracles in the gospel which I had not believed before and I said, 'What a great thing it is for sight to be restored to the blind by the hand of God, if now God's handmaiden makes such cures and has done such a thing through faith, a fact no less impressive than these miracles.' " This was what he told me, and tears fell as he spoke and his voice was choked with emotion. This is the story of the soldier.

I do not think it is wise to add to my story all the other details we heard from those who lived with her and knew her life accurately, for most people judge the credibility of what they hear according to the measure of their own experience, and what is beyond the power of the hearer they insult with the suspicion of falsehood as outside of the truth. Therefore, I pass over that incredible farming phenomenon at the time of the famine when, as the grain was given out in proportion to the need, the amount did not seem to grow smaller, but remained the same as it was before it was given to those asking for it. And after this, there were other events more surprising than these: the healing of disease, the casting out of devils, true prophecies of future events, all of which are believed to be true by those who knew the details accurately, amazing although they are. But for the material-minded, they are beyond what can be accepted. They do not know that the distribution of graces is in proportion to one's faith, meager for those of little faith, great for those who have within themselves great room for faith. So, in order not to do harm to those who have no faith in the gifts of God, I have decided against enumerating the greater miracles, judging it sufficient to end my work about Macrina with what I have already related.

THIRTEENTH SUNDAY OF THE YEAR
Mark 5:25-34

Bernice, a woman whose name we know only from the Acts of Pilate, has been judged ritually unclean for twelve years, possibly because of persistent vaginal bleeding. The power of God goes out from Jesus at her touch and she is cured instantly and completely.

There was a woman who had been suffering from hemorrhages for twelve years. She had endured much under many physicians, and had spent all that she had; and she was no better, but rather grew worse. She had heard about Jesus, and came up behind him in the crowd and touched his cloak, for she said, "If I but touch his clothes, I will be made well." Immediately her hemorrhage stopped; and she felt in her body that she was healed of her disease. Immediately aware that power had gone forth from him, Jesus turned about in the crowd and said, "Who touched my clothes?" And his disciples said to him, "You see the crowd pressing in on you; how can you say, 'Who touched me?' " He looked all around to see who had done it. But the woman knowing what had happened to her, came in fear and trembling, fell down before him, and told him the whole truth. He said to her, "Daughter, your faith has made you well; go in peace, and be healed of your disease."

See Matthew 9:20–22
Luke 8:43–48

THIRTEENTH WEEK OF THE YEAR
Monday
Pseudo-Philo, *Biblical Antiquities* 50:4–8

Hannah, the mother of Samuel, prays fervently to God that she might conceive a child "in her own image." The priest, Eli, then proclaims that her prayer has been answered.

Hannah prayed and said, "Did you not, Lord, search out the heart of all generations before you formed the world? Now what womb is born opened or dies closed unless you wish it? Now let my prayer ascend before you today lest I go down from here empty, because you know my heart, how I have walked before you from the day of my youth." Hannah did not want to pray out loud as all people do (1 Sam 1:13). For then she thought, saying, "Perhaps I am not worthy to be heard, and Peninnah [Pe nin' nah] will then be even more eager to taunt me as she does daily when she says, 'Where is your God in whom you trust?' (Ps 42:3). I know that neither she who has many sons (1 Sam 2:5) is rich nor she who has few is poor, but whoever abounds in the will of God is rich. For who may know what I have prayed for? If they know that I am not heard in my prayer, they will blaspheme. I will not have any witness except in my own soul, because my tears are the servant of my prayers." While she was praying, Eli the priest saw that she was disturbed and acted like a drunken woman, (1 Sam 1:14f) and he said to her, "Go and put your wine away from you." She said, "Is my prayer so heard that I am called a drunken woman? Now I am drunk with sorrow, and I have drunk the cup of my weeping." Eli the priest said to her, "Tell me why you are being taunted." And she said to him, "I am the wife of Elkanah [El ka' nah]; and because God has shut up my womb, I have prayed before God (1 Sam 1:15) that I do not go forth from this world without fruit and that I do not die without having my own image." Eli the priest said to her, "Go, because I know for what you have prayed; your prayer has been heard." (1 Sam 1:17) But Eli the priest did not want to tell her that a prophet had been foreordained to be born from her. For he had heard that when the Lord spoke concerning him. Hannah came into her house, and she was consoled of her sorrow, but she told no one what she had prayed.

THIRTEENTH WEEK OF THE YEAR
Tuesday
Genesis 19:15–26

Does Lot's wife represent the backward glance of reluctance or compassion?

When morning dawned, the angels urged Lot, saying, "Get up, take your wife and your two daughters who are here, or else you will be consumed in the punishment of the city." But he lingered; so the men seized him and his wife and his two daughters by the hand, the Lord being merciful to him, and they brought him out and left him outside the city. When they had brought them outside, they said, "Flee for your life; do not look back or stop anywhere in the Plain; flee to the hills, or else you will be consumed." And Lot said to them, "Oh, no, my lords; your servant has found favor with you, and you have shown me great kindness in saving my life; but I cannot flee to the hills, for fear the disaster will overtake me and I die. Look, that city is near enough to flee to, and it is a little one. Let me escape there—is it not a little one?—and my life will be saved!" He said to him, "Very well, I grant you this favor too, and will not overthrow the city of which you have spoken. Hurry, escape there, for I can do nothing until you arrive there." Therefore the city was called Zoar. The sun had risen on the earth when Lot came to Zoar.

Then the Lord rained on Sodom and Gomorrah [Go mor′ rah] sulfur and fire from the Lord out of heaven; and overthrew those cities, and all the Plain, and all the inhabitants of the cities, and what grew on the ground. But Lot's wife, behind him, looked back, and she became a pillar of salt.

THIRTEENTH WEEK OF THE YEAR
Wednesday
Genesis 21:5, 8–21

Sarah appeals to patriarchal authority to do her dirty work for her. At the same time Hagar demonstrates matriarchal authority in arranging her son's marriage.

Abraham was a hundred years old when his son Isaac was born to him. The child grew, and was weaned; and Abraham made a great feast on the day that Isaac was weaned. But Sarah saw the son of Hagar the Egyptian, whom she had borne to Abraham, playing with her son Isaac. So she said to Abraham, "Cast out this slave woman with her son; for the son of this slave woman shall not inherit along with my son Isaac." The matter was very distressing to Abraham on account of his son. But God said to Abraham, "Do not be distressed because of the boy and because of your slave woman; whatever Sarah says to you, do as she tells you, for it is through Isaac that offspring shall be named for you. As for the son of the slave woman, I will make a nation of him also, because he is your off-spring." So Abraham rose early in the morning, and took bread and a skin of water, and gave it to Hagar, putting it on her shoulder, along with the child, and sent her away. And she departed, and wandered about in the wilderness of Beer-sheba [Be er-she' ba].

When the water in the skin was gone, she cast the child under one of the bushes. Then she went and sat down opposite him a good way off, about the distance of a bowshot; for she said, "Do not let me look on the death of the child." And as she sat opposite him, she lifted up her voice and wept. And God heard the voice of the boy; and the angel of God called to Hagar from heaven, and said to her, "What troubles you, Hagar? Do not be afraid; for God has heard the voice of the boy where he is. Come, lift up the boy and hold him fast with your hand, for I will make a great nation of him." Then God opened her eyes and she saw a well of water. She went, and filled the skin with water, and gave the boy a drink.

God was with the boy, and he grew up; he lived in the wilderness, and became an expert with the bow. He lived in the wilderness of Paran; and his mother got a wife for him from the land of Egypt.

THIRTEENTH WEEK OF THE YEAR
Thursday
Egeria's Travels 16.1–4 (#1 of 2)

One of the most interesting documents of the fourth century is the travel diary of a Spanish nun named Egeria. It is clear from today's reading that all the pilgrims benefited from Egeria's insatiable curiosity about the sacred places.

We travelled through the Jordan valley for a little, and at times the road took us along the river-bank itself. In this valley was the cell of a brother, a monk. You know how inquisitive I am, and I asked what there was about this valley to make this holy monk build his cell there. I knew there must be some special reason, and this is what I was told by those with us who knew the district. "This is the valley of Cherith [Che' rith] (1 Kings 17:3–6). The holy prophet Elijah the Tishbite stayed here in the reign of King Ahab; and at the time of the famine, when God sent a raven to bring him food, he drank water from this brook. For the watercourse you can see running down the valley to the Jordan is Cherith." So we set

off again—as indeed we did every single day—giving renewed thanks to
God for the divine goodness in showing us all the things we wanted to
see, and so much more than we deserved.

THIRTEENTH WEEK OF THE YEAR
Friday
Egeria's Travels 17.1–19.4 (#2 of 2)

---

*Additional opportunities for pilgrimage "inspired by God" are too
tantalizing for Egeria to pass up.*

Since it was already three full years since my arrival in Jerusalem,
and I had seen all the places which were the object of my pilgrimage, I felt
that the time had come to return in God's name to my own country. But
God also moved me with a desire to go to Syrian Mesopotamia.* The
holy monks there are said to be numerous and of so indescribably excellent a life that I wanted to pay them a visit; I also wanted to make a
pilgrimage to the martyrium [mar tyr′ i um] of the holy apostle Thomas,
where his entire body is buried. It is at Edessa [E des′ sa], to which Jesus,
our God, was sending Thomas after his ascension into heaven, as he tells
us in the letter he sent to King Abgar. This letter has been most reverently
preserved at Edessa where they have this martyrium. And, believe me,
loving sisters, no Christian who has achieved the journey to the holy
places and Jerusalem misses going also on the pilgrimage to Edessa. It is
twenty-five staging-posts away from Jerusalem. But Mesopotamia is not
as far from Antioch. So, since my route back to Constantinople took me
back that way, it was very convenient for me at God's bidding to go from
Antioch to Mesopotamia, and that, under God, is what I did.

Fifteen miles after leaving Hierapolis [Hi er ap′ o lis] I arrived in
God's name at the river Euphrates [Eu phra′ tes], and the Bible is right to
call it "the great river Euphrates" (Gen 15:18). It is very big, and really
rather frightening since it flows very fast like the Rhône, but the

---

* This expression renders the Paddan-Aram of Gen 28:12.

Euphrates is much bigger. We had to cross in ships, big ones, and that meant I spent maybe more than half a day there. So, after crossing the river Euphrates, I went on in God's name into the region of Syrian Mesopotamia.

As soon as we arrived in Edessa, we went straight to the church and martyrium of holy Thomas; there we had our usual prayers and everything which was our custom in holy places. And we read also from the writings of holy Thomas himself. The church there is large and beautiful, and built in the new way—just right, in fact, to be a house of God. In this city there was so much I wanted to see that I had to stay there three days.

THIRTEENTH WEEK OF THE YEAR
Saturday
Judges 16:4–21

The devious Delilah, wooed by a bribe, destroys Samson. Money is the root of all evil.

Samson fell in love with a woman in the valley of Sorek, whose name was Delilah [De li' lah]. The lords of the Philistines [Phi lis' tines] came to her and said to her, "Coax him, and find out what makes his strength so great, and how we may overpower him, so that we may bind him in order to subdue him; and we will each give you eleven hundred pieces of silver." So Delilah said to Samson, "Please tell me what makes your strength so great, and how you could be bound, so that one could subdue you." Samson said to her, "If they bind me with seven fresh bowstrings that are not dried out, then I shall become weak, and be like anyone else." Then the lords of the Philistines brought her seven fresh bowstrings that had not been dried out, and she bound him with them. While men were lying in wait in an inner chamber, she said to him, "The Philistines are upon you, Samson!" But he snapped the bowstrings, as a strand of fiber snaps when it touches the fire. So the secret of his strength was not known.

Then Delilah said to Samson, "You have mocked me and told me lies; please tell me how you could be bound." He said to her, "If they bind me with new ropes that have not been used, then I shall become weak, and be like anyone else." So Delilah took new ropes and bound him with them, and said to him, "The Philistines are upon you, Samson!" (The men lying in wait were in an inner chamber.) But he snapped the ropes off his arms like a thread.

Then Delilah said to Samson, "Until now you have mocked me and told me lies; tell me how you could be bound." He said to her, "If you weave the seven locks of my head with the web and make it tight with the pin, then I shall become weak, and be like anyone else." So while he slept, Delilah took the seven locks of his head and wove them into the web, and made them tight with the pin. Then she said to him, "The Philistines are upon you, Samson!" But he awoke from his sleep, and pulled away the pin, the loom, and the web.

Then she said to him, "How can you say, 'I love you,' when your heart is not with me? You have mocked me three times now and have not told me what makes your strength so great." Finally, after she had nagged him with her words day after day, and pestered him, he was tired to death. So he told her his whole secret, and said to her, "A razor has never come upon my head; for I have been a nazirite to God from my mother's womb. If my head were shaved then my strength would leave me; I would become weak, and be like anyone else."

When Delilah realized that he had told her his whole secret, she sent and called the lords of the Philistines, saying, "This time come up, for he has told his whole secret to me." Then the lords of the Philistines came up to her, and brought the money in their hands. She let him fall asleep on her lap; and she called a man, and had him shave off the seven locks of his head. He began to weaken, and his strength left him. Then she said, "The Philistines are upon you, Samson!" When he awoke from his sleep, he thought, "I will go out as at other times, and shake myself free." But he did not know that the Lord had left him. So the Philistines seized him and gouged out his eyes. They brought him down to Gaza and bound him with bronze shackles; and he ground at the mill in the prison.

FOURTEENTH SUNDAY OF THE YEAR
Isaiah 66:10–14

Isaiah's metaphor of Jerusalem as a nursing mother reaches its peak when it shifts to the image of God as a mother comforting her child on her lap.

"Rejoice with Jerusalem, and be glad for her,
    all you who love her;
rejoice with her in joy,
    all you who mourn over her—
that you may nurse and be satisfied
    from her consoling breast;
that you may drink deeply with delight
    from her glorious bosom."

For thus says the Lord:
"I will extend prosperity to her like a river,
    and the wealth of the nations like an overflowing stream;
and you shall nurse and be carried on her arm,
    and dandled on her knees.
As a mother comforts her child,
    so I will comfort you;
    you shall be comforted in Jerusalem.
You shall see, and your heart shall rejoice;
    your bodies shall flourish like the grass;
and it shall be known that the hand of the Lord is with God's servants,
    and God's indignation is against God's enemies."

FOURTEENTH WEEK OF THE YEAR
Monday
Mark 15:40–47

The faithful women disciples were the community's link from Jesus' ministry in Galilee to his death and burial. They will be the first to experience the Easter event.

There were also women looking on from a distance; among them were Mary Magdalene, and Mary the mother of James the younger and of Joses, and Salome. These used to follow Jesus and provided for him when he was in Galilee; and there were many other women who had come up with him to Jerusalem.

When evening had come, and since it was the day of Preparation, that is, the day before the sabbath, Joseph of Arimathea, a respected member of the council, who was also himself waiting expectantly for the kingdom of God, went boldly to Pilate and asked for the body of Jesus. Then Pilate wondered if he were already dead; and summoning the centurion, he asked him whether he had been dead for some time. When he learned from the centurion that he was dead, he granted the body to Joseph. Then Joseph bought a linen cloth, and taking down the body, wrapped it in the linen cloth, and laid it in a tomb that had been hewn out of the rock. He then rolled a stone against the door of the tomb. Mary Magdalene and Mary the mother of Joses saw where the body was laid.

FOURTEENTH WEEK OF THE YEAR
Tuesday
Thunder, Perfect Mind 13.1–14.1 (#1 of 5)

This self-proclamation by a female figure parallels the speeches of Sophia (Lady Wisdom) and the "I am" sayings of Jesus in John's gospel. The antithetical character of the speech signifies the absolute transcendence of the female speaker.

I was sent forth from the power,
   and I have come to those who reflect upon me,
   and I have been found among those who seek after me.
Look upon me, all you who reflect upon me,
   and you hearers, hear me.
   You who are waiting for me, take me to yourselves.
And do not banish me from your sight.
   And do not make your voice hate me, nor your hearing.
   Do not be ignorant of me anywhere or any time. Be on your guard!
   Do not be ignorant of me.

For I am the first and the last.
I am the honored one and the scorned one.
I am the whore and the holy one.
I am the wife and the virgin.
I am the mother and the daughter.
I am the members of my mother.
I am the barren one
   and many are her sons.
I am she whose wedding is great,
   and I have not taken a husband.
I am the midwife and she who does not bear.
I am the solace of my labor pains.
I am the bride and the bridegroom,
   and it is my husband who begot me.
I am the mother of my father
   and the sister of my husband,
   and he is my offspring.
I am the slave of him who prepared me.
I am the ruler of my offspring.

FOURTEENTH WEEK OF THE YEAR
Wednesday
The Thunder, Perfect Mind 14.26–15.16 (#2 of 5)

Using paradox and antithesis, the female speaker continues to proclaim her unfathomable power.

For I am knowledge and ignorance.
I am shame and boldness.
I am shameless; I am ashamed.
I am strength and I am fear.
I am war and peace.
Give heed to me.
I am the one who is disgraced and the great one.

Give heed to my poverty and my wealth.
   Do not be arrogant to me when I am cast out upon the earth,
   and you will find me in those that are to come.
And do not look upon me on the dung-heap
   nor go and leave me cast out,
   and you will find me in the kingdoms.
And do not look upon me when I am cast out among those
   who are disgraced and in the least places,
   nor laugh at me.
And do not cast me out among those who are slain in violence.
But I, I am compassionate and I am cruel.

FOURTEENTH WEEK OF THE YEAR
Thursday
The Thunder, Perfect Mind 15.17–16.5 (#3 of 5)

Proclaiming her wisdom and knowledge, the revealer speaks of her ineffable and mysterious qualities.

Be on your guard!
Do not hate my obedience
    and do not love my self-control.
In my weakness, do not forsake me,
    and do not be afraid of my power.
For why do you despise my fear
    and curse my pride?
But I am she who exists in all fears
    and I am strength in trembling.
I am she who is weak,
    and I am well in a pleasant place.
I am senseless and I am wise.

Why have you hated me in your counsels?
For I shall be silent among those who are silent,
    and I shall appear and speak.
Why then have you hated me, you Greeks?
    Because I am a barbarian among the barbarians?
For I am the wisdom of the Greeks
    and the knowledge of the barbarians.

FOURTEENTH WEEK OF THE YEAR
Friday
The Thunder, Perfect Mind 16.12–36 (#4 of 5)

The female revealer sings of her life-giving power and closeness to Torah in language reminiscent of Jesus. Like the God who is acclaimed in Psalm 139, she is ever-present, and from her no one can hide.

I am the one whom they call Life,
 and you have called Death.
I am the one whom they call Law,
 and you have called Lawlessness.
I am the one whom you have pursued,
 and I am the one whom you have seized.
I am the one whom you have scattered,
 and you have gathered me together.
I am the one before whom you have been ashamed,
 and you have been shameless to me.
I am she who does not keep festival,
 and I am she whose festivals are many.
I, I am godless,
 and I am the one whose God is great.
I am the one whom you have reflected upon,
 and you have scorned me.
I am unlearned,
 and they learn from me.
I am the one whom you have despised,
 and you reflect upon me.
I am the one whom you have hidden from,
 and you appear to me.
But whenever you hide yourselves, I myself will appear.

FOURTEENTH WEEK OF THE YEAR
Saturday
Thunder, Perfect Mind 20.27–35; 21.12–32
(#5 of 5)

The female revealer concludes her speech with a call to hear and learn from her. She claims to speak in the name of the One who created her and promises life to all who heed her call.

Hear me, you hearers,
    and learn of my words, you who know me.
I am the hearing that is attainable to everything;
    I am the speech that cannot be grasped.
I am the name of the sound
    and the sound of the name.
I am the sign of the letter
    and the designation of the division.
And I will speak the name of the One who created me.
Look then at the words
    and all the writings which have been completed.
Give heed then, you hearers
    and you also, the angels and those who have been sent,
    and you spirits who have arisen from the dead.
For I am the one who alone exists,
    and I have no one who will judge me.

For many are the pleasant forms which exist
    in numerous sins,
    and in incontinencies,
    and disgraceful passions,
    and fleeting pleasures,
        which people embrace until they become sober
        and go up to their resting-place.
And they will find me there,
    and they will live,
    and they will not die again.

FIFTEENTH SUNDAY OF THE YEAR
Epitaphs of Sophia, Marin and Rufina

Jewish and Christian funerary inscriptions provide a unique glimpse of women.

Epitaph of Sophia the Deacon, the Second Phoebe
Here lies the servant and bride of Christ
Sophia the deacon, the second Phoebe.
She fell asleep in peace on the 21st of the month of March
in the 11th indiction . . .

See Romans 16:1

Epitaph of a Jewish Priestess from Egypt
O Marin, priestess, worthy one, friend to all, causing pain to no one and friend to your neighbors, farewell. Approximately fifty years old. In the third year of Caesar, on the 13th day of Payni.

Epitaph of Rufina, Head of the Synagogue
Rufina [Ru fi′ na], a Jewess, head of the synagogue, built this tomb for her freed slaves and the slaves raised in her house. No one else has the right to bury anyone here. Anyone who dares to do so, will pay 1500 denaria to the sacred treasury and 1000 denaria to the Jewish people. A copy of this inscription has been placed in the public archives.

FIFTEENTH WEEK OF THE YEAR
Monday
Acts 5:1–11

A business partner with her husband, Sapphira conspires to defraud the church. The story demonstrates that men and women equally are required before God to fulfill the demands of justice.

A man named Ananias [An a ni' as], with the consent of his wife Sapphira [Sap phi' ra], sold a piece of property; with his wife's knowledge, he kept back some of the proceeds, and brought only a part and laid it at the apostles' feet. "Ananias," Peter asked, "why has Satan filled your heart to lie to the Holy Spirit and to keep back part of the proceeds of the land? While it remained unsold, did it not remain your own? And after it was sold, were not the proceeds at your disposal? How is it that you have contrived this deed in your heart? You did not lie to us but to God!" Now when Ananias heard these words, he fell down and died. And great fear seized all who heard of it. The young men came and wrapped up his body, then carried him out and buried him.

After an interval of about three hours his wife came in, not knowing what had happened. Peter said to her, "Tell me whether you and your husband sold the land for such and such a price." And she said, "Yes, that was the price." Then Peter said to her, "How is it that you have agreed together to put the Spirit of the Lord to the test? Look, the feet of those who have buried your husband are at the door, and they will carry you out." Immediately she fell down at his feet and died. When the young men came in they found her dead, so they carried her out and buried her beside her husband. And great fear seized the whole church and all who heard of these things.

FIFTEENTH WEEK OF THE YEAR
Tuesday
Exodus 2:1–10

Three women of varying age, race and class cooperate in saving a life. They are shown to be both clever and gentle in their loving concern to preserve the child.

A man from the house of Levi went and married a Levite woman. The woman conceived and bore a son; and when she saw that he was a fine baby, she hid him three months. When she could hide him no longer she got a papyrus basket for him, and plastered it with bitumen and pitch; she put the child in it and placed it among the reeds on the bank of the river. His sister stood at a distance, to see what would happen to him.

The daughter of Pharaoh came down to bathe at the river, while her attendants walked beside the river. She saw the basket among the reeds and sent her maid to bring it. When she opened it, she saw the child. He was crying, and she took pity on him, "This must be one of the Hebrews' children," she said. Then his sister said to Pharaoh's daughter, "Shall I go and get you a nurse from the Hebrew women to nurse the child for you?" Pharaoh's daughter said to her, "Yes." So the girl went and called the child's mother. Pharaoh's daughter said to her, "Take this child and nurse it for me, and I will give you your wages." So the woman took the child and nursed it. When the child grew up, she brought him to Pharaoh's daughter, and she took him as her son. She named him Moses, "because," she said, "I drew him out of the water."

FIFTEENTH WEEK OF THE YEAR
Wednesday
Exodus 2:15b–22

Reuel's daughters reflect the independence of Bedouin girls who even today tend the flocks, wandering with them in search of water. Yet, in matters of marriage, Zipporah must acquiesce to her father's wishes and become the wife of Moses.

Moses fled from Pharaoh. He settled in the land of Midian [Mid' i an], and sat down by a well. The priest of Midian had seven daughters. They came to draw water, and filled the troughs to water their father's flock. But some shepherds came and drove them away. Moses got up and came to their defense and watered their flock. When they returned to their father Reuel [Reu' el], he said, "How is it that you have come back so soon today?" They said, "An Egyptian helped us against the shepherds; he even drew water for us and watered the flock." He said to his daughters, "Where is he? Why did you leave the man? Invite him to break bread." Moses agreed to stay with the man, and he gave Moses his daughter Zipporah [Zip po' rah] in marriage. She bore a son, and he named him Gershom; for he said, "I have been an alien residing in a foreign land."

FIFTEENTH WEEK OF THE YEAR
Thursday
Exodus 15:19–22

In this powerful and dramatic scene, the prophet Miriam presides triumphantly over the liturgy at the sea. Latin tradition robs Miriam of her role and makes Moses leader of this song (see Ex 15:1).

When the horses of Pharaoh with his chariots and his chariot drivers went into the sea, the Lord brought back the waters of the sea upon them; but the Israelites walked through the sea on dry ground.

The prophet Miriam, Aaron's sister, took a tambourine in her hand; and all the women went out after her with tambourines and with dancing. And Miriam sang to them:

"Sing to the Lord, who has triumphed gloriously;
horse and rider God has thrown into the sea."

Then Moses ordered Israel to set out from the Red Sea, and they went into the wilderness of Shur. They went three days in the wilderness and found no water.

FIFTEENTH WEEK OF THE YEAR
Friday
Numbers 12:1–16, 20:1

The prophet Miriam is partly to blame for the breakdown of relationships among this team of prophetic leaders. Resentment is often the cause of rupture in team ministry.

While they were at Hazeroth [Ha ze' roth], Miriam and Aaron spoke against Moses because of the Cushite woman whom he had married (for he had indeed married a Cushite woman); and they said, "Has the Lord spoken only through Moses? Has the Lord not spoken through us also?" And the Lord heard it. Now the man Moses was very humble, more so than anyone else on the face of the earth. Suddenly the Lord said to Moses, Aaron, and Miriam, "Come out, you three, to the tent of meeting." So the three of them came out. Then the Lord came down in a pillar of cloud, and stood at the entrance of the tent, and called Aaron and Miriam; and they both came forward. And he said, "Hear my words:

When there are prophets among you,
  I the Lord make myself known to them in visions;
  I speak to them in dreams.

Not so with my servant Moses;
   he is entrusted with all my house.
With him I speak face to face—
   clearly, not in riddles;
   and he beholds the form of the Lord.

Why then were you not afraid to speak against my servant Moses?" And the anger of the Lord was kindled against them, and the Lord departed.

When the cloud went away from over the tent, Miriam had become leprous, as white as snow, and Aaron turned towards Miriam and saw that she was leprous. Then Aaron said to Moses, "Oh, my lord, do not punish us for a sin that we have so foolishly committed. Do not let her be like one stillborn, whose flesh is half consumed when it comes out of its mother's womb." And Moses cried to the Lord, "O God, please heal her." But the Lord said to Moses, "If her father had but spit in her face, would she not bear her shame for seven days? Let her be shut out of the camp for seven days." And the people did not set out on the march until Miriam had been brought in again. After that the people set out from Hazeroth and camped in the wilderness of Paran.

The Israelites, the whole congregation, came into the wilderness of Zin in the first month, and the people stayed in Kadesh. Miriam died there, and was buried there.

FIFTEENTH WEEK OF THE YEAR
Saturday
Proverbs 4:5–13

Wisdom is to be prized above all possessions.

Get wisdom; get insight: do not
   forget, nor turn away
   from the words of my mouth.
Do not forsake her, and she will keep you;
   love her, and she will guard you.

The beginning of wisdom is this:
Get wisdom,
and whatever else you get, get insight.
Prize her highly, and she will exalt you;
she will honor you if you embrace her.
She will place on your head a fair garland;
she will bestow on you a beautiful crown.

Hear, my child, and accept my words,
that the years of your life may be many.
I have taught you the way of wisdom;
I have led you in the paths of uprightness.
When you walk, your step will not be
hampered;
and if you run, you will not stumble.
Keep hold of instruction; do not let go;
guard her, for she is your life.

SIXTEENTH SUNDAY OF THE YEAR
Luke 10:38–42

Martha and Mary stand for two complementary sets of gifts and ways of being in the world; what is important is to choose, to live deliberately in the present moment with those gifts and graces uniquely one's own.

Jesus entered a certain village, where a woman named Martha welcomed him into her home. She had a sister named Mary, who sat at the Lord's feet and listened to what he was saying. But Martha was distracted by her many tasks; so she came to him and asked, "Jesus, do you not care that my sister has left me to do all the work by myself? Tell her, then, to help me." But Jesus answered her, "Martha, Martha, you are worried and distracted by many things; there is need of only one thing. Mary has chosen the better part, which will not be taken away from her."

SIXTEENTH WEEK OF THE YEAR
Monday
Micah 6:1–4, 6–8

The leadership of Miriam and her companions is recalled by God as accusation of the people's hard-heartedness. Then the writer proposes a way of justice, love, and humility to re-establish the covenant.

Hear what the Lord says:
    Rise, plead your case before the mountains,
    and let the hills hear your voice.
Hear, you mountains, the controversy of the Lord,
    and you enduring foundations of the earth;
for the Lord has a controversy with the people,
    and God will contend with Israel.
O my people, what have I done to you?
    In what have I wearied you? Answer me!
For I brought you up from the land of Egypt,
    and redeemed you from the house of slavery;
and I sent before you Moses, Aaron, and Miriam.

With what shall I come before the Lord,
    and bow myself before God on high?
Shall I come before God with burnt offerings,
    with calves a year old?
Will the Lord be pleased with thousands of rams,
    with ten thousands of rivers of oil?
Shall I give my firstborn for my transgression,
    the fruit of my body for the sin of my soul?
God has told you, O mortal, what is good;
    and what does the Lord require of you
but to do justice, and to love kindness,
    and to walk humbly with your God?

SIXTEENTH WEEK OF THE YEAR
Tuesday
Mark 3:31–35

Kinship loyalties are superseded by a new understanding of relationships in the Church.

Jesus' mother and his brothers came; and standing outside, they sent to him and called him. A crowd was sitting around him; and they said to him, "Your mother and your brothers and sisters are outside, asking for you." And he replied, "Who are my mother and my brothers?" And looking at those who sat around him, he said, "Here are my mother and my brothers! Whoever does the will of God is my brother and sister and mother."

See Matthew 12:46–50
Luke 8:19–21

SIXTEENTH WEEK OF THE YEAR
Wednesday
Genesis 18:1–15

The courtesy and generosity of Abraham and Sarah are rewarded in an amazing way. The Yahwist writer even adds a very human touch of humor to this story of the cooperation of woman and man in the creation of the family of faith. Some parallels to the visitation narrative may be heard in this story.

The Lord appeared to Abraham by the oaks of Mamre, as he sat at the entrance of his tent in the heat of the day. He looked up and saw three men standing near him. When he saw them, he ran from the tent entrance to meet them, and bowed down to the ground. He said, "My lord, if I find favor with you, do not pass by your servant. Let a little water be brought, and wash your feet, and rest yourselves under the tree. Let me bring a little bread, that you may refresh yourselves, and after that you may pass on—since you have come to your servant." So they said, "Do as you have said." And Abraham hastened into the tent to Sarah, and said, "Make ready quickly three measures of choice flour, knead it, and make cakes." Abraham ran to the herd, and took a calf, tender and good, and gave it to the servant, who hastened to prepare it. Then he took curds and milk and the calf that he had prepared, and set it before them; and he stood by them under the tree while they ate.

They said to him, "Where is your wife Sarah?" And he said, "There, in the tent." Then one said, "I will surely return to you in due season, and your wife Sarah shall have a son." And Sarah was listening at the tent entrance behind him. Now Abraham and Sarah were old, advanced in age; it had ceased to be with Sarah after the manner of women. So Sarah laughed to herself, saying, "After I have grown old, and my husband is old, shall I have pleasure?" The Lord said to Abraham, "Why did Sarah laugh, and say, 'Shall I indeed bear a child, now that I am old?' Is anything too wonderful for the Lord? At the set time I will return to you, in due season, and Sarah shall have a son." But Sarah denied, saying "I did not laugh"; for she was afraid. He said, "Oh yes, you did laugh."

SIXTEENTH WEEK OF THE YEAR
Thursday
Acts of Andrew 2-5, 7 (#1 of 3)

Because of her conversion to Christ, Maximilla refuses the sexual advances of her husband Aegeates, the proconsul, and visits the apostle Andrew in prison in search of his advice.

There was joy among the people of Petrae for many days during which Aegeates [Ae ge' a tes] the Proconsul had no thought of pursuing the charge against the apostle Andrew. So they were then each confirmed in hope toward the Lord; and they gathered fearlessly with Maximilla

[Max i mil'la], Iphidamia [Iph i da mi' a], her friend, and the others into the prison, protected by the guardianship and grace of the Lord.

One day when Aegeates was acting as judge, he remembered the affair of Andrew. And just as if he had become mad he left the case with which he was dealing and rising from the bench went at a run into the praetorium and embraced and flattered Maximilla. She, coming from the prison, had entered the house before him; and when he had come in he said to her:

"Your parents, Maximilla, considered me worthy of marriage with you, and gave you to me as wife, looking neither to wealth nor family nor renown, but perhaps only to the good character of my soul. And intending to pass over much with which I wished to reproach you, both things which I have enjoyed from your parents and things which you enjoyed from me during all our life together, I have come from the court to learn this alone from you; answer me reasonably: if you were the person you used to be, living with me in the way we know, sleeping with me, keeping up marital intercourse with me, bearing my children, then I would treat you well in everything; even more, I would release the stranger whom I have in prison. But if you are not willing, I would not do you any harm, indeed I could not; but the one whom you love more than me, I will torture him so much the more. Consider then, Maximilla, which you wish and answer me tomorrow; for I am completely prepared for it."

And when he had said this he went out. But Maximilla went again at the usual time with Iphidamia to Andrew; and laying his hands on her face she kissed them and began to tell him in full of the demand of Aegeates. And Andrew answered her: But scorn the threats of Aegeates, Maximilla, for you know that we have a God who is merciful to us. And do not let his empty talk move you, but remain chaste; and let him not only punish me with tortures and bonds, but let him even throw me to the beasts or burn me with fire or hurl me from a cliff—what does it matter? Let him ill-treat this body as he wishes, it is only one; it is akin in nature to his own.

SIXTEENTH WEEK OF THE YEAR
Friday
Acts of Andrew 14 (#2 of 3)

Maximilla, impressed by the preaching of Andrew, leaves her husband to pursue a life of chastity.

While the apostle was so speaking, Maximilla was absent. For when she had heard what he answered her and had been in some way impressed by it and had become what the words signified, she had gone out, neither rashly nor without set purpose, and had gone to the praetorium. And she had said farewell to her whole life in the flesh and when Aegeates brought up the same matter which he had told her to consider, that is, whether she was willing to sleep with him, she rejected it; from then on he turned his mind to the murder of Andrew and considered in what way he might kill him. And when crucifixion alone of all deaths mastered him, he went away with some of his friends and dined. But Maximilla, the Lord going before her in the form of Andrew, went with Iphidamia to the prison.

SIXTEENTH WEEK OF THE YEAR
Saturday
Acts of Andrew Martyrdom 2. 10 (#3 of 3)

After the martyrdom of Andrew, Maximilla risks her life and honor by taking and burying the body of the apostle. Her action reminds us of Joseph of Arimathea and his care for the body of Jesus.

After the death of the blessed Andrew, Maximilla came with Stratocles [Strat' o cles] without a thought of those who were standing around and took down the body of Andrew. And when the evening came, she buried him, after she had given the body the customary attention. And she lived apart from Aegeates because of his savage nature and his wicked manner of life; she chose a holy and retired life which she, full of the love of Christ, spent among the brethren. Aegeates urged her strongly, promising her that she would have control over his affairs, but he was not able to persuade her.

SEVENTEENTH SUNDAY OF THE YEAR
Acts of Thomas 6–7

The apostle Thomas sings a hymn to the divine maiden—Sophia/ Wisdom—telling of her beauty and power.

Thomas began to sing this song and to say:
The maiden is the daughter of light,
Upon her stands and rests the majestic effulgence of kings,
Delightful is the sight of her,
Radiant with shining beauty.
Her garments are like spring flowers,
And a scent of sweet fragrance is diffused from them.
In the crown of her head the king is established,
Feeding with his own ambrosia those who are set under him.
Truth rests upon her head,
By the movement of her feet she shows forth joy.
Her mouth is open, and that becomingly,
For with it she sings loud songs of praise.
Thirty and two are they that sing her praises.
Her tongue is like the curtain of the door,
Which is flung back for those who enter in.
Like steps her neck mounts up,
Which the first craftsman wrought.
Her two hands made signs and secret patterns, proclaiming the dance of
        the blessed aeons,
Her fingers open the gates of the city.
Her chamber is full of light,
Breathing a scent of balsam and all sweet herbs,
And giving out a sweet smell of myrrh and aromatic leaves.

Within are strewn myrtle branches and all manner of sweet-smelling
    flowers,
And the portals are adorned with reeds.
Her groomsmen keep her compassed about, whose number is seven,
Whom she herself has chosen;
And her bridesmaids are seven,
Who dance before her.
Twelve are they in number who serve before her
And are subject to her,
Having their gaze and look toward the bridegroom,
That by the sight of him they may be enlightened;
And for ever shall they be with him in that eternal joy,
And they shall be at that marriage
For which the princes assemble together,
And shall linger over the feasting
Of which the eternal ones are accounted worthy,
And they shall put on royal robes
And be arrayed in splendid raiment,
And both shall be in joy and exultation
And they shall glorify the God of all,
Whose proud light they received
And were enlightened by the vision of their Lord,
Whose ambrosial food they received,
Which has no deficiency at all,
And they drank too of his wine
Which gives them neither thirst nor desire;
And they glorified and praised, with the living spirit,
The Father of Truth and the Mother of Wisdom.

SEVENTEENTH WEEK OF THE YEAR
Monday
Matthew 13:31–35

Jesus balances two images, one about a man and the other about a woman, to illustrate the surprising and often hidden growth of God's reign in the midst of ordinary experience.

Jesus put before them this parable: "The reign of God is like a mustard seed that someone took and sowed in a field; it is the smallest of all the seeds, but when it has grown, it is the greatest of shrubs and becomes a tree, so that the birds of the air come and make nests in its branches."

He told them another parable: "The reign of God is like yeast that a woman took and mixed in with three measures of flour until all of it was leavened."

Jesus told the crowds all these things in parables; without a parable he told them nothing. This was to fulfill what had been spoken through the prophet:

"I will open my mouth to speak in parables;
I will proclaim what has been hidden from the foundation of the world."

See Luke 13:20–21

SEVENTEENTH WEEK OF THE YEAR
Tuesday
Genesis 1:26–2:3

Of all creatures, only humankind is made in the image of God, and together women and men mirror the divine image. All other creatures are for their use.

God said, "Let us make humankind in our image, according to our likeness; and let them have dominion over the fish of the sea, and over the birds of the air, and over the cattle, and over all the wild animals of the earth and over every creeping thing that creeps upon the earth."

God created humankind in the divine image, created them in the image of God; male and female God created them.

God blessed them and God said to them, "Be fruitful and multiply, and fill the earth and subdue it; and have dominion over the fish of the sea and over the birds of the air and over every living thing that moves on the earth." God said: "See, I have given you every plant yielding seed that is upon the face of the earth, and every tree with seed in its fruit; you shall have them for food. And to every beast of the earth, and to every bird of the air, and to everything that creeps on the earth, everything that has the breath of life, I have given every green plant for food." And it was so. God saw everything made and indeed, it was very good.

See Genesis 2:18-25

SEVENTEENTH WEEK OF THE YEAR
Wednesday
Sibylline Oracles Book 1:1-18

The prophetic oracles of the female seers known as "sibyls" strongly influenced the eschatological hopes of Jews and Christians alike. This oracle is a retelling of the creation story.

Beginning from the first generation of articulate persons
down to the last, I will prophesy all in turn,
such things as were before, as are, and as will come upon
the world through impiety.
First God bids me tell truly how the world
came to be. But you, devious mortal, so that you may never neglect my
        commands,
attentively make known the most high king. It was God who created
the whole world saying, "Let it come to be" and it came to be.

For God established the earth, draping it around with
Tartarus, and gave sweet light.
God elevated heaven, and stretched out the gleaming sea,
and crowned the vault of heaven amply with bright-shining stars
and decorated the earth with plants. God mixed the sea
with rivers, pouring them in, and with the air mingled fragrances,
and dewy clouds. God placed another species,
fish, in the seas, and gave birds to the winds;
to the woods, also, shaggy wild beasts, and creeping
serpents to the earth; and all things which now are seen.

SEVENTEENTH WEEK OF THE YEAR
Thursday
The Sibylline Oracles Book 3:816–830

The oracle of the sibyl gives an imaginative reinterpretation of the story of the flood.

When everything comes to pass,
then you will remember me and no longer will anyone say that I am
    crazy,
I who am a prophet of the great God.
For God did not reveal to me what God had revealed before to my
    parents
but what happened first, these things my father told me,
and God put all of the future in my mind
so that I prophesy both future and former things
and tell them to mortals. For when the world was deluged
with waters, and a certain single approved man was left
floating on the waters in a house of hewn wood
with beasts, and birds, so that the world might be filled again,
I was God's daughter-in-law and I was of God's blood.
The first things happened to God and all of the latter things have been
    revealed,
so let all these things from my mouth be accounted true.

SEVENTEENTH WEEK OF THE YEAR
Friday
Matthew 13:54–58

Familiarity breeds contempt, even for the followers of Jesus.

Jesus came to his hometown and began to teach the people in their synagogue, so that they were astounded and said, "Where did this man get this wisdom and these deeds of power: Is not this the carpenter's son? Is not his mother called Mary? And are not his brothers James and Joseph and Simon and Judas? And are not all his sisters with us? Where, then, did this man get all this?" And they took offense at him. But Jesus said to them, "Prophets are not without honor except in their own country and in their own house." And he did not do many deeds of power there, because of their unbelief.

See Mark 6:1–6
Luke 4:16–24

SEVENTEENTH WEEK OF THE YEAR
Saturday
Song of Solomon 8:1–5

Reverence for the role of mother comes from both male and female voices in this lovely dialogue from the Song of Solomon.

Oh that you were like a brother to me,
    who nursed at my mother's breast!
If I met you outside, I would kiss you,
    and no one would despise me.
I would lead you and bring you
    into the house of my mother,
    and into the chamber of the one who bore me.

I would give you spiced wine to drink,
  the juice of pomegranates.
Oh that his left hand were under my head,
  and that his right hand embraced me!
I adjure you, O daughters of Jerusalem,
  do not stir up or awaken love until it is ready!

Who is that coming up from the wilderness,
  leaning upon her beloved?

Under the apple tree I awakened you,
There your mother was in labor with you;
  there she who bore you was in labor.

EIGHTEENTH SUNDAY OF THE YEAR
Isaiah 42:14–16

In the very middle of a passage presenting God as warrior-hero, the author shows us the maternal God, in labor for justice.

For a long time I have held my peace,
  I have kept still and restrained myself;
now I will cry out like a woman in labor,
  I will gasp and pant.
I will lay waste mountains and hills,
  and dry up all their herbage;
I will turn the rivers into islands,
  and dry up the pools.
I will lead the blind
  by a road they do not know,
by paths they have not known
  I will guide them.
I will turn the darkness before them into light,
  the rough places into level ground.
These are the things I will do,
  and I will not forsake them.

EIGHTEENTH WEEK OF THE YEAR
Monday
2 Timothy 1:1-8

Timothy learned the faith from his mother and his grandmother. Isn't that often the case among us?

Paul, an apostle of Christ Jesus by the will of God, for the sake of the promise of life that is in Christ Jesus, to Timothy, my beloved child: Grace, mercy, and peace from God and from Christ Jesus our Lord.

I am grateful to God—whom I worship with a clear conscience, as my ancestors did—when I remember you constantly in my prayers night and day. Recalling your tears, I long to see you so that I may be filled with joy. I am reminded of your sincere faith, a faith that lived first in your grandmother Lois and your mother Eunice and now, I am sure, lives in you. For this reason I remind you to rekindle the gift of God that is within you through the laying on of my hands; for God did not give us a spirit of cowardice, but rather a spirit of power and of love and of self-discipline.

Do not be ashamed, then, of the testimony about our Lord or of me his prisoner, but join with me in suffering for the gospel, relying on the power of God.

EIGHTEENTH WEEK OF THE YEAR
Tuesday
Sirach 6:5-17

Wisdom teaches us of true friendship—a gift from God and sign of God's presence. It is placed here as preface to the great narrative of the friendship of Paul and Thecla.

Pleasant speech multiplies friends,
and a gracious tongue multiplies courtesies.

Let those who are friendly with you be many,
  but let your advisers be one in a thousand.
When you gain friends, gain them through testing,
  and do not trust them hastily.
For there are friends who are such when it suits
      them,
  but they will not stand by you in time of trouble.
And there are friends who change into enemies
  and tell of the quarrel to your disgrace.
And there are friends who sit at your table,
  but they will not stand by you in time of trouble.
When you are prosperous, they become your
      second self,
  and lord it over your servants;
but if you are brought low, they turn against you,
  and hide themselves from you.
Keep away from your enemies
  and be on guard with your friends.
Faithful friends are a sturdy shelter;
  whoever finds one has found a treasure.
Faithful friends are beyond price;
  no amount can balance their worth.
Faithful friends are life-saving medicine;
  and those who fear the Lord will find them.
Those who fear the Lord direct their friendship
      aright,
  for as they are, so are their neighbors also.

EIGHTEENTH WEEK OF THE YEAR
Wednesday
Acts of Paul and Thecla 7–10 (#1 of 9)

The figure of Thecla was one of the most appealing for popular devotion in the early church, and was the subject of many stories. Here Thecla, a young woman of Iconium, engaged to Thamyris, is powerfully attracted to the preaching of the apostle Paul on the life of chastity.

While Paul was speaking in the middle of the assembly in the house of Onesiphorus [On e siph' o rus], a certain virgin named Thecla (her mother was Theocleia) [The o cle' i a], who was engaged to a man named Thamyris [Tham' y ris], sat at a nearby window in her house and listened night and day to what Paul said about the chaste life. And she did not turn away from the window but pressed on in the faith, rejoicing exceedingly. Moreover, when she saw many women and virgins going in to Paul, she wished that she, too, be counted worthy to stand before Paul and hear the word of Christ, for she had not yet seen Paul in person but only heard him speak.

But since she did not move from the window, her mother sent to Thamyris. He came joyfully as if he were already taking her in marriage. So Thamyris said to Theocleia, "Where is my Thecla, that I may see her?" And Theocleia said, "I have something new to tell you, Thamyris. Indeed, for three days and three nights Thecla has not risen from the window either to eat or to drink but, gazing intently as if on some delightful sight, she so devotes herself to a strange man who teaches deceptive and ambiguous words that I wonder how one so modest in her virginity can be so severely troubled.

"Thamyris, this man is shaking up the city of the Iconians [I co' ni ans], and your Thecla, too. For all the women and the young men go in to him and are taught by him that it is necessary, as he says, 'to fear one single god only and live a pure life.' And my daughter also, like a spider bound at the window by his words, is controlled by a new desire and a terrible passion. For the virgin concentrates on the things he says and is captivated. But you go and speak to her, for she is engaged to you."

And Thamyris went to her, loving her and yet fearing her distraction, and said, "Thecla, my fiancée, why do you sit like that? and what sort of passion holds you distracted? Turn to your Thamyris and be ashamed." And her mother also said the same thing: "Child, why do you sit like that, looking down and not answering, like one paralyzed?" And they wept bitterly, Thamyris for the loss of a wife, Theocleia for a daughter, the female servants for a mistress. So there was a great commingling of grief in the house. And while that was going on Thecla did not turn away but was concentrating on Paul's word.

EIGHTEENTH WEEK OF THE YEAR
Thursday
Acts of Paul and Thecla 15–19 (#2 of 9)

The story of Thecla's relationship with Paul continues. Paul, arrested because of his preaching, is visited secretly at night by Thecla.

Thamyris rose up early in the morning full of jealousy and wrath and went to the house of Onesiphorus [On e siph' o rus], with rulers and officials and a great crowd, with clubs. He said to Paul, "You have corrupted the city of the Iconians, and my fiancée so that she does not want me. Let us go to governor Castellius [Ca stel' li us]!" And the whole crowd shouted, "Away with the magus [sorcerer], for he has corrupted all our women." And the crowds were persuaded.

And standing before the judgment seat, Thamyris cried out, "Proconsul, this man—we don't know where he comes from—who does not allow virgins to marry, let him declare before you the reasons he teaches these things." And Demas and Hermogenes [Her mog' e nes] said to Thamyris, "Say that he is a Christian, and so you will destroy him." But the governor kept his wits and called Paul, saying to him, "Who are you and what do you teach? For they bring no light accusation against you."

"If I teach the things revealed to me by God, what wrong do I do, Proconsul?" When the governor heard this, he commanded Paul to be bound and to be led off to prison until he could find a convenient time to give him a more careful hearing.

But during the night Thecla removed her bracelets and gave them to the doorkeeper, and when the door was opened for her, she headed off to the prison. Upon giving her silver mirror to the jailer, she went in to Paul and, sitting at his feet, she heard about the mighty acts of God. And Paul feared nothing but continued to live with full confidence in God; and her faith also increased, as she kissed his fetters.

But when Thecla was sought by her own people and by Thamyris, they pursued her through the streets as if she were lost, and one of the doorkeeper's fellow slaves made it known that she had gone out during the night. And they questioned the doorkeeper, and he told them that she had gone to the stranger in prison. And they went, just as he had told them, and found her, so to speak, united with him in loving affection. And they left there, rallied the crowd about them, and relayed this to the governor.

EIGHTEENTH WEEK OF THE YEAR
Friday
Acts of Paul and Thecla 20–22 (#3 of 9)

Thecla is condemned to die, but is miraculously saved from burning through divine intervention. The story portrays her as heroine for Christ in union with Paul.

The governor ordered Paul to be brought to the judgment seat. But Thecla roamed around in the place where Paul was teaching as he sat in the prison, so the governor commanded that she, too, be brought to the judgment seat. And she headed off, joyfully exulting. But when Paul was brought forward again, the crowd shouted out even more, "He is a magus! Away with him!" But the governor gladly listened to Paul concerning the holy works of Christ. When he had taken counsel, he called Thecla, saying, "Why do you not marry Thamyris according to the law of the Iconians?" But she just stood there looking intently at Paul. And when she did not answer, Theocleia, her mother, cried out, saying, "Burn the lawless one! Burn her who is no bride in the midst of the theater in order that all the women who have been taught by this man may be afraid!"

And the governor was greatly moved. He had Paul whipped and threw him out of the city, but Thecla he sentenced to be burned. And immediately the governor arose and went off to the theater, and all the crowd went out to the inevitable spectacle. But Thecla, as a lamb in the wilderness looks around for the shepherd, sought for Paul. And looking over the crowd, she saw the Lord sitting in the form of Paul and said, "As if I were not able to bear up, Paul has come to look after me." And she looked intently at him, but he took off into the heavens.

Now the young men and the virgins brought wood and straw for burning Thecla. And the governor wept and marveled at the power in her. The executioners spread out the wood and ordered her to mount the pyre, and, making the sign of the cross, she mounted up on the wood pile. They put the torch underneath the pile, and although a great fire blazed up, the flame did not touch her. For God in compassion produced a noise below the earth, and a cloud above full of water and hail overshadowed the theater, and all its contents poured out, so that many were in danger and died. The fire was extinguished, and Thecla was saved.

EIGHTEENTH WEEK OF THE YEAR
Saturday
Acts of Paul and Thecla 23–25 (#4 of 9)

The story of Paul and Thecla continues, revealing an affectionate relationship between the two as they are reunited; Thecla asks to be baptized as a sign of her dedication.

Now, Paul was fasting with Onesiphorus and his wife and the children in an open tomb on the road by which they go from Iconium to Daphne [Daph′ ne]. And after many days, as they were fasting, the children said to Paul, "We're hungry." And they had no means to buy bread, for Onesiphorus had left behind worldly things and followed Paul with all his house. But Paul took off his coat and said, "Go, child, sell this, buy several loaves, and bring them back." But while the boy was buying bread he saw his neighbor Thecla; he was astonished and said, "Thecla, where are you going?" And she said, "I am seeking Paul, for I was saved from the fire." And the boy said, "Come, I'll take you to him, for he has been mourning for you and praying and fasting six days already."

Now, when she came to the tomb, Paul was kneeling in prayer and saying, "God of Christ, do not let the fire touch Thecla, but be present with her, for she is yours!" And standing behind him, she cried out, "Maker of heaven and earth, the Father of your beloved child Jesus Christ, I bless you because you saved me from the fire that I might see Paul." And rising up, Paul saw her and said, "God, the knower of hearts,

I bless you that you have so quickly accomplished what I asked, and have listened to me."

And inside the tomb there was much love, with Paul leaping for joy, and Onesiphorus, and everyone. They had five loaves, and vegetables and water, and they were rejoicing over the holy works of Christ. And Thecla said to Paul, "I shall cut my hair short and follow you wherever you go." But he said, "The time is horrible, and you are beautiful. May no other temptation come upon you worse than the first, lest you not bear up but act with cowardice." And Thecla said, "Only give me the seal in Christ, and temptation will not touch me." And Paul said, "Have patience, Thecla, and you will receive the water."

NINETEENTH SUNDAY OF THE YEAR
Acts of Paul and Thecla 26–29 (#5 of 9)

Thecla is again condemned to death, and again miraculously saved through the cooperation of women, including a lioness. The women of the story conspire to protect Thecla from the evil intentions of patriarchal authority.

Paul sent away Onesiphorus with all his house to Iconium, and so taking Thecla he entered Antioch. But just as they came into town a Syrian by the name of Alexander, the first man of the Antiochenes [An ti och' en es], seeing Thecla, desired her and sought to win over Paul with money and gifts. But Paul said, "I don't know the woman of whom you speak, nor is she mine." But he, being a powerful man, embraced her on the open street; she, however, would not put up with it but sought Paul and cried out bitterly, saying, "Force not the stranger, force not the servant of God! I am the first woman of the Iconians, and because I did not wish to marry Thamyris I have been thrown out of the city." And grabbing Alexander, she ripped his cloak, took the crown off his head, and made him a laughing stock.

But he, partly out of love for her and partly out of shame for what had happened to him, brought her before the governor. When she confessed that she had done these things, he sentenced her to the beasts. But the women were horrified and cried out before the judgment seat, "An evil judgment! An impious judgment!" Thecla begged the governor that she might remain pure until her battle with the beasts. And a wealthy woman named Tryphaena [Try phae′ na], whose daughter had died, took her into custody and found comfort in her. When the beasts were led in procession, they bound her to a fierce lioness, and the queen Tryphaena followed her. And as Thecla sat upon the lioness's back, the lioness licked her feet, and all the crowd was astounded. Now the charge on her inscription was "Sacrilegious." But the women with their children cried out from above, saying, "O God, an impious judgment is come to pass in this city!" And after the procession, Tryphaena took her again, for her daughter Falconilla [Fal co nil′ la], who was dead, had spoken to her in a dream: "Mother, the desolate stranger Thecla you will have in my place, in order that she may pray for me and I be translated to the place of the righteous."

So when Tryphaena received her back from the procession she was sorrowful because she was going to battle with the beasts on the following day, but at the same time she loved her dearly like her own daughter Falconilla, and she said, "Thecla, my second child, come and pray for my child, that she may live forever; for this I saw in my dreams." And without hesitation she lifted up her voice and said, "My God, Son of the Most High, who is in heaven, give to her according to her wish, that her daughter Falconilla may live forever!" And when Thecla said this, Tryphaena grieved to think that such beauty was to be thrown to the beasts.

NINETEENTH WEEK OF THE YEAR
Monday
Acts of Paul and Thecla 30–33 (#6 of 9)

Once again Thecla is defended by women, including a lioness who gives her life to defend her. The resistance of the women to patriarchal power continues.

When it was dawn, Alexander came to take her away—for he himself was arranging the hunt—and he said, "The governor has taken his seat, and the crowd is clamoring for us. Give me her who is to battle the beasts, that I may take her away." But Tryphaena cried out so that he fled, saying, "A second mourning for my Falconilla is come upon my house, and there is no one to help; neither child, for she is dead, nor relative, for I am a widow. O God of Thecla my child, help Thecla."

And the governor sent soldiers in order that Thecla might be brought. Tryphaena, however, did not stand aside but, taking her hand, led her up herself, saying, "My daughter Falconilla I brought to the tomb, but you, Thecla, I bring to battle the beasts." And Thecla wept bitterly and groaned to the Lord, saying, "Lord God, in whom I believe, with whom I have taken refuge, who rescued me from the fire, reward Tryphaena, who had compassion upon your servant and because she kept me chaste."

Then there was a clamor, a roaring of the beasts, and a shouting of the people and of the women who sat together, some saying, "Bring the sacrilegious one!" But the women were saying, "Let the city perish for this lawlessness! Slay us all, Proconsul! A bitter spectacle, an evil judgment!"

Now when Thecla was taken out of Tryphaena's hands, she was stripped and thrown into the stadium. And lions and bears were thrown at her, and a fierce lioness ran to her and reclined at her feet. Now, the crowd of women shouted loudly. And a bear ran up to her, but the lioness ran and met it, and ripped the bear to shreds. And again a lion trained against men, which belonged to Alexander, ran up to her, and the lioness wrestled with the lion and perished with it. So the women mourned all the more, since the lioness that helped her was dead.

NINETEENTH WEEK OF THE YEAR
Tuesday
Acts of Paul and Thecla 34–36 (#7 of 9)

The adventures of Thecla continue. Thecla baptizes herself in the seal pond, a passage that made Tertullian repudiate the whole story because some had used it to legitimate the authority of women to baptize (On Baptism 17.4). Still the women cooperate to protect her.

Then they sent in many beasts while she stood and stretched out her hands and prayed. And when she had finished her prayer, she turned and saw a great ditch full of water and said, "Now is the time for me to wash." And she threw herself in, saying, "In the name of Jesus Christ, I baptize myself on the last day!" And when they saw it, the women and the whole crowd wept, saying, "Do not throw yourself into the water!"—so that even the governor wept that such a beauty was going to be eaten by seals. So then she threw herself into the water in the name of Jesus Christ, but the seals, seeing the light of a lightning flash, floated dead on the surface. About her there was a cloud of fire so that neither could the beasts touch her nor could she be seen naked.

Now, the women, as other more terrible beasts were thrown in, wailed, and some threw petals, others nard, others cassia, others amomum, so that there was an abundance of perfumes. And all the beasts, overcome as if by sleep, did not touch her. So Alexander said to the governor, "I have some very fearsome bulls. Let us tie her who battles the beasts to them." Although he was frowning, the governor gave his consent, saying, "Do what you want." And they bound her by the feet between the bulls and prodded them from underneath with red- hot irons at the appropriate spot, that being the more enraged they might kill her. The bulls indeed leaped forward, but the flame that blazed around her burned through the ropes, and it was as if she were not bound.

But Tryphaena fainted as she stood beside the arena, so that her attendants said, "The queen Tryphaena is dead!" The governor observed this, and the whole city was alarmed. And Alexander, falling down at the governor's feet, said, "Have mercy upon me and the city, and set free her who battles the beasts, lest the city also perish with her. For if Caesar hears these things, he will probably destroy both us and the city because his relative Tryphaena has died at the circus gates."

NINETEENTH WEEK OF THE YEAR
Wednesday
Acts of Paul and Thecla 37–39 (#8 of 9)

The power of God and the resistance of the women cause the persecutors of Thecla to cease and release her. She is returned to the community of women.

The governor summoned Thecla from among the beasts and said to her, "Who are you? And what have you about you that not one of the beasts touched you?" She answered, "I am a servant of the living God. As to what I have about me, I have believed in him in whom God is well pleased, his Son, on account of whom not one of the beasts touched me. For he alone is the goal of salvation and the foundation of immortal life. For to the storm-tossed he is a refuge, to the oppressed relief, to the despairing shelter; in a word, whoever does not believe in him shall not live but die for ever."

When the governor heard this, he ordered clothing to be brought and said, "Put on the clothing." But she said, "The one who clothed me when I was naked among the beasts, this one shall clothe me with salvation in the day of judgment." And taking the clothing, she got dressed.

And the governor issued a decree immediately, saying, "I release to you Thecla, the God-fearing servant of God." So all the women cried out with a loud voice and as with one mouth gave praise to God, saying, "One is God who has saved Thecla!"—so that all the city was shaken by the sound.

And when Tryphaena was told the good news, she came to meet her with a crowd. She embraced Thecla and said, "Now I believe that the dead are raised up! Now I believe that my child lives! Come inside, and I will transfer everything that is mine to you." So Thecla went in with her and rested in her house for eight days, instructing her in the word of God, so that the majority of the female servants also believed. And there was great joy in the house.

NINETEENTH WEEK OF THE YEAR
Thursday
Acts of Paul and Thecla 40–43 (#9 of 9)

At the conclusion of the story, Thecla is reunited with Paul, who commissions her as an apostle. She goes alone as an apostle, to become the beloved patron saint of all heroic women in the early church. (See Monday of the 11th Week of the Year; Chrysostom).

Thecla longed for Paul and sought him, sending all around in every direction. And it was made known to her that he was in Myra. So, taking male and female servants, she got herself ready, sewed her tunic into a cloak like a man's, and headed off to Myra. She found Paul speaking the word of God and threw herself at him. But he was astonished when he saw her and the crowd that was with her, wondering whether another temptation was not upon her. So realizing this, she said to him, "I have taken the bath, Paul, for he who worked with you for the gospel has also worked with me for my washing."

And taking her by the hand, Paul led her into the house of Hermias [Her' mi as] and heard everything from her, so that Paul marveled greatly and those who heard were strengthened and prayed on behalf of Tryphaena. And standing up, Thecla said to Paul, "I am going to Iconium." So Paul said, "Go and teach the word of God!" Now, Tryphaena sent her a lot of clothing and gold, so it could be left behind for Paul for the ministry of the poor.

So Thecla herself headed off to Iconium and entered the house of Onesiphorus and threw herself down on the floor where Paul had sat when he was teaching the oracles of God, and wept, saying, "My God, and God of this house where the light shone upon me, Christ Jesus, the Son of God, my help in prison, my help before the governor, my help in the flame, my help among the beasts, you are God, and to you be glory for ever. Amen."

And she found Thamyris dead, but her mother alive. And calling her mother to her, she said to her, "Theocleia, my mother, are you able to believe that the Lord lives in the heavens? Or if you desire your child, behold, I am standing beside you."

And when she had given this witness, she headed off to Seleucia [Se leu' ci a], and after enlightening many with the word of God, she slept with a fine sleep.

NINETEENTH WEEK OF THE YEAR
Friday
Egeria's Travels 22:1–23.6

At the end of the fourth century, a Spanish nun named Egeria visits the shrine of Saint Thecla in her home region and describes it in her diary. Her testimony is continuing evidence of the popularity of Thecla's memory.

When I got back to Antioch, I spent a week there, till we had all we needed for the journey. Then, leaving Antioch, we went on by several staging-posts and reached the province called Cilicia [Ci li' cia]; Tarsus is its capital city, and I had already been there on my way out to Jerusalem. But in Isauria [I sau'ri a], only three staging-posts on from Tarsus, is the martyrium [mar tyr' i um] of holy Thecla, and since it was so close, we were very glad to be able to make the extra journey there.

Leaving Tarsus, but still in Cilicia, I reached Pompeiopolis [Pom pe i op' o lis], a city by the sea, and from there I crossed into Isauria, and spent the night in a city called Corycus [Co' ry cus]. On the third day I arrived at a city called Seleucia [Se leu' ci a] of Isauria, and, when I got there, I called on the bishop, a very godly man who had been a monk, and saw a very beautiful church in the city. Holy Thecla's is on a small hill about a mile and a half from the city, so, as I had to stay somewhere, it was best to go straight on and spend the night there.

Round the holy church there is a tremendous number of cells for men and women. And that was where I found one of my dearest friends, a holy deaconess called Marthana [Mar tha' na]. I had come to know her in Jerusalem when she was up there on pilgrimage. She was the superior of some cells of *apotactites* [ap o tac' tites] or virgins, and I simply cannot tell you how pleased we were to see each other again. But I must get back to the point.

There are a great many cells on that hill, and in the middle a great wall round the martyrium itself, which is very beautiful. The wall was built to protect the church against the Isaurians, who are hostile, and always committing robberies, to prevent them trying to damage the monastery which has been established there. In God's name I arrived at the martyrium, and we had a prayer there, and read the whole Acts of holy Thecla; and I gave heartfelt thanks to God for such mercy in letting me fulfill all my desires so completely, despite all my unworthiness. For two days I stayed there, visiting all the holy monks and apotactites, the men as well as the women; then after praying and receiving Communion, I went back to Tarsus to rejoin my route.

NINETEENTH WEEK OF THE YEAR
Saturday
Proverbs 3:13–18

Those who find wisdom find life.

> Happy are those who find wisdom,
>   and those who get understanding,
> for her income is better than silver,
>   and her revenue better than gold.
> She is more precious than jewels,
>   and nothing you desire can compare with her.
> Long life is in her right hand;
>   in her left hand are riches and honor.
> Her ways are ways of pleasantness,
>   and all her paths are peace.
> She is a tree of life to those who lay hold of her;
>   those who hold her fast are called happy.

TWENTIETH SUNDAY OF THE YEAR
Matthew 15:21–28

The Canaanite woman forces Jesus to face the question whether his mission will include Gentiles. Because of her persistence and cleverness, Jesus' understanding of his mission becomes more inclusive.

Jesus entered the district of Tyre and Sidon and a Canaanite [Ca' naan ite] woman from that region came out and started shouting, "Have mercy on me, Lord, Son of David; my daughter is tormented by a demon." But he did not answer her at all. And his disciples came and urged him, saying, "Send her away, for she keeps shouting after us." He answered, "I was sent only to the lost sheep of the house of Israel." But she came and knelt before him, saying, "Lord, help me." He answered, "It is not fair to take the children's food and throw it to the dogs." She said, "Yes, Lord, yet even the dogs eat the crumbs that fall from their masters' table. Then Jesus answered her, "Woman, great is your faith! Let it be done for you as you wish." And her daughter was healed instantly.

See Mark 7:24–30

TWENTIETH WEEK OF THE YEAR
Monday
Joshua 2:1–21 (#1 of 2)

Rahab, the prostitute, offered hospitality and protection to Joshua's spies. For her heroism she is remembered as a Savior and an example of faith in Judeo-Christian tradition as attested by the authors of the gospel of Matthew, the letter to the Hebrews, and 1 Clement.

Joshua son of Nun sent two men secretly from Shittim as spies saying, "Go, view the land, especially Jericho." So they went, and entered the house of a prostitute whose name was Rahab, and spent the night there. The king of Jericho was told, "Some Israelites have come here tonight to search out the land." Then the king of Jericho sent orders to Rahab, "Bring the men who have come to you, who entered your house, for they have come only to search out the whole land." But the woman took the two men and hid them. Then she said, "True, the men came to me, but I did not know where they came from. And when it was time to close the gate at dark, the men went out. Where the men went I do not know. Pursue them quickly, for you can overtake them." She had, however, brought them up to the roof and hidden them with the stalks of flax that she had laid out on the roof. So the men pursued them on the way to the Jordan as far as the fords. As soon as the pursuers had gone out, the gate was shut.

Before they went to sleep, she came up to them on the roof and said to the men: "I know that the Lord has given you the land, and that dread of you has fallen on us, and that all the inhabitants of the land melt in fear before you. For we have heard how the Lord dried up the water of the Red Sea before you when you came out of Egypt, and what you did to the two kings of the Amorites [Am' o rites] that were beyond the Jordan, to Sihon and Og, whom you utterly destroyed. As soon as we heard it, our hearts melted, and there was no courage left in any of us because of you. The Lord your God is indeed God in heaven above and on earth below. Now then, since I have dealt kindly with you, swear to me by the Lord that you in turn will deal kindly with my family. Give me a sign of good faith that you will spare my father and mother, my brothers and sisters, and all who belong to them, and deliver our lives from death." The men said to her, "Our life for yours! If you do not tell this business of ours, then we will deal kindly and faithfully with you when the Lord gives us the land."

Then she let them down by a rope through the window, for her house was on the outer side of the city wall and she resided within the wall itself. She said to them, "Go toward the hill country, so that the pursuers may not come upon you. Hide yourselves there three days, until the pursuers have returned; then afterward you may go your way." The men said to her, "We will be released from this oath that you have made us swear to you if we invade the land and you do not tie this crimson cord in the window through which you let us down, and you do not gather into your house your father and mother, your brothers and sisters, and all your family. If any of you go out of the doors of your house into the street, they shall be responsible for their own death, and we shall be innocent; but if a hand is laid upon any who are with you in the house, we shall bear the responsibility for their death. But if you tell this business of ours, then we shall be released from this oath that you made us swear to you." She said, "According to your words, so be it." She sent them away and they departed. Then she tied the crimson cord in the window.

See Matthew 1:5
Hebrews 13:31
1 Clement 12.1–8

TWENTIETH WEEK OF THE YEAR
Tuesday
Joshua 6:17–25 (#2 of 2)

Rahab, the prostitute-heroine, receives praise and blessing in Jewish tradition for protecting the Israelite spies. Matthew's genealogy lists her as the wife of Salmon and the mother of Boaz (Mt 1:5). She is, therefore, an ancestress in the Davidic line.

"The city and all that is in it shall be devoted to the Lord for destruction. Only Rahab the prostitute and all who are with her in her house shall live because she hid the messengers we sent. As for you, keep away from the things devoted to destruction, so as not to covet and take any of the devoted things and make the camp of Israel an object for destruction, bringing trouble upon it. But all silver and gold, and vessels of bronze and iron, are sacred to the Lord; they shall go into the treasury of the Lord." So the people shouted, and the trumpets were blown. As soon as the people heard the sound of the trumpets, they raised a great shout, and the wall fell down flat; so the people charged straight ahead into the city and captured it. Then they devoted to destruction by the edge of the sword all in the city, both men and women, young and old, oxen, sheep, and donkeys.

Joshua said to the two men who had spied out the land, "Go into the prostitute's house, and bring the woman out of it and all who belong to her, as you swore to her." So the young men who had been spies went in and brought Rahab out, along with her father, her mother, her brothers and sisters, and all who belonged to her—they brought all her kindred out—and set them outside the camp of Israel. They burned down the city, and everything in it; only the silver and gold, and the vessels of bronze and iron, they put into the treasury of the house of the Lord. But Rahab the prostitute, with her family and all who belonged to her, Joshua spared. Her family has lived in Israel ever since. For she hid the messengers whom Joshua sent to spy out Jericho.

TWENTIETH WEEK OF THE YEAR
Wednesday
Ruth 1:1–9 (#1 of 4)

The courage of Naomi, Ruth and Orpah as they spoke their unselfish concern for one another's well-being took on heroic proportions in a society where women who were not under the protection of a man lived in poverty and were exposed to danger.

In the days when the judges ruled, there was a famine in the land, and a certain man of Bethlehem in Judah went to live in the country of Moab, he and his wife and two sons. The name of the man was Elimelech [E lim' e lech] and the name of his wife Naomi, and the names of his two sons were Mahlon [Mah' lon] and Chilion [Chil' i on]; they were Ephrathites [Eph' ra thites] from Bethlehem in Judah. They went into the country of Moab and remained there. But Elimelech, the husband of Naomi, died, and she was left with her two sons. These took Moabite [Mo' ab ite] wives; the name of the one was Orpah and the name of the other Ruth. When they had lived there about ten years, both Mahlon and Chilion also died, so that the woman was left without her two sons and her husband.

Then she started to return with her daughters-in-law from the country of Moab, for she had heard in the country of Moab that the Lord had considered his people and given them food. So she set out from the place where she had been living, she and her two daughters-in-law, and they went on their way to go back to the land of Judah. But Naomi said to her two daughters-in-law, "Go back each of you to your mother's house. May the Lord deal kindly with you, as you have dealt with the dead and with me. The Lord grant that you may find security, each of you in the house of your husband." Then she kissed them, and they wept aloud.

TWENTIETH WEEK OF THE YEAR
Thursday
Ruth 1:10–22 (#2 of 4)

In the bonding of these two women—Ruth and Naomi—we see a model of female courage and strength in the midst of a patriarchal society.

Ruth and Orpah said to Naomi, "We will return with you to your people." But Naomi said, "Turn back, my daughters, why will you go with me? Do I still have sons in my womb that they may become your husbands? Turn back, my daughters, go your way, for I am too old to have a husband. Even if I thought there was hope for me, even if I should have a husband tonight and bear sons, would you then wait until they were grown? Would you then refrain from marrying? No, my daughters, it has been far more bitter for me than for you, because the hand of the Lord has turned against me." Then they wept aloud again. Orpah kissed her mother-in-law, but Ruth clung to her.

So she said, "See, your sister-in-law has gone back to her people and to her gods; return after your sister-in-law." But Ruth said, "Do not press me to leave you or to turn back from following you!

> Where you go, I will go;
>   Where you lodge, I will lodge;
> Your people shall be my people,
>   and your God my God.
> Where you die, I will die—
>   there will I be buried.
> May the Lord do thus and so to me,
>   and more as well,
> if even death parts me from you!"

When Naomi saw that she was determined to go with her, she said no more to her.

So the two of them went on until they came to Bethlehem. When they came to Bethlehem, the whole town was stirred because of them; and the women said, "Is this Naomi?" She said to them,

> "Call me no longer Naomi,
>   call me Mara,
>   for the Almighty has dealt bitterly with me.
> I went away full,
>   but the Lord has brought me back empty;
> why call me Naomi
>   when the Lord has dealt harshly with me
>   and the Almighty has brought calamity upon me?"

So Naomi returned together with Ruth the Moabite, her daughter-in-law, who came back with her from the country of Moab. They came to Bethlehem at the beginning of the barley harvest.

TWENTIETH WEEK OF THE YEAR
Friday
Ruth 3:1–13 (#3 of 4)

Naomi's ingenuity and resourcefulness combined with the loyalty of Ruth presents Boaz with a challenge to fulfill the levirate law (Deut 25:5–10) to give a child to his kinsman's widow.

Naomi, Ruth's mother-in-law, said to her, "My daughter, I need to seek some security for you, so that it may be well with you. Now here is our kinsman Boaz, with whose young women you have been working. See, he is winnowing barley tonight at the threshing floor. Now wash and anoint yourself, and put on your best clothes and go down to the threshing floor; but do not make yourself known to the man until he has finished eating and drinking. When he lies down, observe the place where he lies; then, go and uncover his feet and lie down; and he will tell you what to do." She said to her, "All that you tell me I will do."

So she went down to the threshing floor and did just as her mother-in-law had instructed her. When Boaz had eaten and drunk, and he was in a contented mood, he went to lie down at the end of the heap of grain. Then she came stealthily and uncovered his feet, and lay down. At midnight the man was startled, and turned over, and there, lying at his feet, was a woman! He said, "Who are you?" And she answered, "I am Ruth, your servant; spread your cloak over your servant, for you are next-of-kin." He said, "May you be blessed by the Lord, my daughter; this last instance of your loyalty is better than the first; you have not gone after young men, whether poor or rich. And now, my daughter, do not be afraid, I will do for you all that you ask, for all the assembly of my people know that you are a worthy woman. But now, though it is true that I am a near kinsman, there is another kinsman more closely related than I. Remain this night and in the morning, if he will act as next-of-kin for you, good; let him do it. If he is not willing to act as next-of-kin for you, then, as the Lord lives, I will act as next-of-kin for you. Lie down until the morning."

TWENTIETH WEEK OF THE YEAR
Saturday
Ruth 4:7–17 (#4 of 4)

Ruth, the Moabite, becomes the mother of Obed and is therefore the great-grandmother of David. Despite her being a non-Israelite, Ruth is singled out in Matthew's genealogy of Jesus as one of the four great woman in the Davidic line.

Now this was the custom in former times in Israel concerning redeeming and exchanging: to confirm a transaction, the one took off a sandal and gave it to the other; this was the manner of attesting in Israel. So when the next-of-kin said to Boaz, "Acquire it for yourself," he took off his sandal. Then Boaz said to the elders and all the people, "Today you are witnesses that I have acquired from the hand of Naomi all that belonged to Elimelech and all that belonged to Chilion and Mahlon. I have also acquired Ruth the Moabite, the wife of Mahlon, to be my wife, to maintain the dead man's name on his inheritance, in order that the name of the dead may not be cut off from his kindred and from the gate of his native place; today you are witnesses." Then all the people who were at the gate, along with the elders, said, "We are witnesses. May the Lord make the woman who is coming into your house like Rachel and Leah, who together built up the house of Israel. May you produce children in Ephrathah and bestow a name in Bethlehem; and through the children that the Lord will give you by this young woman, may your house be like the house of Perez whom Tamar bore to Judah."

So Boaz took Ruth and she became his wife. When they came together, the Lord made her conceive, and she bore a son. Then the women said to Naomi, "Blessed be the Lord, who has not left you this day without next-of-kin, and may God's name be renowned in Israel! God shall be to you a restorer of life and a nourisher of your old age; for your daughter-in-law who loves you, who is more to you than seven sons, has borne him." Then Naomi took the child and laid him in her bosom, and became his nurse. The women of the neighborhood gave him a name, saying, "A son has been born to Naomi." They named him Obed; he became the father of Jesse, who was the father of David.

TWENTY-FIRST SUNDAY OF THE YEAR
2 Corinthians 5:14–17

This passage inspired the first Women's Ordination Conference in the United States, held in Detroit in 1975, and was a reading at the principal liturgy during that historic event.

The love of Christ urges us on, because we are convinced that one has died for all; therefore all have died. And Christ died for all, so that those who live might live no longer for themselves, but for the one who died and was raised for them.

From now on, therefore, we regard no one from a human point of view; even though we once knew Christ from a human point of view, we know Christ no longer in that way. So if anyone is in Christ, there is a new creation: everything old has passed away; see, everything has become new!

TWENTY-FIRST WEEK OF THE YEAR
Monday
Life of Olympias 1–4 (#1 of 6)

Olympias (ca. 365–410 CE) was a noblewoman of the capital city of Constantinople who embraced the monastic life in the middle of the city rather than retreating to the desert. Her biographer here compares her to Thecla [see readings for 18th and 19th Weeks of the Year] and describes her early widowhood and refusal of a second marriage. Like many women of her day, she saw the ascetic life as the best way to follow Christ.

The Kingdom of our Savior Jesus Christ, existing before the ages and shining forth to ages without end, confers immortality on those who have served as its shield-bearers, who have completed the race and kept their faith in God spotless and steadfast. Among them was Thecla, a citizen of heaven, a martyr who conquered in many contests, the holy one among women, who despised wealth and the transitory pleasures of this world. Having followed the teachings of Paul, the blessed apostle, and having taken into her heart the divinely inspired Scriptures, she received the crown of incorruptibility from our Lord and Savior Jesus Christ and to ages without end she rests with all the saints who from eternity have pleased the Lord Jesus Christ. Olympias [O lym′ pi as] walked in the footsteps of this saint, Thecla, in every virtue of the divinely-inspired way of life. Olympias, most serious and zealous for the road leading to heaven, followed the intent of the divine Scriptures in everything and was perfected through these things.

She was daughter, according to the flesh, of Seleucus [Se leu′ cus], one of the *comites* [co′ mi tes] [city assembly member], but according to the spirit, she was the true child of God. It is said that she was descended from Ablabius [Ab la′ bi us] [who was governor] and she was bride for a

few days of Nebridius [Ne bri' di us], the prefect of the city of Constantinople [Con stan ti no' ple]. Through a certain demonic jealousy, it tran-
spired that her untimely widowhood became the subject of mischief. She
was falsely accused before the emperor Theodosius [The o do' si us] of
having dispensed her goods in a disorderly fashion. Since indeed she was
his relation, he took pains to unite her in marriage with a certain Elpidius
[El pid' i us], a Spaniard, one of his own relatives. He directed many
persistent entreaties to her and when he failed to achieve his goal, he was
annoyed.

The emperor, when he had heard the testimony against the pious
Olympias, commanded the man, then prefect of the city, Clementius
[Cle men' ti us], to keep her possessions under guard until she reached
her thirtieth year, that is, her physical prime. And the prefect, having
received the guardianship from the emperor, oppressed her to such a
degree, at Elpidius' urging (she did not have the right either to meet with
the notable bishops nor to come near the church), so that groaning under
the strain, she would meekly bear the option of marriage. But she was
even more grateful to God for the removal of the burden of administration of her property, and hoped further that it could be distributed to the
poor and to the churches.

TWENTY-FIRST WEEK OF THE YEAR
Tuesday
Life of Olympias 5–7 (#2 of 6)

---

*Olympias donates most of her property to the poor and to the
church, and is ordained a deaconess by her friend John Chrysostom.
In spite of her extraordinary wealth, she is attracted to a very simple
lifestyle, for she sees the true value of possessions to benefit others.*

The emperor Theodosius, upon his return from battle, gave the
order that Olympias could exercise control over her own possessions,
since he had heard of the intensity of her ascetic discipline. But she
distributed all of her unlimited and immense wealth and assisted every-

one, simply and without distinction. For the sake of many she surpassed that Samaritan of whom an account is given in the holy Gospels.

Then straightway after the distribution of all her goods, she gave to the archbishop of this royal city, John [Chrysostom], for this holy church (imitating also in this act those ardent lovers and disciples of Christ who in the beginning of salvation's proclamation brought to the feet of the apostles their possessions) ten thousand pounds of gold, twenty thousand of silver and all of her real estate situated in the provinces of Thrace, Galatia [Ga la' ti a], Cappadocia [Cap pa do' ci a] Prima [Pri' ma], and Bithynia [Bi thyn' i a]; and more, the houses belonging to her in the capital city, the one situated near the most holy cathedral, which is called "the house of Olympias"; together with the house of the tribune, complete with baths, and all the buildings near it; a mill; and a house which belonged to her in which she lived near the public baths of Constantinople; and another house of hers which was called the "house of Evander" [E' van der]; as well as all of her suburban properties.

Then by the divine will she was ordained deaconess of this holy cathedral of God and she built a monastery at an angle south of it. She owned all the houses lying near the holy church and all the shops which were at the southern angle mentioned.

The noble servant of God, Olympias, again brought to the above-mentioned hallowed church, through the most holy patriarch, John, the entire remainder of all her real estate, situated in all the provinces, and her interest in the public bread supply. And he also ordained as deaconesses of the holy church her three relatives, Elisanthia [E li san' thi a], Martyria [Mar tyr' i a], and Palladia [Pal la' di a], so that the four deaconesses would be able to be together without interruption in the most sacred monastery founded by her.

TWENTY-FIRST WEEK OF THE YEAR
Wednesday
Life of Olympias 8–10 (#3 of 6)

Olympias' friendship with the bishop, John Chrysostom, gets her involved in the plots against him. Resisting both civil and ecclesiastical pressure, she remains loyal to him and thus she too is exiled.

One was struck with amazement at seeing certain things in the holy chorus and angelic institution of these holy women: the constancy of their praise and thanksgiving to God, their "charity which is the bond of perfection" (Col 3:14), their stillness. For no one from the outside, neither man nor woman, was permitted to come upon them, the only exception being the most holy patriarch John, who visited continuously and sustained them with his most wise teachings. The pious and blessed Olympias (who in these matters, too, imitated the women disciples of Christ who served him from their possessions) prepared for the holy John his daily provisions and sent them to the bishop, for there was not much separation between the episcopal residence and the monastery, only a wall. And she did this not only before the plots against him, but also after he was banished; up to the end of his life, she provided for all his expenses as well as for those who were with him in his exile.

Then the devil could not bear the great and wondrous way of life of these pious women, the way of life, first of all, consistently made straight by God's grace, and secondly, a way made straight by the uninterrupted teaching of the most holy patriarch. He was slandered by them not only in respect to her, but also concerning ecclesiastical affairs; according to their whim, they condemned and exiled him. In that exile he finally died. But this pious woman after his exile did not give way but made a motion for his recall to every royal and priestly person. The opposition encompassed her with numerous evils; they stitched together slanders and untimely abuse against her until the occasion when they made her appear before the city prefect for interrogation by him.

When they saw her openness concerning the truth, they could not bear the nobility and immutability of her love for God. They wished to put a stop to the constant activity in which she was engaged on behalf of the holy John's recall and they sent her as well into exile in Nicomedia [Nic o me' di a], the capital city of the province of Bithynia [Bi thyn' i a]. But she, strengthened by the divine grace, nobly and courageously, for the sake of love of God, bore the storms of trials and diverse tribulations which came upon her.

TWENTY-FIRST WEEK OF THE YEAR
Thursday
Life of Olympias 10–11 (#4 of 6)

At the death of Olympias, miraculous appearances indicated how and where she was to be buried. Soon a popular devotion sprang up and reports of healing multiplied.

The whole rest of her life she passed in the capital city of Nicomedia, performing every ascetic art and maintaining her rule of life unchanged there. Victorious in the good fight, she crowned herself with the crown of patience, having turned over her flock by the divine allotment to Marina [Ma ri' na], among the blessed, who was her relative and spiritual daughter, whom she had received from baptism; she prayed that she in turn be preserved in tranquillity in all things. And Marina did this for Olympias, not only for the remaining time which the holy Olympias passed in the metropolis of Nicomedia, but also after her death. For when the pious woman was about to be with Christ, again she decreed in writing that the aforesaid Marina of divine choice exhibit much care and succor, and committed to her, after God, all the sisters and their care. Having done this, she escaped from the storm of human woes and crossed over to the calm haven of our souls, Christ the God.

But before her holy body was buried, she appeared in a dream to the metropolitan of the same city of Nicomedia, saying, "Place my remains in a casket, put it on a boat, let the boat go adrift into the stream, and at the place where the boat stops, disembark onto the ground and place me there." The metropolitan did what had been told him in the vision concerning Olympias and put the casketed body in the boat and let the boat loose into the stream. Toward the hour of midnight, the boat reached the shore in front of the gallery of the pure house of the holy apostle Thomas, which is in Brochthoi [Broch' thoi], and there it rested without advancing further. At the same hour, an angel of the Lord appeared in a dream to the superior and to the sacristan of the same august house, saying, "Rise and put the casket which you have found in the boat which has come to anchor on the shore in front of the gallery in the sanctuary." When they heard this, they saw all the church gates open by themselves, but since they were still asleep, they thought that the event was an illusion. Having secured the gates again, there appeared to them once more the previous vision. Still a third time, the angel pressed them with much earnestness and said, "Go out and take the casket of the holy Olympias, for she has suffered much for the sake of God, and put the casket in the sanctuary." Then they arose, again saw the gates of the church open, and no longer remained disbelieving. Taking the holy Gospels, the cross, the candelabra with candles, along with the incense, they went out praying into the gallery and found her holy remains in the boat. They called together all the female and male ascetics, and holding the candles and making great praise and thanksgiving to God, they deposited her holy remains in the sanctuary of the house of the holy apostle Thomas in Brochthoi. People could see numerous cures taking place at her holy tomb; impure spirits were banished and many diverse illnesses departed from those afflicted with them. The holy, pious blessed servant of God, Olympias, ended her life in the month of July, on the 25th, in the reign of the emperor Arcadius [Ar ca′ di us]. She is numbered in the choir of the pious confessors and reigns together with the immortal King, Christ our God, for ages without end.

TWENTY-FIRST WEEK OF THE YEAR
Friday
Life of Olympias 12–13 (#5 of 6)

Olympias' life was outstanding for its asceticism and charity, for she understood that the one is of no value without the other.

Let these things be said of Olympias. I have deemed it necessary and entirely useful for the profit of many to run over in the narrative one by one the holy virtues of the noble servant of God, Olympias, who is among the saints. For no place, no country, no desert, no island, no distant setting, remained without a share in the benevolence of this famous woman; rather, she furnished the churches with liturgical offerings and helped the monasteries and convents, the beggars, the prisoners, and those in exile; quite simply, she distributed her alms over the entire inhabited world. And the blessed Olympias herself burst the supreme limit in her almsgiving and her humility, so that nothing can be found greater than what she did. She had a life without vanity, an appearance without pretense, character without affectation, a face without adornment; she kept watch without sleeping, she had a mind without vainglory, intelligence without conceit, an untroubled heart, an artless spirit, charity without limits, unbounded generosity, contemptible clothing, immeasurable self-control, rectitude of thought, undying hope in God, ineffable almsgiving; she was the ornament of all the humble and was in addition worthily honored by the most holy patriarch John.

TWENTY-FIRST WEEK OF THE YEAR
Saturday
Life of Olympias 14–16 (#6 of 6)

Olympias was friend, hostess, and benefactor to some of the most important church leaders of her day, but her concern for the least powerful was just as great.

Olympias looked after the needs of many, including those of blessed John the archbishop. This is no small thing for the workers of Christ who are anxious both night and day for Christ's affairs. As Paul greeted Persis [Per' sis], Tryphaena [Try phae' na], and Tryphosa [Try pho' sa], the pious Olympias, imitator of God, perhaps received the same greeting.

And I know that this completely virtuous and divinely-inspired Olympias provided also for the blessed Nectarius [Nec ta' ri us], the archbishop of Constantinople, who was completely persuaded by her even in the affairs of the church, and for Amphilochius [Am phi lo' chi us], bishop of Iconium [I co' ni um], and Optimus [Op' ti mus], and Peter, and Gregory the brother of the holy Basil, and Epiphanius [Ep i pha' ni us] the archbishop of Constantia [Con stan' ti a] in Cyprus, and many others of the saints and inspired fathers who lived in the capital city. Why is it necessary to say that she also bestowed upon them property in the country and money? And when Optimus died in Constantinople at this time, she shut the eyes of the great man with her own hands. In addition, she relieved the piteous without measure in all ways. She sustained Antiochus [An ti' o chus] of Ptolemais [Ptol e ma' is], and Acacius [A ca' ci us], the bishop of Beroea [Be roe' a], and the holy Severian [Se ve' ri an], the bishop of Gabala [Ga ba' la], and in a word, all the priests residing there, in addition to innumerable ascetics and virgins.

And due to her sympathy for them, she endured many trials by the actions of a willfully evil and vulgar person. She lived full of every reverence, bowing before the saints, honoring bishops and presbyters, welcoming the ascetics, being anxious for the virgins, supplying the widows, raising the orphans, shielding the elderly, looking after the weak, having compassion on sinners, guiding the lost, having pity on all, pity without stinting anything on the poor. Engaging in much catechizing of unbelieving women and making provision for all the necessary things of life, she left a reputation for goodness throughout her whole life which is ever to be remembered.

Having called from slavery to freedom her myriad household servants, she proclaimed them to be of the same honor as her own nobility. Or rather, they appeared more noble in their way of dress than that holy woman. She cultivated in herself a gentleness so that she surpassed even the simplicity of children themselves.

The divine and divinely-inspired Olympias herself was deemed worthy as a confessor on behalf of the truth, and received the many storms of unjust slander; her life was judged to be among the confessors by as many pious people as dwelt in Constantinople. For close to death, she took the risk in the contests for God. Having perfected herself in these, she won the blessed glory and is crowned in an endless age. And she is a member of the chorus in the undefiled mansions where she lives and where she openly demands from the Lord God the recompense for good deeds.

TWENTY-SECOND SUNDAY OF THE YEAR
Matthew 25:1-13

In Matthew the wise and foolish virgins are juxtaposed, to the story of the faithful or the unfaithful servant [24:41-48]. Both parables contrast ways of being faithful in a time of absence.

"The kingdom of heaven will be like this. Ten bridesmaids took their lamps and went to meet the bridegroom. Five of them were foolish, and five were wise. When the foolish took their lamps, they took no oil with them; but the wise took flasks of oil with their lamps. As the bridegroom was delayed, all of them became drowsy and slept. But at midnight there was a shout. 'Look! Here is the bridegroom! Come out to meet him.' Then all those bridesmaids got up and trimmed their lamps. The foolish said to the wise, 'Give us some of your oil, for our lamps are going out.' But the wise replied, 'No! there will not be enough for you and for us; you had better go to the dealers and buy some for yourselves.' And while they went to buy it, the bridegroom came, and those who were ready went with him into the wedding banquet; and the door was shut. Later the other bridesmaids came also, saying, 'Lord, Lord, open to us.' But he replied, 'Truly, I tell you, I do not know you.' Keep awake therefore, for you know neither the day nor the hour."

See Luke 13:35-37

TWENTY-SECOND WEEK OF THE YEAR
Monday
Epiphanius, *Medicine Box* 49.1-2

This hostile description of Montanist groups under a variety of strange names highlights the prominence of women and their feminist biblical exegesis.

Either Quintilla [Quin til' la] or Priscilla [Pri scil' la], I am not sure which, but one of them, was, as they said, sleeping in Pepuza [Pe pu'za] when Christ came to her and lay beside her in the following fashion, as that deluded woman recounted. "In a vision," she said, "Christ came to me in the form of a woman in a bright garment, endowed me with wisdom, and revealed to me that this place is holy, and it is here that Jerusalem is to descend from heaven." Because of this, they say that even to this day some women and men engage in incubation on the spot waiting to see Christ. Some women among them are called prophetesses,

but I do not clearly know whether among them or among the Cataphrygians [Cat a phryg′ i ans]. They are alike and have the same way of
thinking.

They use both the Old and New Testament and also speak in the
same way of a resurrection of the dead. They consider Quintilla together
with Priscilla as founder, the same as the Cataphrygians. They bring with
them many useless testimonies, attributing a special grace to Eve because
she first ate of the tree of knowledge. They acknowledge Miriam, the
sister of Moses, as prophet as support for their practice of appointing
women to the clergy. Also, they say, Philip had four daughters who
prophesied. Often in their assembly seven virgins dressed in white enter
carrying lamps, having come in to prophesy to the people. They deceive
the people present by giving the appearance of ecstasy; they pretend to
weep as if showing the grief of repentance by shedding tears and by their
appearance lamenting human life. Women among them are bishops,
presbyters, and the rest, as if there were no difference of nature. "For in
Christ Jesus there is neither male nor female" (Gal 3:28). These are the
things we have learned about them.

TWENTY-SECOND WEEK OF THE YEAR
Tuesday
Augustine, *Confessions* 9.8 (#1 of 8)

*Augustine, his mother and brother, and a group of friends, are
returning from Italy to Africa when Monica dies along the way at
Ostia. He begins to recount her childhood, narrating as if in conversation with God.*

We started back to Africa. And when we had come as far as Ostia on
the Tiber, my mother died.

I pass over many things, because I am in much haste. Accept my
confessions and my thanksgiving, O my God, for innumerable things of
which I do not speak. But I shall not pass over whatever my soul brings
forth about her, that servant of yours, who brought me forth, giving me

birth in the flesh to this temporal light, and in her heart to eternal light. Not of her gifts do I speak but of your gifts in her. For she did not make herself nor did she bring herself up. You created her, nor did her father or mother know what kind of being was to come forth from them. The rod of your Christ, the discipline of your only-begotten Son, educated her in your fear, in a faithful household worthy to belong to your church. Yet she used to speak not so much of her mother's care in training her, as of the care of an elderly woman servant who had carried her father on her back as a baby, as small children are often carried about on the backs of the grown-up girls. Because of this service and on account of her age and excellent behavior, this servant was greatly respected by her master and mistress in this Christian household. Consequently, she had charge of the daughters of the family, one she fulfilled most conscientiously; in restraining the children when necessary, she acted sternly and with a holy severity, and in teaching them she manifested sound prudence. For example, except at the times they were fed—and very temperately—at their parents' table, she would not even let them drink water, however thirsty they might be, thus guarding against the formation of a bad habit, saying very sensibly: "Now you are drinking water because you are not allowed to have wine. But when you become married and become mistress of your stores and cellars, water will not be good enough for you, but you will have this habit of drinking." By this advice and by the authority she exercised, she brought under control the greediness from which children suffer and disciplined the girls' thirst to a proper moderation so that they no longer wanted what they ought not to have.

TWENTY-SECOND WEEK OF THE YEAR
Wednesday
Augustine, *Confessions* 9.8 (#2 of 8)

Augustine tells a story of his mother's childhood that probably indicates her to have been a recovering alcoholic. According to the thinking of the day, she saw her drinking habit as her fault, but the story, which she later told her son, reveals her strength and simplicity.

Nevertheless, as your servant [Monica] confided in me, her son, there did come upon my mother an inclination toward wine. For when, as the custom was, she as a good sober girl was told by her parents to go and draw some wine from the barrel, she would hold the cup under the tap and then before pouring the cup into the decanter, she would sip a little, just wetting her lips, since she did not like the taste and could not take more. Indeed, she did this not out of any craving for wine, but rather from the excess of childhood's high spirits, which tend to break loose in ridiculous impulses and which in our childhood years are usually kept under restraint by the sobering influence of elders. And so, adding to that daily drop a little more from day to day—for he "who despises small things shall fall little by little" (Sir 19:1)—she fell into the habit, so that greedily she would gulp down cups almost full of wine. Where, then, was that wise old woman with her stern prohibition? What did you do, then, O my God? How did you cure her? How did you make her healthy? Did you not from another soul bring forth a harsh and cutting taunt? For a maidservant, with whom she usually went to the cellar, one day fell into a quarrel with her small mistress when no one else chanced to be about, and hurled at her the most biting insult possible, calling her a drunkard. My mother was pierced to the quick, saw her fault in its true wickedness, and instantly condemned it and gave it up. Just as the flatteries of a friend will pervert, so the insults of an enemy will sometimes correct. Nor do you, O God, reward people for what you do through them, but according to what they themselves intended. For that maid, being in a temper, wanted to hurt her young mistress, not to cure her, for she did it when no one else was there, either because of the time and place where the quarrel started, or because she feared that the elders would be angry that she had not mentioned it sooner. But you, O Lord, Ruler of heavenly and earthly things, who turn to your own purposes the very depths of the torrents as they run and order the turbulence of the flow of time, brought health to one soul by means of the unhealthiness of another, showing us that if someone is improved by any word of ours, we must not attribute this to our own power, even if we intended this result to occur.

TWENTY-SECOND WEEK OF THE YEAR
Thursday
Augustine, *Confessions* 9.9 (#3 of 8)

Monica was psychologically abused by her pagan husband, but by her strength of character avoided the physical abuse so common among her friends. As a woman of her time, she accepted her husband's dominance but knew how to work with it as her society and her own intelligence allowed.

My mother was educated, therefore, in a modest sober way, being rather made obedient to her parents by you than to you by her parents. And when she reached marriageable age, she was given to a husband whom she served "as her lord." She tried to win him to you, preaching you to him by her behavior in which you had made her beautiful to her husband, reverently lovable and admirable in his sight. So she tolerated his infidelities and never had a jealous scene with her husband about them. She awaited your mercy upon him, that he might grow chaste through faith in you. Although an extremely kind man by nature, he was, in fact, also very hot-tempered. Only when he had calmed down and had become quiet, when she saw an opportunity, she would explain her actions, if perchance he had been aroused to anger unreasonably. Indeed there were many wives with much milder husbands who bore the marks of beatings, even in the form of facial disfigurement, and coming together to talk, they would complain of their husbands' behavior. Yet my mother, speaking lightly but seriously, warned them that the fault was in their tongues. And they were often amazed, knowing how violent a husband she had to live with, that it had never been heard of, nor had there been any evidence to show that Patricius [Pa tric' i us] had ever beaten his wife or that there had been a family quarrel that had lasted as much as a single day.

TWENTY-SECOND WEEK OF THE YEAR
Friday
Augustine, *Confessions* 9.9 (#4 of 8)

Monica's gift of reconciliation and personal example brought about her husband's conversion.

This great gift also, O my God, my mercy, you gave to your good servant, in whose womb you created me, that she showed herself, wherever possible, a peacemaker between people quarreling and minds at discord. But my mother would never report to one woman what had been said about her by another except insofar as what had been said might help to reconcile the two. I might consider this a small virtue if I had not had the sad experience of knowing innumerable people who, through some horrible infection of sin, not only tell others who are angry what their enemies said about them in anger, but actually add things which never were said. Whereas ordinary humanity would seem to require not merely restraining from exciting or increasing wrath among people by evil tongues, but that we endeavor to extinguish anger by speaking kindly. This is what my mother did, and you were the master who, deep in the school of her heart, taught her this lesson.

Finally, toward the end of his earthly life, she won her husband over to you, and now that he was a believer, she no longer had to lament the things she had to tolerate when he was not yet a believer. She was also the servant of your servants. Whoever knew her praised many things in her, and honored and loved you, because they felt your presence in her heart, through the fruitful evidence of her saintly manner of life. She had been the wife of one husband, had requited her parents, had governed her house piously, was well reported of for good works; she had "brought up her children" as often "travailing in birth of them" as she saw them straying away from you (1 Tim 5:9; Gal 4:19).

Finally, Lord, of all of us—since by your gift we are allowed to speak—who before her death were living together after receiving the grace of baptism, she took as much care as though she were the mother of us all, and served us as though she were the daughter of us all.

TWENTY-SECOND WEEK OF THE YEAR
Saturday
Augustine, *Confessions* 9.10 (#5 of 8)

Augustine describes the experience of deep prayer he shared with his mother a few days before she died.

The day was now approaching on which my mother was to depart this life—the day you knew though we did not—it came about, as, I believe, by your secret arrangement that she and I stood alone leaning in a window which looked onto the garden inside the house where we were staying, at Ostia on the Tiber where, apart from the group, we were resting for the sea voyage after the weariness of our long journey by land. There we conversed, she and I alone, very sweetly, and "forgetting the things that were behind and straining forward to those ahead" (Phil 3:13), we were discussing in the presence of Truth, which you are, what the eternal life of the saints would be like, "which eye has not seen nor ear heard, nor has it entered into the human heart" (1 Cor 2:9). But with the mouth of our heart we also panted for the supernal streams from your fountain, the fountain of life which is with you (Ps 35:10).

And while we were speaking and panting for wisdom, we did with the whole impulse of the heart slightly touch it. We sighed and left behind "the first fruits of the Spirit" (Rom 8:23) which were bound there, and returned to the sound of our own tongue where the spoken word has both beginning and ending. How is it like your word, our Lord, "remaining ageless in itself and renewing all things" (Wis 7:27)? We said therefore: If to anyone the uproar of the flesh grew silent, silent the images of earth and sea and air; and if the heavens also grew silent and the very soul grew silent to itself, and by not thinking of self ascended beyond self; if all dreams and imagined revelations grew silent, and every tongue and every sign and everything created to pass away were completely silent—since if one hears them, they all say this: We did not make ourselves, but God who abides forever made us. Suppose that, having said this and directed our attention to God who made them, they also were to become hushed and God alone were to speak, not by their voice but in

God's own, and we were to hear God's Word, not through any tongue of flesh or voice of an angel or sound of thunder or involved allegory, but that we might hear God whom in all these things we love, might hear God without these things, just as a moment ago we two, as it were, rose beyond ourselves and in a flash of thought touched the Eternal Wisdom abiding over all. If this were to continue and other quite different visions disappear, leaving only this one to ravish and absorb and enclose its beholder in inward joys so that life might forever be such as that one moment of understanding for which we had been sighing, would not this surely be: "Enter into the joy of Your Lord" (Matt 25:21)? But when shall it be? Perhaps when "we shall all rise again" and "shall not all be changed" (1 Cor 15:51)?

TWENTY-THIRD SUNDAY OF THE YEAR
Augustine, *Confessions* 9.10–11 (#6 of 8)

As so often happens at death, the dying Monica has let go of her previous plans for her place of burial. She can even joke that God will know where to find her.

O Lord, you know that on that day when we talked of these things the world with all its delights seemed worthless to us, even as we were speaking of it. Then my mother said: "Son, as for me, I no longer take delight in anything in this life. What I am doing here now, and why I am here I do not know, now that I have nothing else to hope for in this world. There was only one reason why I wanted to remain a little longer in this life, that I should see you a Catholic Christian before I died. This God has granted me superabundantly. What am I doing here?"

What I answered to this I do not clearly remember; within five days or not much longer she fell into a fever. And in that sickness she one day fainted away and for the moment lost consciousness. We ran to her, but she quickly regained consciousness, and seeing my brother and me standing by her, she said to us, as though seeking an answer to some question, "Where am I?" Then gazing intently upon us as we stood speechless in our grief, she said: "Bury your mother here." I was silent and restrained my weeping; but my brother said something about hoping that she would have the good fortune to die in her own country and not in a foreign land. But when she heard this, she looked anxious and gave him a reproachful look because he still relished earthly things. Then she looked into my face and said: "See how he talks." Soon she said to both of us: "You may lay this body of mine anywhere: Do not worry at all about that. All I ask you is this: that wherever you may be, you will remember me at the altar of the Lord." And when she had expressed this wish in such words as she could, she fell silent as the agony of her sickness grew stronger upon her.

I rejoiced and gave thanks to you, recalling that I knew how worried and anxious she had always been about the question of her burial. She had already provided herself and prepared a tomb close to that of her husband. Since they had lived together in such harmony, she had wished —so little is the human mind capable of grasping things divine—that it should be granted her as an addition to her happiness and to have it spoken of, that after her pilgrimage across the sea the earthly part of both man and wife should lie covered under the same earth. Just when this desire began to leave her heart through the plenitude of your goodness, I did not know; but I was pleased and surprised that it had now vanished, although in that conversation of ours together in the window, when she said: "What am I still doing here?" she had shown no desire to die in her own country. Furthermore, I later heard that when we were at Ostia, she spoke one day to some of my friends, as a mother speaking to her children, and they inquired whether she was not afraid to leave her body so far from her own city. "Nothing," she said, "is far from God and I do not fear that God will not know at the end of the world from what place to raise me up." And so on the ninth day of her illness, in the fifty-sixth year of life and the thirty-third of mine, that religious and holy soul was released from the body.

TWENTY-THIRD WEEK OF THE YEAR
Monday
Augustine, *Confessions* 9.12 (#7 of 8)

Augustine recounts his grief and loss at his mother's death, remembering her last words of gratitude to him and her directions about burial arrangements. He is unable at first to express his grief.

I closed her eyes; and an immense wave of sorrow flooded my heart and would have overflowed in tears. But my eyes under the mind's strong constraint seemed to pump that fountain dry, and in that struggle it was agony for me. Then as soon as she had breathed her last, the boy Adeodatus [A de o da' tus] (Augustine's son) broke out in lamentation until, constrained by all of us, he grew silent. But in this very deed, the childish element in me which was breaking out in tears was checked and silenced by the manlier voice of my mind. For we felt that it was not appropriate that her funeral should be marked with moaning and weeping and lamentation, because these are the way people grieve for an utter wretchedness in death or a kind of total extinction. But she had not died miserably nor did she wholly die. Of this we had good reason to be certain from the evidence of her way of living and from her "unfeigned faith" (1 Tim 1:5).

What was it, then, that grieved my heart so deeply except the freshness of the wound, in finding the custom I had so loved, of living with her, suddenly snapped short? I rejoiced in the testimony she gave me in the very last days of her illness when, as I was doing what service I could for her, she spoke so affectionately to me, calling me her good and dutiful son, with such great love, she told me that she had never once heard me say a word to her that was hard or bitter. And yet, my God, who made us, what comparison was there between the honor I showed her and the service she rendered me?

Because I had now lost the great comfort of her, my soul was wounded and my very life torn asunder, for it had been one life made up of hers and mine together. And when it was known what we were doing, many brethren and religious women gathered. And while those whose function it was made arrangements for the burial, I with some of my friends who thought I should not be left alone found another part of the house where we could properly be, and there I spoke to them on such subjects as I thought appropriate for the occasion.

When the body was carried to the grave, we went and returned without tears. During the prayers we poured forth to you when the sacrifice of our redemption was offered for her—while the body, as was customary there, lay by the grave before it was actually buried—during those prayers I did not weep. Yet all that day I was heavy with hidden grief and in my troubled mind I begged you, as best I could, to heal my sorrow; but you did not.

TWENTY-THIRD WEEK OF THE YEAR
Tuesday
Augustine, *Confessions* 9.12–13 (#8 of 8)

Augustine grieves for his mother and gives his final tribute to her, commending both his parents to the prayers of his friends and readers.

Little by little I began to recover my former feelings about your handmaid, Monica, her devout and holy behavior in regard to you, her saintly kindness and benevolence toward us, of which I was suddenly deprived. And I found solace in weeping in your sight both about her and for her, about myself and for myself. So I allowed the tears which I had been holding back to fall, and I let them flow as they would, making them a pillow for my heart, and my heart rested on them, since only your ears were there, not those of someone who would have scornfully misunderstood my tears.

Let her, therefore, rest in peace with her husband, before or after whom she had no other, whom she obeyed, "with patience bringing forth fruit" for you, so that she might win him for you also. And inspire, my Lord and my God, inspire your servants, whom I serve with heart and voice and pen, so that as many as shall read this may remember at your altar Monica, your servant, with Patricius her husband, through whose flesh you introduced me into this life, though how I know not. May they with holy affection remember those who were my parents in this transitory light, and my fellow citizens in the eternal Jerusalem which your people sigh after in their pilgrimage from the beginning of their journey until their return, so that what my mother in her extremity asked of me may be fulfilled for her more fully through my confessions by the prayers of many, rather than through my prayers alone.

TWENTY-THIRD WEEK OF THE YEAR
Wednesday
Proverbs 6:20–23

It is Wisdom which tutors the heart.

> My child, keep your father's commandment,
>   and do not forsake your mother's teaching.
> Bind them upon your heart always;
>   tie them around your neck.
> When you walk, they will lead you;
>   when you lie down, they will watch over you;
>   and when you awake, they will talk with you.
> For the commandment is a lamp
>   and the teaching a light,
> and the reproofs of discipline are the way of life.

TWENTY-THIRD WEEK OF THE YEAR
Thursday
Genesis 29:4–12 (#1 of 3)

As Bedouin women still do, Rachel tended the flocks of her father Laban, bringing them to the well to drink. Could she not also be an image of the "good shepherd"?

Jacob said to the shepherds, "My brothers, where do you come from?" They said, "We are from Haran." He said to them, "Do you know Laban, son of Nahor?" They said, "We do." He said to them, "Is it well with him?" "Yes," they replied, "and here is his daughter Rachel, coming with the sheep." He said, "Look, it is still broad daylight; it is not time for the animals to be gathered together. Water the sheep, and go, pasture them." But they said, "We cannot, until all the flocks are gathered together and the stone is rolled from the mouth of the well; then we water the sheep."

While he was still speaking with them, Rachel came with her father's sheep; for she kept them. Now when Jacob saw Rachel, the daughter of his mother's brother Laban, and the sheep of his mother's brother Laban, Jacob went up and rolled the stone from the well's mouth, and watered the flock of his mother's brother Laban. Then Jacob kissed Rachel and wept aloud. And Jacob told Rachel that he was her father's kinsman, and he was Rebekah's son; and she ran and told her father.

TWENTY-THIRD WEEK OF THE YEAR
Friday
Genesis 29:13–30 (#2 of 3)

The "bride-price" for Rachel was seven years of service which Jacob willingly paid, out of his love for her. But Laban's treachery gave Jacob Leah as his wife, and, only in return for more service, also Rachel. The plight of Leah is tragic; she not only becomes the unloved wife but also the reminder of Laban's deception.

When Laban heard the news about his sister's son Jacob, he ran to meet him; he embraced him and kissed him, and brought him to his house. Jacob told Laban all these things, and Laban said to him, "Surely you are my bone and my flesh!" And he stayed with him a month.

Then Laban said to Jacob, "Because you are my kinsman, should you therefore serve me for nothing? Tell me, what shall your wages be?" Now Laban had two daughters; the name of the elder was Leah, and the name of the younger was Rachel. Leah's eyes were lovely, and Rachel was graceful and beautiful. Jacob loved Rachel; so he said, "I will serve you seven years for your younger daughter Rachel." Laban said, "It is better that I give her to you than I should give her to any other man; stay with me." So Jacob served seven years for Rachel, and they seemed to him but a few days because of the love he had for her.

Then Jacob said to Laban, "Give me my wife that I may go in to her, for my time is completed." So Laban gathered together all the people of the place, and made a feast. But in the evening he took his daughter Leah and brought her to Jacob; and he went in to her. When morning came, it was Leah! And Jacob said to Laban, "What is this you have done to me? Did I not serve with you for Rachel? Why then have you deceived me?" Laban said, "This is not done in our country—giving the younger before the firstborn. Complete the week of this one, and we will give you the other also in return for serving me another seven years." Jacob did so, and completed her week; then Laban gave him his daughter Rachel as a wife. So Jacob went in to Rachel also, and he loved Rachel more than Leah. He served Laban for another seven years.

TWENTY-THIRD WEEK OF THE YEAR
Saturday
Genesis 35:16–21 (#3 of 3)

After Rachel died in childbirth, Jacob changed the name she gave her son, preferring to name him Benjamin—"Son of my right hand." The exact location of Rachel's tomb is unknown, but "to this day" pilgrims visit the site of "Rachel's tomb" near the village of Bethlehem.

Jacob, and all the people with him, journeyed from Bethel; and when they were still some distance from Ephrath [Eph' rath], Rachel was in childbirth, and she had hard labor. When she was in her hard labor, the midwife said to her, "Do not be afraid; for now you will have another son." As her soul was departing (for she died), she named him Ben-oni ("Son of my sorrow"); but his father called him Benjamin ("Son of my right hand"). So Rachel died, and she was buried on the way to Ephrath (that is, Bethlehem), and Jacob set up a pillar at her grave; it is the pillar of Rachel's tomb, which is there to this day. Israel journeyed on, and pitched his tent beyond the tower of Eder.

TWENTY-FOURTH SUNDAY OF THE YEAR
Luke 8:1–3

Contrary to the popular image of "the twelve," some of Jesus' itinerant disciples—those who left everything to follow him—were women.

Jesus went on through cities and villages, proclaiming and bringing the good news of the kingdom of God. The twelve were with him, as well as some women who had been cured of evil spirits and infirmities: Mary, called Magdalene, from whom seven demons had gone out, and Joanna, the wife of Herod's steward Chuza, and Susanna, and many others, who provided for them out of their resources.

See Mark 15:40–41

TWENTY-FOURTH WEEK OF THE YEAR
Monday
Esther 1:5–22 passim (#1 of 13)

The book of Esther begins with the story of Queen Vashti whose refusal to comply with patriarchal power sends shock waves throughout the empire.

King Ahasuerus [A ha su' e rus] gave for all the people present in the citadel of Susa, both great and small, a banquet lasting for seven days, in the court of the garden of the king's palace. There were white cotton curtains and blue hangings tied with cords of fine linen and purple to silver rings and marble pillars. There were couches of gold and silver on a mosaic pavement of porphyry, marble, mother-of-pearl, and colored stones. Drinks were served in golden goblets, goblets of different kinds, and the royal wine was lavished according to the bounty of the king. Drinking was by flagons, without restraint; for the king had given orders to all the officials of his palace to do as each one desired. Furthermore, Queen Vashti gave a banquet for the women in the palace of King Ahasuerus.

On the seventh day, when the king was merry with wine, he commanded the seven eunuchs who attended him to bring Queen Vashti before the king, wearing the royal crown, in order to show the peoples and the officials her beauty, for she was fair to behold. But Queen Vashti refused to come at the king's command conveyed by the eunuchs. At this the king was enraged, and his anger burned within him.

Then the king consulted the sages who knew the laws (for this was the king's procedure toward all who were versed in law and custom). One of the officials said in the presence of the king and the officials, "Not only has Queen Vashti done wrong to the king, but also to all the officials and all the peoples who are in all the provinces of King Ahasuerus. For this deed of the queen will be made known to all women, causing them to look with contempt on their husbands. This very day the noble ladies of Persia and Media who have heard of the queen's behavior will rebel against the king's officials, and there will be no end of contempt and wrath! If it pleases the king, let a royal order go out from him, and let it be written among the laws of the Persians and Medes so that it may not be altered, that Vashti is never again to come before King Ahasuerus; and let the king give her royal position to another who is better than she. So when the decree made by the king is proclaimed throughout all his kingdom, vast as it is, all women will give honor to their husbands, high and low alike."

This advice pleased the king and the officials, and the king did as proposed; he sent letters to all the royal provinces, to every people in its own language, declaring that every man should be master in his own house.

TWENTY-FOURTH WEEK OF THE YEAR
Tuesday
Esther 2:1–11 (#2 of 3)

Esther appears among all the beautiful, young women assembled like chattel for the king's pleasure.

After these things, when the anger of King Ahasuerus had abated, he remembered Vashti and what she had done and what had been decreed against her. Then the king's servants who attended him said, "Let beautiful young virgins be sought out for the king. And let the king appoint commissioners in all the provinces of his kingdom to gather all the beautiful young virgins to the harem in the citadel of Susa under custody of Hegai, the king's eunuch, who is in charge of the women; let their cosmetic treatments be given them, and let the girl who pleases the king be queen instead of Vashti." This pleased the king, and he did so.

Now there was a Jew in the citadel of Susa whose name was Mordecai [Mor' de cai], a Benjaminite [Ben' ja mi nite]. His father had been carried away from Jerusalem among the captives carried away with King Jeconiah of Judah, whom King Nebuchadnezzar [Neb u chad nez' zar] of Babylon had carried away. Mordecai had brought up Hadassah, that is Esther, his cousin, for she had neither father nor mother. The girl was fair and beautiful, and when her father and her mother died, Mordecai adopted her as his own daughter. So when the king's order and his edict were proclaimed, and when many young women were gathered in the citadel of Susa in custody of Hegai, the eunuch in charge of women, Esther also was taken. The girl pleased Hegai and won his favor, and he quickly provided her with her cosmetic treatments and her portion of food, and with seven chosen maids from the king's palace, and advanced her and her maids to the best place in the harem. Esther did not reveal her people or kindred, for Mordecai had charged her not to tell. Every day Mordecai would walk around in front of the court of the harem, to learn how Esther was and how she fared.

TWENTY-FOURTH WEEK OF THE YEAR
Wednesday
Esther 2:12–18 passim (#3 of 13)

Esther replaces Vashti on the throne.

The turn came for each girl to go in to King Ahasuerus, after being twelve months under the regulations for the women, since this was the regular period of their cosmetic treatment, six months with oil of myrrh and six months with perfumes and cosmetics for women. When the girl went in to the king she was given whatever she asked for to take with her from the harem to the king's palace. In the evening she went in; then in the morning she came back to the second harem in custody of Shaashgaz [Sha ash' gaz], the king's eunuch, who was in charge of the concubines; she did not go in to the king again, unless the king delighted in her and she was summoned by name.

When the turn came for Esther, daughter of Abihail [A' bi ha il] the uncle of Mordecai, who had adopted her as his own daughter, to go in to the king, she asked for nothing except what Hegai advised. Now Esther was admired by all who saw her. When Esther was taken to King Ahasuerus in his royal palace in the tenth month, which is the month of Tebeth in the seventh year of his reign, the king loved Esther more than all the other women; of all the virgins, she won his favor and devotion, so that he set the royal crown on her head and made her queen instead of Vashti. Then the king gave a great banquet to all his officials and ministers—"Esther's banquet." He also granted a holiday to the provinces, and gave gifts with royal liberality.

TWENTY-FOURTH WEEK OF THE YEAR
Thursday
Esther 2:19–23 (#4 of 13)

Esther, with the help of her cousin, exposes a plot to assassinate her husband.

When the virgins were being gathered together, Mordecai was sitting at the king's gate. Now Esther had not revealed her kindred or her people, as Mordecai had charged her; for Esther obeyed Mordecai just as when she was brought up by him. In those days while Mordecai was sitting at the king's gate, two of the king's eunuchs, who guarded the threshold, became angry and conspired to assassinate King Ahasuerus. But the matter came to the knowledge of Mordecai, and he told it to Queen Esther, and Esther told the king in the name of Mordecai. When the affair was investigated and found to be so, both the men were hanged on the gallows. It was recorded in the book of the annals in the presence of the king.

TWENTY-FOURTH WEEK OF THE YEAR
Friday
Esther 3:1–4:8 passim (#5 of 13)

Haman, an official in the favor of the king, plots to destroy the Jews. Only Esther can save them.

King Ahasuerus promoted Haman, and advanced him and set his seat above all the officials who were with him. But Mordecai would not bow down or do obeisance to Haman. So, having been told who Mordecai's people were, Haman plotted to destroy all the Jews, the people of Mordecai, throughout the whole kingdom of Ahasuerus.
    When Mordecai learned of these plans, he tore his clothes and put

on sackcloth and ashes, and went through the city, wailing with a loud and bitter cry; he went up to the entrance of the king's gate, for no one might enter the king's gate clothed with sackcloth. In every province, wherever the king's command and his decree came, there was great mourning among the Jews, with fasting and weeping and lamenting, and most of them lay in sackcloth and ashes.

When Esther's maids and her eunuchs came and told her, the queen was deeply distressed; she sent garments to clothe Mordecai, so that he might take off his sackcloth; but he would not accept them. Then Esther called for one of the king's eunuchs, who had been appointed to attend her, and ordered him to go to Mordecai to learn what was happening and why. The eunuch went out to Mordecai in the open square of the city, in front of the king's gate, and Mordecai told him all that had happened to him and the exact sum of money that Haman had promised to pay into the king's treasuries for the destruction of the Jews. Mordecai also gave him a copy of the written decree issued in Susa for the destruction of the Jews, that he might show it to Esther, explain it to her, and charge her to go to the king to make supplication to him and entreat him for her people.

TWENTY-FOURTH WEEK OF THE YEAR
Saturday
Esther 4:9–16 (#6 of 13)

Esther, together with the whole Jewish community, prepares herself by prayer and fasting to undertake a courageous action to save her people.

The eunuch went and told Esther what Mordecai had said. Then Esther gave him a message for Mordecai, saying, "All the king's servants and the people of the king's provinces know that if any man or woman goes to the king inside the inner court without being called, there is but one law—all alike are to be put to death. Only if the king holds out the golden scepter to someone, may that person live. I myself have not been called to come in to the king for thirty days." When they told Mordecai what Esther had said, Mordecai told them to reply to Esther, "Do not think that in the king's palace you will escape any more than all the other Jews. For if you keep silence at such a time as this, relief and deliverance will rise for the Jews from another quarter, but you and your father's family will perish. Who knows? Perhaps you have come to royal dignity for just such a time as this." Then Esther said in reply to Mordecai, "Go, gather all the Jews to be found in Susa, and hold a fast on my behalf, and neither eat nor drink for three days, night or day. I and my maids will also fast as you do. After that, I will go to the king, though it is against the law; and if I perish, I perish." Mordecai then went away and did everything as Esther had ordered him.

TWENTY-FIFTH SUNDAY OF THE YEAR
Esther, Addition D 15:1–16 (#7 of 13)*

Despite her terror, Esther confronts the king.

On the third day, when Esther ended her prayer, she took off the garments in which she had worshiped, and arrayed herself in splendid attire. Then, majestically adorned, after invoking the aid of the all-seeing God and Savior, she took two maids with her; on one, she leaned gently for support, while the other followed, carrying her train. She was radiant with perfect beauty, and she looked happy, as if beloved, but her heart was frozen with fear. When she had gone through all the doors, she stood before the king. He was seated on his royal throne, clothed in the full array of his majesty, all covered with gold and precious stones. He was most terrifying.

Lifting his face, flushed with splendor, he looked at her in fierce anger. The queen faltered, and turned pale and faint, and collapsed on the head of the maid who went in front of her. Then God changed the spirit of the king to gentleness, and in alarm he sprang from his throne

---

* The Hebrew text of Esther has been augmented in the Greek version by several additions.

and took her in his arms until she came to herself. He comforted her with soothing words, and said to her, "What is it, Esther? I am your husband. Take courage; you shall not die, for our law applies only to our subjects. Come near."

Then he raised the golden scepter and touched her neck with it; he embraced her, and said, "Speak to me." She said to him, "I saw you like an angel of God, and my heart was shaken with fear at your glory. For you are wonderful, and your countenance is full of grace." And while she was speaking, she fainted and fell. Then the king was agitated, and all his servants tried to comfort her.

TWENTY-FIFTH WEEK OF THE YEAR
Monday
Esther 5:3–8 (#8 of 13)

Esther postpones her confrontation with the king while plying him with food and drink.

The king said to Esther, "What is it, Queen Esther? What is your request? It shall be given you, even to the half of my kingdom." Then Esther said, "If it pleases the king, let the king and Haman come today to a banquet that I have prepared for the king." Then the king said, "Bring Haman quickly, so that we may do as Esther desires." So the king and Haman came to the banquet that Esther had prepared. While they were drinking wine, the king said to Esther, "What is your petition? It shall be granted you. And what is your request? Even to the half of my kingdom, it shall be fulfilled." Then Esther said, "This is my petition, and request: let the king and Haman come tomorrow to the banquet that I will prepare for them, and then I will do as the king has said."

TWENTY-FIFTH WEEK OF THE YEAR
Tuesday
Esther 5:9-14 (#9 of 13)

Esther's cousin Mordecai remains a thorn in Haman's side. Haman himself is taken in by Esther's ploy.

Haman went out that day happy and in good spirits. But when Haman saw Mordecai in the king's gate, and observed that he neither rose nor trembled before him, he was infuriated with Mordecai; nevertheless Haman restrained himself and went home. Then he sent and called for his friends and his wife Zeresh, and Haman recounted to them the splendor of his riches, the number of his sons, all the promotions with which the king had honored him, and how he had advanced him above the officials and ministers of the king. Haman added, "Even Queen Esther let no one but myself come with the king to the banquet that she prepared. Tomorrow also I am invited by her, together with the king. Yet all this does me no good so long as I see the Jew Mordecai sitting at the king's gate." Then his wife Zeresh and all his friends said to him, "Let a gallows fifty cubits high be made, and in the morning tell the king to have Mordecai hanged on it; then go with the king to the banquet in good spirits." This advice pleased Haman, and he had the gallows made.

TWENTY-FIFTH WEEK OF THE YEAR
Wednesday
Esther 6:1-14 passim (#10 of 13)

Mordecai escapes Haman's treachery.

On that night the king could not sleep, and he gave orders to bring the book of records, the annals, and they were read to the king. It was found written how Mordecai had told about two of the king's eunuchs, who guarded the threshold, and who had conspired to assassinate King Ahasuerus. Then the king said, "What honor or distinction has been bestowed on Mordecai for this?" The king's servants who attended him said, "Nothing has been done for him." The king said, "Who is in the court?" Now Haman had just entered the outer court of the king's palace to speak to the king about having Mordecai hanged on the gallows that he had prepared for him. So the king's servants told him, "Haman is there, standing in the court." The king said, "Let him come in." The king said to him, "What shall be done for the man whom the king wishes to honor?" [After Haman spoke] the king said, "Quickly, take the robes and the horse, as you have said, and honor the Jew Mordecai. Leave out nothing that you have mentioned." So Haman took the robes and the horse and robed Mordecai and led him riding through the open square of the city, proclaiming, "Thus shall it be done for the man whom the king wishes to honor."

Then Mordecai returned to the king's gate, but Haman hurried to his house, mourning and with his head covered. When Haman told his wife Zeresh and all his friends everything that had happened to him, his advisers and his wife Zeresh said to him, "If Mordecai, before whom your downfall has begun, is of the Jewish people, you will not prevail against him, but will surely fall before him." While they were still talking with him, the king's eunuchs arrived and hurried Haman off to the banquet that Esther had prepared.

TWENTY-FIFTH WEEK OF THE YEAR
Thursday
Esther 7:1–10 (#11 of 13)

Esther intercedes on behalf of her people and Haman gets his just desserts.

The king and Haman went in to feast with Queen Esther. On the second day, as they were drinking wine, the king again said to Esther, "What is your petition, Queen Esther? It shall be granted you. Even to the half of my kingdom, it shall be fulfilled." Then Queen Esther answered, "If it pleases the king, let my life be given me—that is my petition—and the lives of my people—that is my request. For we have been sold, I and my people, to be destroyed, to be killed, and to be annihilated. If we had been sold merely as slaves, men and women, I would have held my peace; but no enemy can compensate for this damage to the king." Then King Ahasuerus said to Queen Esther, "Who is he, and where is he, who has presumed to do this?" Esther said, "A foe and enemy, this wicked Haman!" Then Haman was terrified before the king and the queen. The king rose from the feast in wrath and went into the palace garden, but Haman stayed to beg his life from Queen Esther, for he saw that the king had determined to destroy him. When the king returned from the palace garden to the banquet hall, Haman had thrown himself on the couch where Esther was reclining; and the king said, "Will he even assault the queen in my presence, in my own house?" As the words left the mouth of the king, the servants covered Haman's face. Then one of the eunuchs in attendance on the king, said, "Look, the very gallows that Haman has prepared for Mordecai, whose word saved the king, stands at Haman's house, fifty cubits high." And the king said, "Hang him on that." So they hanged Haman on the gallows that he had prepared for Mordecai. Then the anger of the king abated.

On that day King Ahasuerus gave to Queen Esther the house of Haman, the enemy of the Jews; and Mordecai came before the king, for Esther had told what he was to her. Then the king took off his signet ring, which he had taken from Haman, and gave it to Mordecai. So Esther set Mordecai over the house of Haman.

TWENTY-FIFTH WEEK OF THE YEAR
Friday
Esther 8:3–10 passim (#12 of 13)

Esther is invested with royal authority.

Esther spoke again to the king; she fell at his feet, weeping and pleading with him to avert the evil design of Haman and the plot that he had devised against the Jews. The king held out the golden scepter to

Esther, and Esther rose and stood before the king. She said, "If it pleases the king, let an order be written to revoke the letters devised by Haman, which he wrote giving orders to destroy the Jews who are in all the provinces of the king. For how can I bear to see the calamity that is coming on my people? Or how can I bear to see the destruction of my kindred?" Then King Ahasuerus said to Queen Esther and to the Jew Mordecai, "See, I have given Esther the house of Haman, and they have hanged him on the gallows, because he plotted to lay hands on the Jews. You may write as you please with regard to the Jews, in the name of the king, and seal it with the king's ring for an edict written in the name of the king and sealed with the king's ring cannot be revoked."

Mordecai wrote letters in the name of King Ahasuerus, sealed them with the king's ring, and sent them by mounted couriers riding on fast steeds bred from the royal herd.

TWENTY-FIFTH WEEK OF THE YEAR
Saturday
Esther 9:20–32 passim (#13 of 13)

Esther is responsible for establishing the Jewish feast of Purim.

Mordecai recorded these things and sent letters to all the Jews who were in all the provinces of King Ahasuerus, both near and far, enjoining them that they should keep the fourteenth day of the month of Adar and also the fifteenth day of the same month, year by year, as the days on which the Jews gained relief from their enemies, and as the month that had been turned for them from sorrow into gladness and from mourning into a holiday; that they should make them days of feasting and gladness, days for sending gifts of food to one another and presents to the poor. So the Jews adopted as a custom what they had begun to do after their victory.

Haman, the enemy of all the Jews, had cast Pur—that is "the lot"— to crush and destroy them. Therefore these days are called Purim, from the word Pur, and should be remembered and kept throughout every generation, in every family, province, and city; and these days of Purim should never fall into disuse among the Jews, nor should the commemoration of these days cease among their descendants.

Then the command of Queen Esther also fixed these practices of Purim, and it was recorded in writing.

TWENTY-SIXTH SUNDAY OF THE YEAR
Jerome, *Life of Marcella* 1–2 (#1 of 6)

Marcella, a wealthy Roman noblewoman of the late fourth–early fifth century, was both orphaned and widowed at an early age. Taking her early widowhood as a sign from God, like many highborn women of her day, she dedicated herself to chastity and a life of prayer.

You have besought me often and earnestly, Principia [Prin cip′ i a], virgin of Christ, to dedicate a letter to the memory of that holy woman Marcella [Mar cel′ la], and to set forth the goodness long enjoyed by us for others to know and to imitate. I am so anxious myself to do justice to her merits that it grieves me that you should spur me on and fancy that your entreaties are needed when I do not yield even to you in love of her. In putting upon record her signal virtues I shall receive far more benefit myself than I can possibly confer upon others. If I have hitherto remained silent and have allowed two years to go without making any sign, this has not been owing to a wish to ignore her as you wrongly suppose, but to an incredible sorrow which so overcame my mind that I judged it better to remain silent for a while than to praise her virtues in inadequate language. Neither will I now follow the rules of rhetoric in eulogizing one so dear to both of us and to all the saints, Marcella the glory of her native Rome. I will not set forth her illustrious family and the lofty lineage, nor will I trace her pedigree through a line of consuls and praetorian prefects. I will praise her for nothing but the virtue which is her own and which is the more noble, because forsaking both wealth and rank she has sought the true nobility of poverty and lowliness.

Her father's death left her an orphan, and she had been married less than seven months when her husband was taken from her. Then, as she was young and highborn, as well as distinguished for her beauty—always an attraction to men—and her self-control, an illustrious consular named Cerealis [Ce re a' lis] paid court to her with great assiduity. Being an old man he offered to make over to her his fortune so that she might consider herself less his wife than his daughter. Her mother Albina [Al bi' na] went out of her way to secure for the young widow so exalted a protector. But Marcella answered, "Had I a wish to marry and not rather to dedicate myself to perpetual chastity, I should look for a husband and not for an inheritance." And when her suitor argued that sometimes old men live long while young men die early, she cleverly retorted, "A young man may indeed die early, but an old man cannot live long." This decided rejection of Cerealis convinced others that they had no hope of winning her hand.

In the gospel according to Luke we read the following passage: "There was one Anna, a prophet, the daughter of Phanuel [Pha' nu el], of the tribe of Aser: she was of great age, and had lived with a husband seven years from her virginity; and she was a widow of about fourscore and four years, who did not depart from the temple but served God with fastings and prayers night and day" (Luke 2:36). It was no marvel that she won the vision of the Saviour, whom she sought so earnestly.

TWENTY-SIXTH WEEK OF THE YEAR
Monday
Jerome, *Life of Marcella* 3–4 (#2 of 6)

Marcella showed her wisdom, discretion, and administrative ability in her life of asceticism, and established a pattern of generosity to the poor.

In a slander-loving community such as Rome, filled as it formerly was with people from all parts, and bearing the palm for wickedness of all kinds, detraction assailed the upright and strove to defile even the pure and the clean. In such an atmosphere it is hard to escape from the breath of calumny. Who ever heard a slander of Marcella that deserved the least credit? Or who ever credited such without being guilty of malice and defamation? No; she put the pagans to confusion by showing them the nature of that Christian widowhood which her conscience and mien alike set forth. Our widow's clothing was meant to keep out the cold and not to show her figure. Of gold she would not wear so much as a seal-ring, choosing to store her money in the stomachs of the poor rather than to keep it at her own disposal. She went nowhere without her mother, and would never see without witnesses such monks and clergy as the needs of a large house required her to interview. Her train was always composed of virgins and widows, and these women were serious and staid; for, as she well knew, the levity of the attendants speaks ill for the mistress and a woman's character is shown by her choice of companions.

Marcella practiced fasting, but in moderation. She abstained from eating flesh, and she knew rather the scent of wine than its taste, touching it only for her stomach's sake and for her frequent infirmities. She seldom appeared in public and took care to avoid the houses of great ladies, that she might not be forced to look upon what she had once and for all renounced. She frequented the basilicas of apostles and martyrs that she might escape from the throng and give herself to private prayer. So obedient was she to her mother that for her sake she did things of which she herself disapproved. For example, when her mother, careless of her own offspring, was for transferring all her property from her children and grandchildren to her brother's family, Marcella wished the money to be given to the poor instead, and yet could not bring herself to thwart her parent. Therefore she made over her ornaments and other effects to persons already rich, content to throw away her money rather than to sadden her mother's heart.

TWENTY-SIXTH WEEK OF THE YEAR
Tuesday
Jerome, *Life of Marcella* 5 (#3 of 6)

Marcella first heard of the monastic life in Egypt from some of its greatest admirers, and Jerome, in the midst of a Christian society biased against women, showed an unusual appreciation of their importance.

In those days no highborn lady at Rome had made profession of the monastic life, or had ventured—so strange and ignominious and degrading did it then seem—publicly to call herself a nun. It was from some priests of Alexandria, and from pope Athanasius [Ath a na' si us] (bishop of Alexandria), and subsequently from Peter, who, to escape the persecution of the Arian heretics, had all fled for refuge to Rome as the safest haven in which they could find communion—it was from these that Marcella heard of the blessed Antony [An' to ny], then still alive, and of the monasteries in the Thebaid [The ba' id] founded by Pachomius [Pa cho' mi us], and of the discipline laid down for virgins and for widows. Nor was she ashamed to profess a life which she had thus learned to be pleasing to Christ. Many years after, her example was followed first by Sophronia [So phro' ni a] and then by others.

My revered friend Paula was blessed with Marcella's friendship, and it was in Marcella's cell that Eustochium [Eu sto' chi um], that paragon of virgins, was gradually trained. Thus it is easy to see of what type the mistress was who found such pupils.

The unbelieving reader may perhaps laugh at me for dwelling so long on the praises of mere women; yet if you will but remember how holy women followed our Lord and Saviour and ministered to him of their substance (Luke 8:2-3), and how the three Marys stood before the cross (John 19:25) and especially how Mary Magdalene—called the tower from the earnestness and glow of her faith*—was privileged to see the rising Christ first of all before the very apostles (John 20:11-18), you will convict yourself of pride sooner than me of folly. For we judge of people's virtue not by their sex but by their character, and hold those to be worthy of the highest glory who have renounced both rank and wealth.

---

* A word play on her name; Migdal (Hebrew) or Magdala (Aramaic) means "tower." It is the name of the village on the west coast of the Lake of Galilee from which she came.

TWENTY-SIXTH WEEK OF THE YEAR
Wednesday
Jerome, *Life of Marcella* 6–7 (#4 of 6)

Marcella was so tireless in her study of the scriptures that she became widely recognized and consulted for her learning.

Marcella then lived the ascetic life for many years, and found herself old before she bethought herself that she had once been young. She often quoted with approval Plato's saying that philosophy consists in meditating on death. She passed her days and lived always in the thought that she must die. Her very clothing was such as to remind her of the tomb, and she presented herself as a living sacrifice, reasonable and acceptable, to God (Rom 12:1).

When the needs of the Church at length brought me to Rome in company with the reverend pontiffs, Paulinus [Pau li' nus] and Epiphanius [Ep i pha' ni us]—the first of whom ruled the church of the Syrian Antioch while the second presided over that of Salamis [Sal' a mis] in Cyprus—I in my modesty was for avoiding the eyes of highborn ladies, yet she pleaded so earnestly, "both in season and out of season" (2 Tim 4:2), as the apostle says, that at last her perseverance overcame my reluctance. And, as in those days my name was held in some renown as that of a student of the scriptures, she never came to see me that she did not ask me some question concerning them, nor would she at once acquiesce in my explanations but on the contrary would dispute them; not, however, for argument's sake but to learn the answers to those objections which might, as she saw, be made to my statements. How much virtue and ability, how much holiness and purity I found in her I am afraid to say; both lest I may exceed the bounds of belief and lest I may increase your sorrow by reminding you of the blessings that you have lost. This much only will I say, that whatever in me was the fruit of long study and as such made by constant meditation a part of my nature, this she tasted, this she learned and made her own. Consequently after my departure from Rome, in case of a dispute arising as to the testimony of scripture on any subject, recourse was had to her to settle it. And so wise was she and so well did she understand what philosophers call *to prepon*, that is, "the becoming," in what she did, that when she answered questions she gave her own opinion not as her own but as from me or someone else, thus admitting that what she taught she had herself learned from others. For she knew that the apostle had said: "I suffer not a woman to teach" (1 Tim 2:12), and she would not seem to inflict a wrong upon the male sex many of whom (including sometimes priests) questioned her concerning obscure and doubtful points.

TWENTY-SIXTH WEEK OF THE YEAR
Thursday
Jerome, *Life of Marcella* 8–10 (#5 of 6)

Marcella in Rome and Jerome in Bethlehem kept up frequent correspondence, and he attributed to her the initiative for mounting the theological attack against the Origenist revival of these years. As such, she is recognized as a leading teacher and theologian of Rome. Jerome's efforts to disassociate himself from the Origenists are ironic, since he had previously been enamored of their position.

I am told that my place with Marcella was immediately taken by you (Principia, Marcella's disciple), that you attached yourself to her, and that, as the saying goes, you never let even a hair's breadth come between her and you. You both lived in the same house and occupied the same room so that every one in the city knew for certain that you had found a mother in her and she a daughter in you. In the suburbs you found for yourselves a monastic seclusion, and chose the country instead of the town because of its loneliness. For a long time you lived together, and as many ladies shaped their conduct by your examples, I had the joy of seeing Rome transformed into another Jerusalem. Monastic establishments for virgins became numerous, and of hermits there were countless numbers. Meantime we consoled each other for our separation by words of mutual encouragement. We always went to meet each other's letters, tried to outdo each other in attentions, and anticipated each other in courteous inquiries. Not much was lost by a separation thus effectually bridged by a constant correspondence.

While Marcella was thus serving the Lord in holy tranquillity, there arose in these provinces a tornado of heresy which threw everything into confusion; indeed so great was the fury into which it lashed itself that it spared neither itself nor anything that was good. And as if it were too little to have disturbed everything here, it introduced a ship freighted with blasphemies into the port of Rome itself. It was then that the holy Marcella, who had long held back lest she should be thought to act from party motives, threw herself into the breach. Conscious that the faith of Rome —once praised by an apostle—was now in danger, and that this new heresy was drawing to itself not only priests and monks but also many of the laity, besides imposing on the bishop who fancied others are guileless as he was himself, she publicly withstood its teachers, choosing to please God rather than human beings.

You will say, what has this to do with the praises of Marcella? I reply, she it was who originated the condemnation of the heretics. She it was who furnished witnesses, first taught by them and then carried away by their heretical teaching. She it was who showed how large a number they had deceived, and who brought up against them the impious books *On First Principles*, books which were passing from hand to hand after being "improved" by the hand of the scorpion (Jerome's rival, Rufinus [Ru fi' nus]). She it was lastly who called on the heretics in letter after letter to appear in their own defense. They did not indeed venture to come, for they were so conscience-stricken that they let the case go against them by default rather than face their accusers and be convicted by them. This glorious victory originated with Marcella; she was the source and cause of this great blessing. You who shared the honour with her know that I speak the truth. You know too that out of many incidents I only mention a few, not to tire out the reader by a wearisome recapitulation. Were I to say more, ill-natured persons might fancy me, under pretext of commending a woman's virtues, to be giving vent to my own rancour.

TWENTY-SIXTH WEEK OF THE YEAR
Friday
Jerome, *Life of Marcella* 13–14 (#6 of 6)

Marcella died in the arms of her disciple Principia during the sack of Rome by the Goths, 410 CE. At the end, she rejoiced to have one further way to share the suffering of Christ.

As was natural in a scene of such confusion as the sack of Rome, one of the bloodstained victors found his way into Marcella's house. Now be it mine to say what I have heard, to relate what holy people have seen; for there were some such present and they say that you too were with her in the hour of danger. When the soldiers entered she is said to have received them without any look of alarm; and when they asked her for gold she pointed to her coarse dress to show them that she had no buried treasure. However, they would not believe in her self-chosen poverty, but scourged her and beat her with cudgels. She is said to have felt no pain but to have thrown herself at their feet and to have pleaded with tears for you, that you might not be taken from her, or, owing to your youth, have to endure what she as an old woman had no occasion to fear. Christ softened their hard hearts and, even among bloodstained swords, natural affection asserted its rights. The barbarians conveyed both you and her to the basilica of the apostle Paul, that you might find there either a place of safety or, if not that, at least a tomb. Hereupon Marcella is said to have burst into great joy and to have thanked God for having kept you unharmed in answer to her prayer. She said she was thankful too that the taking of the city had found her poor, not made her so, that she was not in want of daily bread, that Christ satisfied her needs so that she no longer felt hunger, that she was able to say in word and in deed: "naked I came out of my mother's womb, and naked shall I return there: the Lord gave and the Lord has taken away; blessed be the name of the Lord" (Job 1:21).

After a few days she fell asleep in the Lord; but to the last her powers remained unimpaired. You she made the heir of her poverty, or rather the poor through you. When she closed her eyes, it was in your arms; when she breathed her last breath, your lips received it; you shed tears but she smiled, conscious of having led a good life and hoping for her reward hereafter.

In one short night I have dictated this letter in honour of you, revered Marcella, and of you, my daughter Principia, not to show off my own eloquence but to express my heartfelt gratitude to you both; my one desire has been to please both God and my readers.

TWENTY-SIXTH WEEK OF THE YEAR
Saturday
Job 42:10–17

This narrative of Job departs from the conventional mores of his day in two significant ways: naming the daughters and not the sons, and stipulating that the daughters would also receive an inheritance.

The Lord restored the fortunes of Job when he had prayed for his friends; and the Lord gave Job twice as much as he had before. Then there came to him all his brothers and sisters and all who had known him before, and they ate bread with him in his house; they showed him sympathy and comforted him for all the evil that the Lord had brought upon him; and each of them gave him a piece of money and a gold ring. The Lord blessed the latter days of Job more than his beginning; and he had fourteen thousand sheep, six thousand camels, a thousand yoke of oxen, and a thousand donkeys. He also had seven sons and three daughters. He named the first Jemimah [Je mi' mah], the second Keziah [Ke zi' ah], and the third Keren-happuch [Kar' en-hap' puch]. In all the land there were no women so beautiful as Job's daughters; and their father gave them an inheritance along with their brothers. After this Job lived one hundred and forty years, and saw his children, and his children's children, four generations. And Job died, old and full of days.

TWENTY-SEVENTH SUNDAY OF THE YEAR
Genesis 2:18–25

The Yahwist story of creation tells that the woman was created from the man. "Bone of my bone and flesh of my flesh" highlights the equality of the couple.

The Lord God said, "It is not good that the man should be alone; I will make him a helper as his partner." So out of the ground the Lord God formed every animal of the field and every bird of the air, and brought them to the man to see what he would call them; and whatever the man called every living creature, that was its name. The man gave names to all cattle, and to the birds of the air, and to every animal of the field; but for the man there was not found a helper as his partner. So the Lord God caused a deep sleep to fall upon the man, and he slept; then he took one of his ribs and closed up its place with flesh. And the rib that the Lord God had taken from the man God made into a woman and brought her to the man. Then the man said,

> "This at last is bone of my bones
>   and flesh of my flesh;
> this one shall be called Woman,"
>   for out of Man this one was taken.

Therefore a man leaves his father and his mother and clings to his wife, and they become one flesh. And the man and his wife were both naked, and were not ashamed.

TWENTY-SEVENTH WEEK OF THE YEAR
Monday
Life of Adam and Eve 9–11

*One legend has it that after leaving the garden Adam went to the
Jordan River and Eve to the Tigris, both seeking God's mercy by
standing in the waters up to the neck. Eve agreed to remain silently
in the river for thirty-seven days, Adam for forty.*

Eighteen days went by. Then Satan was angry and transformed
himself into the brightness of angels and went away to the Tigris River to
Eve and found her weeping. The devil himself, as if to grieve with her,
began to weep and said to her, "Step out of the river and cry no more.
Cease now from sadness and sighs. Why are you and your husband Adam
disturbed? The Lord God has heard your sighs and accepted your repentance; and all we angels have entreated for you and interceded with the
Lord, and he sent me to bring you up from the water and give you food
which you had in Paradise, and for which you have been lamenting. Now
therefore come out of the water and I will lead you to the place where
your food has been prepared."

Now when Eve heard this she believed and came out of the water of
the river, and her flesh was as grass from the cold of the water. When she
came out, she fell on the ground and the devil raised her and led her to
Adam. But when Adam saw her and the devil with her, he cried out with
tears and said, "O Eve, Eve, where is the work of your penitence? How
have you again been seduced by our enemy by whom we have been
deprived of our dwelling in Paradise and of spiritual joy?"

When Eve heard this, she knew that the devil had persuaded her to
come out of the river, and she fell on her face to the ground, and her
sorrow and sighing and lamenting were doubled. She cried out, saying,
"Woe to you, O devil. Why do you assault us for nothing? What have
you to do with us? What have we done to you, that you should pursue us
with deceit? Why does your malice fall on us? Have we stolen your glory
and made you to be without honor? Why do you treacherously and
enviously pursue us, O enemy, all the way to death?"

TWENTY-SEVENTH WEEK OF THE YEAR
Tuesday
Shepherd of Hermas, Vision 1.2.2–3; 3.3–4.3 (#1 of 4)

The visionary Hermas sees an old woman, symbol of the church, who reveals to him some of the hidden things of God. This vision and those which follow on the next three days deal with the regeneration of the church.

As I was reflecting on what had happened and discerning in my heart, I saw in front of me a large white chair made of snow-white wool, and an older woman in a shining robe approached with a book in her hands. She sat down by herself and greeted me: "Hello, Hermas."

Sad and weeping, I responded: "Hello, lady."

She said to me: "Why are you so downcast, Hermas? Would you like to hear me read?"

I answered: "I would like that, lady."

She said: "Then become a listener, and listen to the glory of God." I heard great awesome things that I could not remember, for it was all too frightening for human comprehension. So I remembered the last words, because they were helpful and easy: "Behold, the God whom I love, with great power and understanding created the world and by glorious intent surrounded it with beauty, and with powerful word established the heaven and founded the earth upon the waters, and with wisdom foreordained the holy church, to give to the holy ones the promise made with great glory and joy to those who keep the law of God, which they received with great faith."

When she finished reading and rose from the chair, four young men came to take it up and went off toward the East. She called me, touched my chest and said: "Did my reading please you?"

I answered: "Lady, these last things pleased me, but the first things were difficult to understand."

"These last things are for the just," she answered, "but the first things for outsiders and apostates."

While she was still speaking with me, there came two men who took her by the arms and they went away to the East, in the same direction in which the chair had been taken. But she left in good spirits and said to me as she left: "Be of good courage, Hermas."

TWENTY-SEVENTH WEEK OF THE YEAR
Wednesday
Shepherd of Hermas, Vision 3.1.1–6 (#2 of 4)

Hermas recounts two visions of the beautiful elder lady, symbol of the church, which prompt him to prayer and confession of sinfulness. She suggests that he focus rather on broader and more positive issues of justice.

Now I saw the following. When I was fasting a great deal and asking the Lord to interpret the revelation that had been promised to me through the elder lady, that night I saw her, and she said to me: "Since you are so eager and need to know everything, go to the field where you farm, and in the late morning I will appear to you and show you what you want to see."

I asked her: "Lady, to what part of the field?"

"Wherever you want," she answered.

I found a lovely secluded place. But even before I had told her the place, she said: "I will be there, wherever you want."

So, friends, I went to the field and waited for the right time, then went to the place where I had arranged that she would come. There I saw an ivory couch set up, upon the couch a linen pillow, and a piece of good linen covering it. When I saw all this set out, but no one there, I was seized with terror and began trembling so that my hair stood on end. I was panic stricken because I was alone. When I came to myself and took courage, remembering God's glory, I fell to my knees and once more acknowledged my sinfulness. Then she came with the same six young men for escorts, and stood by listening to my prayer and confession of sin. Finally she touched me and said: "Hermas, stop concentrating on your sins, and ask instead about justice, in order to take this concern back to your household."

TWENTY-SEVENTH WEEK OF THE YEAR
Thursday
Shepherd of Hermas, Vision 3.8.1–10 (#3 of 4)

The elder lady, symbol of the church, shows Hermas a tower being built, sustained by seven women who represent virtues. The tower, too, symbolizes the church, which is being built up until the end time. Those who live by these key virtues belong in the tower.

When I had stopped asking the lady all my questions, she said to me: "Would you like to see something else?" I was eager to see it, and got excited. She looked at me smiling and said: "Do you see seven women surrounding a tower?"

"Yes, I do," I said.

"This tower is being sustained by them, according to God's design. Now listen to what they are. The first one, the one clasping her hands together, is called Faith. Through her the chosen ones of God are saved. The other is called Moderation. She is Faith's daughter. Whoever follows her will be happy in this life, and will hold off from doing evil, believing that the one who refrains from all evil desires will inherit eternal life."

"But who are the others?"

"They are daughters of one another. Their names are Simplicity, Understanding, Innocence, Holiness, and Love. When you do their mother's works, you will live. From Faith is born Moderation, from Moderation Simplicity, from Simplicity Innocence, from Innocence Holiness, from Holiness Understanding, and from Understanding Love. Whoever is devoted to these women and can embrace their works shall have a dwelling in the tower with God's holy ones. But when the construction of the tower is completed, the end will come. These things were not revealed only for you, but for you to interpret them to everyone."

TWENTY-SEVENTH WEEK OF THE YEAR
Friday
Shepherd of Hermas, Vision 3.10.1–13.4 (#4 of 4)

The woman of Hermas' vision, a woman who images the church, has become progressively younger throughout the series of visions. He asks why, and discovers that she grows younger as the church is spiritually renewed.

When the lady finished talking to me, the six young men came to take her away to the tower, and another four took up the couch to the tower as well. But as she was leaving I asked her to reveal to me why she appeared in three different ways. She answered: "About this you must ask someone else to show you."

Friends, at first I had seen her rather old and sitting in a chair. The next time, her face was younger but her flesh and hair were old, and she was standing, but she looked happier than before. But in the third vision she was much younger, very lovely, and only her hair looked old. She was very happy and seated on a dining couch. I fasted, and one night a young man appeared to me and said: "Why are you, Hermas, always asking for revelations? Why did she first appear to you older and seated in a chair? Because the spirit of your church members is old and already fainting away because of your weakness and divided self. You have been weakened by worldly concerns and have not 'cast your worries upon God' (Ps 55:22). In the second vision, Hermas, you saw her standing, looking younger and happier. Even so, when you heard the revelation that God had mercy on you, your spirit was renewed, and you were strengthened. In the third vision you saw her younger, happy, and lovely in appearance. She was sitting on a couch, a very secure position. Just so, those who completely repent will be made new and securely founded, if they repent with their whole heart. This is the entire revelation; do not ask for anything more."

TWENTY-SEVENTH WEEK OF THE YEAR
Saturday
Luke 11:27–28

This text does not undermine Mary's maternity but rather empha-
sizes her role as disciple.

While Jesus was speaking, a woman in the crowd raised her voice
and said to him, "Blessed is the womb that bore you and the breasts that
nursed you!" But he said, "Blessed rather are those who hear the word of
God and obey it!"

TWENTY-EIGHTH SUNDAY OF THE YEAR
Dhuoda, *On John 15 to Her Son*

Dhuoda, a gifted woman of the Carolingian period, suffered violent
treatment from her husband and his political allies; when her sons
were removed from her by their father and she herself was exiled for
protesting the barbarous realities of the period, she sought comfort
by writing a treatise to her son about Christ, the living tree.

The true tree, together with the vine that is in concord with it, is our
Lord Christ. That is, the Lord Jesus, from whom all chosen trees arise
and vineshoots burgeon, has deigned to choose the worthy branches that
will bring forth beautiful fruit. Christ himself says, "I am the true vine and
you are the vineshoots." And again, "I have chosen you from the world
so that you may go and bear fruit and that your fruit shall remain. Who
remains with me and I in them, will bear much fruit" (John 15:5, 16),
and so forth.

It is to such a tree, therefore, that I urge you to graft yourself, so that
you may cleave to Christ without fail, and—since fruit means good deeds
—you will be able to bring forth much fruit. Those who behold Christ

and have sure trust in him are compared to this saintly tree which is transplanted beside the flowing water (Ps 1:3). Those trees which have deeply and profoundly fixed their roots in the moisture will not grow dry in the summer season (Jer 17:8). Their leaves will always be green and abundant and they will never fail to produce fruit.

And so that you may know which trees are worthy of yielding their fruits in abundance, hear the Apostle when he says, "The fruits of the spirit are charity, joy, peace, forbearance, kindness, gentleness, patience, chastity, self-control, modesty, sobriety, vigilance, and wisdom" (Gal 5:22–23), and other virtues like these. Since those who practice such virtues will deserve to attain quite readily to the kingdom of God, graft those fruits in your mind and body, and bring them forth and meditate upon them continually. In this way, with the fruit and perseverance of good works, you will deserve on the day of tribulation and adversity to be sheltered and supported by the True Tree.

TWENTY-EIGHTH WEEK OF THE YEAR
Monday
Acts of Perpetua and Felicitas 2–3 (#1 of 10)

Perpetua, a young woman of distinguished family, and the slave Felicitas are among a group of young catechumens arrested and imprisoned for being Christians in Carthage, North Africa, in 203 CE. Perpetua herself tells of her fear, her troubles with her family because of her arrest, and her concern for her nursing baby. (These readings would also be appropriate for Lent.)

A number of young catechumens were arrested, Revocatus [Re vo ca' tus] and his fellow slave Felicitas [Fe li' ci tas], Saturninus [Sa tur ni' nus] and Secundulus [Se cun' du lus], and with them Vivia [Viv' i a] Perpetua [Per pet' u a], a newly married woman of good family and upbringing. Her mother and father were still alive and one of her two brothers was a catechumen like herself. She was about twenty-two years old and had an infant son at the breast. (Now from this point on the entire account of her ordeal is her own, according to her own ideas and in the way that she herself wrote it down.)

While we were still under arrest (she said), my father out of love for me was trying to persuade me and shake my resolution. "Father," said I, "do you see this vase here, for example, or waterpot or whatever?"

"Yes, I do," said he.

And I told him: "Could it be called by any other name than what it is?"

And he said: "No."

"Well, so, too, I cannot be called anything other than what I am, a Christian."

At this my father was so angered by the word "Christian" that he moved towards me as though he would pluck my eyes out. But he left it at that and departed, vanquished along with his diabolical arguments.

For a few days afterwards I gave thanks to the Lord that I was separated from my father, and I was comforted by his absence. During these few days I was baptized, and I was inspired by the spirit not to ask for any other favour after the water but simply the perseverance of the flesh. A few days later we were lodged in the prison; and I was terrified, as I had never before been in such a dark hole. What a difficult time it was! With the crowd, the heat was stifling; then there was the extortion of the soldiers; and to crown all, I was tortured with worry for my baby there.

Then Tertius [Ter' ti us] and Pomponius [Pom po' ni us], those blessed deacons who tried to take care of us, bribed the soldiers to allow us to go to a better part of the prison to refresh ourselves for a few hours. All then left that dungeon and shifted for themselves. I nursed my baby, who was faint from hunger. In my anxiety I spoke to my mother about the child, I tried to comfort my brother, and I gave the child into their charge. I was in pain because I saw them suffering out of pity for me. These were the trials I had to endure for many days. Then I got permission for my baby to stay with me in prison. At once I recovered my health, relieved as I was of my worry and anxiety over the child. My prison had suddenly become a palace, so that I wanted to be there rather than anywhere else.

TWENTY-EIGHTH WEEK OF THE YEAR
Tuesday
Acts of Perpetua and Felicitas 4 (#2 of 10)

While in prison Perpetua tells of her first dream-vision, full of signifi-cant symbols and a fine example of how God speaks to us in dreams.

My brother said to me: "Dear sister, you are greatly privileged; surely you might ask for a vision to discover whether you are to be condemned or freed."

Faithfully I promised that I would, for I knew that I could speak with the Lord, whose great blessings I had come to experience. And so I said: "I shall tell you tomorrow." Then I made my request and this was the vision I had.

I saw a ladder of tremendous height made of bronze, reaching all the way to the heavens, but it was so narrow that only one person could climb up at a time. To the sides of the ladder were attached all sorts of metal weapons: there were swords, spears, hooks, daggers, and spikes; so that if anyone tried to climb up carelessly or without paying attention, they would be mangled and their flesh would adhere to the weapons.

At the foot of the ladder lay a dragon of enormous size, and it would attack those who tried to climb up and try to terrify them from doing so. And Saturus [Sa' tur us] was the first to go up, he who was later to give himself up of his own accord. He had been the builder of our strength, although he was not present when we were arrested. And he arrived at the top of the staircase and he looked back and said to me: "Perpetua, I am waiting for you. But take care; do not let the dragon bite you."

"He will not harm me," I said, "in the name of Christ Jesus."

Slowly, as though he were afraid of me, the dragon stuck his head out from underneath the ladder. Then using it as my first step, I trod on his head and went up.

Then I saw an immense garden, and in it a grey-haired man sat in shepherd's garb; tall he was, and milking sheep. And standing around him were many thousands of people clad in white garments. He raised his head, looked at me, and said: "I am glad you have come, my child."

He called me over to him and gave me, as it were, a mouthful of the milk he was drawing; and I took it into my cupped hands and consumed it. And all those who stood around said: "Amen!" At the sound of this word I came to, with the taste of something sweet still in my mouth. I at once told this to my brother, and we realized that we would have to suffer, and that from now on, we would no longer have any hope in this life.

TWENTY-EIGHTH WEEK OF THE YEAR
Wednesday
Acts of Perpetua and Felicitas 5–6 (#3 of 10)

Perpetua has a painful encounter with her father, who is later humiliated during her makeshift trial. Sometimes fidelity to the gospel causes deep family divisions.

A few days later there was a rumour that we were going to be given a hearing. My father also arrived from the city, worn with worry, and he came to see me with the idea of persuading me. "Daughter," he said, "have pity on my grey head—have pity on me your father, if I deserve to be called your father, if I have favoured you above all your brothers, if I have raised you to reach this prime of your life. Do not abandon me to be the reproach of men. Think of your brother, think of your mother and your aunt, think of your child, who will not be able to live once you are gone. Give up your pride! You will destroy all of us! None of us will ever be able to speak freely again if anything happens to you."

This was the way my father spoke out of love for me, kissing my hands and throwing himself down before me. With tears in his eyes he no longer addressed me as his daughter but as a woman. I was sorry for my father's sake, because he alone of all my kin would be unhappy to see me suffer.

I tried to comfort him saying: "It will all happen in the prisoner's dock as God wills; for you may be sure that we are not left to ourselves but are all in God's power."

And he left in great sorrow.

One day while we were eating breakfast, we were suddenly hurried off for a hearing. We arrived at the forum, and straight away the story went about the neighbourhood near the forum and a huge crowd gathered. We walked up to the prisoner's dock. All the others when questioned admitted their guilt. Then, when it came my turn, my father appeared with my son, dragged me from the step, and said; "Perform the sacrifice—have pity on your baby!"

Hilarianus [Hi la ri a' nus], the governor, who had received his judicial powers as the successor of the late proconsul Minucius [Mi nu' ci us] Timinianus [Ti mi ni a' nus], said to me: "Have pity on your father's grey head; have pity on your infant son. Offer the sacrifice for the welfare of the emperors."

"I will not," I retorted.

"Are you a Christian?" said Hilarianus.

And I said: "Yes, I am."

When my father persisted in trying to dissuade me, Hilarianus ordered him to be thrown to the ground and beaten with a rod. I felt sorry for father, just as if I myself had been beaten. I felt sorry for his pathetic old age.

Then Hilarianus passed sentence on all of us: we were condemned to the beasts, and we returned to prison in high spirits. But my baby had got used to being nursed at the breast and to staying with me in prison. So I sent the deacon Pomponius [Pom po' ni us] straight away to my father to ask for the baby. But father refused to give him over. But as God willed, the baby had no further desire for the breast, nor did I suffer any inflammation; and so I was relieved of any anxiety for my child and of any discomfort in my breasts.

TWENTY-EIGHTH WEEK OF THE YEAR
Thursday
Acts of Perpetua and Felicitas 7–9 (#4 of 10)

Perpetua has two touching dreams of her deceased little brother, showing the strong Christian belief in the power of intercessory prayer. Even one of the prison guards begins to believe in the spiritual power of the martyrs.

Some days later when we were all at prayer, suddenly while praying I spoke out and uttered the name Dinocrates [Di no' cra tes]. I was surprised; for the name had never entered my mind until that moment. And I was pained when I recalled what had happened to him. At once I realized that I was privileged to pray for him. I began to pray for him and to sigh deeply for him before the Lord. That very night I had the following vision. I saw Dinocrates, coming out of a dark hole, where there were many others with him, very hot and thirsty, pale and dirty. On his face was the wound he had when he died.

Now Dinocrates had been my brother according to the flesh; but he had died horribly of cancer of the face when he was seven years old, and his death was a source of loathing to everyone. Thus it was for him that I made my prayer. There was a great abyss between us: neither could approach the other. Where Dinocrates stood there was a pool full of water; and its rim was higher than the child's height, so that Dinocrates had to stretch himself up to drink. I was sorry that, though the pool had water in it, Dinocrates could not drink because of the height of the rim. Then I woke up, realizing that my brother was suffering. But I was confident that I could help him in his trouble; and I prayed for him every day until we were transferred to the military prison. For we were supposed to fight with the beasts at the military games to be held on the occasion of the emperor Geta's [Ge' ta's] birthday. And I prayed for my brother day and night with tears and sighs that this favour might be granted me.

On the day we were kept in chains, I had this vision shown to me. I saw the same spot that I had seen before, but there was Dinocrates all clean, well dressed, and refreshed. I saw a scar where the wound had been; and the pool that I had seen before now had its rim lowered to the level of the child's waist. And Dinocrates kept drinking water from it, and there above the rim was a golden bowl full of water. And Dinocrates drew close and began to drink from it, and yet the bowl remained full. And when he had drunk enough of the water, he began to play as children do. Then I awoke, and I realized that he had been delivered from his suffering.

Some days later, an adjutant named Pudens, who was in charge of the prison, began to show us great honour, realizing that we possessed some great power within us. And he began to allow many visitors to see us for our mutual comfort.

Now the day of the contest was approaching, and my father came to see me overwhelmed with sorrow. He started tearing the hairs from his beard and threw them on the ground; he then threw himself on the ground and began to curse his old age and to say such words as would move all creation. I felt sorry for his unhappy old age.

TWENTY-EIGHTH WEEK OF THE YEAR
Friday
Acts of Perpetua and Felicitas 10 (#5 of 10)

Perpetua has another dream in which she fights the power of evil as a gladiator, and triumphs. Faced with imminent death in a violent world, she is assured through her dream-vision that death means victory.

The day before we were to fight with the beasts I saw the following vision. Pomponius, the deacon, came to the prison gates and began to knock violently. I went out and opened the gate for him. He was dressed in an unbelted white tunic, wearing elaborate sandals. And he said to me: "Perpetua, come; we are waiting for you."

Then he took my hand and we began to walk through rough and broken country. At last we came to the amphitheatre out of breath, and he led me into the centre of the arena.

Then he told me: "Do not be afraid. I am here, struggling with you." Then he left.

I looked at the enormous crowd who watched in astonishment. I was surprised that no beasts were let loose on me; for I knew that I was condemned to die by the beasts. Then out came an Egyptian against me, of vicious appearance, together with his seconds, to fight with me. There also came up to me some handsome young men to be my seconds and assistants.

My clothes were stripped off, and suddenly I was a man. My seconds began to rub me down with oil (as they are wont to do before a contest). Then I saw the Egyptian on the other side rolling in the dust. Next there came forth a man of marvellous stature, such that he rose above the top of the amphitheatre. He was clad in a beltless purple tunic with two stripes, one on either side, running down the middle of his chest. He wore sandals that were wondrously made of gold and silver, and he carried a wand like an athletic trainer and a green branch on which there were golden apples.

And he asked for silence and said: "If this Egyptian defeats her, he will slay her with the sword. But if she defeats him, she will receive this branch." Then he withdrew.

We drew close to one another and began to let our fists fly. My opponent tried to get hold of my feet. Then I was raised up into the air and I began to pummel him without as it were touching the ground. Then when I noticed there was a lull, I put my two hands together linking the fingers of one hand with those of the other and thus I got hold of his head. He fell flat on his face and I stepped on his head.

The crowd began to shout and my assistants started to sing psalms. Then I walked up to the trainer and took the branch. He kissed me and said to me: "Peace be with you, my daughter!" I began to walk in triumph towards the Gate of Life. Then I awoke. I realized that it was not with wild animals that I would fight but with the Devil, but I knew that I would win the victory. So much for what I did up until the eve of the contest. About what happened at the contest itself, let the one write of it who will.

TWENTY-EIGHTH WEEK OF THE YEAR
Saturday
Acts of Perpetua and Felicitas 15 (#6 of 10)

The slave woman Felicitas gives birth prematurely in prison because of the prayer of her companions, so that she will be able to join them in the arena. She knows that when we suffer for the name of Christ, it is Christ who suffers in us (see Gal 2:20).

As for Felicitas, she, too, enjoyed the Lord's favour in this wise. She had been pregnant when she was arrested, and was now in her eighth month. As the day of the spectacle drew near, she was very distressed that her martyrdom would be postponed because of her pregnancy; for it is against the law for women with child to be executed. Thus she might have to shed her holy, innocent blood afterwards along with others who were common criminals. Her comrades in martyrdom were also saddened; for they were afraid that they would have to leave behind so fine a companion to travel alone on the same road to hope. And so, two days before the contest, they poured forth a prayer to the Lord in one torrent of common grief. And immediately after their prayer the birth pains came upon her. She suffered a good deal in her labour because of the natural difficulty of an eight months' delivery.

Hence one of the assistants of the prison guards said to her: "You suffer so much now—what will you do when you are tossed to the beasts? Little did you think of them when you refused to sacrifice."

"What I am suffering now," she replied, "I suffer by myself. But then another will be inside me who will suffer for me, just as I shall be suffering for him."

And she gave birth to a girl; and one of the sisters brought her up as her own daughter.

TWENTY-NINTH SUNDAY OF THE YEAR
Acts of Perpetua and Felicitas 16–17 (#7 of 10)

> *Perpetua and her companions prepare for their ordeal. Their courage and joy are a source of amazement and inspiration to the curious who flock to see them. Their final meal together in prison must have been consciously reminiscent of Jesus' last meal with his disciples.*

Since the Holy Spirit has permitted the story of this contest to be written down, and by so permitting has willed it, we shall carry out the command or, indeed, the commission of the most saintly Perpetua, however unworthy I might be to add anything to this glorious story. At the same time I shall add one example of her perseverance and nobility of soul.

The military tribune had treated them with extraordinary severity because, on the information of certain very foolish people, he became afraid that they would be spirited out of the prison by magical spells.

Perpetua spoke to him directly. "Why can you not even allow us to refresh ourselves properly? For we are the most distinguished of the condemned prisoners, seeing that we belong to the emperor; we are to fight on his very birthday. Would it not be to your credit if we were brought forth on the day in a healthier condition?"

The officer became disturbed and grew red. So it was that he gave the order that they were to be more humanely treated; and he allowed her brothers and other persons to visit, so that the prisoners could dine in their company. By this time the adjutant who was head of the jail was himself a Christian.

On the day before, when they had their last meal, which is called the free banquet, they celebrated not a banquet but rather a love feast. They spoke to the mob with the same steadfastness, warned them of God's judgement, stressing the joy they would have in their suffering, and ridiculing the curiosity of those that came to see them. Saturus said: "Will not tomorrow be enough for you? Why are you so eager to see something that you dislike? Our friends today will be our enemies on the morrow. But take careful note of what we look like so that you will recognize us on the day." Thus everyone would depart from the prison in amazement, and many of them began to believe.

TWENTY-NINTH WEEK OF THE YEAR
Monday
Acts of Perpetua and Felicitas 18 (#8 of 10)

Perpetua demonstrates her leadership and strong character by insisting that she and her companions not be forced, while dying for Christ, to wear costumes of pagan gods. Her insistence prevails.

The day of their victory dawned, and they marched from the prison to the amphitheatre joyfully as though they were going to heaven, with calm faces, trembling, if at all, with joy rather than fear. Perpetua went along with shining countenance and calm step, as the beloved of God, as a wife of Christ, putting down everyone's stare by her own intense gaze. With them also was Felicitas, glad that she had given birth so that now she could fight the beasts, going from one blood bath to another, from the midwife to the gladiator, ready to wash after childbirth in a second baptism.

They were then led up to the gates and the men were forced to put on the robes of priests of Saturn, the women the dress of the priestesses of Ceres. But the noble Perpetua strenuously resisted this to the end.

"We came to this of our own free will, that our freedom should not be violated. We agreed to pledge our lives provided that we would do no such thing. You agreed with us to do this."

Even injustice recognized justice. The military tribune agreed. They were to be brought into the arena just as they were. Perpetua then began to sing a psalm: she was already treading on the head of the Egyptian. Revocatus, Saturninus, and Saturus began to warn the onlooking mob. Then when they came within sight of Hilarianus, they suggested by their motions and gestures: "You have condemned us, but God will condemn you" was what they were saying.

At this the crowds became enraged and demanded that they be scourged before a line of gladiators. And they rejoiced at this: that they had obtained a share in the Lord's sufferings.

TWENTY-NINTH WEEK OF THE YEAR
Tuesday
Acts of Perpetua and Felicitas 19–20 (#9 of 10)

The two young women are tossed by a mad heifer in a sadistic use of femininity. The vulnerability of a nursing mother and a woman who has just given birth are an ironic contrast to the brute power of their persecutors. Even in shock from her ordeal, Perpetua is a source of encouragement for others.

The one who said, "Ask and you shall receive" (John 16:24), answered their prayer by giving each one the death he or she had asked for. For whenever they would discuss among themselves their desire for martyrdom, Saturninus indeed insisted that he wanted to be exposed to all the different beasts, that his crown might be all the more glorious. And so at the outset of the contest he and Revocatus were matched with a leopard, and then while in the stocks they were attacked by a bear. As for Saturus, he dreaded nothing more than a bear, and he counted on being killed by one bite of a leopard. Then he was matched with a wild boar; but the gladiator who had tied him to the animal was gored by the boar and died a few days after the contest, whereas Saturus was only dragged along. Then when he was bound in the stocks awaiting the bear, the animal refused to come out of the cages, so that Saturus was called back once more unhurt.

For the young women, however, the Devil had prepared a mad heifer. This was an unusual animal, but it was chosen that their sex might be matched with that of the beast. So they were stripped naked, placed in nets and thus brought out into the arena. Even the crowd was horrified when they saw that one was a delicate young girl and the other was a woman fresh from childbirth with the milk still dripping from her breasts. And so they were brought back again and dressed in unbelted tunics.

First the heifer tossed Perpetua and she fell on her back. Then sitting up she pulled down the tunic that was ripped along the side so that it covered her thighs, thinking more of her modesty than of her pain. Next she asked for a pin to fasten her untidy hair: for it was not right that a martyr should die with her hair in disorder, lest she might seem to be mourning in her hour of triumph.

Then she got up. And seeing that Felicitas had been crushed to the ground, she went over to her, gave her her hand, and lifted her up. Then the two stood side by side. But the cruelty of the mob was by now appeased, and so they were called back through the Gate of Life.

Then Perpetua was held up by a man named Rusticus who was at the time a catechumen and kept close to her. She awoke from a kind of sleep (so absorbed had she been in ecstasy in the Spirit) and she began to look about her. Then to the amazement of all she said: "When are we going to be thrown to that heifer or whatever it is?"

When told that this had already happened, she refused to believe it until she noticed the marks of her rough experience on her person and her dress. Then she called for her brother and spoke to him, together with the catechumens, and said: "You must all stand fast in the faith and love one another, and do not be weakened by what we have gone through."

TWENTY-NINTH WEEK OF THE YEAR
Wednesday
Acts of Perpetua and Felicitas 21 (#10 of 10)

The martyrs are finally killed by the sword. Even at the end, Perpetua shows her outstanding courage.

They were thrown unconscious in the usual spot to have their throats cut. But the mob asked that their bodies be brought out into the open that their eyes might be the guilty witnesses of the sword that pierced their flesh. And so the martyrs got up and went to the spot of their own accord as the people wanted them to, and kissing one another they sealed their martyrdom with the ritual kiss of peace. The others took the sword in silence and without moving, especially Saturus, who being the first to climb the stairway was the first to die. For once again he was waiting for Perpetua. Perpetua, however, had yet to taste more pain. She screamed as she was struck on the bone; then she took the trembling hand of the young gladiator and guided it to her throat. It was as though so great a woman, feared as she was by the unclean spirit, could not be dispatched unless she herself were willing.

Ah, most valiant and blessed martyrs! Truly are you called and chosen for the glory of Christ Jesus our Lord! And anyone who exalts, honours, and worships his glory should read for the consolation of the Church these new deeds of heroism which are no less significant than the tales of old. For these new manifestations of virtue will bear witness to one and the same Spirit who still operates, and to God the almighty, to Jesus Christ our Lord, to whom is splendour and immeasurable power for all the ages. Amen.

TWENTY-NINTH WEEK OF THE YEAR
Thursday
Judges 11:29–40

Jephthah's rash vow costs his daughter her life. Hereafter, Israelite women keep her memory for four days each year.

The spirit of the Lord came upon Jephthah [Jeph' thah], and he passed through Gilead [Gil' e ad] and Manasseh [Ma nas' seh]. He passed on to Mizpah of Gilead, and from Mizpah of Gilead he passed on to the Ammonites [Am' mon ites]. And Jephthah made a vow to the Lord, and said, "If you will give the Ammonites into my hand, then whoever comes out of the doors of my house to meet me, when I return victorious from the Ammonites, shall be the Lord's to be offered up by me as a burnt offering." So Jephthah crossed over to the Ammonites to fight against them; and the Lord gave them into his hand. He inflicted a massive defeat on them from Aroer to the neighborhood of Minnith, twenty towns, and as far as Abel-keramim [A bel-ker' a mim]. So the Ammonites were subdued before the people of Israel.

Then Jephthah came to his home at Mizpah; and there was his daughter coming out to meet him with timbrels and with dancing. She was his only child; he had no son or daughter except her. When he saw her, he tore his clothes, and said, "Alas, my daughter! You have brought me very low; you have become the cause of great trouble to me. For I have opened my mouth to the Lord, and I cannot take back my vow." She said to him, "My father, if you have opened your mouth to the Lord, do to me according to what has gone out of your mouth, now that the Lord has given you vengeance against your enemies, the Ammonites." And she said to her father, "Let this thing be done for me: Grant me two months, so that I away go and wander on the mountains, and bewail my virginity, my companions and I." "Go," he said and sent her away for two months. So she departed, she and her companions, and bewailed her virginity on the mountains. At the end of two months, she returned to her father, who did with her according to the vow he had made. She had never slept with a man. So there arose an Israelite custom that for four days every year the daughters of Israel would go out to lament the daughter of Jephthah, the Gileadite.

TWENTY-NINTH WEEK OF THE YEAR
Friday
Pseudo-Philo, *Biblical Antiquities* 40:1–3 (#1 of 2)

The anonymous "daughter of Jephthah" (Judges 11:29–40) in Pseudo-Philo is identified by her name: Seila. Here, Seila expressed forgiveness for her father's careless vow which meant Seila's own death.

Jephthah [Jeph' thah] came and attacked the sons of Ammon, and the Lord delivered them into his hands, and he struck down sixty of their cities. And Jephthah returned in peace, and women came out to meet him in song and dance. And it was his only daughter who came out of the house first in the dance to meet her father. And when Jephthah saw her, he grew faint and said, "Rightly was your name called Seila [Sei' la], that you might be offered in sacrifice. And now who will put my heart in the balance and my soul on the scale? And I will stand by and see which will win out, whether it is the rejoicing that has occurred or the sadness that befalls me. Because I opened my mouth to my Lord in song with vows, I cannot call that back again" (Judg 11:36). Seila his daughter said to him, "Who is there who would be sad in death, seeing the people freed? Or do you not remember what happened in the days of our fathers when the father placed the son as a holocaust (Gen 22), and he did not refuse him, but gladly gave consent to him, and the one being offered was ready, and the one who was offering was rejoicing? Now do not annul everything you have vowed, but carry it out. Yet, one request I ask of you before I die, a small demand I seek before I give back my soul: that I may go into the mountains and stay in the hills and walk among the rocks, I and my virgin companions (Judg 11:36–38). I will pour out my tears there and tell of the sadness of my youth. The trees of the field will weep for me, and the beasts of the field will lament over me. For I am not sad because I am to die nor does it pain me to give back my soul, but because my father was caught up in the snare of his vow; and if I did not offer myself willingly for sacrifice, I fear that my death would not be acceptable or I would lose my life in vain. These things I will tell the mountains, and afterward I will return."

TWENTY-NINTH WEEK OF THE YEAR
Saturday
Pseudo-Philo, *Biblical Antiquities* 40:4–8 (#2 of 2)

Seila, Jephthah's daughter, weeps in lamentation before her death. Together the virgins of Israel weep for the death of their sister.

Seila's father said, "Go" (Judg 11:38). Seila the daughter of Jephthah, she and her virgin companions, went out and came and told it to the wise ones of the people and no one could respond to her word. Afterward, she came to Mount Stelac, and the Lord thought of her by night and said, "Behold now I have shut up the tongue of the wise of my people for this generation so that they cannot respond to the daughter of Jephthah, to her word, in order that my word be fulfilled and my plan that I thought out not be foiled. I have seen that the virgin is wise in contrast to her father and perceptive in contrast to all the wise ones who are here. Now, let her life be given at his request, and her death will be precious before me (Ps 116:15) always, and she will go away and fall into the bosom of her mothers."

When the daughter of Jephthah came to Mount Stelac, she began to weep, and this is her lamentation that she lamented and wept over herself before she departed. She said,

"Hear, you mountains, my lamentation;
and pay attention, you hills, to the tears of my eyes;
and be witnesses, you rocks, of the weeping of my soul.
Behold how I am put to the test!
But not in vain will my life be taken away.
May my words go forth in the heavens,
and my tears be written in the firmament!
That a father did not refuse the daughter whom he had sworn to
      sacrifice,
that a ruler granted that his only daughter be promised for sacrifice.
But I have not made good on my marriage chamber,
and I have not retrieved my wedding garlands.
For I have not been clothed in splendor while sitting in my
      woman's chamber,
I have not used the sweet-smelling ointment,
And my soul has not rejoiced in the oil of anointing that has been
      prepared for me.
O Mother, in vain have you borne your only daughter,
because Sheol has become my bridal chamber,
and on earth there is only my woman's chamber.
May all the blend of oil that you have prepared for me be poured
      out,
and the white robe that my mother has woven, the moth will eat it.
The crown of flowers that my nurse plaited for me for the festival,
      may it wither up;
and the coverlet that she wove of hyacinth and purple in my
      woman's chamber, may the worm devour it.
May my virgin companions tell of me in sorrow and weep for me
      through the days.
You trees, bow down your branches and weep over my youth,
You beasts of the forests, come and bewail my virginity,
for my years have been cut off
and the time of my life grown old in darkness."

On saying these things, Seila returned to her parents, and her father did everything that he had vowed and offered the holocausts (Judg

11:39f). Then all the virgins of Israel gathered together and buried the daughter of Jephthah and wept for her. The children of Israel made a great lamentation and established that in that month on the fourteenth day of the month they should come together every year and weep for Jephthah's daughter for four days. They named her tomb in keeping with her name: Seila.

THIRTIETH SUNDAY OF THE YEAR
Luke 13:10–17

Jesus "breaks the sabbath" in the eyes of some onlookers. He touches a woman and frees her from a spirit that has crippled her for eighteen years.

Jesus was teaching in one of the synagogues on the sabbath. And just then there appeared a woman with a spirit that had crippled her for eighteen years. She was bent over and was quite unable to stand up straight. When Jesus saw her, he called her over and said, "Woman, you are set free from your ailment." When he laid his hands on her, immediately she stood up straight and began praising God. But the leader of the synagogue, indignant because Jesus had cured on the sabbath, kept saying to the crowd, "There are six days on which work ought to be done; come on those days and be cured, and not on the sabbath day." But Jesus answered him and said, "You hypocrites! Does not each of you on the sabbath untie his ox or his donkey from the manger, and lead it away to give it water? And ought not this woman, a daughter of Abraham whom Satan bound for eighteen long years, be set free from this bondage on the sabbath day?" When he said this, all his opponents were put to shame; and the entire crowd was rejoicing at all the wonderful things that he was doing.

THIRTIETH WEEK OF THE YEAR
Monday
Luke 15:1-10

Parallel stories about a man and a woman provide images of God's love for sinners.

All the tax collectors and sinners were coming near to listen to Jesus. And the Pharisees and the scribes were grumbling and saying, "This fellow welcomes sinners and eats with them."

So he told them this parable: "Which one of you, having a hundred sheep and losing one of them, does not leave the ninety-nine in the wilderness and go after the one that is lost until he finds it? When he has found it, he lays it on his shoulders and rejoices. And when he comes home, he calls together his friends and neighbors, saying to them, 'Rejoice with me, for I have found my sheep that was lost.' Just so, I tell you, there will be more joy in heaven over one sinner who repents than over ninety-nine righteous persons who need no repentance.

"Or what woman having ten silver coins, if she loses one of them, does not light a lamp, sweep the house, and search carefully until she finds it? When she has found it, she calls together her friends and neighbors, saying, 'Rejoice with me, for I have found the coin that I had lost.' Just so, I tell you, there is joy in the presence of the angels of God over one sinner who repents."

THIRTIETH WEEK OF THE YEAR
Tuesday
Life of Leoba, by Rudolph, Monk of Fulda
(#1 of 12)

The eighth century Anglo-Saxon nun, Leoba, missionary to Germany with St. Boniface, was trained in a famous English monastery before beginning her missionary life. The abbess Tetta, her tutor, governed monasteries of both women and men.

The small book which I have written about the life and virtues of the holy and revered virgin Leoba [Le′ o ba] has been dedicated to you, O Hadamout [Had′ a mout], virgin of Christ, in order that you may have something to read with pleasure and imitate with profit.

Before I begin to write the life of the blessed and venerable virgin Leoba, I invoke her spouse, Christ, our Lord and Saviour, who gave her the courage to overcome the powers of evil, to inspire me with eloquence sufficient to describe her outstanding merits. I have been unable to discover all the facts of her life. I shall therefore recount the few that I have learned from the writings of others, venerable men who heard them from four of her disciples, Agatha, Thecla, Nana and Eoloba [E o lo′ ba]. Each one copied them down according to her ability and left them as a memorial to posterity. . . .

But before I begin the narration of her remarkable life and virtues, it may not be out of place if I mention a few of the many things I have heard about her spiritual mistress and mother, who first introduced her to the spiritual life and fostered in her a desire for heaven. In this way the reader who is made aware of the qualities of this great woman may give credence to the achievements of the disciple more easily the more clearly one sees that she learned the elements of the spiritual life from so noble a mistress.

In the island of Britain, which is inhabited by the English nation, there is a place called Wimbourne, an ancient name which may be translated "Winestream." It received this name from the clearness and sweetness of the water there, which was better than any other in that land. In olden times the kings of that nation had built two monasteries in the place, one for men, the other for women, both surrounded by strong and lofty walls and provided with all the necessities that prudence could devise.

It was over this monastery, in succession to several other abbesses and spiritual mistresses, that a holy virgin named Tetta was placed in authority, a woman of noble family (for she was a sister of the king), but more noble in her conduct and good qualities. Over both the monasteries she ruled with consummate prudence and discretion. She gave instruction by deed rather than by words, and whenever she said that a certain course of action was harmful to the salvation of souls she showed by her own conduct that it was to be shunned. There are many instances of the virtues of this woman which the virgin Leoba, her disciple, used to recall with pleasure when she told her reminiscences.

THIRTIETH WEEK OF THE YEAR
Wednesday
Life of Leoba, by Rudolf, Monk of Fulda (#2 of 12)

As with so many famous ancient and medieval people, Leoba's was believed to be a miraculous birth in her parents' old age and was accompanied by a prophetic dream-vision.

We will now pursue our purpose of describing the life of her (the abbess Tetta's) spiritual daughter, Leoba, the virgin.

As we have already said, her parents were English, of noble family and full of zeal for religion and the observance of God's commandments. Her father was called Dynno [Dyn' no], her mother Aebba [Aeb' ba]. But as they were barren, they remained together for a long time without children. After many years had passed and the onset of old age had deprived them of all hope of offspring her mother had a dream in which she saw herself bearing in her bosom a church bell, which on being drawn out with her hand rang merrily. When she woke up she called her old nurse to her and told her what she had dreamt. The nurse said to her: "We shall yet see a daughter from your womb and it is your duty to consecrate her straightway to God. And as Anna offered Samuel to serve God all the days of his life in the temple (1 Sam 1:23), so you must offer her, when she has been taught the Scripture from her infancy, to serve God in holy virginity so long as she shall live." Shortly after the woman had made this vow, she conceived and bore a daughter, whom she called Thrutgeba [Thrut ge'ba], surnamed Leoba because she was beloved, for this is what Leoba means. And when the child had grown up her mother consecrated her and handed her over to Mother Tetta to be taught the sacred sciences. And because the nurse had foretold that she should have such happiness, Aebba gave her her freedom.

THIRTIETH WEEK OF THE YEAR
Thursday
Life of Leoba, by Rudolf, Monk of Fulda (#3 of 12)

According to medieval custom, Leoba as a young girl is entrusted to a woman's monastery for her education. She was characterized by moderation, common sense, charity, and a love of learning, in part because her sisters modeled such virtues.

The girl grew up and was taught with such care by the abbess and all the nuns that she had no interest other than the monastery and the pursuit of sacred knowledge. She took no pleasure in aimless jests and wasted no time on girlish romances, but, fired by the love of Christ, fixed her mind always on reading or hearing the Word of God. Whatever she heard or read she committed to memory, and put all that she learned into practice. She exercised such moderation in her use of food and drink that she eschewed dainty dishes and the allurements of sumptuous fare, and was satisfied with whatever was placed before her. She prayed continually, knowing that in the Epistles the faithful are counselled to prayer without ceasing (1 Thess 5:17). When she was not praying she worked with her hands at whatever was commanded her, for she had learned that the one who will not work should not eat (2 Thess 3:10). However, she spent more time in reading and listening to Sacred Scripture than she gave to manual labour. She took great care not to forget what she had heard or read, observing the commandments of the Lord and putting into practice what she remembered of them. In this way she so arranged her conduct that she was loved by all the sisters. She learned from all and obeyed them all, and by imitating the good qualities of each one she modelled herself on the continence of one, the cheerfulness of another, copying here a sister's mildness, there a sister's patience. One she tried to equal in attention to prayer, another in devotion to reading. Above all, she was intent on practicing charity, without which, as she knew, all other virtues are void.

THIRTIETH WEEK OF THE YEAR
Friday
Life of Leoba, by Rudolf, Monk of Fulda (#4 of 12)

A strange dream interpreted by a wise old nun indicates the future importance of Leoba. The imagery follows the ancient belief that the bowels were the location of what today is centered in the heart: emotions and courage.

When Leoba had succeeded in fixing her attention on heavenly things, by these and other practices in the pursuit of virtue, she had a dream in which one night she saw a purple thread issuing from her mouth. It seemed to her that when she took hold of it with her hand and tried to draw it out there was no end to it; and as if it were coming from her very bowels, it extended little by little until it was of enormous length. When her hand was full of thread and it still issued from her mouth, she rolled it round and round and made a ball of it. The labour of doing this was so tiresome that eventually, through sheer fatigue, she woke from her sleep and began to wonder what the meaning of the dream might be. She understood quite clearly that there was some reason for the dream, and it seemed that there was some mystery hidden in it. Now there was in the same monastery an aged nun who was known to possess the spirit of prophecy, because other things that she had foretold had always been fulfilled. As Leoba was diffident about revealing the dream to her, she told it to one of her disciples just as it had occurred and asked her to go to the old nun and describe it to her as a personal experience and learn from her the meaning of it. When the sister had repeated the details of the dream as if it had happened to her, the nun, who could foresee the future, angrily replied: "This is indeed a true vision and presages that good will come. But why do you lie to me in saying that such things happened to you? These matters are no concern of yours: they apply to the beloved chosen by God." In giving this name, she referred to Leoba. "These things," she went on, "were revealed to the person whose holiness and wisdom make her a worthy recipient, because by her teaching and good example she will confer benefits on many people. The thread which came from her bowels and issued from her mouth signifies the wise counsels that she will speak from the heart. The fact that it filled her hand means that she will carry out in her actions whatever she expresses in her words. Furthermore, the ball which she made by rolling it round and round signifies the mystery of the divine teaching, which is set in motion by the words and deeds of those who give instruction and which turns earthwards through active works and heavenwards through contemplation, at one time swinging downwards through compassion for one's neighbour, again swinging upwards through the love of God. By these signs God shows that your mistress will profit many by her words and example, and the effect of them will be felt in other lands afar off whither she will go." That this interpretation of the dream was true later events were to prove.

THIRTIETH WEEK OF THE YEAR
Saturday
Life of Leoba, by Rudolf, Monk of Fulda (#5 of 12)

Leoba has become so famous in her monastery that Boniface explicitly asks for her to accompany him as his partner in mission to Germany.

At the time when the blessed virgin Leoba was pursuing her quest for perfection in the monastery the holy martyr Boniface [Bon' i face] was being ordained by Gregory, Bishop of Rome and successor to Constantine [Con' stan tine], in the apostolic See. His mission was to preach the Word of God to the people in Germany. When Boniface found that the people were ready to receive the faith and that, though the harvest was great, the labourers who worked with him were few, he sent messengers and letters to England, his native land, summoning from different ranks of the clergy many who were learned in the divine law and fitted both by their character and good works to preach the Word of God.

Likewise, he sent messengers with letters to the abbess Tetta, of whom we have already spoken, asking her to send Leoba to accompany him on this journey and to take part in this embassy: for Leoba's reputation for learning and holiness had spread far and wide and her praise was on everyone's lips. The abbess Tetta was exceedingly displeased at her departure, but because she could not gainsay the dispositions of divine providence she agreed to his request and sent Leoba to the blessed man. Thus it was that the interpretation of the dream which she had previously received was fulfilled. When she came, the man of God received her with the deepest reverence, holding her in great affection, not so much because she was related to him on his mother's side as because he knew that by her holiness and wisdom she would confer many benefits by her word and example.

THIRTY-FIRST SUNDAY OF THE YEAR
Life of Leoba, by Rudolf, Monk of Fulda (#6 of 12)

Leoba, established as superior of a new monastery in Germany, continues to be a model to all of simplicity, wisdom, and strength.

In furtherance of his aims, Boniface appointed persons in authority over the monasteries and established the observance of the Rule: he placed Sturm as abbot over the monks and Leoba as abbess over the nuns. He gave her the monastery at a place called Bischofsheim [Bis' chofs heim], where there was a large community of nuns. These were trained according to her principles in the discipline of monastic life and made such progress in her teaching that many of them afterwards became superiors of others, so that there was hardly a convent of nuns in that part which had not one of her disciples as abbess. She was a woman of great virtue and was so strongly attached to the way of life she had vowed that she never gave thought to her native country or her relatives. She expended all her energies on the work she had undertaken in order to appear blameless before God and to become a pattern of perfection to those who obeyed her in word and action. She was ever on her guard not to teach others what she did not carry out herself. In her conduct there was no arrogance or pride; she was no distinguisher of persons, but showed herself affable and kindly to all. In appearance she was angelic, in word pleasant, clear in mind, great in prudence, catholic in faith, most patient in hope, universal in her charity. But though she was always cheerful, she never broke out into laughter through excessive hilarity. No one ever heard a bad word from her lips; the sun never went down upon her anger.

THIRTY-FIRST WEEK OF THE YEAR
Monday
Life of Leoba, by Rudolf, Monk of Fulda (#7 of 12)

Leoba proves to be a wise monastic superior who leads with moderation. She is more learned than most women of her day, and she encourages her sisters in the same learned pursuits.

In the matter of food and drink Leoba always showed the utmost understanding for others but was most sparing in her own use of them. She had a small cup from which she used to drink and which, because of the meagre quantity it would hold, was called by the sisters "the Beloved's little one." So great was her zeal for reading that she discontinued it only for prayer or for the refreshment of her body with food or sleep: the Scriptures were never out of her hands. For, since she had been trained from infancy in the rudiments of grammar and the study of the other liberal arts, she tried by constant reflection to attain a perfect knowledge of divine things so that through the combination of her reading and her quick intelligence, by natural gifts and hard work, she became extremely learned. She read with attention all the books of the Old and New Testaments and learned by heart all the commandments of God. To these she added, by way of completion, the writings of the church fathers, the decrees of the Councils, and the whole of ecclesiastical law. She observed great moderation in all her acts and arrangements and always kept the practical end in view, so that she would never have to repent of her actions through having been guided by impulse. She was deeply aware of the necessity for concentration of mind in prayer and study, and for this reason took care not to go to excess either in watching or in other spiritual exercises. Throughout the summer both she and all the sisters under her rule went to rest after the midday meal, and she would never give permission to any of them to stay up late, for she said that lack of sleep dulled the mind, especially for study.

THIRTY-FIRST WEEK OF THE YEAR
Tuesday
Life of Leoba, by Rudolf, Monk of Fulda (#8 of 12)

A story of unwanted pregnancy and infanticide threatens to destroy the reputation of Leoba's monastery. Thanks to her prayer, the situation is resolved peacefully.

There was a certain poor little crippled girl, who sat near the gate of the monastery begging alms. Every day she received her food from the abbess's table, her clothing from the nuns, and all other necessities from them; these were given to her from divine charity. It happened that after some time, deceived by the suggestions of the devil, she committed fornication, and when her appearance made it impossible for her to conceal that she had conceived a child, she covered up her guilt by pretending to be ill. When her time came, she wrapped the child in swaddling clothes and cast it at night into a pool by the river which flowed through that place. When day dawned, another woman came to draw water and, seeing the corpse of the child, was struck with horror. Burning with womanly rage, she filled the whole village with her uncontrollable cries and reproached the holy nuns with these indignant words: "Oh, what a chaste community! How admirable is the life of nuns, who beneath their veils give birth to children and exercise at one and the same time the function of mother and priest, baptizing those to whom they have given birth. Now go and ask those women to remove this corpse from the river and make it fit for us to use again. Look for the one who is missing from the monastery and then you will find out who is responsible for this crime." At these words all the crowd was set in uproar and everybody, of whatever age or sex, ran in one great mass to see what had happened. As soon as they saw the corpse they denounced the crime and reviled the nuns. When the abbess heard the uproar and learned what was afoot she called the nuns together, told them the reason, and discovered that no one was absent except Agatha, who a few days before had been summoned to her parents' house on urgent business: but she had gone with full permission. A messenger was sent to her without delay to recall her to the monastery, as Leoba could not endure the accusation of so great a crime to hang over them. When Agatha returned and heard of the deed that was charged against her she fell on her knees and gazed up to heaven, crying: "Almighty God, who know all things before they come to pass, show your mercy to this community gathered together in your name but unmask and make known for the praise and glory of your name the person who has committed this misdeed."

On hearing this, the venerable superior, being assured of her innocence, ordered them all to go to the chapel and to go around the monastic buildings in procession with the crucifix at their head, calling upon God to free them from this accusation. When they had done this the blessed Leoba went straight to the altar and, standing before the cross, stretched out her hands towards heaven, and with tears and groans prayed, saying: "O Lord Jesus Christ, unconquerable God, manifest your power and deliver us from this charge, because the reproaches of those who reproached you have fallen upon us" (Rom 15:3). Immediately after she had said this, that wretched little woman, the dupe and the tool of the devil, calling out the name of the abbess, confessed to the crime she had committed. Then a great shout rose to heaven: the vast crowd was astounded at the miracle, the nuns began to weep with joy, and all of them with one voice gave expression to the merits of Leoba and of Christ our Saviour.

So it came about that the reputation of the nuns, which the devil had tried to ruin by his sinister rumour, was greatly enhanced and praise was showered on them in every place. Even before this, God had performed many miracles through Leoba, but they had been kept secret. This one was her first in Germany and, because it was done in public, it came to the ears of everyone.

THIRTY-FIRST WEEK OF THE YEAR
Wednesday
Life of Leoba, by Rudolf, Monk of Fulda (#9 of 12)

To Leoba, as to Jesus, is attributed the miraculous calming of a storm in the presence of terrified villagers.

I think it should be counted among the virtues of Leoba also that one day, when a wild storm arose and the whole sky was obscured by such dark clouds that day seemed turned into night, terrible lightning and falling thunderbolts struck terror into the stoutest hearts and everyone was shaking with fear. At first the people drove their flocks into the houses for shelter so that they should not perish; then, when the danger increased and threatened them all with death, they took refuge with their wives and children in the church, despairing of their lives. They locked all the doors and waited there trembling, thinking that the last judgment was at hand. In this state of panic they filled the air with the din of their mingled cries. Then the holy virgin went out to them and urged them all to have patience. She promised them that no harm would come to them; and after exhorting them to join with her in prayer, she fell prostrate at the foot of the altar. Then the mob, unable to endure the suspense any longer, rushed to the altar to rouse her from prayer and seek her protection. Thecla, her kinswoman, spoke to her first, saying: "Beloved, all the hopes of these people lie in you: you are their only support. Arise, then, and pray to the Mother of God, your mistress, for us, that by her intercession we may be delivered from this fearful storm." At these words Leoba rose up from prayer and, as if she had been challenged to a contest, flung off the cloak which she was wearing and boldly opened the doors of the church. Standing on the threshold, she made a sign of the cross, opposing to the fury of the storm the name of the High God. Then she stretched out her hands towards heaven and three times invoked the mercy of Christ, praying that through the intercession of Holy Mary, the Virgin, he would quickly come to the help of his people. Suddenly God came to their aid. The sound of thunder died away, the winds changed direction and dispersed the heavy clouds, the darkness rolled back and the sun shone, bringing calm and peace. Thus did divine power make manifest her merits. Unexpected peace came to the people and fear was banished.

THIRTY-FIRST WEEK OF THE YEAR
Thursday
Life of Leoba, by Rudolf, Monk of Fulda (#10 of 12)

Boniface, before leaving for a new mission, affirms his respect for Leoba and requests that they be buried near to each other.

Blessed Boniface, the archbishop, was preparing to go to Frisia [Fris′ i a], having decided to preach the Gospel to this people. He summoned Leoba to him and exhorted her not to abandon the country of her adoption and not to grow weary of the life she had undertaken, but rather to extend the scope of the good work she had begun. He commended her to Lull and to the senior monks of the monastery who were present, admonishing them to care for her with reverence and respect and reaffirming his wish that after his death her bones should be placed next to his in the tomb, so that they who had served God during their lifetime with equal sincerity and zeal should await together the day of resurrection.

After these words he gave her his cowl and begged and pleaded with her not to leave her adopted land. And so, when all necessary preparations had been made for the journey, he set out for Frisia, where he won over a multitude of people to the faith of Christ and ended his labours with a glorious martyrdom. His remains were transported to Fulda and there, according to his previous wishes, he was laid to rest with worthy tokens of respect.

The blessed virgin Leoba, however, persevered unwaveringly in the work of God. She had no desire to gain earthly possessions but only those of heaven, and she spent all her energies on fulfilling her vows. Her wonderful reputation spread abroad and her holiness and wisdom drew to her the affections of all.

THIRTY-FIRST WEEK OF THE YEAR
Friday
Life of Leoba, by Rudolf, Monk of Fulda (#11 of 12)

Leoba's fame and friendship extended to royalty, including Emperor Charlemagne and his Queen Hiltigard. Both rulers and bishops sought her counsel, an extraordinary tribute to her wisdom and holiness.

Leoba was held in veneration by all who knew her, even by kings. Pippin, King of the Franks, and his sons Charles and Carloman [Carl' o man] treated her with profound respect, particularly Charles, who, after the death of his father and brother, with whom he had shared the throne for some years, took over the reins of government. Many times he summoned the holy virgin to his court, received her with every mark of respect and loaded her with gifts suitable to her station. Queen Hiltigard [Hil' ti gard] also revered her with a chaste affection and loved her as her own soul. She would have liked her to remain continually at her side so that she might progress in the spiritual life and profit by her words and example. But Leoba detested the life at court like poison. The princes loved her, the nobles received her, the bishops welcomed her with joy. And because of her wide knowledge of the Scriptures and her prudence in counsel they often discussed spiritual matters and ecclesiastical discipline with her. But her deepest concern was the work she had begun. She visited the various convents of nuns and, like a mistress of novices, stimulated them to vie with one another in reaching perfection.

Sometimes she came to the Monastery of Fulda to say her prayers, a privilege never granted to any woman either before or since, because from the day that monks began to dwell there, entrance was always forbidden to women. Permission was only granted to her, for the simple reason that the holy martyr St. Boniface had commended her to the seniors of the monastery, and because he had ordered her remains to be buried there. When she was an old woman and became decrepit through age she put all the convents under her care on a sound footing and then, on Bishop Lull's advice, went to a place four miles south of Mainz. There she took up residence with some of her nuns and served God night and day in fasting and prayer.

THIRTY-FIRST WEEK OF THE YEAR
Saturday
Life of Leoba, by Rudolf, Monk of Fulda (#12 of 12)

Leoba's final visit to the queen reveals their deep affection for one another as well as Leoba's awareness that her death is near. After her simple death, she is buried at the men's monastery at Fulda near the tomb of St. Boniface, according to both their wishes, to await together the day of resurrection.

While King Charles was staying in the palace at Aachen [Aa' chen], Queen Hiltigard sent a message to Leoba begging her to come and visit her, if it were not too difficult, because she longed to see her before she passed from this life. And when the queen importuned her to stay a few days longer she refused; but, embracing her friend rather more affectionately than usual, she kissed her on the mouth, the forehead and the eyes and took leave of her with these words: "Farewell for evermore, my dearly beloved lady and sister; farewell, most precious half of my soul. May Christ, our Creator and Redeemer, grant that we shall meet again without shame on the day of judgment. Never more on this earth shall we enjoy each other's presence."

So Leoba returned to the convent, and after a few days she was stricken by sickness and was confined to her bed. When she saw that her ailment was growing worse and that the hour of her death was near she sent for a saintly English priest who had always been at her side and ministered to her with respect and love, and received from him the viaticum of the body and blood of Christ. She died in the month of September, the fourth of the kalends of October. Her body, followed by a long cortège of noble persons, was carried by the monks of Fulda to their monastery with every mark of respect. Thus the seniors there remembered what St. Boniface had said, namely, that it was his last wish that her remains should be placed next to his bones. They buried her on the north side of the altar which the martyr St. Boniface had himself erected and consecrated in honour of our Saviour and the twelve Apostles.

THIRTY-SECOND SUNDAY OF THE YEAR
Mark 12:38–44

The sacrifice of the widow stands in stark contrast to the ostentation and hypocrisy of some of the scribes. The placement of this story before the passion suggests that Mark recognized in the generosity of the widow a hint of Jesus' own self-donation.

As Jesus taught, he said, "Beware of the scribes, who like to walk around in long robes, and to be greeted with respect in the marketplaces, and to have the best seats in the synagogues and places of honor at banquets! They devour widows' houses and for the sake of appearance say long prayers. They will receive the greater condemnation."

He sat down opposite the treasury, and watched the crowd putting money into the treasury. Many rich people put in large sums. A poor widow came and put in two small copper coins, which are worth a penny. Then he called his disciples and said to them, "Truly I tell you, this poor widow has put in more than all those who are contributing to the treasury. For all of them have contributed out of their abundance; but she out of her poverty has put in everything she had, all she had to live on."

See Luke 21:1–4

THIRTY-SECOND WEEK OF THE YEAR
Monday
Sayings of the Desert Mother Sarah

Among the famous figures in the early monastic movement, there were some women recognized for their outstanding qualities of virtue and leadership, among them Amma Sarah (fifth cent. CE).

It was related of Amma Sarah that for thirteen years she waged warfare against the demon of fornication. She never prayed that the warfare should cease but she said, "O God, give me strength."

Once the same spirit of fornication attacked her more intently, reminding her of the vanities of the world. But she gave herself up to the fear of God and to asceticism and went up onto her little terrace to pray. Then the spirit of fornication appeared corporally to her and said, "Sarah, you have overcome me." But she said, "It is not I who have overcome you but my master, Christ."

Amma Sarah said, "If I prayed God that all should approve of my conduct, I should find myself a penitent at the door of each one, but I shall rather pray that my heart may be pure towards all."

She also said, "I put out my foot to ascend the ladder, and I place death before my eyes before going up it."

She also said, "It is good to give alms to those in need. Even if it is only done to please people, through it one can begin to seek to please God."

THIRTY-SECOND WEEK OF THE YEAR
Tuesday
Jerome, *Letter 77 on Fabiola* 2 (#1 of 8)

Jerome writes in praise of the well-known Roman matron Fabiola who, after two aristocratic marriages, embraced the ascetic life and was an example of love of the poor. The letter was written in 399 CE, soon after her death.

Today you give me as my theme Fabiola [Fab i' o la], the praise of the Christians, the marvel of the gentiles, the sorrow of the poor, and the consolation of the monks. Whatever point in her character I choose to treat of first, pales into insignificance compared with those which follow after. Shall I praise her fasts? Her alms are greater still. Shall I commend her lowliness? The glow of her faith is yet brighter. Shall I mention her studied plainness in dress, her voluntary choice of plebeian costume and the garb of a slave that she might put to shame silken robes? To change one's disposition is a greater achievement than to change one's dress. It is harder for us to part with arrogance than with gold and gems. For, even though we throw away these, we plume ourselves sometimes on a meanness that is really ostentatious. But a virtue that seeks concealment and is cherished in the inner consciousness appeals to no judgement but that of God. Thus the eulogies which I have to bestow upon Fabiola will be altogether new. Another writer would perhaps bring forward the whole Fabian [Fa' bi an] family, and would exult that Fabiola had come to us through a line so noble, showing that qualities not apparent in the branch still existed in the root. But as I am a lover of the inn at Bethlehem and of the Lord's stable in which the virgin travailed and gave birth to an infant God, I shall deduce the lineage of Christ's handmaid not from a stock famous in history but from the lowliness of the church.

THIRTY-SECOND WEEK OF THE YEAR
Wednesday
Jerome, *Letter 77 on Fabiola* 3 (#2 of 8)

After a civil divorce from an abusive husband, Fabiola remarried, contrary to church law. Jerome's discussion of the situation shows an awareness of the sexual double standard operating in the culture.

Because at the very outset there is a rock in the path and Fabiola is overwhelmed by a storm of censure, for having forsaken her first husband and having taken a second, I will not praise her for her conversion till I have first cleared her of this charge. So terrible then were the faults imputed to her former husband that not even a prostitute or a common slave could have put up with them. If I were to recount them, I should undo the heroism of the wife who chose to bear the blame of a separation rather than to blacken the character and expose the stains of him who was one body with her. I will only urge this one plea which is sufficient to exonerate a chaste matron and a Christian woman. The Lord has given commandment that a wife must not be put away "except for fornication, and that if put away, she must remain unmarried" (Matt 19:9).

Now a commandment which is given to men logically applies to women also. For it cannot be that, while an adulterous wife is to be put away, an incontinent husband is to be retained. The apostle says: "he who is joined to a harlot is one body" (1 Cor 6:16). Therefore, she also who is joined to a whoremonger and unchaste person is made one body with him. The laws of Caesar are different, it is true, from the laws of Christ. Earthly laws give a free rein to the unchastity of men, merely condemning seduction and adultery; lust is allowed to range unrestrained among brothels and slave girls, as if the guilt were constituted by the rank of the person assailed and not by the purpose of the assailant. But with us Christians what is unlawful for women is equally unlawful for men, and as both serve the same God both are bound by the same obligations. Fabiola then has put away—they are quite right—a husband that was a sinner, guilty of this and that crime, sins—I have almost mentioned their names—with which the whole neighbourhood resounded but which the wife alone refused to disclose.

THIRTY-SECOND WEEK OF THE YEAR
Thursday
Jerome, *Letter 77 on Fabiola* 3–5 (#3 of 8)

After the death of her second husband, Fabiola did public penance for her violation of church law, as was the custom. For an aristocrat to make such a public display of shame was considered high virtue.

The apostle wills that the younger widows should marry, bear children, and give no occasion to the adversary to speak reproachfully (1 Tim 5:14). Fabiola therefore was fully persuaded in her own mind: she thought she had acted legitimately in putting away her husband, and that when she had done so, she was free to marry again.

But why do I linger over old and forgotten matters, seeking to excuse a fault for which Fabiola has herself confessed her penitence? Who would believe that, after the death of her husband at a time when most widows, having shaken off the yoke of servitude, grow careless and allow themselves more liberty than ever, frequenting the baths, flitting through the streets, showing their faces everywhere; that at this time Fabiola came to herself? Yet it was then that she put on sackcloth to make public confession of her error. It was then that in the presence of all Rome (in the basilica which formerly belonged to that Lateranus [La ter a' nus] who perished by the sword of Caesar) she stood in the ranks of the penitents and exposed before bishop, presbyters, and people—all of whom wept when they saw her weep—her dishevelled hair, pale features, and soiled hands. What sins would such a penance fail to purge away?

But this one thing I will say, for it is at once useful to my readers and pertinent to my present theme. As Fabiola was not ashamed of the Lord on earth, so he shall not be ashamed of her in heaven (Luke 9:26).

THIRTY-SECOND WEEK OF THE YEAR
Friday
Jerome, *Letter 77 on Fabiola* 6 (#4 of 8)

Instead of only giving alms to help the poor and sick, Fabiola nursed them herself.

Restored to communion before the eyes of the whole church, what did Fabiola do? In the day of prosperity she was not forgetful of affliction; and having once suffered shipwreck, she was unwilling again to face the risks of the sea. Instead, therefore, of re-embarking on her old life, she broke up and sold all that she could lay hands on of her property (it was large and suitable to her rank), and turning it into money, she laid out this for the benefit of the poor. She was the first person to found a hospital, into which she might gather sufferers out of the streets, and where she might nurse the unfortunate victims of sickness and want. Often did she carry on her own shoulders persons infected with jaundice or with filth. Often, too, did she wash away the matter discharged from wounds which others, even men, could not bear to look at. She gave food to her patients with her own hand, and moistened the scarce breathing lips of the dying with sips of liquid. I know of many wealthy and devout persons who, unable to overcome their natural repugnance to such sights, perform this work of mercy by the agency of others, giving money instead of personal aid. I do not blame them and am far from construing their weakness of resolution into a want of faith. While, however, I pardon such squeamishness, I extol to the skies the enthusiastic zeal of one who is above it. A great faith makes little of such trifles.

> Not with a hundred tongues or throat of bronze
> Could I exhaust the forms of fell disease
>
> (Virgil, *Aeneid* 6,625–27)

which Fabiola so wonderfully alleviated in the suffering poor that many of the healthy fell to envying the sick. However, she showed the same liberality towards the clergy and monks and virgins. Was there a monastery which was not supported by Fabiola's wealth? Was there a naked or bedridden person who was not clothed with garments supplied by her? Were there ever any in want to whom she failed to give a quick and unhesitating supply? Even Rome was not wide enough for her pity. Either in her own person or else through trustworthy agents, she went from island to island and carried her bounty wherever communities of monks are to be found.

THIRTY-SECOND WEEK OF THE YEAR
Saturday
Jerome, *Letter 77 on Fabiola* 7 (#5 of 8)

Fabiola impetuously decided to sail from Rome to the Holy Land to visit Paula and Jerome. The latter relates how insistent Fabiola was to understand the Scriptures.

Suddenly Fabiola made up her mind, against the advice of all her friends, to take ship and to come to Jerusalem. Here she was welcomed by a large concourse of people and for a short time took advantage of my hospitality. Indeed, when I call to mind our meeting, I seem to see her here now instead of in the past. Blessed Jesus, what zeal, what earnestness she bestowed upon the sacred books! In her eagerness to satisfy what was a veritable craving, she would run through Prophets, Gospels, and Psalms, she would suggest questions and treasure the answers. And yet this eagerness to hear did not bring with it any feeling of satiety, and by casting oil upon the flame, she did but supply fuel for a still more burning zeal. One day we had before us the book of Numbers written by Moses, and she modestly questioned me as to the meaning of the great mass of names there to be found. Why was it, she inquired, that single tribes were differently associated in this passage and in that, how came it that the soothsayer Balaam in prophesying of the future mysteries of Christ spoke more plainly of him than almost any other prophet? I replied as best I could and tried to satisfy her enquiries. And when she asked me the meaning and reason, I spoke doubtfully about some things, dealt with others in a tone of assurance, and in several instances simply confessed my ignorance. Hereupon she began to press me harder still, expostulating with me as though it were a thing unallowable that I should be ignorant of what I did not know. In a word, I was ashamed to refuse her request and allowed her to extort from me a promise that I would devote a special work to this subject for her use.

THIRTY-THIRD SUNDAY OF THE YEAR
Proverbs 31:13–31

The traditional reference to this woman of Proverbs has been to "the valiant woman." This woman is a successful independent business woman. Her participation in the economy of her day, while juggling family responsibilities, might today win her the names "bold," "intrepid," "fearless"—even "gutsy."

A capable wife seeks wool and flax,
   and works with willing hands.
She is like the ships of the merchant,
   she brings her food from far away.
She rises while it is still night
   and provides food for her household
   and tasks for her servant girls.

She considers a field and buys it;
  with the fruit of her hands she plants a vineyard.
She girds herself with strength,
  and makes her arms strong.
She perceives that her merchandise is profitable.
  Her lamp does not go out at night
She puts her hands to the distaff,
  and her hands hold the spindle.
She opens her hand to the poor,
  and reaches out her hands to the needy.
She is not afraid for her household when it snows,
  for all her household are clothed in crimson.
She makes herself coverings;
  her clothing is fine linen and purple.
Her husband is known in the city gates,
  taking his seat among the elders of the land.
She makes linen garments and sells them;
  she supplies the merchant with sashes.
Strength and dignity are her clothing,
  and she laughs at the time to come.
She opens her mouth with wisdom,
  and the teaching of kindness is on her tongue.
She looks well to the ways of her household
  and does not eat the bread of idleness.
Her children rise up and call her happy;
  her husband too, and he praises her;
"Many women have done excellently,
  but you surpass them all."
Charm is deceitful, and beauty is vain,
  but a woman who fears the Lord is to be praised.
Give her a share in the fruit of her hands,
  and let her works praise her in the city gates.

THIRTY-THIRD WEEK OF THE YEAR
Monday
Jerome, *Letter 77 on Fabiola* 8–9 (#6 of 8)

*Fabiola considered staying in Bethlehem, but never adapted to the
solitude of the monastic life as it was lived there. The threat of
invasion by the Huns provided the occasion for her to return home.
When she got there, she was still restless. Fabiola's high-strung
personality seeps through Jerome's defense of her.*

While I was in search of a suitable dwelling for so great a lady, whose
only conception of the solitary life included a place of resort like Mary's
inn, suddenly messengers flew this way and that, and the whole East was
terror-struck. For news came that the hordes of the Huns had poured
forth in our direction, and that they were filling all the world with panic
and bloodshed. It was generally agreed that the goal of the invaders was
Jerusalem and that it was their excessive desire for gold which made them
hasten to this particular city. I myself clung to my long-settled abode in
the East and gave way to my deep-seated love for the holy places. Fabiola,
used as she was to moving from city to city and having no other property
but what her baggage contained, returned to her native land; to live in
poverty where she had once been rich, to lodge in the house of another,
she who in old days had lodged many guests in her own, and—not unduly
to prolong my account—to bestow upon the poor before the eyes of
Rome the proceeds of that property which Rome knew her to have sold.
  This only do I lament: that in her the holy places lost a necklace of
the loveliest. Rome recovered what it had previously parted with, and the
wanton and slanderous tongues of the heathen were confuted by the
testimony of their own eyes. Others may commend her pity, her humility, her faith; I will rather praise her ardour of soul. The letter in which as
a young man I once urged Heliodorus [He li o do' rus] to the life of a
hermit, she knew by heart, and whenever she looked upon the walls of
Rome she complained that she was in a prison. Forgetful of her sex,
unmindful of her frailty, and only desiring to be alone, she was in fact
there where her soul lingered. The counsels of her friends could not hold
her back; so eager was she to burst from the city as from a place of

bondage. Nor did she leave the distribution of her alms to others for the sake of Christ. In such haste was she and so impatient of delay that you would fancy her on the eve of her departure. As she was always ready, death could not find her unprepared.

THIRTY-THIRD WEEK OF THE YEAR
Tuesday
Jerome, *Letter 77 on Fabiola* 10 (#7 of 8)

Fabiola and the widowed senator Pammachius, a close friend of Jerome, worked together to found a famous hospice at Portus, near Ostia. Even to the end of her life, Fabiola was searching out new charitable projects.

As I pen Fabiola's praises, my dear friend Pammachius [Pam ma' chi us] seems suddenly to rise before me. His wife Paulina [Pau li' na] sleeps that he may keep vigil; she has gone before her husband that he remaining behind may be Christ's servant. Although he was his wife's heir, others—I mean the poor—are now in possession of his inheritance. He and Fabiola contended for the privilege of setting up a tent like that of Abraham at Portus. The contest which arose between them was for the supremacy in showing kindness. Each conquered and each was overcome. Both admitted themselves to be at once victors and vanquished; for what each had desired to effect alone, both accomplished together. They united their resources and combined their plans that harmony might forward what rivalry must have brought to nought. No sooner was the scheme broached than it was carried out. A house was purchased to serve as a shelter, and a crowd flocked into it. "There was no more travail in Jacob nor distress in Israel" (Num 23:21). The seas carried voyagers to find a welcome here on landing. Travellers left Rome in haste to take advantage of the mild coast before setting sail. What Publius [Pub' li us] once did in the island of Malta for Paul (Acts 28:7), Fabiola and Pammachius have done over and over again for large numbers; and not only have they supplied the wants of the destitute, but so universal has been their munificence that they have provided additional means for those who have something already. The whole world knows that a home for strangers has been established at Portus.

THIRTY-THIRD WEEK OF THE YEAR
Wednesday
Jerome, *Letter 77 on Fabiola* 11–12 (#8 of 8)

At her death Fabiola's funeral attracted throngs of those who had been her friends and the recipients of her generosity. Jerome acknowledges her as not without fault, but with a generous heart.

In the death of this noble lady Fabiola, we have seen a fulfilment of the apostle's words:—"All things work together for good to those who fear God" (Rom 8:28; note that Jerome substitutes "fear" for "love"). Having a presentiment of what would happen, she had written to several monks to come and release her from the burden under which she laboured (the remnant of her fortune). They came to her and she made them her friends; she fell asleep in the way that she had wished, and having at last laid aside her burden she soared more lightly up to heaven. How great a marvel Fabiola had been to Rome while she lived came out in the behavior of the people now that she was dead. Hardly had she breathed her last breath, hardly had she given back her soul to Christ whose it was when the entire city gathered to attend her obsequies. I seem to hear even now the squadrons which led the van of the procession, and the sound of the feet of the multitude which thronged in thousands to attend her funeral. The streets, porches, and roofs from which a view could be obtained were inadequate to accommodate the spectators. On that day Rome saw all her peoples gathered together in one.

I give you this, Fabiola, the best gift of my aged powers, to be as it were a funeral offering. Oftentimes have I praised virgins and widows and married women who have kept their garments always white and who follow the Lamb wherever he goes (Rev 14:4). Happy indeed is she in her encomium who, throughout her life, has been stained by no defilement. But let envy depart and censoriousness be silent.

THIRTY-THIRD WEEK OF THE YEAR
Thursday
Epitaph of Arsinoe

A young Egyptian Jewish woman named Arsinoe died during her first childbirth in the first century BCE. Her family erected this moving tribute.

This is the grave of Arsinoe [Ar si' no e], wayfarer. Stand by and weep for her, unfortunate in all things, whose lot was hard and terrible. For I was bereaved of my mother when I was a little girl, and when the flower of my youth made me ready for a bridegroom, my father married me to Phabeis [Pha' be is], and Fate brought me to the end of my life in bearing my firstborn child. I had a small span of years, but great grace flowered in the beauty of my spirit. This grave hides in its bosom my chaste body, but my soul has flown to the holy ones. Lament for Arsinoe. In the 25th year, the second day of the month of Mechir.

THIRTY-THIRD WEEK OF THE YEAR
Friday
2 Samuel 13:1–14 (#1 of 2)

Like thousands of young women before and after her, Tamar is a victim of incest.

David's son Absalom [Ab' sa lom] had a beautiful sister whose name was Tamar; and David's son Amnon fell in love with her. Amnon was so tormented that he made himself ill because of his sister Tamar, for she was a virgin, and it seemed impossible to Amnon to do anything to her. But Amnon had a friend whose name was Jonadab, the son of David's brother Shimeah [Shim' e ah]; and Jonadab was a very crafty man. He said to him, "O son of the king, why are you so haggard morning after morning? Will you not tell me?" Amnon said to him, "I love Tamar, my brother Absalom's sister." Jonadab said to him, "Lie down on your bed, and pretend to be ill; and when your father comes to see you, say to him, 'Let my sister Tamar come and give me something to eat, and prepare the food in my sight, so that I may see it and eat it from her hand.' " So Amnon lay down, and pretended to be ill; and when the king came to see him, Amnon said to the king, "Please let my sister Tamar come and make a couple of cakes in my sight, so that I may eat from her hand." Then David sent home to Tamar, saying, "Go to your brother Amnon's house, and prepare food for him." So Tamar went to her brother Amnon's house, where he was lying down. She took dough, kneaded it, made cakes in his sight, and baked the cakes. Then she took the pan and set them out before him, but he refused to eat. Amnon said, "Send out everyone from me." So everyone went out from him. Then Amnon said to Tamar, "Bring the food into the chamber, so that I may eat from your hand." So Tamar took the cakes she had made, and brought them into the chamber to Amnon her brother. But when she brought them near him to eat, he took hold of her, and said to her, "Come, lie with me, my sister." She answered him, "No, my brother, do not force me; for such a thing is not done in Israel; do not do anything so vile! As for me, where could I carry my shame? And as for you, you would be as one of the scoundrels in Israel. Now therefore, I beg you, speak to the king; for he will not withhold me from you." But he would not listen to her; and being stronger than she, he forced her and lay with her.

THIRTY-THIRD WEEK OF THE YEAR
Saturday
2 Samuel 13:15–22 (#2 of 2)

Even though David's son Amnon had violated Tamar, his sister, the king gave no response because his son was considered too valuable to be punished. Later Absalom, Tamar's half-brother, redresses the wrong by killing Amnon.

Then Amnon was seized with a very great loathing for her; indeed, his loathing was even greater than the lust he had felt for her. Amnon said to her, "Get out!" But she said to him, "No, my brother; for this wrong in sending me away is greater than the other that you did to me." But he would not listen to her. He called the young man who served him and said, "Put this woman out of my presence, and bolt the door after her." (Now she was wearing a long robe with sleeves; for this is how the virgin daughters of the king were clothed in earlier times.) So his servant put her out, and bolted the door after her. But Tamar put ashes on her head, and tore the long robe that she was wearing; she put her hand on her head, and went away, crying aloud as she went.

Her brother Absalom said to her, "Has Amnon your brother been with you? Be quiet for now, my sister, he is your brother; do not take this to heart." So Tamar remained, a desolate woman in her brother Absalom's house. When King David heard of all these things, he became very angry, but he would not punish his son Amnon, because he loved him, for he was his firstborn. But Absalom spoke to Amnon neither good nor bad; for Absalom hated Amnon because he had raped his sister Tamar.

See 1 Kings 13:30

THIRTY-FOURTH SUNDAY OF THE YEAR
See Solemnity of Corpus Christi (p. 161)

THIRTY-FOURTH WEEK OF THE YEAR
Monday
Luke 21:1–4

While exemplifying extraordinary generosity, this text also highlights the oppressive social condition of poverty suffered especially by women.

Jesus looked up and saw rich people putting their gifts into the treasury; he also saw a poor widow put in two small copper coins. He said, "Truly I tell you, this poor widow has put in more than all of them; for all of them have contributed out of their abundance, but she out of her poverty has put in all she had to live on."

See Mark 12:41–44

THIRTY-FOURTH WEEK OF THE YEAR
Tuesday
Martyrdom of Saints Agape, Irene, Chione, and Companions 1–2 (#1 of 4)

Three women of Thessalonica try to flee the persecution of Diocletian and Maximian but are captured and condemned to death. They seem to have lived or worked together and to have held responsible positions in the church.

Since the advent and the presence on earth of our Lord and Saviour Jesus Christ, the greater the grace of those of old, so much the greater was the victory of the holy ones. For instead of those visible enemies, we have now begun to crush enemies that cannot be seen with bodily eyes, and the invisible substance of the demons has been handed over to the flames by pure and holy women who were full of the Holy Spirit. Such were the three saintly women who came from the city of Thessalonica [Thes sa lo' ni ca], the city that the inspired Paul celebrated when he praised its faith and love, saying, "Your faith in God has gone out to every place" (1 Thess 1:8). And elsewhere he says, "Of charity for your brothers and sisters I have no need to write to you; for you yourselves have learned from God to love one another" (1 Thess 4:9).

When the persecution was raging under the Emperor Maximian [Max im' i an], these women, who had adorned themselves with virtue, following the precepts of the Gospel, abandoned their native city, their family, property, and possessions because of their love of God and their expectation of heavenly things, performing deeds worthy of their father

Abraham. They fled the persecutors, according to the commandment, and took refuge on a high mountain. There they gave themselves to prayer: though their bodies resided on a mountain top, their souls lived in heaven.

At any rate, they were here captured and brought to the official who was conducting the persecution, that, by thus fulfilling the rest of the divine commands and loving their Master even unto death, they might weave for themselves the chaplet of immortality. Of these three, one had preserved the shining purity of her baptism according to the holy prophet who said: "You will wash me and I shall be whiter than snow" (Ps 51:7), and she was called Chione [Chi o' ne] (snow). The second possessed the gift of our God and Saviour within herself and manifested it to everyone according to the word, "My peace I give you" (John 14:27), and she was called Irene [I re' ne] (peace) by everyone. The third possessed the perfection of the Gospel, loving God with her whole heart and her neighbour as herself, in accord with the holy Apostle who says, "The aim of our charge is love" (1 Tim 1:5), and she was appropriately named Agape [Ag' a pe] (love). When these three were brought before the magistrate and refused to sacrifice, he sentenced them to the fire, in order that thus by a short time in the fire, they might overcome those that are devoted to fire, that is, the Devil and all his heavenly host of demons, and, attaining the incorruptible crown of glory, they might endlessly praise, along with the angels, the God who had showered this grace upon them. The record that was taken down in their case is the material of our account.

THIRTY-FOURTH WEEK OF THE YEAR
Wednesday
Martyrdom of Saints Agape, Irene, Chione, and Companions 3–4 (#2 of 4)

To the original group of three women, four more are added, one of them pregnant. Agape and Chione are sentenced to death, the others kept temporarily in prison. The narrative is probably based on

the actual court record of their interrogation. It is a remarkable story
of women resisting oppressive political power. (This reading would
be very effective read in parts.)

The prefect Dulcitius [Dul ci' ti us] was sitting on the tribunal, and
the court clerk Artemisius [Ar te mi' si us] spoke, "With your permission,
I shall read the charge which was sent to you by the guard, here present,
in connection with the parties in court."

"You may read it," said the prefect Dulcitius. And the charge was
duly read: "To you, my lord, greetings from Cassander [Cas san' der],
staff-officer. This is to inform you, Sir, that Agatho [Ag' a tho], Irene,
Agape, Chione, Cassia [Cas' si a], Philippa [Phi lip' pa], and Eutychia [Eu
ti' chi a] refuse to eat sacrificial food, so I have referred them to you."

"What is this insanity," said the prefect Dulcitius, "that you refuse
to obey the order of our most religious emperors and Caesars?" And
turning to Agatho, he said, "When you came to the sacrifices, why did
you not perform the cult practices like other religious people?"

"Because I am a Christian," said Agatho.

The prefect Dulcitius said, "Do you still remain in the same
mind today?"

"Yes," said Agatho.

The prefect Dulcitius said, "What do you say, Agape?"

"I believe in the living God," replied Agape, "and I refuse to destroy my conscience."

"What do you say, Irene?" asked the prefect Dulcitius. "Why did
you disobey the command of our lords the emperors and Caesars?"

"Because of my fear of God," said Irene.

"What do you say, Chione?" asked the prefect.

"I believe in the living God," replied Chione, "and I refuse to
do this."

The prefect said, "And how about you, Cassia?"

"I wish to save my soul," said Cassia.

The prefect said, "Are you willing to partake of the sacrificial meat?"

"I am not," said Cassia.

The prefect said, "And what say you, Philippa?"

"I say the same," said Philippa.

"What do you mean, the same?" said the prefect.

Said Philippa, "I mean, I would rather die than partake."

"Eutychia," said the prefect, "what do you say?"

"I say the same," said Eutychia; "I would rather die."

The prefect said, "Do you have a husband?"

"He is dead," said Eutychia.

"When did he die?" asked the prefect.

"About seven months ago," said Eutychia.

The prefect said, "I urge Eutychia to cease this madness and to return to sound reason. What do you say? Will you obey the imperial command?"

"No, I will not," said Eutychia. "I am a Christian, a servant of almighty God."

The prefect said, "Since Eutychia is pregnant, she shall be kept meanwhile in jail." Then he added, "What say you, Agape? Will you perform all the actions which religious persons perform in honour of our lords the emperors and Caesars?"

Agape replied, "It is not at all in Satan's power. He cannot move my reason; it is invincible."

The prefect said, "What say you, Chione?"

Chione said, "No one can change my mind."

The prefect said, "Do you have in your possession any writings, parchments, or books of the impious Christians?"

Chione said, "We do not, Sir. Our present emperors have taken these from us."

"Who was it who gave you this idea?" asked the prefect.

"God almighty," said Chione.

The prefect said, "Who was it who counselled you to commit such folly?"

"It was almighty God," answered Chione, "and our Lord Jesus Christ."

The prefect Dulcitius said, "It is clear to all that you are all liable to the crime of treason against our lords the emperors and Caesars. But seeing that you have persisted in this folly for such a long time, in spite of strong warnings and so many decrees, sanctioned by stern threats, and have despised the command of our lords the emperors and Caesars, remaining in this impious name of Christian, and seeing that even today when you were ordered by the soldiers and officials to deny your belief and signify this in writing, you refused—therefore you shall receive the punishment appropriate for you."

Then he read the sentence written on a sheet, "Whereas Agape and Chione have with malicious intent acted against the divine decree of our lords the Augusti and Caesars, and whereas they adhere to the worthless and obsolete worship of the Christians which is hateful to all religious people, I sentence them to be burned." Then he added, "Agatho, Irene, Cassia, Philippa, and Eutychia, because of their youth, are to be put in prison in the meanwhile."

THIRTY-FOURTH WEEK OF THE YEAR
Thursday
Martyrdom of Saints Agape, Irene, Chione, and Companions 5 (#3 of 4)

Irene is interrogated alone. Her testimony is evidence of the unusual independence from family with which Christian women often operated. They were even entrusted with keeping the copies of the scriptures when legal orders required their confiscation. Instead of the death sentence, she is consigned to a brothel, a punishment intended to break down her resistance.

After the most holy women were consumed in the flames, the saintly Irene was once again brought before the court on the following day. Dulcitius said to her, "It is clear from what we have seen that you are determined in your folly, for you have deliberately kept even till now so many tablets, books, parchments, codices, and pages of the writings of the former Christians of unholy name; even now, though you denied each time that you possessed such writings, you did show a sign of recognition when they were mentioned. You are not satisfied with the punishment of your sister, nor do you keep before your eyes the terror of death. Therefore you must be punished.

"It would not, however, seem out of place to show you some measure of mercy: if, even now, you would be willing to recognize the gods, you will be released from all danger and punishment. Now what do you say? Will you do the bidding of our emperors and Caesars? Are you prepared to eat the sacrificial meats and to sacrifice to the gods?"

"No," said Irene, "I am not prepared, for the sake of the God almighty who 'has created heaven and earth and the seas and all that is in them' (Acts 4:24). For those who transgress the word of God there awaits the great judgement of eternal punishment."

The prefect Dulcitius said, "Who was it that advised you to retain those parchments and writings up to the present time?"

"It was almighty God," said Irene, "who bade us to love unto death. For this reason we did not dare to be traitors, but we chose to be burned alive or suffer anything else that might happen to us rather than betray the writings."

The prefect said, "Was anyone else aware that the documents were in the house where you lived?"

"No one else saw them," said Irene, "save almighty God who knows all things. But no stranger. As for our own relatives, we considered them worse than our enemies, in fear that they would denounce us. Hence we told no one."

"Last year," said the prefect, "when this edict of our lords the emperors and Caesars was first promulgated, where did you hide?"

"Wherever God willed," said Irene. "We lived on the mountains, in the open air, as God is my witness."

"Whom were you living with?" asked the prefect.

Irene answered, "I swear out of doors in different places among the mountains."

The prefect said, "Who supplied you with bread?"

Irene answered, "God, who supplies all."

"Was your father aware of this?" asked the prefect.

Irene answered. "I swear by almighty God, he was not aware; he knew nothing at all about it."

"Were any of your neighbours aware of this?" asked the prefect.

Irene answered, "Go and question our neighbours, and inquire about the area to see whether anyone knew where we were."

Dulcitius the prefect said, "Your sisters, in accordance with my commands in their regard, have received their sentence. I do not wish you to die immediately in the same way. Instead I sentence you to be placed naked in the brothel with the help of the public notaries of this city and of Zosimus [Zos' i mus] the executioner; and you will receive merely one loaf of bread from our residence, and the notaries will not allow you to leave."

THIRTY-FOURTH WEEK OF THE YEAR
Friday
Martyrdom of Saints Agape, Irene, Chione, and Companions 6 (#4 of 4)

Irene is miraculously preserved from harm in the brothel, and finally condemned to death by burning on April 1, 304 CE. These martyrs are one of the few known groups composed only of women who were tried and executed together.

After the notaries and the slave Zosimus, the executioner, were brought in, the prefect said, "Be it known to you that if ever I find out from the troops that this girl was removed from the spot where I have ordered her to be even for a single instant, you will immediately be punished with the most extreme penalties."

After those who were put in charge had taken the girl off to the public brothel in accordance with the prefect's order, by the grace of the Holy Spirit which preserved and guarded her pure and inviolate for the God who is the lord of all things, no man dared to approach her or so much as tried to insult her in speech. Hence the prefect Dulcitius called back this most saintly girl, had her stand before the tribunal, and said to her, "Do you still persist in the same folly?"

But Irene said to him, "It is not folly, but piety."

"It was abundantly clear from your earlier testimony," said the prefect Dulcitius, "that you did not wish to submit religiously to the bidding of the emperors; and now I perceive that you are persisting in the same foolishness. Therefore you shall pay the appropriate penalty."

He then asked for a sheet of papyrus and wrote the sentence against her as follows, "Whereas Irene has refused to obey the command of the emperors and to offer sacrifice, and still adheres to a sect called Christians, I therefore sentence her to be burned alive, as I did her two sisters before her."

After this sentence had been pronounced by the prefect, the soldiers took the girl and brought her to a high place, where her sisters had been martyred before her. They ignited a huge pyre and ordered her to climb up on it. And the holy woman Irene, singing and praising God, threw herself upon it and so died. It was in the ninth consulship of Diocletian Augustus, in the eighth of Maximian Augustus (304 CE), on the first day of April, in the reign of our Lord Christ Jesus, who reigns for ever, with whom there is glory to God with the Holy Spirit for ever. Amen.

THIRTY-FOURTH WEEK OF THE YEAR
Saturday
Sibylline Oracles Book 2:1–31

The Sibyl's apocalyptic description of the disasters of the end time challenges us to live in justice as we await God's final coming.

When indeed God stopped my most perfectly wise song
as I prayed many things, God also again placed in my breast
a delightful utterance of wondrous words.
I will speak the following with my whole person in ecstasy.
For I do not know what I say, but God bids me utter each thing.

But when on earth there are raging earthquakes
and thunderbolts, thunders, and lightnings . . . and mildew of the land
and frenzy of jackals and wolves, and slaughters
and destruction and bellowing oxen,
four-footed cattle and laboring mules
and goats and sheep, then much farmland
will be left barren through neglect,
and fruits will fail. Selling of free persons into slavery
will be practiced among very many people, and robbing of temples.
Then indeed the tenth generation of people will also appear
after these things, when the earth-shaking lightning-giver
will break the glory of idols and shake the people of
seven-hilled Rome. Great wealth will perish,
burned in a great fire by the flame of Hephaestus [He phaes' tus].
Then there will be bloody precipitation from heaven . . .

but the entire world of innumerable people
will kill each other in madness. In the tumult
God will impose famines and pestilence and thunderbolts
on people who adjudicate without justice.
There will be a scarcity of people throughout the whole world
so that if one were to see a person's footprint on the ground, one would
      wonder.
Then further, the great God who lives in the sky
will be a savior of pious people in all respects.
Then also there will be deep peace and understanding,
and the fruitful earth will again bear more numerous fruits,
being neither divided nor in servitude any longer.

Appendixes

APPENDIX I
Sanctoral Calendar
[Taken from *The Sacramentary* and the *Roman Martyrology*]

JANUARY
1 Motherhood of Mary
2
3 Angela of Foligno
  Genevieve, Patroness of Paris
4 Elizabeth Ann Seton
5
6
7
8
9
10
11
12
13 Veronica of Binasso
14 Macrina, the Elder
15 Ita, Abbess
16
17
18 Prisca
19 Martha with her martyr companions
20
21 Agnes
22
23 Emerentiana
  Mary Ward, Foundress
24

25
26
27   Angela Merici
28   Margaret of Hungary
29
30   Martina
31   Marcella, Hostess of Jerome in Rome

FEBRUARY
1 Brigid
2 Purification of Mary
   Jeanne de Lestonnac, Foundress
3
4 Joan of France
5 Agatha
6 Dorothy
7
8
9 Apollonia
10 Scholastica
11 Our Lady of Lourdes
12 Marina, "Monk"—disguised as a boy
13 Katherine dei Ricci
14
15 Jovita with companion, Faustinus
16 Juliana
17
18
19
20 Mildred
21
22 Margaret of Cortona
23 Mildburga, Abbess
24
25
26
27
28 Antoinette
29

MARCH

1   Antonia
2
3   Cunegundis, Empress
4
5
6   Colette
7   Perpetua and Felicitas
8
9   Frances of Rome
10
11
12
13   Euphrasia
14   Matilda, Queen
15   Louise de Marillac
16
17   Gertrude of Nivelles
18
19
20   Alexandra
21
22   Catherine of Sweden
23
24   Katherine of Vadstena
25   Annunciation of Mary
26
27
28
29
30
31

APRIL

1
2
3 Agape, Chionia, Irene
4
5
6
7
8
9 Mary Cleophas
10 Mechtild of Hackenborn
11 Gemma Galgani
12
13 Hermenegild
14
15 Octavia
16 Bernadette Soubirous
17
18 Anthia
19
20 Agnes of Montepulciano
21
22 Pherbutha
23
24
25
26 Our Lady of Good Counsel
27
28
29 Catherine of Siena
30

MAY
1
2
3
4
5   Jutta
6
7
8
9
10
11
12   Domitilla
13
14   Mary Mazzarello
15   Dympna
16
17
18
19   Pudentiana
20
21
22   Rita of Cascia
23
24   Our Lady, Help of Christians
25   Mary Magdalene de Pazzi
       Mary, Mother of James
       Madeleine Sophie Barat, Foundress
26   Mariana of Quito
27
28
29
30   Joan of Arc
31   Visitation of Mary
       Petronilla

JUNE

1
2 Blandina
3 Clotilda
4
5
6
7
8 Melania, the Elder
9
10 Margaret of Scotland
11
12
13
14
15 Edburga of Winchester, Abbess
16
17
18 Elizabeth of Schönau
19 Juliana of Falconieri
20
21
22
23 Agrippina
    Etheldreda
24
25 Febronia
26
27 Our Lady of Perpetual Help
28 Irene
29
30
Saturday after solemnity of the Sacred Heart—Immaculate Heart
    of Mary

JULY

1
2
3
4　Elizabeth of Portugal
5　Philomena
6　Maria Goretti
7
8
9　Anatolia
　　Veronica Giuliani
10　Rufina and Secunda
11　Olga
12　Veronica who wiped the face of Jesus
13　Mildred, Abbess
14　Blessed Kateri Tekakwitha
15　Edith
16　Our Lady of Mount Carmel
17
18　Symphorosa and her children
19　Macrina the Younger
20　Margaret (Marina)
21　Praxedes
22　Mary Magdalene
23　Bridget
24　Christina
25
26　Anne, wife of Joachim
27　Anthusa
28
29　Martha of Bethany
　　Beatrice and companions
30
31

AUGUST

1 Faith, Hope, Charity (daughters of Wisdom)
2
3
4
5 Dedication of the Church of Saint Mary Major
6
7
8
9
10
11 Clare
   Susanna
12
13
14
15 Assumption of Mary
16
17
18 Helena, Empress
19
20
21
22 Queenship of Mary
23 Rose of Lima
24 Joan Thouret, Foundress
25
26 Mary of Czestochowa
27 Monica
28 Joaquina, Foundress
29 Sabina
30
31

SEPTEMBER

1   Anna, the Prophetess
2
3   Erasma
    Cuthburga
4   Rosalie
5
6
7   Regina
8   Birth of Mary
9
10 Pulcheria
11
12 Name of Mary
13 Notburga
14
15 Our Lady of Sorrows
16 Euphemia
17 Hildegard of Bingen
18
19 Emily de Rodat
20
21
22
23 Thecla
24 Our Lady of Ransom
25
26 Justina
27
28 Leoba, Abbess
29
30 Sophia

OCTOBER

1 Theresa of the Child Jesus
2
3 Josepha Rosello, Foundress
4
5
6 Blessed Marie Rose Durocher
7 Our Lady of the Rosary
8 Brigid of Sweden, Foundress
9
10
11
12 Ethelburga of Barking
13
14
15 Teresa of Avila
16 Margaret Mary Alacoque
   Hedwig
17 Audrey
18
19
20
21 Ursula and her companions
22 Mary Salome
23
24
25 Daria
26
27
28 Anastasia
29
30
31

NOVEMBER
1 All Saints
2 All Souls
3 Winifred
4
5 Elizabeth, wife of Zachary
6
7
8
9
10 Nympha
11
12
13 Frances Cabrini
14
15
16 Gertrude of Helfta
17 Elizabeth of Hungary, Queen
18 Philippine Duchesne
19
20
21 Presentation of Mary
22 Cecilia
23 Felicity
24
25 Catherine of Alexandria
26
27
28 Catherine Labouré
29
30

DECEMBER

 1 Natalia
 2 Vivian
 3
 4 Barbara
 5 Crispina
 6
 7
 8 Immaculate Conception
 9 Leocadia
10 Eulalia
11
12 Our Lady of Guadalupe
   Jane Frances de Chantal
13 Lucy
14
15
16 Adelaide
17
18 Expectation of Blessed Virgin Mary
19 Fausta
20
21
22
23 Victoria
24
25
26
27 Fabiola
28
29
30
31

APPENDIX II
Scriptures Cited

Hebrew Scriptures

Genesis 1:26–2:3
   Seventeenth Week of the Year—Tuesday

Genesis 2:18–25
   Twenty-seventh Sunday of the Year

Genesis 16:1–12, 15–16
   Second Sunday of Advent

Genesis 18:1–15
   Sixteenth Week of the Year—Wednesday

Genesis 19:15–26
   Thirteenth Week of the Year—Tuesday

Genesis 20:1–18
   Fourth Week of the Year—Saturday

Genesis 21:5, 8–21
   Thirteenth Week of the Year—Wednesday

Genesis 24:10–28
   Fifth Week of the Year—Thursday

Genesis 24:42–49
   Fifth Week of the Year—Friday

Genesis 24:50–67
    Fifth Week of the Year—Saturday

Genesis 25:19–28
    Seventh Week of the Year—Monday

Genesis 29:4–12
    Twenty-third Week of the Year—Thursday

Genesis 29:13–20
    Twenty-third Week of the Year—Friday

Genesis 35:16–21
    Twenty-third Week of the Year—Saturday

Genesis 38:13–18, 24–27
    Third Week of Advent—Wednesday

Exodus 1:15–22
    December 27

Exodus 2:1–10
    Fifteenth Week of the Year—Tuesday

Exodus 2:15b–22
    Fifteenth Week of the Year—Wednesday

Exodus 15:19–22
    Fifteenth Week of the Year—Thursday

Numbers 12:1–16; 20:1
    Fifteenth Week of the Year—Friday

Numbers 27:1–8
    Eighth Week of the Year—Wednesday

Joshua 2:1–21
    Twentieth Week of the Year—Monday

Joshua 6:17–25
Twentieth Week of the Year—Tuesday

Judges 4:4–16
First Week of the Year—Tuesday

Judges 4:17–22
First Week of the Year—Wednesday

Judges 5:1, 6–9, 12–15b, 24–31
First Week of the Year—Thursday

Judges 11:29–40
Twenty-ninth Week of the Year—Thursday

Judges 16:4–21
Thirteenth Week of the Year—Saturday

Ruth 1:1–9
Twentieth Week of the Year—Wednesday

Ruth 1:10–22
Twentieth Week of the Year—Thursday

Ruth 3:1–13
Twentieth Week of the Year—Friday

Ruth 4:7–17
Twentieth Week of the Year—Saturday

1 Samuel 1:1–8
Eighth Week of the Year—Thursday

1 Samuel 1:9–20
Eighth Week of the Year—Friday

1 Samuel 21:21–28
Eighth Week of the Year—Saturday

1 Samuel 2:1–10
    Ninth Sunday of the Year

1 Samuel 4:4–22
    December 18

1 Samuel 25:2–42 passim
    Sixth Week of the Year—Wednesday

1 Samuel 28:5–8, 11–14, 20, 24–25
    Fourth Week of the Year—Thursday

2 Samuel 6:12–23
    January 10

2 Samuel 11:1–17, 26–27
    January 11

2 Samuel 13:1–14
    Thirty-third Week of the Year—Friday

2 Samuel 13:15–22
    Thirty-third Week of the Year—Saturday

1 Kings 10:1–10, 13
    Fifth Week of the Year—Wednesday

1 Kings 17:7–16
    Tenth Week of the Year—Tuesday

1 Kings 17:17–24
    Tenth Week of the Year—Wednesday

1 Kings 21:1–11, 14–16
    Tenth Week of the Year—Saturday

2 Kings 4:1–7
    Fifth Week of Lent—Thursday

2 Kings 4:8–17
    Fifth Week of Lent—Friday

2 Kings 4:18–37
    Fifth Week of Lent—Saturday

2 Kings 11:1–4, 9–16, 20
    January 12—Saturday after Epiphany

2 Kings 22:8, 11–20
    Second Week of Advent—Friday

Esther (Greek) 14:18b, 3–5, 12–15a
    First Week of Lent—Thursday

Esther 1:5–22 passim
    Twenty-fourth Week of the Year—Monday

Esther 2:1–11
    Twenty-fourth Week of the Year—Tuesday

Esther 2:12–18 passim
    Twenty-fourth Week of the Year—Wednesday

Esther 2:19–23
    Twenty-fourth Week of the Year—Thursday

Esther 3:1–4:8 passim
    Twenty-fourth Week of the Year—Friday

Esther 4:9–16
    Twenty-fourth Week of the Year—Saturday

Esther Addition D 15:1–16
    Twenty-fifth Sunday of the Year

Esther 5:3–8
    Twenty-fifth Week of the Year—Monday

Esther 5:9-14
  Twenty-fifth Week of the Year—Tuesday

Esther 6:1–14 passim
  Twenty-fifth Week of the Year—Wednesday

Esther 7:1–10
  Twenty-fifth Week of the Year—Thursday

Esther 8:3–10
  Twenty-fifth Week of the Year—Friday

Esther 9:20–32 passim
  Twenty-fifth Week of the Year—Saturday

Job 19:25–27
  Trinity Sunday—Vigil

Job 42:10–17
  Twenty-sixth Week of the Year—Saturday

Proverbs 3:13–18
  Nineteenth Week of the Year—Saturday

Proverbs 4:5–13
  Fifteenth Week of the Year—Saturday

Proverbs 6:20–23
  Twenty-third Week of the Year—Wednesday

Proverbs 8:22–31
  Second Week of Easter—Thursday

Proverbs 9:1–6
  Twelfth Sunday of the Year

Proverbs 31:13–31
  Thirty-third Sunday of the Year

Song of Solomon 3:1–4
  Octave of Easter—Tuesday

Song of Solomon 8:1–5
  Seventeenth Week of the Year—Saturday

Isaiah 42:14–16
  Eighteenth Sunday of the Year

Isaiah 46:3–4
  Second Week of Lent—Monday

Isaiah 54:7–8
  December 20

Isaiah 66:10–14
  Fourteenth Sunday of the Year

Daniel 13:1–9, 15–17, 19–27
  Fifth Week of Lent—Monday

Daniel 13:28–30, 33–43
  Fifth Week of Lent—Tuesday

Daniel 13:44–60, 62–63
  Fifth Week of Lent—Wednesday

Hosea 11:1–9
  January 2

Micah 6:1–4, 6–8
  Sixteenth Week of the Year—Monday

Zephaniah 3:14–18
  December 21

Judith 13:18–20
  Fourth Sunday of the Year

Wisdom of Solomon 6:12–19
    Thursday after Ash Wednesday

Wisdom of Solomon 7:7–14b
    Friday after Ash Wednesday

Wisdom of Solomon 7:21–28
    Baptism of the Lord

Sirach 1:1–10
    First Week of Advent—Tuesday

Sirach 4:11–18
    First Week of Advent—Wednesday

Sirach 6:5–17
    Eighteenth Week of the Year—Tuesday

Sirach 6:18–31
    First Week of Advent—Thursday

Sirach 24:1–12
    First Week of Advent—Friday

Sirach 24:13–14, 19–21
    First Week of Advent—Saturday

Sirach 51:12b–20
    December 17

Christian Scriptures

Matthew 1:18–23
    December 23

Matthew 8:14–15—See Mark 1:29–31

Matthew 9:18–19, 23–26—See Luke 8:40–42, 49–56

Matthew 9:20–22—See Mark 5:25–34

Matthew 12:46–50—See Mark 3:31–35

Matthew 13:31–35—See Luke 13:20–21; Mark parallel, no woman
    Seventeenth Week of the Year—Monday

Matthew 13:54–58
    Seventeenth Week of the Year—Friday

Matthew 14:3–12—See Mark 6:14–29

Matthew 15:21–28—See Mark 7:24–30
    Twentieth Sunday of the Year

Matthew 20:17–28—See Mark 10:35–45
    Second Week of Lent—Wednesday

Matthew 25:1–13 No parallel exactly, but see Luke 13:35–37
    Twenty-second Sunday of the Year

Matthew 26:6–13
    Sixth Sunday of Year

Matthew 26:69–75—See Mark 14:66–72

Matthew 27:15–26
    Monday of Holy Week

Matthew 27:55–61
    Octave of Easter—Thursday

Matthew 28:1–10
    Sixth Sunday of Easter

Mark 1:29–39—See Matthew 8:14–15; Luke 4:38–39
    Fifth Sunday of the Year

Mark 3:31–35—See Matthew 12:46–50
  Sixteenth Week of the Year—Tuesday

Mark 5:25–34—See Matthew 9:20–22; Luke 8:43–48
  Thirteenth Sunday of the Year

Mark 5:21–24, 35–43—See Luke 8:41–56

Mark 6:1–6—See Matthew 13:54–58

Mark 6:14–29—See Matthew 14:3–12
  Fourth Week of the Year—Friday

Mark 7:24–30
  Seventh Sunday of the Year

Mark 10:35–45—See Matthew 20:17–28

Mark 12:38–44—See Luke 21:1–4
  Thirty-second Sunday of the Year

Mark 14:3–9—See John 12:1–8; Matthew 26:6–13
  Passion [Palm] Sunday

Mark 14:66–72
  Wednesday of Holy Week

Mark 15:40–47
  Fourteenth Week of the Year—Monday

Mark 16:1–8
  Fifth Week of Easter—Tuesday

Mark 16:9–13
  Octave of Easter—Saturday

Luke 1:26–38
  Third Sunday of Advent

Luke 1:39–56
Fourth Sunday of Advent

Luke 2:1–14
Christmas Day

Luke 2:15–19
December 28

Luke 2:22–35
December 29

Luke 2:36–40
December 30

Luke 2:41–52
December 31

Luke 4:16–24—See Matthew 13:54–58

Luke 4:38–44—See Mark 1:29–31

Luke 7:11–16a—See Matthew 8:14–15
Tenth Sunday of the Year

Luke 7:36–50
Eleventh Sunday of the Year

Luke 8:1–3
Twenty-fourth Sunday of the Year

Luke 8:19–21
Eighth Sunday of the Year

Luke 8:40–42, 49–56—See Mark 5:21–24, 35–43; Matthew 9:18–19, 23–26
Fourth Week of the Year—Tuesday

Luke 8:43–48—See Mark 5:25–34; Matthew 9:20–22

Luke 10:38–42
Sixteenth Sunday of the Year

Luke 11:27–28
Twenty-seventh Week of the Year—Saturday

Luke 13:10–17
Thirtieth Sunday of the Year

Luke 13:20–21—See Matthew 13:31–35

Luke 15:1–10
Thirtieth Week of the Year—Monday

Luke 21:1–4
Thirty-fourth Week of the Year—Monday

Luke 22:54–62—See Mark 14:66–72

Luke 23:26–31
Tuesday of Holy Week

Luke 24:1–12
Easter Vigil Gospel

John 2:1–11
Third Sunday of the Year

John 4:5–30, 39–42
Third Sunday of Lent

John 8:2–11
Fifth Sunday of Lent

John 11:1–6
Fourth Week of Easter—Thursday

John 11:17–27
Fourth Week of Easter—Friday

John 11:28-37
Fourth Week of Easter—Saturday

John 11:38-45
Fifth Sunday of Easter

John 12:1-8
Corpus Christi—Vigil

John 16:20-22
Second Week of Advent—Saturday

John 18:15-18, 25-27—See Mark 14:66-72

John 19:25-27
Mass of the Lord's Supper

John 20:1-2, 11-18
Easter Sunday

Acts 1:12-14
Seventh Week of Easter—Monday

Acts 5:1-11
Fifteenth Week of the Year—Monday

Acts 9:36-42
Third Week of Easter—Saturday

Acts 12:11-17
Fifth Week of Easter—Monday

Acts 16:16-18
Sixth Week of Easter—Monday

Acts 16:11-15
Second Week of Easter—Tuesday

Acts 18:1–4
   Sixth Week of Easter—Friday

Acts 18:18–28
   Sixth Week of Easter—Saturday

Acts 21:8–14
   Third Week of Advent—Thursday

Romans 8:35–39
   December 19

Romans 16:1–16
   Seventh Week of the Year—Thursday

2 Corinthians 5:14–17
   Twenty-first Sunday of the Year

Galatians 3:23–28
   January 9

Galatians 4:4–7
   December 22

Galatians 4:24–5:1
   Second Week of Lent—Saturday

Philippians 4:1–9
   First Week of Lent—Wednesday

2 Timothy 1:1–8
   Eighteenth Week of the Year—Monday

James 3:13–18
   Saturday after Ash Wednesday

Revelation 12:1–6
   First Sunday of Advent

APPENDIX III
Sources

Acts of Andrew. Trans. M. Hornschuh, *New Testament Apocrypha*, ed. Wilhelm Schneemelcher. Eng. trans. edited by R. McL. Wilson. Vol. 2: *Writings Relating to the Apostles; Apocalypses and Related Subjects* (Philadelphia: The Westminster Press, 1963) pp. 403–425.
Date: ca. 150–190 CE
Provenance: Greece or Asia Minor
Description: This document belongs to the collection of apocryphal "Acts of the Apostles" written during the latter half of the second century. The Acts of Andrew narrates the activities of the apostle Andrew, brother of Simon Peter, and his eventual martyrdom by crucifixion. The material in these Acts is sometimes fanciful but represents the attempt of early Christians to preserve the memory of their apostolic heroes.

Acts of John. Trans. K. Schäferdiek and G.C. Stead. Edgar Hennecke, *New Testament Apocrypha*, ed. Wilhelm Schneemelcher. Eng. trans. edited by R. McL. Wilson. Vol. 2: *Writings Relating to the Apostles; Apocalypses and Related Subjects* (Philadelphia: The Westminster Press, 1963) pp. 215–259.
Date: second century CE
Provenance: Asia Minor or Syria
Description: This is a composite collection of traditions and legends about the apostle John in which John demonstrates his extraordinary powers to heal and raise from the dead. This text is an early witness to the heterodox nature of the Johannine community in the second century and it perhaps gives voice to the "opponents" against whom the author of the First Letter of John writes.

Acts of the Martyrs of Lyon and Vienne. See Eusebius

Acts of Paul. Trans. W. Schneemelcher and R. McL. Wilson, Edgar Hennecke, *New Testament Apocrypha*, ed. Wilhelm Schneemelcher. Eng. trans. edited by R. McL. Wilson. Vol. 2: *Writings Relating to the Apostles; Apocalypses and Related Subjects* (Philadelphia: The Westminster Press, 1963) pp. 352–390.

Date: second century CE
Provenance: ? Asia Minor
Description: This collection of legendary stories about the missionary activities of Paul includes a portion entitled The Acts of Paul and Thecla (see below). Besides Thecla, other women became disciples and co-workers with Paul, sharing their prophecy and teaching with others.

Acts of Paul and Thecla. Trans. R. Kraemer, *Maenads, Martyrs, Matrons, Monastics*, ed. Ross S. Kraemer (Philadelphia: Fortress, 1988) pp. 280–288.

Date: second century CE
Provenance: ? Asia Minor
Description: The story of the conversion and passion of Thecla was immensely popular in the early church for many centuries, and she may well have been the best known woman saint in the east, even though there is no positive evidence of her historical existence. Tertullian (*On Baptism,* 17) relates that the story of Paul and Thecla was written in his day by a presbyter in Asia Minor, who was deposed from office for his trouble, though he protested that he had written it out of love for Paul. In Tertullian's church, women were citing it as authorization for them to baptize, something to which Tertullian was opposed. The story is a remarkable indication of how popular imagination could exalt the memory of an apostolic woman, even at a time when such freedom for women was no longer encouraged. Cf. Life of Macrina, 11th–12th Weeks of the Year; Life of Olympias, 21st Week of the Year.

Acts of Perpetua and Felicitas. Trans. H. Musurillo, *The Acts of the Christian Martyrs* (Oxford: Clarendon, 1972) pp. 107–131.

Date: c. 200 CE
Provenance: Carthage, North Africa
Description: This stirring account of the death of several martyrs in the amphitheatre of Carthage consists of an introduction, Perpetua's own narration of their imprisonment and her dreams, and the continuation of

the story of their deaths by another writer. Because of the insistence on the revelatory qualities of prophecy and dreams, the story may have originated in a Montanist community and may depict the death of Montanist martyrs. Though the text never mentions Tertullian, he was a prominent presbyter of Carthage at the time, very influenced by Montanism. The fact that Perpetua, a freeborn woman, and the slave woman Felicitas are the central figures indicates their importance in the community, and may be further evidence of Montanism, which favored the leadership of women.

Acts of Peter. Trans. C. Schmidt, et al., Edgar Hennecke, *New Testament Apocrypha*, ed. Wilhelm Schneemelcher. Eng. trans. edited by R. McL. Wilson. Vol. 2: *Writings Relating to the Apostles; Apocalypses and Related Subjects* (Philadelphia: The Westminster Press, 1963) pp. 276–322.
Date: ca. 180 CE
Provenance: ? Asia Minor
Description: Another example of the genre of apocryphal acts of the apostles, the Acts of Peter recounts Peter's missionary travels, his dispute with Simon the Magician, his miracles and preaching.

Acts of Thomas. Trans. G. Bornkamm and R. McL. Wilson, Edgar Hennecke, *New Testament Apocrypha*, ed. Wilhelm Schneemelcher. Eng. trans. edited by R. McL. Wilson. Vol. 2: *Writings Relating to the Apostles; Apocalypses and Related Subjects* (Philadelphia: The Westminster Press, 1963) pp. 442–531.
Date: third century CE
Provenance: Syria
Description: This Christian gnostic text presents the deeds and missionary activities of Thomas, the Twin. The text includes several stories of women converts, like Mygdonia, or Thecla in the Acts of Paul, who renounce marriage in favor of a life of sexual continence and become missionaries with the apostle. The beautiful Hymn of Bride and Groom excerpted from this text is reminiscent of the language of the Song of Songs.

Apocalypse of Elijah. Trans. O.S. Wintermute, *The Old Testament Pseudepigrapha*, Vol. 1, ed. James H. Charlesworth (Garden City, NY: Doubleday, 1983) pp. 721–753.

Date: ca. 150–275 CE
Provenance: ? Alexandria
Description: This is an apocalyptic work from the second or third century CE portraying various events of the final days, including the martyrdom of several Jewish and Christian figures.

Apostolic Constitutions 2.26; 8.19–20, Text: F.X. Funk (Paderborn, 1905) pp. 105, 524. Trans. Carolyn Osiek.
Date: third to fourth century CE.
Provenance: Syria
Description: The Apostolic Constitutions or Teaching of the Holy Apostles is a fourth century Syrian compilation of liturgical and disciplinary canons, partially based on earlier collections like the first to second century Didache, the third century Apostolic Tradition of Hippolytus, and the third century Didascalia Apostolorum. It contains valuable evidence about church practice and theology of the period.

Augustine, *Confessions.* Trans. Mary T. Clark (Paulist, 1984) pp. 110–121.
Date: 354–430 CE
Provenance: North Africa
Description: One of the best known and most influential writers of the western church, Augustine dominates the theology of Europe well into the middle ages. His well-known autobiography, though intended as a "confession" of praise to God, has been called the first modern writing because of the author's unusual capacity for introspection and self-awareness.

Biblical Antiquities. See Pseudo-Philo

Catherine of Siena: Dialogue. Translation and Introduction by Suzanne Noffke, O.P. (New York: Paulist, 1980) p. 131.
Date: 1347–1380
Provenance: Italy
Description: The declaration of Catherine of Siena as doctor of the church in 1970 is but one tribute to her extraordinary influence on Christian thought. She lived but a half of a turbulent century, but left her mark, through her *Dialogue* and her tireless efforts to reform her order, her local church, the clergy, and the papacy. That there is an active

school of Catherinian studies is tribute to the power of God at work in her short life of thirty-three years. One of the most striking of images in her *Dialogue* is her portrayal of Christ as bridge.

Church History. See Socrates Scholasticus

Clement of Alexandria, *Who Is the Rich One Who Can Be Saved?* *Clement of Alexandria,* Loeb Classical Library (Cambridge, MA: Harvard University, 1968). Trans. C. Osiek.
Date: ca. 160–215 CE
Provenance: Alexandria, Egypt
Description: Clement was a learned Christian teacher who attempted to integrate classical Greek culture with the developing Christian intellectual tradition of his day. Unlike most early Christian theologians, he was a married man, and his teaching is noted for its moderate approach to asceticism. This treatise explores the tension between the radical gospel call to dispossession in the story of the rich young man (Mk 10:17–22) and the practical life of relatively affluent Alexandrian Christians.

Confessions. See Augustine

Dhuoda's epitaph. Katharina M. Wilson, ed. *Medieval Women Writers* (Athens: University of Georgia Press, 1984) pp. 25–26.
Date: late eighth, early ninth centuries CE
Provenance: Southern France
Description: Dhuoda, sometimes referred to as Dhuodana, wrote a moral guide book (*Manual*) which reveals amazing information about the Carolingian period. A learned lay woman, she was held under virtual house arrest in a castle in southern France, simply because her husband found it politically convenient. Not only does the *Manual* reveal what sources she used to formulate her spirituality but, even more importantly, it reveals how a private person viewed the turbulent Carolingian period.

Dhuoda, *On John 15 to Her Son.* Translation and Introduction by Morsel Thiébaux (New York: Garland Publishing Company, 1987) pp. 77–78, 133, 143–144.
Date: late eighth, early ninth centuries CE
Provenance: Southern France
Description: Dhuoda, a learned lay woman of the Carolingian period,

wrote a work entitled *Manual* which was intended as a kind of moral guidebook. It is remarkable in its scope of topics and its extensive references to scripture and to patristic teaching. Much of it was written for her sons, who were taken from her because of the jealousy and the political ambitions of her husband.

Dialogue. See Catherine of Siena

Ecclesiastical History. See Eusebius.

Egeria's Travels. Trans. J. Wilkinson, *Egeria's Travels to the Holy Land* (rev. ed.; Jerusalem: Ariel, 1981) pp. 93–144.
Date: Late 4th c. CE
Provenance: Western Europe.
Description: We do not know exactly where this intrepid pilgrim came from, nor even her name; the weight of evidence suggests that she was a nun from Gaul or Spain named Egeria. In her extensive journeys through biblical lands, her travelogue supplied her sisters back home with information. Only the middle of her text is preserved, discovered in the last century after having been lost for several centuries. It is a major source of information for Holy Week liturgy in late fourth century Jerusalem, which she described in detail.

1 Enoch. Trans. E. Isaac, *The Old Testament Pseudepigrapha*, Vol. 1, ed. James H. Charlesworth (Garden City, NY: Doubleday, 1983) pp. 13–89.
Date: second century BCE–first century CE
Provenance: Judea
Description: This composite collection of apocalyptic (revelatory) writings spans the time period from the second century BCE to the first century CE. The writings are attributed to Enoch, of whom it was said in Genesis 5:24: "Enoch walked with God; and he was not, for God took him." Jews believed, therefore, that Enoch could reveal to them the heavenly mysteries.

Epiphanius, *Medicine Box* 48, 49, 78, 79 on the Montanists. Trans. R. Kraemer (#48) and C. Osiek, *Maenads, Martyrs, Matrons, Monastics*, ed. Ross S. Kraemer (Philadelphia: Fortress, 1988) pp. 50, 58, 226–227, 230.

Date: 4th c. CE
Provenance: Cyprus
Description: Epiphanius (c. 315–403) was bishop of Salamis in Cyprus. Of questionable scholarly ability, nevertheless he wrote an extended compendium on heresies, the *Panarion* or *Medicine Box*, which is considered a major historical source for the period. It is always to be used with caution.

Eusebius, *Ecclesiastical History* 5.16.17 on the Montanists
Date: early fourth century CE
Provenance: Palestine
Description: Eusebius (c. 260–340) was bishop of Caesarea in Palestine and the foremost historian of the early church. He was a witness to some of the last great persecutions of Christians in the early fourth century and an uncritical admirer of Constantine. His massive *Ecclesiastical History* is *the* major source for information on the church through the early fourth century.

Acts of the Martyrs of Lyon and Vienne. Eusebius, *Ecclesiastical History* 5.1.3–2.8. Trans. H. Musurillo, *The Acts of the Christian Martyrs* (Oxford: Clarendon, 1971) pp. 63–85.
Date: 177 CE
Provenance: Gaul
Description: In the summer of 177 in the Roman center of Lugdunum (Lyon), popular resentment against the largely Greek-speaking immigrant Christian community seems to have erupted into a trial and condemnation of some of them, and their death during games held in the local amphitheatre. The story is told from the perspective of the surviving persecuted Christians who write a letter back to their home churches in Asia Minor. It is one of the earliest full martyrdom accounts, and is very revealing of the growing glorification of martyrdom. Here the slave woman Blandina, of uncertain age, emerges as the symbol of courage and hope for all who shared her faith.

Martyrdom of Potamiaena and Basilides. Eusebius, *Ecclesiastical History* 6.5. Trans. H. Musurillo, *The Acts of the Christian Martyrs* (Oxford: Clarendon, 1972) pp. 133–135.
Date: Early third century CE
Provenance: Alexandria, Egypt

Description: This story of three Alexandrian martyrs includes a mother and daughter and the soldier who led them to execution, said by Eusebius between his conversion and execution to have been a catechetical student of the great Origen. The focus of the story is on Potamiaena, and it includes detailed descriptions of her tortures and defense of her chastity, both common elements of martyrdom stories by the fourth century when the account is recorded. The most interesting part of the story is her appearance in a dream to Basilides, welcoming him to her company in heaven, and the subsequent reports of conversions attributed to her appearance in dreams.

Funerary Inscriptions of Christian Female Deacons and a Jewish Woman. Arsinoe, Athanasia: *Maenads, Martyrs, Matrons, Monastics,* ed. Ross S. Kraemer (Philadelphia: Fortress, 1988) pp. 84, 223. Trans. R. Kraemer. Maria: G.H.R. Horsley, *New Documents Illustrating Early Christianity* (Sydney: Macquarie University, 1982) 2.109, trans. C. Osiek. Regina: *Corpus Inscriptionum Judaicarum* 476, trans. C. Osiek.
Date: second, fifth to sixth centuries CE
Provenance: Athanasia (immortality) from fifth century Delphi in Greece; Maria from sixth century Archelais, Cappadocia in central Asia Minor; Regina from second century Rome; Arsinoe from first century BCE Egypt.
Description: These inscriptions from various times and places are examples of a number of known inscriptions from early Christianity and Judaism testifying to the presence of women leaders and devotees in church and synagogue. The responsibilities of the deacons may have differed according to place and time, but probably included various kinds of ministry to women. The threat to anyone tampering with Athanasia's tomb is commonplace in funerary inscriptions. The description of Maria's ministry is a quotation from 1 Timothy 5:10. The eulogies of Regina and Arsinoe are typical of domestic ideals for women from all faiths at the time.

Gospel of Bartholomew. Trans. F. Scheidweiler, Edgar Hennecke, *New Testament Apocrypha,* ed. Wilhelm Schneemelcher. Eng. trans. edited by R. McL. Wilson. Vol. 1: *Gospels and Related Writings* (Philadelphia: The Westminster Press, 1963) pp. 486–503.
Date: third century CE
Provenance: Uncertain

Description: This revelatory text describes the meeting between the risen Jesus and Bartholomew in which Jesus reveals the mystery of his death, his descent to the underworld, and the resurrection. Later the text recounts a similar discussion between Bartholomew and Mary in which she reveals to him and the other disciples the ineffable mystery of Jesus' conception and birth.

Gospel of Mary [Magdalene]. Trans. George MacRae and R. McL. Wilson, *Nag Hammadi Library in English*, ed. James M. Robinson (San Francisco: Harper and Row, 1977) pp. 472–473.

Date: second century CE
Provenance: Egypt
Description: This Christian, gnostic text is an example of the genre of gnostic dialogue, in which the Christian disciples discuss together the meaning of Jesus' life and resurrection. It preserves, as other early Christian texts do (viz. The Gospel of Thomas, Pistis Sophia, The Gospel of the Egyptians) the confrontation between Mary Magdalene and Peter and reflects the ongoing debate between orthodox traditions and those of gnostic Christianity which accorded special prominence to Mary Magdalene as the beloved friend of Jesus.

Hippolytus, *Refutation of All Heresies* 8.19. Trans. C. Osiek.

Date: c. 170–236 CE
Provenance: Rome
Description: A brilliant theologian and biblical scholar, Hippolytus is also the author of the *Apostolic Tradition*, an important liturgical source, as well as other treatises and a *Commentary on Daniel*, the oldest surviving Christian biblical commentary. Unhappy with the governance of the Roman church, he formed a breakaway schismatic movement and probably died a martyr. One of the Roman catacombs bears his name.

Life of St. Macrina by Gregory of Nyssa. Trans. Virginia Woods Callahan, Gregory of Nyssa, *Ascetical Works* (Fathers of the Church; Washington, DC: Catholic University, 1967) pp. 163–191.

Date: late fourth century
Provenance: Cappadocia, Asia Minor.
Description: Macrina was the oldest of ten children, including two of the famous Cappadocian theologians, Basil the Great and Gregory of Nyssa.

Gregory narrates the life and death (for which he was present) of his elder sister, whom he revered as the holiest and strongest member of the family. It was she who led most of the family into a life of prayer and asceticism, and she whom Gregory describes as his "teacher in all things." Already during her life miracles were attributed to her. After writing her life, Gregory wrote his Dialogue on the Soul and Resurrection, a recreation of his conversations with her before her death.

Hadewijch: The Complete Works. Translation and Introduction by Mother Columbia Hart, O.S.B. (New York: Paulist, 1980) pp. 73, 162–165, 206–207, 210, 297.

Date: thirteenth century CE
Provenance: Belgium and Holland
Description: Though Hadewijch's works were published in the fourteenth century, they have enjoyed wide circulation only since their "rediscovery" in Belgium in 1838. Her complete works include poems, visions, letters, and dialogues, and all the works are grounded in a love mysticism, common to her day, but highly developed by Hadewijch. She is acknowledged as a superb lyricist and is credited with developing a new genre, the religious love lyric.

Hildegard of Bingen, Translation and Introduction by Marcelle Thiébaux. *The Writings of Medieval Women* (New York: Garland Publishing Co., 1987) pp. 133, 143–144.

Date: 1098–1179 CE
Provenance: Germany
Description: Known primarily for the record of her visions in the primary work, *Scivias*, Hildegard was prolific in many other areas, writing poems, letters, songs (both words and music), homilies, a morality play, and books on medicine and natural history. Honored for her contemplative visions, she was sought after, by many different audiences, for her spiritual guidance. She even invented a language of her own, for diversion!

Homily on Romans. See John Chrysostom

Jerome, Letters. Trans. *Nicene and Postnicene Fathers*, ser. 2, vol. 6, pp. 157–163, 195–212, 253–258.

Date: 347–420 CE
Provenance: Bethlehem
Description: Jerome, irascible character, secretary to a pope, spiritual guide of aristocratic Roman women, eminent biblical scholar, and monk of Bethlehem, wrote these tributes to his women friends Marcella, Paula, and Fabiola after their deaths. He wrote these from his monastery in Bethlehem where he had settled in 386 and remained until his death.

John Chrysostom (c. 347–407 CE), Homily on Romans 16:1–2, 5–6. *Patrologia Graeca* 60.663–70. Trans. C. Osiek.
Date: late fourth century CE
Provenance: Syrian Antioch
Description: John, presbyter of Antioch at the time of this homily, was in 398 forced into accepting the episcopacy of Constantinople, where he formed his deep friendship with the deaconess Olympias (cf. Life of Olympias, 21st Week of the Year) that remained throughout his life. The fiery preaching of moral reformation that had made him so popular in Antioch backfired in the cosmopolitan atmosphere of political intrigue in the capital. In 403 he was deposed and in 404 forced to go into exile, where he died a few years later. By the sixth century he was given the name Chrysostom ("golden-mouthed"), and has been an enduringly popular church writer.

Joseph and Aseneth. Trans. C. Burchard, *The Old Testament Pseudepigrapha*, Vol. 2, ed. J.H. Charlesworth (Garden City, NY: Doubleday, 1985) pp. 202–247.
Date: first century BCE–second century CE
Provenance: ? Egypt
Description: This text is a Hellenistic Jewish romance—a love story about Jacob's son, Joseph, and his marriage to Aseneth (Gen 41:45). Stories such as these were used by Jews to teach virtues and moral principles that all Jews should follow.

Julian of Norwich, *Showings*. Translated by Edmund Colledge, O.S.A. and James Walsh, S.J. (New York: Paulist Press, 1978) pp. 264, 285, 294–298 passim
Date: 1340–1413
Provenance: England

Description: Though Julian's work has been read and revered since her "long Text" was published in 1670, the Paulist edition becomes both critical edition and commentary, and reveals Julian's extraordinarily creative mystical theology in all its breadth. Though the work is celebrated on many counts, and Julian's language is often compared to Chaucer's for its striking images, it is her mystical sense of the motherhood of God and the feminine nature in Christ which has so enriched western mystical theology and given courage to those who know that this feminine aspect of God has been sorely neglected in the western church.

Life of Adam and Eve. Trans. M.D. Johnson, *The Old Testament Pseudepigrapha,* Vol. 2, ed. J.H. Charlesworth (Garden City, NY: Doubleday, 1985) pp. 258–295.
Date: ca. 100 CE
Provenance: Palestine
Description: This text is a midrash (an expanded interpretation) on the story of the first creatures of the Genesis 1–3 accounts. It most likely served as both an entertaining and a didactic source among Jews of the first century. Like many Pharisaic documents it teaches that the dead will be raised on the last day.

Life of Léoba. See Rudolf, Monk of Fulda

Life of Macrina. See Gregory of Nyssa

Life of Olympias (c. 365–410) Deaconess of the Cathedral of Constantinople. Trans. E. Clark, *Jerome, Chrysostom and Friends* (Lewiston, NY: Edwin Mellen, 1979) pp. 127–142.
Date: fifth century CE
Provenance: Constantinople
Description: Nothing is known of the anonymous author of the Life, obviously an admirer of John Chrysostom as well. Olympias was a wealthy young widow of the capital city who, like so many of her day, chose the ascetic life rather than remarriage. In her position as deaconess of the great church of Hagia Sophia and head of an adjoining monastery, she associated with and gave hospitality to most of the prominent church leaders of the day. The Life stresses her qualities of character and her friendship with John, which cost her exile along with him.

Martyrdom of Saint Crispina. Trans. H. Musurillo, *The Acts of the Christian Martyrs* (Oxford: Clarendon, 1972) pp. 303–309.

Date: December 5, 304 CE, during the Great Persecution of Diocletian and Maximian

Provenance: North Africa

Description: Though we know very little about Crispina, her memory remained alive in the North African church along with that of other African martyrs like Perpetua and Felicitas, as evidenced for example in the later sermons of Augustine. The account of her trial is a typical martyr story in which the political-legal questions of the magistrate are countered by theological answers from the accused, revealing the entirely different level on which the Christians understood the meaning of their lives and their deaths.

Martyrdom of Saints Agape, Irene, Chione and Companions at Thessalonica. Trans. H. Musurillo, *The Acts of the Christian Martyrs* (Oxford: Clarendon, 1972) pp. 281–293.

Date: Spring 304 CE, during the Great Persecution of Diocletian and Maximian

Provenance: Thessalonica, Greece

Description: The account of the trial of these women martyrs includes three sessions, and is presumably taken directly from the court record. The details of their situation are not clear, but it seems that they were living as a group outside the city to escape persecution, even though one of them, Eutychia, is widowed and pregnant. One of Irene's crimes is to have concealed Christian books (probably the scriptures) in defiance of the imperial edict to surrender them for burning. This may indicate that she held a position of responsibility in the church.

Mechtild, "True Sorrow," "The Soul and God," "Praise of God." Ed. H.A. Reinhold, *The Soul Afire: Revelations of the Mystics* (New York: Pantheon Books, 1944) pp. 113, 139–240, 310.

Date: 1207–1282

Provenance: Germany

Description: Mechtild's writing is characterized by strong and fresh images and by dialogues between the soul and God. Though the date of her death is uncertain, her life spanned most of the thirteenth century and she is celebrated by most medievalists as the greatest of the German mystic women writers. It is significant to note that she is the first mystic to write in her own vernacular (German) rather than in Latin.

Medicine Box. See Epiphanius

A Montanist Visionary. See Tertullian

Odes of Solomon. Trans. J.H. Charlesworth, *The Old Testament Pseud-epigrapha*, Vol. 2, ed. J.H. Charlesworth (Garden City, NY: Doubleday, 1985) pp. 735–771
Date: Late first and early second century CE
Provenance: ? Antioch
Description: The Odes are early Christian (? Jewish-Christian) hymns praising God and giving thanks for the coming of the messiah. They were composed in Syriac and seem to have originated in the same milieu as the letters of Ignatius of Antioch and perhaps the gospel of John.

On John 15 to Her Son. See Dhuoda

The Protoevangelium of James. Trans. O. Cullman and A.J.B. Higgins. Edgar Hennecke, *New Testament Apocrypha*, ed. Wilhelm Schneemelcher. Eng. trans. edited by R. McL. Wilson. Vol. 1: *Gospels and Related Writings* (Philadelphia: The Westminster Press, 1963) pp. 374–388.
Date: ca. 150 CE
Provenance: ? Syria
Description: This text is an infancy gospel recording the birth of Mary to Joachim and Anne and her dedication at the temple. It recounts, as well, the gospel story of the birth of Jesus combining and expanding the traditions preserved in the gospels of Matthew and Luke.

Pseudo-Philo, *Biblical Antiquities*. Trans. Daniel J. Harrington, *The Old Testament Pseudepigrapha*, Vol. 2, ed. J.H. Charlesworth (Garden City, NY: Doubleday, 1985) pp. 304–377.
Date: first century CE
Provenance: ? Palestine
Description: This text retells the biblical story beginning with Abraham to the death of Saul. It freely adapts the canonical tradition, often adding

and interpolating prayers, speeches, and narrative expansions. These expansions are evident especially in the greater attention paid to female characters from the Bible, such as the daughter of Jephthah of Judges 11.

Rudolf, Monk of Fulda, Life of Léoba, *The Anglo-Saxon Missionaries in Germany,* ed. and trans. Charles H. Talbot (New York: Sheed and Ward, 1954) pp. 205–226.
Date: ca. 838 CE
Provenance: Germany
Description: Rudolf (d. 862), teacher and chronicler in the Benedictine monastery of Fulda, was one of the most distinguished scholars of his time. At the suggestion of Rabanus Maurus, his teacher, he compiled from notes of the priest Mego and from the memories of four nuns of Bischofsheim, Léoba's abbey, a life of St. Léoba who had died about 779. Thus the *Life* is written by one with no first-hand knowledge of Léoba, but is based on records of those who knew her.

St. Gertrude, "Spiritual Exercises," *The Fire and the Cloud: An Anthology of Catholic Spirituality,* ed. David Fleming, S.M. (New York: Paulist, 1978) p. 96
Date: 1256–1302 CE
Provenance: Germany
Description: Gertrude's (The Great) primary work, *The Spiritual Exercises,* is a record of her visions of Christ. She was highly influenced by Cistercian thought, but recounts her visions as all stemming from her "conversion"—a moment of intense union with Christ which changed her life. Her revelations contain the seeds for what will later flower into devotion to Christ's humanity under the rubric of "devotion to the Sacred Heart."

Sayings of the Desert Mothers Sarah, Syncletica, and Theodora. Trans. Benedicta Ward, *The Desert Christian: Sayings of the Desert Fathers; The Alphabetical Collection* (New York: Macmillan, 1975) pp. 82–84, 229–235.
Date: fifth century CE?
Provenance: Egypt
Description: It is difficult to assign dates to the sayings in the collections from the desert. They began as oral tradition, were preserved by disciples, and eventually were formed into a number of literary collections and so

passed to the west by scholars like John Cassian, Jerome, and Palladius. Our three desert mothers are presumed to have lived in the fifth century, by which time the heremetical life was evolving into more communal forms of monasticism, more suitable to assure safety to women. There were also, however, some women who braved the solitary desert life in the earlier years.

The Shepherd of Hermas. Trans. C. Osiek
Date: Early second century CE
Provenance: Rome
Description: This Jewish-Christian apocalypse contains long passages of moral teaching and was well-known in the early church. It was especially popular in Egypt, and was considered scripture by some Christian writers. The name of the work derives from the name of the recipient of revelation, Hermas, and the description of the heavenly revealer in the second and third parts of the book, The Mandates and Parables. In the first part, the Visions, the heavenly revealer is the feminine figure who is the church.

Showings. See Julian of Norwich

Sibylline Oracles. Trans. John J. Collins, *The Old Testament Pseudepigrapha*, Vol. 1, ed. James H. Charlesworth (Garden City, NY: Doubleday, 1983) pp. 317–472.
Date: Books I and II, ca. 30 BCE–150 CE
Book III, ca. 35 BCE
Book IV, ca. 300 BCE; edited ca. 80 CE
Provenance: Books I and II, Asia Minor
Book III, Egypt
Book IV, Syria
Description: This collection of prophetic oracles is attributed to female seers or prophets known as "sibyls." Originally Jewish writings, these prophetic oracles were later adapted by Christian prophets.

Sibylline Oracles, Book VIII. Trans. John J. Collins, *The Old Testament Pseudepigrapha*, Vol. 1, ed. James H. Charlesworth (Garden City, NY: Doubleday, 1983) pp. 456–480.
Date: ca. 175 CE
Provenance: ? Egypt

Description: This prophetic oracle is against the greed and social injustice of the Roman empire. There are striking parallels in the text to the Christian book of Revelation.

Socrates Scholasticus, *Church History.* Trans. *Nicene and Postnicene Fathers,* ser. 2, vol. 2, pp. 21–22.
Date: c. 380–450 CE
Provenance: Constantinople
Description: A lawyer and lay Christian scholar of the capital city, Socrates wrote his history about 430 in seven books covering the lives of seven emperors. It covers the years 305–439 and so picks up where Eusebius left off. His work is highly regarded for its accuracy and objectivity.

"Spiritual Exercises." See St. Gertrude

A Montanist Visionary. **Tertullian** (c. 160–212) *On the Soul* #9. Trans. *Ante-Nicene Fathers* 3.181–235.
Date: early third century CE
Provenance: Carthage, North Africa
Description: Quintus Septimius Florens Tertullianus was a convert to Christianity in his native Carthage, after being trained in rhetoric and law and perhaps practicing at Rome. He was probably a presbyter, and his writings indicate that he was married, though he opposed second marriages. Sometime in mid-career, he became increasingly influenced by Montanism (see Acts of Perpetua and Felicitas, which took place at Carthage during his lifetime), with its heightened emphasis on visions and prophecies. Nothing certain is known about his death.

Testament of Abraham, Trans. E.P. Sanders, *The Old Testament Pseudepigrapha,* Vol. 1, ed. James H. Charlesworth (Garden City, NY: Doubleday, 1983) pp. 871–902.
Date: ca. 100 CE
Provenance: ? Egypt
Description: This is a Jewish text of the first century CE which presents a picture of a "universalistic and generalized Judaism" in which Jew and Gentile are accorded equal place in the judgment and reign of God. The "testamentary form" flourished in this period. It is characterized by

speeches of famous ancestors as they prepare for death. This form is widely attested in the Old Testament (Gen 47:29–31; Gen 48–49; Deut) and in Jesus' farewell address in John 14–17.

Testament of Job. Trans. R.P. Spittler, *The Old Testament Pseudepigrapha*, Vol. 1, ed. James H. Charlesworth (Garden City, NY: Doubleday, 1983) pp. 829–868.
Date: ca. first century BCE or CE
Provenance: Egypt
Description: A retelling and expansion of the biblical story of Job, this text stresses Job's virtue of endurance and exhorts us to imitate Job's fidelity. More striking is its attention to the women—Job's wife and daughters who remain silent and nameless in the biblical text but who play active and significant roles in the Testament of Job.

Testaments of the Twelve Patriarchs. Trans. Howard C. Kee, *The Old Testament Pseudepigrapha*, Vol. 1, ed. James H. Charlesworth (Garden City, NY: Doubleday, 1983) pp. 775–828.
Date: ca. 150 BCE with Christian additions
Provenance: ? Syria
Description: The documents purport to be the final testaments of the twelve sons of Jacob. In fact, they combine ethical exhortations and eschatological expectations typical of Hellenistic Judaism in the first century BCE.

Thunder, Perfect Mind. Trans. George W. MacRae and Douglas M. Parrott, *Nag Hammadi Library in English*, Rev. Ed., ed. James M. Robinson (San Francisco: Harper and Row, 1977) pp. 271–274.
Date: uncertain
Provenance: Egypt
Description: The discourse of a female revealer is spoken in the first person, and marked by repeated self-proclamations of antithetical character. This work shares the revelatory character of Jewish wisdom literature, such as Sirach and the Wisdom of Solomon, the hymns (aretologies) of the goddess Isis, and the "I am" sayings of Jesus in the gospel of John. Though found among the collections of the gnostic library of Nag Hammadi, it exhibits none of the mythological speculations of the other gnostic documents at Nag Hammadi.

Who Is the Rich One Who Can Be Saved. See Clement of Alexandria

Women of the Syrian Orient: Anahid, Elizabeth, Martha, Ruhn. Introduction and Translation by Sevastian P. Broch and Susan Asbrook Harvey. *Holy Women of the Syrian Orient* (Berkeley: University of California Press, 1987) pp. 67–68, 93, 105–106, 112–113.
Date: fourth to seventh centuries CE
Provenance: Iran, Iraq, Saudi Arabian Peninsula
Description: These lives of Persian and Syrian women, most of them martyrs, were based on eyewitness accounts, and provide an excellent picture of religious themes and struggles in late antiquity in the Syrian Orient. Written originally in the Syriac language, they were recently (1887) translated and edited with the intent of showing how valuable to the larger Church is the memory of these courageous, believing women of the fourth to seventh century CE.

NOTES ON THE EDITORS

Barbara E. Bowe, R.S.C.J., received both a master's and a doctorate in New Testament and Christian Origins from Harvard University, and also holds a master's degree in Religious Education from Boston College. Her dissertation on First Clement, A *Church in Crisis: Ecclesiology and Paraenesis in Clement of Rome* was published by Fortress Press in 1988 as part of the Harvard Dissertations in Religion Series. In 1989, she returned to the U.S. from the Philippines where she taught for three years at Maryhill School of Theology and the Sister Formation Institute in Manila. She is a member of the Catholic Biblical Association, The Chicago Society of Biblical Research, and the Society of Biblical Literature. She is currently Associate Professor of Biblical Studies at the Catholic Theological Union in Chicago where she teaches courses in New Testament and early Christianity.

Kathleen Hughes, R.S.C.J., earned a doctorate in Liturgical Studies from the University of Notre Dame. She is currently Professor of Liturgy at the Catholic Theological Union, past president of the North American Academy of Liturgy, has served as advisor to the U.S. Bishops' Committee on the Liturgy, and is in her second term on the International Commission on English in the Liturgy (ICEL). Among her publications, the most recent are *The Monk's Tale: A Biography of Godfrey Diekmann, O.S.B.* and *Living No Longer for Ourselves: Liturgy and Justice in the 90's*, the latter edited with Mark Francis. She has also published a monograph: *Lay Presiding: The Art of Leading Prayer*, and her articles have appeared in more than twenty journals.

Sharon Karam, R.S.C.J., a native of Louisiana, is a member of the Society of the Sacred Heart and has been a teacher and administrator in high schools run by the order for the past 25 years. She holds an M.A. from Washington University in St. Louis in the field of English, an M.Ed. from Tulane University in Administration and Supervision, and a Certificate in Pastoral Studies from Catholic Theological Union.

Carolyn Osiek, R.S.C.J., is Professor of New Testament Studies at Catholic Theological Union, Chicago. She holds a doctorate in New Testament and Christian Origins from Harvard University, and is an associate editor of *The Bible Today*, and *New Theology Review*, as well as New Testament Book Review editor of *Catholic Biblical Quarterly*. Her publications include *What Are They Saying About the Social Setting of the New Testament?* (Paulist, 2nd ed., 1992) and commentaries on Galatians, 1 Corinthians, and Philippians, as well as numerous articles on biblical studies, spirituality, women in the church, and the social world of early Christianity.